# THE GOOD NEWS ACCORDING TO LUKE

# THE
# GOOD
# NEWS
## ACCORDING TO
# LUKE

---

## Eduard Schweizer

TRANSLATED BY DAVID E. GREEN

John Knox Press
ATLANTA

**Library of Congress Cataloging in Publication Data**

Schweizer, Eduard, 1913–
   The Good news according to Luke.

   Translation of Das evangelium nach Lukas.
   Scripture and Apocrypha quotations are from the
Revised Standard version of the Holy Bible.
   Bibliography: p.
   Includes index.
   1. Bible. N.T. Luke—Commentaries. I. Bible.
N.T. Luke. English. Revised Standard. 1984.
II. Title.
BS2595.3.S3713 1984     226'.4077     83-22237
ISBN 0-8042-0249-4

Translated from the German with the permission of Vandenhoeck & Ruprecht, Publishers, Göttingen. © Vandenhoeck & Ruprecht in Göttingen.

Published simultaneously in Great Britain by S.P.C.K., London, and in the United States of America by John Knox Press, Atlanta, Georgia.

Translation © copyright John Knox Press 1984
10  9  8  7  6  5  4  3  2  1
Printed in the United States of America
John Knox Press
Atlanta, Georgia 30365

# LIST OF ABBREVIATIONS

## Old Testament

| | | | |
|---|---|---|---|
| Gen. | Genesis | Eccles. | Ecclesiastes |
| Exod. | Exodus | Song of Sol. | Song of Solomon |
| Lev. | Leviticus | Isa. | Isaiah |
| Num. | Numbers | Jer. | Jeremiah |
| Deut. | Deuteronomy | Lam. | Lamentations |
| Josh. | Joshua | Ezek. | Ezekiel |
| Judg. | Judges | Dan. | Daniel |
| Ruth | Ruth | Hos. | Hosea |
| 1 Sam. | 1 Samuel | Joel | Joel |
| 2 Sam. | 2 Samuel | Amos | Amos |
| 1 Kings | 1 Kings | Obad. | Obadiah |
| 2 Kings | 2 Kings | Jon. | Jonah |
| 1 Chron. | 1 Chronicles | Mic. | Micah |
| 2 Chron. | 2 Chronicles | Nah. | Nahum |
| Ezra | Ezra | Hab. | Habakkuk |
| Neh. | Nehemiah | Zeph. | Zephaniah |
| Esther | Esther | Hag. | Haggai |
| Job | Job | Zech. | Zechariah |
| Ps. (pl. Pss.) | Psalms | Mal. | Malachi |
| Prov. | Proverbs | | |

## Apocrypha

| | | | |
|---|---|---|---|
| Bar. | Baruch | Jth. | Judith |
| Ecclus. | Ecclesiasticus (Sirach) | 1 Macc. | 1 Maccabees |
| 1 Esd. | 1 Esdras | 2 Macc. | 2 Maccabees |
| 2 Esd. | 2 Esdras | Tob. | Tobit |
| Wisd. | Wisdom of Solomon | | |

## New Testament

| | | | |
|---|---|---|---|
| Matt. | Matthew | 1 Tim. | 1 Timothy |
| Mark | Mark | 2 Tim. | 2 Timothy |
| Luke | Luke | Titus | Titus |
| John | John | Philem. | Philemon |
| Acts | Acts of the Apostles | Heb. | Hebrews |
| Rom. | Romans | James | James |
| 1 Cor. | 1 Corinthians | 1 Pet. | 1 Peter |
| 2 Cor. | 2 Corinthians | 2 Pet. | 2 Peter |
| Gal. | Galatians | 1 John | 1 John |
| Eph. | Ephesians | 2 John | 2 John |
| Phil. | Philippians | 3 John | 3 John |
| Col. | Colossians | Jude | Jude |
| 1 Thess. | 1 Thessalonians | Rev. | Revelation |
| 2 Thess. | 2 Thessalonians | | |

## General

| | |
|---|---|
| Bill. | H. L. Strack and P. Billerbeck, *Kommentar zum Neuen Testament aus Talmud und Midrasch* ([5]1969). |
| Hennecke | E. Hennecke and W. Schneemelcher, *Neutestamentliche Aprokryphen* ([2]1924, [3]1959–1964); English trans., *New Testament Apocrypha* (1963–1965). |
| Hercher | *Erotici* |
| HTK | Herders theologisches Kommentar |
| L | Luke's special material (see section 1 of the Introduction). |
| LXX | The Septuagint (Greek translation of the Old Testament) |
| NTD | Das Neue Testament Deutsch |
| Q | Sayings Source used by Matthew and Luke |

## Jewish Documents (Pseudepigrapha), 200–1 B.C.

| | |
|---|---|
| Ahikar | A collections of proverbs from seventh century B.C. |
| Aris. | Letter of Aristeas, contains legend of how LXX was composed |
| Bk. Jub. | Book of Jubilees, originated among priestly circles, second century B.C. |
| En. | Enoch, sometimes referred to as Ethiopic or Ethiopian Enoch or 1 Enoch; cf. Sl. En. |
| 3 Macc. | 3 Maccabees (LXX) |
| 4 Macc. | 4 Maccabees (LXX) |
| Ps. Sol. | Psalms of Solomon (LXX) |
| Sl. En. | Slavonic Enoch, "The Book of the Secrets of Enoch," or 2 Enoch |

| Test. XII | Testaments of the Twelve Patriarchs, could be Jewish or Christian |
| Test. G. | Testament of Gad |
| Test. Isaac | Testament of Isaac |
| Test. Jud. | Testament of Judah |
| Test. Levi | Testament of Levi |
| Test. N. | Testament of Naphtali |
| Test. Sol. | Testament of Solomon |

### Dead Sea Scrolls (Qumran)

| CD | Damascus Document |
| 1QGen Apoc. | Genesis Apocryphon |
| 1QH | Hymns of Thanksgiving |
| 1QM | The Wars of the Sons of Light Against the Sons of Darkness |
| 1QMelch | Melchizedek Document |
| 1QpHab | Commentary (Pesher) on Habakkuk |
| 1QS | Manual of Discipline or Rule of the Community |
| 1QSa | Rule of the Congregation |
| 1Q27 | Book of Mysteries |
| 2QFlor. | The Blessing of Jacob or The Florilegium |
| 4QPatr | The Patriarchensegen (Blessings of the Patriarchs) |
| 4QTest | The "Testimonia" |
| 11QtgJob | Targum of Job |

### Jewish Documents (Pseudepigrapha), A.D. 1–200

| Apoc. Bar. | Apocalypse of Baruch, also known as the Syrian or Syriac Apocalypse of Baruch. There is also a Greek Apocalypse of Baruch. Both are to be distinguished from the apocryphal Baruch. |
| Apoc. Ezra | Apocalypse of Ezra |
| Apoc. Moses | Apocalypse of Moses |
| Asc. Mose | Ascension of Moses |
| B. Sukk. | Babylonian Talmud, tractate Sukkoth |
| Jos. As. | Joseph and Aseneth (influenced by Christian Gnosticism?) |
| Josephus (ca. 37–ca. 100), Jewish historian | |
| Ant. | *Antiquitates judaicae, Antiquities of the Jews* |
| Ap. | *Contra Apionem* |
| De bello jud. | *De bello judaico* |
| Pes. R. | Pesikta Rabba |
| Philo (ca. 20 B.C.–ca. A.D. 50), Jewish philosopher and exegete | |
| Abel | *De Sacrificiis Abelis et Caini* |
| Dreams | *De Somniis* |
| Drunkenness | *De Ebrietate* |

| | |
|---|---|
| *Emb.* | *Embassy to Gaius* |
| *Hypothet.* | *Hypothetica* |
| *Vit. Mos.* | *De Vita Mosis*, *Life of Moses* |
| Ps. Philo | Pseudo-Philo, *Antiquities* (influenced by Qumran) |
| Sib. Or. | Sibylline Oracles, a collection of Hellenistic Jewish and Christian prophecies |
| Sifre Deut. | Sifre on Deuteronomy |
| Targ. Jon. | Targum Jonathan, a free Aramaic translation of Genesis 1—5 |
| Vita Adami | Life of Adam and Eve, related to the Apocalypse of Moses |

## Christian Documents

| | |
|---|---|
| A. Barn. | Acts of Barnabas |
| A. Thomas | Acts of Thomas |
| Apost. Const. | Apostolic Constitutions (fourth century, Syrian, probably includes earlier material) |
| 1 Clem. | 1 Clement, first epistle of Clement, bishop of Rome, to the Corinthians, end of the first century |
| Cyril of Alexandria (d. 444) | |
| *Hom.* | *Homilies* |
| Did. | Didache, or Teachings of the Twelve Apostles, end of the first century, Syrian? |
| | Didascalia, chapters 1—6 of the Apostolic Constitutions, third century, Syrian. |
| Epiphanius | (ca. 315–403), bishop of Salamis and metropolitan of Cyprus |
| *Haer.* | *Panarion seu adversus lxxx haereses*, attacking heresies known to him |
| Eu. Heb. | Gospel According to the Hebrews |
| Eu. Thom. | Gospel of Thomas |
| Eusebius | (ca. 260–ca. 340), bishop of Caesarea |
| *Hist. eccl.* | *Historia ecclesiastica*, *Church History* |
| Hermas | Second century writer |
| *Prayer* | |
| *Sim.* | *Similitudes*, part of *The Shepherd* |
| Ignatius | (ca. 35–ca. 107), Ignatius of Antioch, bishop of Antioch |
| *Eph.* | *Epistula ad Ephesios* |
| *Magn.* | *Epistula ad Magnesios* |
| *Polyc.* | *Epistula ad Polycarpum*, "Letter to Polycarp" |
| *Smyrn.* | *Epistula ad Smyraneos* |
| *Trall.* | *Epistula ad Trallianos* |
| Irenaeus | (ca. 130–ca. 200), bishop of Lyons |
| | *Adversus omnes haereses* |

Justin  (ca. 100–ca. 200), Justin Martyr, Christian apologist
    *Dial.*      *Dialogus cum Tryphone*, "Dialogue with Trypho the
               Jew
Marcion  Second century figure in Rome who rejected the Old Testament
Mart. Is.      Martyrdom of Isaiah
Odes of Sol.      Odes of Solomon

Origen  (185–254), Alexandrian theologian
               *Contra Celsum, Against Celsus*
Protev. James      Protevangelium of James, an infancy narrative of Jesus,
               end of the second century
Ps. Clem.      Pseudo-Clement, about 300
   *Hom.*      *Homilies*
Ps. Cyprian      *Centesima*, a work erroneously ascribed to Cyprian,
               third century
Terullian  (ca. 160–ca, 225)
   *Jej.*      *De jejuniis*

## Greek and Roman Authors

### Pre-Christian

Aristophanes (ca. 448–ca. 380 B.C.), Greek satirical dramatist
   *Birds*      *The Birds*
Cicero  (106–43 B.C.), Roman orator and Stoic philosopher
   *Fam.*      *Epistulae ad familiares*
   *Ligarius*      *Pro Ligario*
Dionysus of Halicarnassus  (ca. 54–ca. 7 B.C.), Greek historian and
               rhetorician
   *Ant. Rom.*      *Antiquitates Romanae*
Epictetus  (ca. A.D. 50–ca. 130), Stoic philosopher
Epicurus  (342–270 B.C.), Greek philosopher
   *Diogenes*
Euripides  (fifth century B.C.), Greek tragic dramatist
   *Fr.*      *Frogs*
   *Hel.*      *Helena*
   *Or.*      *Orestes*
   *Tr.*      *The Trojan Women*
Herodotus  (fifth century B.C.), Greek historian
Homer  (eighth century B.C.), Greek epic poet
   *Od.*      *Odyssey*
Livy  (59 B.C.–A.D. 17), Roman historian
Sophocles  (ca. 496–ca. 406.B.C.), Greek tragic dramatis
   *Oed. Col.*      *Oedipus Coloneus*
Virgil  (70–19 B.C.), Roman poet
   *Aen.*      *Aeneid*

Xenophon    (ca. 434–ca. 355 B.C.), Greek general and historian
   *Cyrop.*      *Cyropaedia*
               *Cyrus*
   *Hell.*       *Hellenica*

## A.D. 1–200

Aelian    (ca. 170–235), Greek philosopher
Charitonos    (second century), Greek novelist
               *Chaereas and Callirhoe*
Diodorus Siculus    (first century), Sicilian historian
Lucian    (ca. 115–ca. 200), Lucian of Samosata (Syria), pagan satirist
   *Hist.*       *Historia*
   *Pereg.*     *De peregrini morte*
   *Pseudolog.*   *Pseudologista*
Plutarch    (ca. 46–120), Greek biographer and moralist
               *Education of Children*
   *Is. et Os.*   *De Iside et Osiride*
   *Rom.*      *Quaestiones Romanae*
Seneca    (ca. 4 B.C.–A.D. 65), Lucius Annaeus Seneca, Roman moralist
   *Agam.*    *Agammemnon*
   *Ep.*       Epistles, apocryphal letters to St. Paul
   *Heracles Oet.*   *Hercules Oetaeus*
Suetonius    (first century), Roman historian
   *Vitae*      *Lives of the Caesars*

## Later Writers

Libanius    (314–ca. 393), Greek rhetorician
               *Orationes*
Philostratus    (third century), Greek Sophist
   *Apoll.*      *Life of Apollonius*
Simplicius    (sixth century), Platonist and commentator on Aristotle

# CONTENTS

**Introduction**     **1**

**Preface: Luke's Purpose (1:1–4)**     **10**

**I. Infancy Narratives: John and Jesus (1:5—2:52)**     **15**

  A. ANNUNCIATION (1:5–38)     18
    God's New Beginning: Annunciation of John
    (1:5–25) ................................................ 18
    God's New Creation: The Annunciation of Jesus
    (1:26–38) ............................................ 24

  B. THE ENTWINING OF GOD'S TWO ACTS: THE MEETING
    OF MARY AND ELIZABETH, THE MAGNIFICAT
    (1:39–56)     32

  C. BIRTH—NAMING—PRAISE OF GOD (1:57—2:40)     37
    Fulfillment of the Promise: Birth and Naming
    (1:57–66) ............................................ 37
    Benedictus (1:67–80) ................................. 39
    God's Visitation of His People (2:1–20) ............. 45
    The Presentation: Nunc Dimittis (2:21–40) .......... 53

  D. JESUS, AT HOME WITH GOD AND HUMANITY
    (2:41–52)     61

**II. The Growth of the Community (3:1—9:50)**     **68**

  A. PREPARATION: APPEARANCE AND MESSAGE OF THE
    BAPTIST AND JESUS (3:1—4:30)     68
    The Forerunner (3:1–6) .............................. 69
    The Gospel of the Baptist (3:7–20) ................. 71

The Son of God Is Proclaimed: Jesus' Baptism and
  Genealogy (3:21–38) .............................. 77
The Temptation of Jesus (4:1–13) ..................... 81
Jesus Programmatic Sermon (4:14–30) ............... 84

B. "THROUGHOUT ALL JUDEA, BEGINNING FROM
  GALILEE" (Acts 10:37) (4:31–5:11)           96
The Good News of the Kingdom of God (4:31–44) .. 97
God's Call to Discipleship (5:1–11) ................... 100

C. THE GROWTH OF THE COMMUNITY (5:12—6:11)      107
  Conflict (5:12—6:11) ................................ 107

D. CALL AND INSTRUCTION (6:12–49)              113
Call to Disciples and People (6:12–19) ............... 114
The Sermon on the Plain (6:20–49) .................. 116
  (1) God's Partisanship on Behalf of the Poor
    (6:20–26) ..................................... 118
  (2) The Central Commandment of Love
    (6:27–36)                                  122
  (3) Love That Does Not Judge (6:37–42) .......... 124
  (4) Roots and Foundations (6:43–49) ............. 127

E. CALL TO ASSEMBLE (7:1—9:50)                 128
The Faith of the Centurion (7:1–10) ................. 130
Power over Death (7:11–17) .......................... 132
God's Astonishing Work in the Baptist and in Jesus
  (7:18–35) ...................................... 134
The Friend of Sinners (7:36–50) ..................... 137
Women Follow Jesus (8:1–3) ......................... 141
The Parable of Those Who Hear the Word
  (8:4–21)                                      143
Jesus' Authority over Storm, Demons, and Death
  (8:22–56) ..................................... 147
The Sending of the Twelve (9:1–6) .................. 151
Who Is This? (9:7–9) ................................ 153
Jesus' Authority in the Feeding of the Five Thousand
  (9:10–17) ..................................... 154

Who Is This?—The Answer (9:18–27) ............... 155
God's Affirmation of Jesus' Suffering (9:28–36) ...... 158
The Incomprehension of the Disciples (9:37–50) ..... 161

## III. The Road to Jerusalem (9:51—19:27)  165

A. THE COMING KINGDOM: CALL TO DISCIPLESHIP
   (9:51—11:36)  167
To Jerusalem (9:51–56) .................................. 168
Discipleship (9:57–62) .................................. 171
Mission of the Seventy (10:1–16) ...................... 172
The Fall of Satan (10:17–20) ........................... 178
The Presence of Salvation (10:21–24) ................. 182
The Chance to Love (10:25–37) ....................... 184
The Chance to Have Faith (10:38–42) ................ 188
The Chance to Pray (11:1–13) ......................... 190
The Chance to Encounter Jesus (11:14–36) .......... 193

B. TRUE DISCIPLESHIP IN CONTRAST TO PHARISEES AND
   SCRIBES (11:37—12:59)  197
Conflict with Pharisees and Scribes (11:37—12:1) ... 198
Discipleship Without Anxiety (12:2–12) .............. 203
A Bad Investment (12:13–21) .......................... 206
Freedom from Anxiety (12:22–34) ..................... 209
Openness to Whatever Comes (12:35–48) ............ 211
Trial by Fire and Baptism (12:49–53) ................. 214
Blindness to God's Signs (12:54–59) ................. 216

C. REPENTANCE AND THE COMING KINGDOM (13:1–21) 218
Time to Repent (13:1–9) ............................... 218
The Sabbath as a Sign of God's New Creation
   (13:10–17) ........................................... 220
The Littleness and Greatness of the Kingdom of God
   (13:18–21) ........................................... 223

D. JERUSALEM: CITY OF DECISION (13:22–35) 224
The Nearness to Jesus of the Distant (13:22–30) ..... 224
Jerusalem, City of Decision (13:31–35) .............. 228

E. THE JOY OF REPENTANCE (14:1—15:32) .................... 232
  Table Conversation as Call to the Kingdom of God
    (14:1–24) ............................................. 233
    (1) Sabbath Healing (14:1–6) ...................... 233
    (2) The Life Shaped by the Coming Kingdom
        (14:7–14) ...................................... 234
    (3) The Kingdom of God as a Banquet
        (14:15–24) ..................................... 237
  Considered Discipleship (14:25–35) ................... 240
  Two Seekers (15:1–10) ............................... 242
  The Powerless Almighty Father (15:11–32) .......... 246

F. DISCIPLESHIP AND POSSESSIONS (16:1—17:10) ......... 252
  Liberation for God's Future (16:1–13) ................ 253
  The Function of the Law (16:14–18) .................. 256
  Wealth as Separation from God (16:19–31) ........... 259
  The Life of a Disciple (17:1–10) ...................... 262

G. JERUSALEM AND GOD'S FINAL JUDGMENT
    (17:11—19:27) ....................................... 265
  Healing and Salvation (17:11–19) ..................... 266
  Present and Future of the Kingdom (17:20–37) ...... 269
  Perseverance in Prayer (18:1–8) ...................... 277
  Right Self-Assessment Before God (18:9–14) ........ 280
  Childlikeness and Freedom from Possessions
    (18:15–30) ........................................... 284
  Blindness to God (18:31–43) .......................... 287
  The Repentance of Those Far Off (19:1–10) .......... 289
  Life That Looks for God's Coming (19:11–17) ....... 292

IV. Passion and Resurrection (19:28—24:53) .............. 297

A. DAYS IN JERUSALEM (19:28—21:38) ................... 297
  Jesus Takes Possession of the Temple (19:28–48) .... 297
  Jesus' Teaching in the Temple (20:1—21:4) .......... 302
    (1) The Authority of His Teaching (20:1–8) ....... 302
    (2) The Parable of the Rejected Messenger
        (20:9–19) ...................................... 303

(3) A Trick Question: Religion and Politics
(20:20–26) .....................................  305
(4) The Theology of the Resurrection (20:27–40)    306
(5) Jesus' Counterquestions (20:41—21:4) ........  308
Presence and Future of God's Kingdom (21:5–38) ...  309

B. JESUS' PASSION (22:1—23:56)                     329
Passover Preparations in the Shadow of the Cross
(22:1–13) ...........................................  329
Passover (22:14–38) ...................................  330
Jesus' Struggle with God's Will (22:39–46) ..........  342
The Hour of Darkness (22:47–53) .....................  344
Peter's Denial and Jesus' Confession (22:54–71) .....  345
"Before King and Governor" (23:1–25) ...............  349
The End as a Sign of the New Beginning
(23:26–56)                                         356
(1) The Way of the Cross (23:26–32) ..............  356
(2) Jesus' Crucifixion and Death (23:33–49) ......  358
(3) The Burial of Jesus (23:50–56) .................  363

C. NEW BEGINNING—GIFT OF THE RISEN LORD
(24:1–53)                                          364
God's Message to the Women (24:1–12) ..............  365
Word and Sacrament—Gift of the Risen Lord
(24:13–35) .........................................  367
The Road into the Future—Gift of the Risen Lord
(24:36–53) .........................................  374

Retrospect                                         381

Indexes
Index of Names and Subjects                        386
Index of Excursuses                                xvi

# INDEX OF EXCURSUSES

Christology of the Infancy Narrative, The            65

Final Coming and Eschatological History             323

Israel and the Nations                               58

Luke's Special Source (L)                           354

Sacred History                                       92

Significance of Israel, The                         318

Understanding Jesus' Death on the Cross             338

# INTRODUCTION

## 1

Like Matthew, Luke begins with stories of Jesus' infancy. Then, apart from a few interpolations, he follows Mark up to 9:50 and from 18:15 to the end. In between comes the so-called journey narrative, comprising special material and sections related to Matthew. This section stresses that Jesus is on his way to Jerusalem. It is therefore likely that Luke was familiar with both Mark and the Sayings Source, which we will refer to as Q although it was probably not a single source (see §§ 2 and 3 of the introduction to *The Good News According to Matthew*).

The sections dealing with common material presuppose the discussion of Mark and Matthew and merely point out Lukan peculiarities. The most important parallels are always cited at the beginning of each section. In the purely Lukan sections, those based on Luke's special material (L), the translation is followed by an introduction discussing the structure and history of the text (which may be skipped by the reader who is merely interested in the message of the text), the exegesis proper, and a conclusion.

On the question of whether the Gospel presents a true account, see §5 of the introduction to *The Good News According to Mark*. Luke's theology is discussed in a retrospective conclusion and in several excursuses (see the Index of Excursuses, p. xvi). His purpose is discussed in the conclusion at 1:1–4.

## 2

(a) The extent to which Luke drew on other sources is an insoluble problem. Of course he did not make up his special material—but was his tradition written or oral? It is almost impossible to decide on linguistic grounds. Comparison with Mark and (Q) shows how much he reproduces his sources in his own style. The sources in 3:16–22; 8:22–25; 9:28–36 could hardly be recovered if we did not have Mark

(and Matthew). On the other hand, he also imitates stylistic peculiarities of his sources when he is formulating his own material (cf.
17:25 with Mark 8:31; 24:7 with Mark 14:41 [omitted by Luke];
10:25*b* with Mark 10:17 [Luke 18:18]; 11:16 with Mark 8:11 [?];
12:11–12 and 21:14–15 with Mark 13:11; 14:26 [brothers and sis-
ters] with Mark 10:29 [Luke 18:29]). In the case of parallel traditions he is also influenced by the other text (see the discussion of
17:23 and 9:8/19; 9:1–6/10:1–12). In 8:16 and 11:43, for example,
un-Lukan idioms appear together with Mark and Q; Mark or Q idioms appear in 11:33 and 20:46.

Furthermore, Luke sometimes writes in a consciously archaic style.
Normally he speaks of the devil but occasionally of Satan (Acts 5:3;
26:18) a term that he otherwise uses only when it is present in the
tradition (11:18; from L: 10:18; 13:16; 22:3, 31). The sacred scriptural form "Hierosolyma" appears at times in Acts instead of the
Lukan "Hierusalem."

The presence of Lukan idioms therefore does not prove that no
source is involved; neither do un-Lukan idioms prove the presence
of a source. But in 3:3–16*a* or 10:21–24, for example, there is so
much un-Lukan material that we would hypothesize the use of sources
even if we did not have Mark, Q, or the Septuagint (LXX).

(b) Luke 1:1 speaks of "many" predecessors. Even if this is a
commonplace of rhetorical style, more than Mark and Q must be
involved. Even if Luke had been familiar with a basic document that
was also available to Mark and Q (which is highly unlikely), such a
document could not have been an actual Gospel. Luke might have
known individual sayings and stories from oral tradition, for example from the liturgy, but also from the Hellenistic Jewish synagogue. The nucleus of 24:13–35, for instance, could have been
recounted orally in highly fixed form. A similar situation could hold
for parables and sayings of Jesus although comparison with Mark
shows how little Luke alters such material. Such sayings, however,
could have been transformed in the course of oral tradition before
Luke, especially under the influence of Greek thought.

There are, however, sections in which we can recognize the various strata of tradition or tensions between the textual basis and its
interpretation: 1—2; 3:23–38; 4:14–30; 5:1–11; 7:36–50; 19:1–10;

the three healings on the sabbath; the Passion and Easter narratives (see the excursus following 23:25); parables like 10:25–37; 11:5–8; 16:1–15; 18:1–8; 19:11–27; discourses like 13:23–29, 31–33; 17:20–37; 21. In addition, bits of Lukan framework or comment can be distinguished clearly from the tradition (7:29–30[?]; 11:37–41; 12:13–21, 41; 14:7–14; see also the discussion of 7:11–17; 15:1–3; 18:9–14). Oral tradition is not sufficient to explain these observations. It is also inconceivable that Luke possessed a stack of separate leaves containing stories, parables, and discourses.

This makes it relatively likely that most of the L passages were drawn from a coherent written source. This is also suggested by their style which is strongly assimilated to that of the Greek Bible; in Acts similar idioms appear almost exclusively in the context of specific citations.

Behind L there certainly stands a tradition that exhibits many points of contact with the Fourth Gospel without any direct dependence of one on the other. This is true of the Passion narrative (see the excursus following 23:25) but also of John's refusal to be identified as the Messiah (Luke 3:15/John 1:20), the names Mary and Martha (and Lazarus; see the discussion of 8:2), and miracles as the motivation for the rejoicing at Jesus' triumphal entry (Luke 19:37/John 12:17–18).

More important are the centrality of Israel to Christology, the absence of any contact between Jesus and Gentiles before his passion despite their openness to him (Luke 7:3; cf. the discussion of 8:39/John 12:20–32), the fall of Satan (Luke 10:18/John 12:31), Jesus' intercession for his disciples (Luke 22:31–32/John 17:15), the Holy Spirit as Jesus' gift to his disciples (Luke 11:13; 24:44/John 14:16–17; 20:21–22), and the idea of death as the transition to glory together with the importance of Jesus' exaltation (Luke 24:26, 51; Acts 1:9; 2:33; 5:31). As in John, Samaria plays an important part in L; Jesus appears to have an extended ministry there and in Judea (Luke 9:51–52; 17:11; 19:47; 21:37–38; 22:39; see the discussion of 22:1). Galilee is mentioned in Acts only in 9:31 (cf. the discussion of Luke 21:4, 44; 24:6); Samaria appears in Acts 1:8; 8:1–14; 15:3.

Are L and John possibly drawing on a tradition of Judean disciples who are also perhaps described in the missionary discourse of 10:1–

12 (in L following the departure for Samaria and Jerusalem), while 9:1–6 concerns a Galilean group whose voice we hear in Mark and Q?

Other characteristics of L include a special concern for women and the poor (shared by Q in 6:20; 12:34; Luke in 16:14; 18:22; Acts 16:13–18), the notion of an extensive (inner) circle of disciples, rejection of merit and reward (10:20; 15:25–32; 17:5–10), and the gift of salvation to the people (1:68; 2:32, 38; 7:16), whereas Luke stresses the decision of each individual.

A special place belongs to the infancy narratives, which intertwine the lives of Jesus and John the Baptist and strongly imitate the style of the LXX (see also the discussion of 9:51). Here "Lord" is used twenty-six times for God (for Christ in 1:43), a usage found elsewhere only in Luke 5:17. Luke 8:39 even eliminates the expression found in Mark 5:19. Are these narratives the nucleus or a highly stylized late element of L, which comprises most of the special material from 3:10–14, 23–38 on and continues on into a Passion narrative (see the excursus following 23:25)? It is impossible to be certain because we must reckon in any case with the influence that such a source had on Luke himself. But there is much evidence to support the theory.

(c) It is much harder to evaluate the Q passages. They exhibit several stylistic peculiarities that appear otherwise only in L but not in Acts or in Markan passages borrowed by Luke (and altered). Since they do not appear in Matthew but agree with L, they must go back to this source or to Luke himself. The list includes the following: "I say to you" (not found in Mark, Matthew, or John), e.g., 6:27; (7:9); 11:9; 12:4, 5, 51, 14:24; 15:7; 17:34; 19:26, 40; "turning," 7:9; 10:23; "no, but . . . ," 12:51 (see 1:60; 13:3, 5; 16:30; always expressed differently in Acts); unemphatic "begin" (removed from Mark ten times by Luke), especially with reference to judgment, 13:25, 26 (14:18); negated participle with article, 12:48; 19:27 (L 3:11; 22:36; Q 11:23; 19:26); "however," fourteen or fifteen times, only Q and L (once in another sense in Acts).

Luke places numerals before their nouns (forty-four times in Acts, in comparison to eleven cases where the numeral follows), even changing Mark five times and biblical quotations twice. The numeral follows in 12:6, 52; 19:13–25 (eight times); 22:30. But Luke also eliminates all nine Markan combinations with "summon," while using the term in Acts and redactionally in Luke 7:18(?); 18:16; in L 15:26; 16:5. "Lord" is used of the earthly Jesus fifteen times in Luke and five in John (Mark 11:3 and Matt. 24:43 in a different sense); it never appears interpolated into material from Mark (19:34 merely repeats vs. 31); it does appear in Q 7:19; 10:1; 13:39; as a term of address in 7:6; 17:37; and apparently redactionally in L (10:17; 11:1; 12:41–42; 13:23; 17:5–6; 19:8; 24:3).

Such non-Lukan features appear prominently in 10:23–24; 12:49–53; 14:15–24; 17:34–37; 19:12–27 (in L, e.g., 7:12–16; 22:14–18, 21–38; 23:28–31, 39–43), where the wording and sequence also clearly differ from Matthew. This argues that Luke used a form of Q that had already undergone further development, influenced by the style of the author of L. This would mean that, besides Mark, Luke was familiar with a Gospel that had incorporated the Q material. Such a Gospel, like John, would have born the mark of Samaritan-Judean tradition and would have exhibited the peculiarities mentioned above, especially concern for women and the poor, and emphasis on the close association of the group of Jesus' followers with Israel.

Of course caution is required, as the usage of "summon" and "Lord" shows. Some material could have been drawn from oral tradition while reaching Matthew in a different way. In markedly divergent Q passages, only the initial root of the tradition may have been common to both. Parables could have existed in a special collection independent of Q. Matthew or Luke could have omitted something in Q or replaced it with something else. Luke undoubtedly followed Mark's structural lead, so that if his source (L + Q) really did exist, he imposed Mark's structure upon it. But the above-mentioned tensions between the textual basis and Luke's redaction make it highly unlikely that Luke himself was responsible for most of the special material and the alterations in Q, relying at most upon oral tradition. Since, on the other hand, a large number of short passages in writing is almost out of the question, the theory of a special source L + Q remains probable. A discussion of Q as known to Matthew before its possible incorporation into L is found in §2 of the introduction to *The Good News According to Matthew*. This stratum is most clearly visible in 3:7—7:10 but can be traced as far as 17:37.

## 3

(a) Who is Luke? His name does not appear in the text; it is first mentioned toward the end of the second century by Irenaeus (*Adv. haer*. 3. 1. 1) and in a list of canonical books. Both identify him with the Gentile Christian (cf. Col. 4:11) physician mentioned in Philemon 24 and Colossians 4:14 as a companion of Paul. This identification, however, is unlikely since Acts disagrees at many points with the information provided by Paul's letters and has little to say about the long stay in Ephesus when Luke was with Paul. It is conceivable that the short "we" passages in Acts (and the account of Paul's journey to Rome?) go back to a list of stopping places with brief notes made by Luke, with the result that the later double work of Gospel and Acts was ascribed to him. Medical terminology appears occasionally in the work of other contemporary writers who were not physicians (see *NTD*, Ergänzungsreihe, vol. 5:142).

Where Luke did his writing cannot be determined. Antioch is a possibility but is not mentioned until the fourth century (Eusebius *Hist. eccl.* 2. 4. 6). He knows and uses the Greek Bible and its style. Before his baptism he may have been a proselyte, i.e., a Gentile who attended Jewish worship and kept the major commandments without accepting circumcision (see the discussion of 24:47). According to 1:1–4 he was not an eyewitness, and he can hardly have come from Palestine (see the discussion of 4:44 and 17:11).

Since 21:20–24 not only presupposes the siege and fall of Jerusalem but reinterprets the Markan text on the basis of these events, the Gospel must have been written after the year 70 (cf. also 19:43–44; 23:28–31; 13:1–5) but also before Acts (1:1–2). Since Acts treats Paul as a central figure but knows nothing of his letters, it can hardly have been written later than the end of the first century. Thus the most likely date for the Gospel is around 80.

It is sometimes suggested that Luke was familiar not only with Q but also with Matthew; this is most unlikely. How could he have ignored Matthew's totally different infancy narratives, the riches of the Sermon on the Mount, the guide to the Christian community with its impressive parable of forgiveness (Matthew 18), the parables of judgment (Matthew 25), or changed sayings like Matthew 12:28?

(b) It is impossible to define Luke's enemies clearly. Was he attacking extreme Paulinists, predecessors of Marcion (see the discussion of 4:31)? However, in the second half of Acts, Paul alone is seen as the one who determines the subsequent history of the Christian community; he shows no sign of being dependent on the Twelve. And how could Luke in this case have included the speech of Stephen (Acts 7)? It is even less conceivable that he was attacking Judaism: he stresses that Jesus preached repeatedly in the context of Jewish worship. The danger of Gnosticism is never mentioned, above all not in the "testament" of Paul, Acts 20:18–35. Nor is the length of time before Jesus' final coming a pressing issue (see the excursus after 21:38, a).

(c) It is clear that the same author wrote Acts. There are minor stylistic changes; the construction "and it happened . . ." is somewhat different, a word such as "likewise" appears eleven times in Luke, never in Acts, etc. But it is certainly the same author who obviously wrote the second book after a short break. But it was probably planned from the beginning. Luke 24:47–49 indicates clearly that the story of Jesus cannot be understood correctly apart from the history of its outcome. It is possible that in writing 22:66–71, Luke left out Jesus' prophecy against the temple because it appears in similar form in the trial of Stephen (Acts 6:13–14). Of course later influence is also conceivable (cf. Mark 5:40; 14:2 with Acts 9:40; 12:4). But the preface was written for the first book alone; see the discussion of 1:1. On the whole subject, see *NTD* 5, Introduction, especially §2; also 3; 4. 6. 2; 5; and 7. 2; with bibliography.

## 4

I was able to revise my commentary during my recent stay as visiting lecturer at Southern Baptist Theological Seminary in Louisville, Kentucky, testing it in dialogue with good friends and enriching it in a well-appointed library through further reading, primarily of English-language materials (including a photocopy of an unpublished theology of Luke by R. Maddox). I am therefore pleased to dedicate it to the Society of Biblical Literature in North America and especially to my personal friends among its members. It is a small token of gratitude for having been made an honorary member on the occasion of its centennial.

The author wishes also to express his thanks for a grant from the Schweizerischer Nationalfond, which made possible the help of an assistant, especially for checking references, even after retirement.

## 5

## BIBLIOGRAPHY

Scholarly commentaries: J. M. Creed, *The Gospel According to St. Luke* (1930); E. E. Ellis, *The Gospel of Luke* (1966); J.A. Fitzmyer, *The Gospel According to Luke* (AB, 1981-   ); W. Grundmann, *Das Evangelium nach Lukas* (THNT, [6]1971); I. H. Marshall, *Commentary on Luke* (1978); H. Schürmann, *Das Lukasevangelium, Kap. 1, 1—9,50* (HTK, 1969).

More popular commentaries: H. W. Bartsch, *Wachet aber zu jeder Zeit* (1963); J. Ernst, *Das Evangelium nach Lukas* (RNT, 1977); R. Gutzwiller, *Meditation über Lukas I–II* (1965); K. H. Rengstorf, *Das Evangelium nach Lukas* (NTD, [1]1937—[17]1978); W. Schmithals, *Das Evangelium nach Lukas* (ZB, 1980); G. Schneider, *Das Evangelium nach Lukas* I–II (OTK, 1977).

Monographs: F. Bovon, *Luc le théologien, 25 ans de recherches* (1978); G. Braumann, ed., *Das Lukasevangelium* (1974); R. E. Brown, *The Birth of the Messiah* (1977); H. Conzelmann, *Die Mitte der Zeit* ([5]1964); M. Dömer, *Das Heil Gottes* (1978); J. Drury, *Tradition and Design in Luke's Gospel* (1976); J. Jeremias, *Die Sprache des Lukasevangeliums* (1980); J. Jervell, *Luke and the People of God* (1972); L. E. Keck and J. L. Martyn, ed., *Studies in Luke-Acts* (1966); R. Maddox, *The Purpose of Luke-Acts* (1982); F. Neirynck, ed., *L'évangile de Luc* (1973); E. Rasco, *La teologia de Lucas* (1976); C. H. Talbert, ed. *Perspectives on Luke-Acts* (1978); *La Parole de Grâce, Études lucaniennes à la mémoire d'A. George* (*RSR* 69, 1981); E. Schweizer, "Zur Frage der Quellenbenutzung durch Lukas" and other essays, *Neues Testament und Christologie im Werden* (1982).

Apocrypha and Pseudepigrapha: E. Kautzsch, *Die Apokryphen und Pseudepigraphen des Alten Testaments, I–II (²1921); P. Riessler, Altjüdisches Schrifltum ausserhalb der Bibel (1928); E. Hennecke and W. Schneemelcher, Neutestamentliche Apokryphen* (²1924, ³1959–1964).

Dead Sea Scrolls: J. Maier, *Die Texte vom Toten Meer*, I,–II (1960); *Die Tempelrolle vom Toten Meer (UTB*, 1978); E. Lohse, *Die Texte aus Qumran, hebräisch und deutsch* (²1971); also *NTS* 20 (1974), 386–94, 404–406; *Discoveries in the Judean Desert* (1955–    ); cf. also Fitzmyer.

Rabbinic texts: (H. L. Strack and) P. Billerbeck, *Kommentar zum Neuen Testament aus Talmud und Midrasch* (⁵1969) (cited as "Bill." without page number for discussion of Lukan passages); tractates not in Billerbeck are cited from various editions.

Also helpful are good modern translations such as Today's English Version or the Jerusalem Bible, and a synopsis, in which the texts of the first three Gospels are printed in parallel columns.

The List of Abbreviations (pp. v–x) indicates whether a given text is Jewish, Christian, or pagan, and its approximate date.

# PREFACE
## LUKE'S PURPOSE
### (1:1—4)

---

[1]Inasmuch as many have already undertaken to compile a narrative of the events which have been accomplished among us—[2]just as those who from the beginning had been eyewitnesses and ministers of the word delivered to us—[3]it seemed good to me also, having followed all things carefully from the beginning, to write a sequential account for you, dear Theophilus, [4]that you may know the truth of the words in which you have been instructed.

[In this and all subsequent passages, divergences from the Revised Standard Version are the author's.]

In an artful Greek sentence that differs markedly from the style of the narrative to follow, Luke writes his preface. It resembles similar prefaces in contemporary historical works (e.g., Arist. 1—2) but at the same time mentions typical theological questions of Luke's day. While Mark almost attacks his reader with his abrupt "good news," Luke bridges the gap between himself and his readers in the manner of a cultured contemporary.

"Many" tried (Greek aorist) to describe the saving event which, though past, still lives in the present (Greek perfect). Even these had to rely on the choir of eyewitnesses who, in service to the word, handed the past on to the present (aorist). At this point the main clause begins with Luke in the dative ("to me"). He, too, stands between the past (the completed study on which his writing is based [perfect]) and the goal of his writing, which lies in the future: that Theophilus will be assured of what he has heard (aorist). The line from the past through the present to the future is artfully presented: the saving event, institution of witnesses, their tradition, previous attempts, Luke's Gospel, the assurance of faith. That the object, the events to be comprehended in words, is mentioned before the evangelist is no accident. Only the saving act itself and Luke's thorough study of it appear in the perfect tense, as elements of the past that continue to live in the present (cf. the discussion of 4:21).

[1] That "many" (often a convention) "undertook" the task of writing an account does not necessarily imply that they failed (Acts 9:29; 19:13; but cf. Josephus *Contra Ap.* 2. 1–2). But a new attempt was not unnecessary. The tradition had already become problematic, probably on account of its variety. It is not meant to be simply a proclamation of faith and a call to faith but a "narrative of events" (cf. Diodorus *Hist.* 11. 20. 1). In these events, however, something was "accomplished." This can mean the end of a certain period of time (as in Acts 14:26; 19:21; 24:24, 27), but it usually refers to the will of God (Luke 8:31; 21:24; 22:16; Acts 7:23; 9:23) already announced in the Old Testament (Luke 4:21; 24:44; Acts 1:16; 3:18; 13:27). The latter is probably the meaning here. The two views are not contradictory if God controls the course of the ages.

"Among us" does not mean that God's history was brought to a close among those named in Acts. God's history is not yet at an end. Although Luke almost certainly had his second book in mind from the outset, he did not write his preface for them both. The "many" precursors can only be the evangelists. In addition, the further development of Luke's style shows that Acts was written later, after some interval. Luke thus has in mind all for whom Jesus has become this fulfillment—as Justin Martyr, writing in the second century, says that John the Baptist appeared "among us" (*Dial.* 81. 4).

[2] Luke himself is not among the eyewitnesses, nor does he know any Gospel ascribed to an eyewitness. He must rely on the tradition of the "events" of a specific period (Acts 1:22: from Jesus' baptism by John to his resurrection), not merely the present voice of the Spirit or the new understanding of God shared by the Apostles. An Apostle, however is not a guarantor of the course of historical events but a "witness to the resurrection" (Acts 1:22; cf. 4:33 with 31). According to Luke 1:2, the eyewitnesses were appointed "ministers of the word," probably at Easter (aorist; Acts 10:41; 13:31). Thus beyond being an eyewitness, there must also be a special call to hand down the tradition of the gospel (selection of the Twelve; Pentecost;

cf. Luke 24:31, 34; Acts 1:21–23, with reference to the risen Lord). The function of the Apostles is thus not merely to give a historically accurate account of what has taken place (like witnesses at the scene of an accident) but at the same time to proclaim it as an act of God (cf. Josephus *De bello jud.* 6. 134: "eyewitness and witness"). There is no room for self-serving propaganda: the real agent of their witness is the Spirit of God (Acts 1:2; 5:32). Only the Spirit gives knowledge of what is truly taking place (cf. 2:11–12, etc.). Even Herod and Pilate were outward witnesses. The two go together: an event in the course of earthly history is understood to be God's act that interrupts the whole earthly course of history, not just a symbol or example of an independently valid truth (cf. the excursus following 4:30). Central to Luke is therefore the "word," in which there begins to speak not the depths of our hearts or the ideas of someone exceptionally wise, but that which God has done in history.

[3] Unlike Josephus (*De bello jud.* Preface 1. 1), Luke says nothing about himself. He is a member of the Christian community—nothing else matters. Four expressions characterize his work. "From the beginning" may refer to Luke 1—2, though without insisting that there is something lacking in a Gospel that does not include a preliminary history. The word used could also be translated "once again" or "thoroughly," but the meaning given above is probably correct here. "Sequential" suggests a train of events (Acts 3:24; 18:23), perhaps with secondary stress on completeness but hardly can refer to a sequence of eras in sacred history. "The following" (instead of "sequential") is out of the question since there is no article. The statement that Luke has followed "all things" may be directed against the recent appearance of secret traditions (Acts 20:20, 27). The word "followed" might suggest direct personal witness, which could refer only to some parts of Acts; vs. 2 excludes this possibility for the Gospel, indeed for "all things" recounted there, so that the author's studies must be meant. According to the preface in Acts 1:1, these studies embrace the tradition of Jesus to the time of his ascension. Finally, Luke does all this "carefully" as befits a historian.

A dubious tradition (Pseudo-Clement, 10. 71) has it that Theophilus later became a bishop in Antioch. The term "dear" (literally "honored") is conventional; it would be inappropriate to conclude from it that Theophilus was a high Roman official (the same form of address appears in Acts 23:26; 24:3; 26:25) or joined the Christian community between the dates of Luke 1:3 and Acts 1:1 (where the epithet does not occur). The Greek name, which means "beloved of God," would also be appropriate for a Jew.

[4] He is "instructed" or "informed" concerning the gospel. We may therefore think of him as sharing the Christian faith; the formal address is unusual but may be due to the conventional style of a preface. In any case the Gospel is not intended as an apologia addressed to Roman officials—would any of them plow through so much material to find a few details bearing on the question of whether or not this group was dangerous? It is also highly dubious that the readers are threatened by Roman persecution (see the discussion of 21:12 and cf. the discussion of 4:6).

Faith cannot be Christian faith apart from God's action in the history of Israel, Jesus Christ, and the Christian community. On the other hand, no accurate historical account as such can ever give "assurance" of faith. But Luke presupposes the actual proclamation of the Christian faith and recalls the "words" that Theophilus already knows. God's concrete—and therefore historical—act of love cannot be reduced to an abstract doctrine; therefore the Gospel is a historical account. But at the same time this act must be proclaimed as God's act and pronounced as salvation for the reader.

It is unlikely that Luke is defending this "assurance" against some explicit heresy. The heretics in Acts 20:29–30 are described in very general terms without mention of any specific error. According to vss. 33–34, the problem seems to lie more in the realm of ethical conduct. There is not the slightest hint that Paul might be misunderstood in the Christian community; on the contrary, he is the model for the coming battle against false doctrine (Acts 20:17–36). Acts 14:4, 14 also shows that Luke does not hesitate to give Paul the title "Apostle."

In the final analysis, then, Luke understands his work as laying a foundation for Christianity as a whole. It is written in the modern language of educated and demanding contemporaries, possibly to "compete" for the attention of cultured readers. When he incorporates archaic biblical expressions from his tradition, he does so deliberately, like the builder of a neo-Gothic church, in order to add a sacred dimension that cannot be comprehended in everyday language. He presupposes a knowledge of the Old Testament and Christian history (cf. the discussion of 1:7; 4:38) and seeks to reinforce existing knowledge of the faith; he therefore is thinking in terms of dissemination within the Christian community.

The mode of expression resembles that of the scientific historian: "The only goal and the only purpose of history is to be useful, and this can come only. from the truth. . . . It is the sole task of the historian to describe things precisely as they happened . . . , in order that, when similar circumstances arise, people may learn from description of the past how they should act in present need" (Lucian *Historia* 9. 39, 42). In substance, Luke's purpose is entirely different. Even Old Testament historiography does not look for examples of constantly repeating actions but rather for purposive acts of God, unique, differing in every period, albeit performed in constant faithfulness. Here the past is not an instructive example but a foundation upon which one lives in the present and from which one approaches the consummation of the end. Therefore Luke cannot maintain the purely objective, historical presentation suggested in his preface, nor does he wish to do so. In Acts 1:1–5, also, Luke's concern for the Christian faith disrupts the elegant literary form of his preface. The outline of his work follows that of Mark, which is kerygmatic, and illustrates the theologically important determination of Jesus to go to Jerusalem (Luke 9:51—19:28). The resurrection at the conclusion of the Gospel points forward to what God will do (described in Acts).

Also the Gospels before Luke have a kerygmatic purpose in their narrative (cf. the Introduction to *The Good News According to Mark*, §6). Luke, however, clearly sees the problem of tradition, that is, how to link events of the past with the message of today. Of course the past cannot simply be the guarantee of the present, but it can prevent faith from degenerating into superstition, correct it and reshape it, even as its own significance is revealed only by the witness of faith (see the excursus following 4:30).

# I
## INFANCY NARRATIVES
## JOHN AND JESUS
### 1:5—2:52

---

In chapters 1—2, the infancy narratives of John and Jesus are closely interwoven; they are clearly separated from later events by 3:1–2, which marks a new beginning. The sequence is as follows:

A. Annunciation (1:5–25/1:26–38)
   Transition (Visitation, Thanksgiving; 1:39–56)
B. (1:57–80/2:1–40)
   (a) Birth (1:57–58/2:1–20)
   (b) Circumcision and naming (1:59–66/2:21–24)
   (c) Thanksgiving and prophecy (1:67–79/2:25–39)
   (d) Growth (1:80/2:40)
   Transition (Jesus in the temple; 2:41–52).

Noteworthy are the extended account of Jesus' birth (2:6–7 would have been an adequate parallel) and the elaboration of the narrative in 2:21–39, where the presentation of Jesus and the prophecy of Anna go beyond the parallel account of John. There are corresponding "comings" and "goings" in 1:9/23, 28/38, 39/56; 2:9/15, 16/20, 22/39, 41/51.

Luke 1:5–24a(25), 57–66 probably originated among followers of John the Baptist who did not recognize Jesus as Messiah (cf. Mark 2:18; Luke 7:16; Acts 19:2). They awaited only God's final coming, not the Messiah (see the discussion of 1:17). The same is probably true of the hymns in 1:46–55 (as a hymn of Elizabeth without vs. 48b?) and 1:68–75 (without vss. 76–79); these differ in structure but exhibit the same vocabulary (see the discussion). It is therefore highly unlikely that the story of John was shaped after the story of Jesus. In addition, vs. 26a presupposes vs. 24. If the hymn of Zechariah were contemporary with the story, it would have to follow vs. 64; it has also been expanded in vss. 76–79 by the addition of a stylistically distinct Christian strophe (see the introduction to vss. 57–66 and 67–80). If the Christian passages in vss. 26–56 are omitted, vs. 57 continues naturally from vs. 25; the Old Testament flavor is then even more distinct. At one time the narrative may also have told how the mother learned of the promise (vs. 60).

Whether it was a pre-Lukan Jewish Christian or Luke himself who expanded this tradition by added parallel Jesus narratives surpassing the story of John is hard to determine, as is the extent to which the two accounts had already been assimilated to each other in the oral stage. This process probably antedates Luke: he holds Mary in high esteem (Acts 1:14; also Luke 8:19, 21 in contrast with Mark 3:22, 33; cf. also 11:27–28), and 2:19, 51b appear to originate with him, but he never refers subsequently to the virgin birth (see the discussion of 2:12), not even in summaries of the faith (Acts 10:34, 43; 13:16–41; etc.).

In addition, he actually reduces the parallelism between John and Jesus: Jesus is depicted as Elijah, but this is no longer true of John; Mark 9:11–13 and Matthew 11:14 are lacking, as well as the account of John's martyrdom. Almost certainly 2:8–20 was already extant as a separate unit (see the introduction to 2:1–20), together with a tradition comprising roughly 2:3(or 6)–7, 22–38, 42–51a, although here certainty is impossible. This unit would already have been understood as a supplement to a Gospel (Mark? L?). When the two traditions were linked, vs. 21 was added as a parallel to 1:59. Groups of two are common in the Bible (Elijah/Elisha, Moses/Joshua, Moses/Elijah, Peter/Paul), but the second does not regularly surpass the first. Luke might have connected John and Jesus by means of vss. 39–45, placed vss. 46–55 in Mary's mouth, and written 2:21; but vss. 39–46a contain un-Lukan expressions, so that he may only have added isolated passages (1:48b, 80; 2:1–2, 19, 40, 51b?) and given his style to the whole.

The stories about John stress his connection with Israel, especially the priestly tradition of Jerusalem; the hymns have more the flavor of Jewish messianism. The same is true of the stories about Jesus (2:21–38, 41–51, and 2:32–33). The story of the shepherds, however, has certain unique features. The early tradition is characterized by incomprehension of God's miracles; whoever linked the two strands also introduced Mary's understanding faith and incorporated expectations that were cherished at Qumran (see the discussion of 1:34–35).

Stylistically, chapters 1—2 differ markedly from the preface; they exhibit a solemn biblical form that itself influenced Luke. Only in 1:80; 2:52; and the addition 1:76–79 do they refer to what follows. Luke sees them as an introduction to chapters 3—24, just as Acts 1—2 is an introduction to 3—28.

The very fact that we are told of Jesus' infancy is important. In the case of most of the prophets, we know only the message that was theirs to deliver; there is no infancy narrative for any of them (but cf. Exod. 2:1–10; Josephus *Ant.* 2. 215–16; 5. 276; Enoch 106; Book of Jubilees 2). In Jesus, God became not just word but flesh. That a human life was lived, from a mother's womb to death and resurrection, with all that such a life implies, is important to Luke. God has become solidary with humankind, or, better expressed, the life of God is such that it can take form in a human life, totally permeated by God's love, like that lived by Jesus of Nazareth.

This is why Jesus' life is so intimately interwoven with the human life of John the Baptist. Luke's interest here is not biographical but to proclaim the miracle that a totally human life means the salvation of the world. He intends his text to awaken the acceptance of faith not satisfy curiosity. Therefore he uses a narrative form because God's salvation is found in a historical human life, not in great ideas or dogmatic propositions. And this salvation is to live on in the totality of a human life, so that it seeks acceptance by mind, will, and heart.

The stories are not legends meant to illustrate the truth of an idea; they describe in legendary form what really happened: God did not remain in a distant heaven far above the world but became a real presence within the world and therefore seeks also to become a real presence in the life of the reader. Just as the Baptist's life was meaningless by itself—he was executed before he had a chance to really accomplish anything—so is every life that is not filled in all its light and shadows by Jesus. Since God's love took form in him, the possibility and blessing of God's love also invades such lives that, humanly speaking, end unfulfilled (cf. Retrospect).

# A. ANNUNCIATION
## (1:5–38)

A    5–7/–: General situation: Date, place, persons, need.

B    8–11/26–28: Specific situation: Date, place, persons, appearance of the angel.

C    12–13a/29–30a: Reaction and reassurance.

D    13b–17/30b–33: Promise of birth and its meaning for many.

C′    18–20/34–37: Reaction and angelic sign.

B′    21–22/38: Silence/confession.

A′    23–25/–: Fulfillment, resolution of need.

There are several expressions repeated almost identically: in C, "was troubled," "the angel said to him/her, 'Fear not, [Name]'"; in D: "she/you will bear a son, and you shall call his name," "he will be great"; in C′: "said to the angel," "and behold." In addition, the name Gabriel is mentioned in both accounts. The promise "he will be called the Son of the Most High" may be compared to vs. 76: "you [John] will be called the prophet of the Most High." Significant differences are discussed in the context of 1:26–38. The complex of angelic appearance, fear, question of how, and sign also appears in Genesis 17:1–21; 18:1–15; Judges 13:3–22, sometimes in different sequence.

## God's New Beginning: The Annunciation of John (1:5–25)

[5]It happened in the days of Herod, king of Judea, that there was a priest with the name Zechariah, of the division of Abijah; and he had a wife of the daughters of Aaron, and her name was Elizabeth. [6]There were both righteous before God, walking in all the commandments and ordinances of the Lord blameless. [7]And they had no child because Elizabeth was barren and both were advanced in years.

[8]Then it happened, while he was serving as priest before God [9]according to the order of his division, according to the custom of the priesthood it fell to him by lot to enter the temple of the Lord to offer incense, [10]and the whole multitude of the people were praying outside at the hour of incense offering. [11]There appeared to him an angel of the

Lord standing on the right side of the altar of incense. ¹²And Zechariah was troubled when he saw it, and fear fell upon him. ¹³But the angel said to him, "Do not be afraid, Zechariah, for your prayer has been heard, and your wife Elizabeth will bring a son into the world for you, and you shall call his name John.

¹⁴And he will bring you joy and gladness,
  and many will rejoice at his birth.
¹⁵For he will be great before the Lord,
  and he will not drink wine or strong drink,
  and he will be filled with Holy Spirit,
  even in his mother's womb.
¹⁶And he will turn many of the sons of Israel to the Lord their God,
¹⁷and he will go before him in the spirit and power of Elijah,
  to turn the hearts of the fathers to the children,
  and disobedient to the wisdom of the just,
  to make ready for the Lord a people prepared."

¹⁸And Zechariah said to the angel, "How shall I know this? For I am old and my wife is advanced in years." ¹⁹And the angel answered and said to him, "I am Gabriel, who stands before God, and was sent to speak to you, and to bring you this good news. ²⁰And behold, you will be silent and unable to speak until the day that these things come to pass because you did not believe my words, which will be fulfilled in their time." ²¹And the people were waiting for Zechariah, and they wondered at his delay in the temple. ²²But when he came out, he could not speak to them, and they perceived that he had seen a vision in the temple; and he made signs to them and remained silent. ²³And it happened that the days of his service were fulfilled and he went to his home.

²⁴After these days his wife Elizabeth conceived and hid herself for five months, and said, ²⁵"Thus the Lord has done to me in the days when he looked on me, to take away my reproach among the people."

(Vs. 5—1 Chron. 24:10. Vss. 7, 18—Gen. 18:11–12; 1 Sam. 1:2. Vs. 13—Dan. 10:12. Vs. 15—Num. 6:3; Judg. 13:4. Vs. 17—Mal. 4:5–6.)

This is the story of a miracle, but it differs from the run of miracle stories. An angel is the agent of the miracle, rather than Jesus, for obvious reasons. What is unusual is that the resistance, Zechariah's doubt, comes only after the promise. This feature recalls the style of call narratives (Exod. 3:11—4:13; Jer. 1:6; cf. Isa. 6:5), just as the opening of the story suggests a much broader future than just help for a childless couple. In addition, their righteousness is emphasized, but the promise of a miracle is met not with faith but rather with doubt on the part of the righteous man. The sign sent by God is thus both a punishment and an aid to faith; it underlines the totally unexpected and unbelievable way God acts in the world.

It is possible that Luke added details like vss. 10, 21; for the most part, however, his contribution is only stylistic. Vss. 24–25 were added when this section was connected with the story of Jesus, which was not originally in mind (vs. 17). A summary statement like vs. 24a (and 25?) was probably followed originally by vs. 57 (cf. also the discussion of vss. 46–55).

[5] Herod wanted to be considered a Davidic king (Josephus *Ant.* 14. 9) and possibly even something like a Messiah. This is the earthly human history in which God intervenes. The names are significant: Zechariah = "The Lord has remembered"; Elizabeth = "God's oath" (or: happiness? perfection?); John = "The Lord is merciful." "Judea" means the whole land, as in 4:44 and 23:5; only in 3:1 does it designate the Roman province.

God's history begins in the temple, which is for Israel a sign of God's presence. [6] We sense the Old Testament delight in the law without critical comment. Both parents are "blameless" with respect to the law like Paul (Phil. 3:6) and Job (LXX)—"before God," who alone is competent to judge. The author has no schema for measuring such righteousness, as was the case at Qumran and among the Pharisees. Their piety finds expression in the cult, again without criticism or rigoristic intensity (again as at Qumran and among the Pharisees). But the living spirit of God and wisdom also play an important role (1:15, 80; 2:25, 40, 47).

[7] The situation of John's parents resembles that of Isaac's (Gen. 17:17; cf. 18:11, "advanced in age" [literally: in "days"]), Samson's (Judg. 13:2; similarly vs. 5), and Samuel's (1 Sam. 1:1–2). What they suffered, only to see transformed into joy and thanksgiving, is here concentrated once more in the fate of John's parents, with the suggestion that the meaning of all these human experiences will be fulfilled. Their wound is not yet healed, the promise of salvation is

not yet fulfilled. In their private life as in the life of Israel, everything is still totally open to the future.

[8] Each of the twenty-four divisions of priests served for a week (1 Chronicles 24), during which its members came to Jerusalem from their regular homes. Within these divisions, each family was assigned to a day. According to a later regulation, a priest's offering of incense was the high point of his life; he could do it only once as long as there were others to whom the lot had not yet fallen. After the general prayer "May the God of mercy come into the sanctuary and accept with pleasure the sacrifice of his people" (Bill. 2. 79), the priest presses the bowl of incense down on the coals in the holy place behind the outer curtain. This takes place in the morning before the sacrifice of burnt offering in the outer court and afterward at about 3:00 P.M., when the crowd was especially large (vs. 10; cf. 1 Kings 8:5, 10–14). Josephus (*Ant.* 13. 282) also tells of God's voice speaking when the high priest offers incense.

[11] The prayer for God's coming is visibly answered (cf. Ps. 141:1–2). The temple, the petrified tent of meeting, is filled with God's life and set in motion, as was typical of the tent of meeting in the desert. There is a new, direct irruption of God's presence, taking its most concentrated form not in the prophetic word—Zechariah remains silent—but in the angel.

[12] Fear is the normal human reaction in the face of the unexpected and inexplicable (Judg. 6:22–23; 13:6, 22; Dan. 8:17; 10:11–19; Tob. 12:16; Mark 16:5; etc.). It is fear that comes over someone when God, who normally plays such a minor role in life, suddenly becomes inescapably present. But the first words that introduce the new covenant free the listener from fear—in particular, the listener who accepts the encounter with God and does not retreat from it (cf. the discussion of 1:29).

[13] The divine promise takes Zechariah wholly by surprise; he had not reckoned concretely with the fulfillment of his prayer (for a child or for God's salvation? cf. Gen. 17:19; Dan. 9:20–23) (vs. 18). What he had ardently believed in theory he had never pictured in concrete terms. It was customarily a father's right to name his child and thus determine the nature of the one to come; God preempts this right (cf. Gen. 16:11; 17:19; Isa. 7:14; 1 Kings 13:2).

[14] Although later the preaching of repentance is stressed, the crucial message is one of joy, indeed of eschatological "rejoicing" on the part of "many." God's first word is thus liberation from fear, fulfillment of supplications, eschatological joy, "gospel" (vs. 19). The reader is already invited to join these "many" to whom the promise is given.

[15] The basis of this promise is the fact that John "will be great before the Lord (i.e., God; vs. 16)." Jesus himself explicitly affirms John's greatness (7:26–28), which is not simply in human eyes. It is described in vss. 15b–16 and again in 17a–17b as a gift and a commission. Even before his birth and through no choice of his own (cf. Isa. 49:1; Jer. 1:5; Ecclus. 49:7; 1QH 9:29–31), he is one set apart by God like the Nazirites, who renounced cutting their hair, drinking wine, and eating meat in order to show that there is more to life than the enjoyment of civilization (Num. 6:2–5; Judg. 13:4–7; 16:17). Prophet and Nazirite were originally distinct figures although later they were assimilated to each other (Amos 2:11–12). And yet John is not really a Nazirite: nothing is said about cutting his hair (also 1 Sam. 1:11), and the promise of the Spirit throughout his lifetime is new. We see at once in a single sign the Lord's purpose for God's people: the day of salvation is at hand (Joel 2:32–36; opposite, Ps. 74:2, 9). [16] John's commission is to call Israel back to its "Lord." Salvation is thus the gift to men and women of the strength and the repose to return, to change.

[17] Vs. 17 develops this theme. "Spirit" and "power" often occur together, especially in Luke and Paul (but also in Isaiah 11:2 and 1QH 7:6). As in the case of Elijah (cf. the discussion of 1:76; 3:19–20), the Spirit brings about a real change in the sick body and the sick heart. The expectation of reconciliation between generations (Mal. 4:6) is here expressed in fact as a hope for a younger generation that, in contrast to an older generation set in its ways, will heed the call to something new (similar statements already appear in the LXX and Ecclus. 48:10; Bk. Jub. 23:16, 26; En. 90:6–7). The earlier generation will then join God's revolution. Is Luke thinking in terms of the Gentiles and Israel (cf. 3:8)? Or are the "disobedient" to be identified with the new generation, the "just" with their parents, so that the double movement is preserved? But such readings are not in

the text. Vs. 16 had already made it clear that the point is repentance and return to God, not just a compromise in the conflict between generations.

As a forerunner of the "Lord" (clearly identified as God in vs. 16), John is seen as a kind of messianic figure in Luke's source (see the discussion of 1:76). According to Malachi 3:1, 23, Elijah plays the same role (also Test. Sim. 6:5; made to refer to the incarnate Lord by Christian copyists). Luke undoubtedly had Jesus in mind (cf. 1:43; 2:11)—and rightly so because God's coming was realized in him.

[18] So startling is the angel's message that, like his predecessors in the Old Testament, Zechariah is unprepared for it (cf. Gen. 15:8, "how am I to know?"; Judg. 6:36–40; 1 Sam. 10:2–7; 2 Kings 20:8–9; Isa. 7:11). [19] But God will not be held back by human lack of faith. The emphatic "*I* am old" is countered by an equally emphatic "*I* am Gabriel." The very name of the angel ("Man of God," according to En. 40:9 the one who stands "before God's face" above all powers; cf. Bill.) and above all the reference to God who sent him (as in Dan. 10:11 and especially Tob. 12:14–15) are meant to make great the little faith of Zechariah to receive the "good news," the "gospel." In Judaism both noun and verb refer to the message of a prophet or an angel, even of God or the Messiah, a message of either judgment (2 Macc. 3:29) or salvation (Ezek. 3:26; 24:27; cf. also Rev. 14:6). [20] Therefore the sign vouchsafed to Zechariah, though revealing his lack of faith, is at the same time an aid of faith. A salvation that does not reveal and thereby change what stands in its way would not be real salvation (see the discussion of Rom. 1:18). That God opens someone's eyes to that which is distorted in such a way that the person is re-formed, not simply shattered, is a demonstration of the living God.

[21] Even the high priest was charged not to stay too long in the sanctuary, lest the people be worried (Bill. 2. 77). Israel knew that God's presence is like a "devouring fire" (Deut. 4:24; Isa. 33:14)!

[22] In the face of God's amazing act, a human being is reduced to silence (cf. Dan. 10:15–16). This silence is the space for God's saving acts: God alone has the floor. [23] Zechariah can only return to the mountain village (vs. 39) where he lives and practice his sec-

ular profession. **[24]** God's promise is "fulfilled" (see the discussion of vs. 57), and Elizabeth, too, withdraws into a seclusion broken only by the angel (vs. 36). Now that God has begun to work with her, the only appropriate human response is thanksgiving.

Thus the beginning of God's new history is rooted in the joy given by the law and Israel's temple but also, as Luke sees it, in openness to God's future actions. At the high point of a priest's life, God begins—quite on divine initiative and unexpectedly—to become reality, initially in the lives of two human beings and their distress. Nothing is said yet about the Messiah but rather of God's coming, which will reach far beyond the single individual and recall all Israel to its Lord.

At this very point we see how little human lives are ready for God's new act, even the lives of those who live not for themselves and for human morality but in openness to God. The coming of the real God, not as expected, strikes dumb even the upright and devout, who suddenly discover their lack of faith and see that with all their sincerely held beliefs they did not really reckon on a transforming irruption of God. But God, who puts human history at divine service, shaped as it is by chance and by good and evil actions, overcomes even Zechariah and Elizabeth. They understand that God has laid claim on them and given them grace; their silence and retreat is the appropriate consequence. They are incorporated into the good news by God's own act, which both bewilders them and comforts them, which goes forward despite all human resistance. For this reason the beginning of Elizabeth's pregnancy is included here although we would not expect it until vs. 57.

### God's New Creation: The Annunciation of Jesus (1:26–38)

[26]In the sixth month the angel Gabriel was sent from God to a city of Galilee named Nazareth, [27]to a virgin betrothed to a man named Joseph, of the house of David; and the virgin's name was Mary. [28]And when he came to her, he said, "Hail to you, O favored one, the Lord is with you!" [29]But she was greatly troubled at the saying, and considered what sort of greeting this might be. [30]And the angel said to her, "Do not be

afraid, Mary, for you have found favor with God. [31]And 'behold, you will conceive in your womb and bear a son, and you shall call his name' Jesus.
[32]He will be great, and will be called the Son of the Most High;
  and the Lord God will give to him the throne of David his father,
[33]and he will reign over the house of Jacob for ever;
  and of his reign [or: of his kingdom] there will be no end."
[34]Then Mary said to the angel, "How will this be, since I do not know any man?" [35]And the angel answered and said to her,
  "Holy Spirit will come upon you,
  and the power of the Most High will overshadow you;
  therefore what will be born will be called holy,
  God's son.
[36]And behold, Elizabeth, your kinswoman, she too has conceived a son in her old age; and this is the sixth month for her who was called barren. [37]'For with God nothing is impossible.'" [38]Then Mary said, "Behold, the handmaid of the Lord; let it be to me according to your word." And the angel departed from her.

(Vs. 31—Judg. 13:3; Isa. 7:14. Vs. 32—Isa. 9:6; 2 Sam. 7:12–16. Vs. 33—Mic. 4:7; Dan. 7:14. Vs. 37—Gen. 18:14; Jer. 32:17.)


Comparison with vss. 5–25 (see the discussion of 1:5–38) reveals significant differences. There is no description of need because no need exists; nothing is said of the parents' righteousness because here there is infinitely more emphasis on the grace of God alone (A). Therefore the angel takes center stage. He is subject; Mary comes in afterward as the one to whom he is sent. There is likewise no mention of the miracle's taking place because the response of faith in vs. 38 makes it unnecessary (A').

The emphasis is on the woman (see the discussion of 8:3) as receiver of the promise. She will give the child his name; in contrast to vs. 13, she will not bear a son "for her husband." In place of Zechariah's silence we have her acceptance in faith (B'). Her question, which parallels the doubt of Zechariah, is answered by a reference to the creative power of the Holy Spirit, which thus shifts from section D (vss. 15, 17) to C' (vs. 35) because it performs a different function. In 1:15, 17, 41, 67, 80; 2:25–27, we have the Spirit of prophecy in the style of the Old Testament; the creator Spirit of 1:35, however, introduces a new act on the part of God (see the discussion of 3:21–22). Mary, too, is promised a sign, but she does not need one and sees it only after the acceptance in vs. 38. All of this places the miracle in bold relief as an act of God's pure grace. Contrary to every expectation the central character is a woman; there is no introduction involving unusual righteousness or the persistent prayer of a sufferer. A free creative act of God, as at the beginning of the world, brings into being one who this time is not the forerunner of a yet greater event, one whose reign knows no end.

As many have pointed out, there seems to be conflict between hope for a Davidic king (vss. 32–33) and expectation of the Son of God, born of the Spirit (vs. 35); either vss. 34–35 or the introduction of Joseph coupled with the typically Davidic expectation may be viewed as secondary. In the latter case, Mary's statement that she does not know any man (vs. 34) would make sense and Luke would also be responsible for introducing the Son of David (Acts 13:23), with his "throne" and "kingship" (Acts 2:30; Luke 22:30; 23:42). On the other hand, "come upon you—Holy Spirit—power—Most High—overshadow" are Lukan expressions, and vss. 34–35 are more likely to be Hellenistic than is the Davidic hope (see the discussion of Mark 12:37). Nevertheless the verse is not Lukan since he never refers back to it, not even in 2:1–20. "Come upon you" (the Spirit, Isa. 32:15; cf. Job 1:19; 4:15; Num. 5:14, 30; 1 Sam. 11:7) and "overshadow" (Exod. 40:35; Num. 10:36; see the discussion of vs. 35) are Old Testament terms. "Spirit" and "power" draw on 1:17; the "Most High" is also mentioned in vss. 32 and 76. Above all, Qumran texts (4Q243 1:7; 2:1) now show that similar ideas were borrowed by contemporary Palestinian Judaism, possibly from its Hellenistic environment: "He will be great. . . . He will be called God's Son, and they will name him Son of the Most High." A "reign" (Luke 1:33) is also mentioned (4Q243 2:2). In 1:1 we find the statement, "She will descend upon you." It is uncertain who is meant, but the Hebrew word for "spirit" is feminine. That an angel should beget a human being is quite conceivable in Judaism (see Gen. 6:4 and 1QGenApoc 2:1); another Qumran text (1QSa 2:11–12) may even attest to the begetting of the Messiah by God. "Son of David" and "Son of God" appear together in Romans 1:3–4 although here the latter title is reserved for the risen Lord. Above all, the two are linked in 2 Samuel 7:12–14 and so probably go together from the beginning. Whoever linked the traditions of John and Jesus and wrote vss. 26–38 to outdo vss. 5–25 probably combined the two ideas since vss. 27–31 refer to Mary alone, with the intent of surpassing the miracle in vss. 7 and 13. In vss. 32b–33, an oral tradition preserving an oracle related to the Davidic Messiah may have been used and in vss. 34–35 the tradition of the virgin birth, whose substance also appears in Matthew 1:18.

[26] The reference to the sixth month of (Elizabeth's!) pregnancy links the two stories. From the very beginning the two lives are interwoven. According to Book of Jubilees 16:12, Sarah became pregnant in the sixth month of the year. According to a rabbinic text (RH 10b, 11a; cf. Bill. 1. 50, 918; 4. 1006), however, the barrenness of the mothers of Isaac, Jacob, and Samuel was ended at the beginning of the sacral year (end of September). This would fit with the traditional date for the Nativity of St. John the Baptist (24 June) and thus also with 24/25 December as the feast of Christ's Nativity (both first attested in the fourth century). But who might have known this tradition and performed the calculation? Probably 25 December was chosen because 25 March was considered the first day of creation and thus also the day when Jesus was begotten (Julius Africanus, A.D. 221) or because Rome celebrated the winter solstice toward the end of December, so that Jesus was born when the light of the sun begins to increase, John when it begins to decrease (John 3:30).

Here an angel comes to Mary, whereas in 1:9 Zechariah goes where God's presence is expected. In 1:23, accordingly, Zechariah "went," while according to 1:38 the angel "departs" from Mary.

[27] The beginning is much more modest: a girl in an insignificant village rather than a priest in the temple at the capital. In this case, too, the vision is not described. All that matters is the message. The reference to Davidic descent is associated with Joseph (as in 3:23). Betrothal incorporates Mary legally into this lineage; in this period, the legal act was more important than first intercourse—for example, virgins who lost their betrothed before marriage were con-

sidered widows. Not until Ignatius (Eph. 18. 2) and Justin (*Dial.* 43, etc.) is Mary spoken of as a descendant of David.

[28] The same Greek root is present in both "hail" and "favored"; the play on words emphasizes God's act of grace in choosing her. This salutation, together with vs. 42, constitutes the "Hail Mary." Her name, her human individuality, is not mentioned at first but rather what has befallen her, what is happening to her: the promise of the Lord's presence. She is the daughter of grace not the mother. It is unlikely that we have here an echo of the promise to the "daughter of Zion" in Zephaniah 3:14–17 ("the Lord . . . is in your midst" [Heb. also: "within your body"]). In any case, Luke 19:28–40 differs from Matthew 21:5 who makes reference to the visitation of the daughter of Zion by the humble king at his coming (Zech. 9:9).

[29] Mary's confusion at the unexpected greeting emphasizes God's elective act. In contrast to 1:6, 13, nothing is said of Mary's spirituality and prayers; there is certainly no hint that she was sinless from birth. She, too, first finds God a stranger in their encounter, but fear of God—that is, fear of missing the life God offers by making anything more important than God's grace—and trust in that grace are one and the same (Ps. 33:18). This recalls Abraham (Gen. 18:3, 14 = Rom. 4:1, 21; cf. Luke 1:37, 55), but nothing is said about Mary's faith. Everything is "from the Lord."

[31] The mother also names her child in the case of Hagar (Gen. 16:11) because the father will not be present (cf. also Gen. 4:25; 30:21; Judg. 13:24) and probably in the Hebrew text of Isaiah 7:14, where the Greek translation reads "virgin" instead of "young woman" (see the discussion of Matt. 1:21 and 23).

[32] A term used otherwise only of God is applied to Jesus: he will be "great" (cf. 1:15, with the addition of "before the Lord" ["God"]). While still unbegotten (future tense in vs. 31), he is laid claim to by God. What had been awaited of the coming descendant of David since 2 Samuel 7:12–16 is fulfilled in him: he will reign for ever (cf. Apoc. Bar. 40:3; 2 Esd. 7:29, where this reign, however, is conceived in earthly terms and is delimited by the eschaton), and God will be his father (Ps. 89:27–29; 2:7; Isa. 55:3; Ps. Sol. 17:3–4; 18; 2QFlor 1:10 ff.; 4QPatr 1–7). There is no conflict between human parentage (see the discussion of vs. 27) and divine sonship.

What was said of John is here clearly surpassed. Even if "Son of the Most High" is taken as a reference to the function of the reigning king as in Psalm 2:7 (see the discussion of Mark 15:39, excursus), no higher claim can be made in terms of the Davidic expectation. But the unusual term "Most High" itself already suggests the ideas presented in vs. 35 (cf. also Luke 22:70 together with vs. 67).

[33] In any case, the message speaks of God's unique irruption into human history and this in terms of Jesus' sovereignty not his Passion. Luke probably has in mind the lordship of the risen Christ over his community, which reaches its consummation in the Kingdom of God (cf. Acts 1:6–8), thus uniting Christmas and Easter, God's coming and the call for certain decisions and actions on the part of the community. Whether he is also thinking of Jesus' last coming, bringing to a close the age of salvation, the work of both the earthly and the exalted Christ, is uncertain.

There is no mention of asceticism (cf. 5:33; 7:33–34), i.e., human efforts to gain assurance of God. The Qumran sect looked for both a priestly and a royal Messiah, ranking the former above the latter. There is no trace of such an ideology here. In vss. 31–33, Jesus is already clearly distinguished from John; they are not put on the same plane.

[34] Mary shows no enthusiasm, but also, in agreement with the passage as a whole, she offers no resistance. Her astonishingly sober question is: "How?" This is psychologically odd; she must surely have thought of her imminent marriage. But the statement is only meant as an introduction to vs. 35. In the case of a male, "know" refers to sexual intercourse; the same is probably true here. Mary's statement emphasizes the miracle.

[35] In Judaism generative power is not associated with the Spirit but rather creation (Ps. 33:6; Gen. 1:2) and new creation (Ezek. 37:14). Here, then, is where the emphasis lies. Mary experiences what took place when the Spirit caused the world to arise out of chaos and life out of dried bones. It has nothing to do with her virtue or her nature nor with the active procreative will of Joseph. The presence of God "overshadows" Mary just at the cloud of God overshadowed the tent of meeting (cf. the introduction above; also LXX Pss. 91 [90]: 4; 140 [139]: 8; Prov. 18:11). In Luke 9:34, too, the

terrifying presence of God comes to the disciples in a cloud; the idea is fundamentally the same as what is described here although 9:35 implies that the new life is to be expected from Jesus' words. A common religious notion (see the excursus on Matt. 1:18, 23) is thus borrowed and transformed.

The section as a whole emphasizes the unmerited, unmotivated, gracious coming of God; vs. 35*b* focuses on the uniqueness of Jesus. The translation given above is appropriate since "to be called holy" means to be set apart for the service of God (Isa. 4:3; cf. 35:8; 62:12; Exod. 13:12; Lev. 23:2, 37 LXX). In other words, the child will be God's son as something set apart by the deity. Faith in God—who creates life, even when there is no human expectation of life, as in the case of Sarah, the wife of Manoah, or Hannah—is here linked with faith in the Spirit, marking the beginning of a new creation. This helped the community to maintain the full humanity of the Son of God: "Jesus Christ . . . of Mary, who was truly born, ate and drank. . . ." (Ignatius *Trall.* 9. 1).

[36] Mary learns to trust in God even without a sign (vs. 38) and then later to accept God's aid to faith thankfully and with open eyes (vs. 39). [37] The statement from the story of Abraham (Gen. 18:14) that no "word" (literally; but the effect is included) is impossible with God is borrowed by Mary without actually being quoted. [38] She is open to the effectual creative word of God to which she can only be handmaid, standing at its service. Here all discussion ceases. For this very reason she is great in faith. Neither grounds for faith nor grounds for doubt are important—only the act of God on which the human response is grounded.

The whole section leads up to these words of Mary. There is nothing comparable in 1:20. At the end Mary is indeed highly favored just as the angel promised at the beginning. If the virgin birth originally expressed the uniqueness of the Son of God, for the first narrator of our story it served far more to express the grace and favor of the word of God, which calls forth life out of nothing.

In contrast to 1:5–25, everything begins with the angel; nothing exceptional is said of the girl in the village of Nazareth. The visit of the angel is as perplexing to her as it would be to anyone; for her, too, it evokes the uncomprehending question of how it is all to happen. Her true greatness resides in her faith awakened by God's word, a faith that can be silent before God and accede to God's will.

A virgin birth was for the contemporary world an extraordinary but not totally singular event. A proper understanding of the text therefore does not concentrate on this question but on the question of the incomprehensible but real act of God's grace. And of course there is not a word about Mary's perpetual virginity (see the discussion of Mark 6:3). Such an ideal would be Greek, not Israelite. What Mark expressed by citing the Old Testament (Mark 1:2–3), John by speaking of the eternal Word of God which became flesh (John 1:1–14), and Paul by speaking of the sending of God's Son (Gal. 4:4), Luke 1:35 describes in language that attempts to characterize God's mystery by recalling the unique act of creation at the beginning of the world. Even before creation, God is life and movement, not simply a self-contained "person," eternal and unmoved, standing exalted over the suffering of the world. As Spirit God is always coming to meet us, entering into the created world (Gen. 1:2; Ps. 33:6 [Heb. "breath" = "spirit"]) and into the life of Jesus as the beginning of a new creation.

The unity of God can be captured in the image of a single "person," the "Father." But it is impossible to be a person unless life goes forth from us, unless we see, hear, and address other people and other things. The church attempted to express this fact in the image of three "persons": in God the flow of love has been present from the beginning, from the "Father" to the "Son" and back, shining forth into creation in the "Spirit." This flow of love took shape in the life of Jesus and will one day find perfection in the Kingdom of God (see the excursus on Matt. 28:19). In Mary, humanity is represented as the recipient of this life and love from God. With her quiet awaiting of God's act she is the figure of Advent, the opposite of the nervous activity of modern society. Therefore the later church formulated its belief: "conceived by the Holy Spirit" (not simply engendered, as in pagan myths), "born of Mary" (without active human participation). What is important is the change imposed on the common idea of the begetting of a child by a god or its spirit, not the idea itself, which, as Justin comments, is also a commonplace for

Greek heroes and is therefore not peculiar to the Christian faith (*Apol.* 1. 21; *Dial.* 48. 2; cf. the excursus on Matt. 1:18, 23).

# B. THE ENTWINING OF GOD'S TWO ACTS: THE MEETING OF MARY AND ELIZABETH, THE MAGNIFICAT (1:39–56)

[39]In those days Mary arose and went with haste into the hill country, to a city of Judah, [40]and she entered the house of Zechariah and greeted Elizabeth. [41]And it happened, when Elizabeth heard the greeting of Mary, the babe leaped in her womb; and Elizabeth was filled with Holy Spirit, [42]and lifted up her voice with a loud cry and said: "Blessed are you among women, and blessed is the fruit of your womb! [43]And why is this granted me, that the mother of my Lord should jome to me? [44]For behold, when the voice of your greeting came to my ears, the babe in my womb leaped for joy. [45]And blessed is she who believed, for fulfillment will come upon what has been spoken to her from the Lord." [46]And Mary said:

"'My soul' magnifies 'the Lord,'
[47]and my spirit 'rejoices in God my Savior,'
[48]for 'he has regarded the low estate of his handmaiden.'
For behold, henceforth all generations will call me blessed;
[49]for 'he who is mighty has done great things for me,
and holy is his name,
[50]and his mercy' is upon generations and generations
'for those who fear him.'
[51]Strength 'he has showed with his arm.
He has scattered the proud' in the imagination of their hearts,
[52]the mighty 'he has toppled from their thrones,
and exalted those of low degree;
[53]he has filled the hungry with good things,' and 'the rich he has sent empty away.'
[54]'He has espoused the cause of Israel his servant,
in remembrance of his mercy,
[55]as' he spoke 'to our fathers,
to Abraham and his posterity for ever.'"

[56]Then Mary remained with her about three months, and returned to her home.

(Vs. 46—Ps. 35:9. Vs. 47—Hab. 3:18. Vs. 48—1 Sam. 1:11; 9:16. Vs. 49—Ps. 111:9. Vs. 50—Ps. 103:13, 17; 89:2. Vs. 51—Ps. 89:11. Vs. 52—Ecclus. 10:14; Ezek. 21:31. Vs. 53—Ps. 107:9. Vs. 54—Isa. 41:8–9; Ps. 98:3. Vs. 55—Mic. 7:20; 2 Sam. 22:51.)

This section links the two narrative strands. At the beginning Mary comes to Elizabeth and greets her, but she immediately becomes the receiver: the greeting of the unborn child and the blessing pronounced by her kinswoman show where the emphasis lies—not, of course, on Mary herself but on God's unprecedented act involving her. This focus is underlined once more in the hymn that is interpolated into the narrative like Exodus 15:1–18; Numbers 23—24; Deuteronomy 32–33; Judges 5; 2 Samuel 22—23; Jonah 2; Judith 16; Daniel 3:23 LXX; etc.

It moves in three stages from personal experience of God expressed in the first person (vss. 46–49a) through universal experience of God expressed in the third person (vss. 49b–53) to the experience of God in history, where the first person plural appears (vss. 54–55). If we omit vs. 48b, vss. 46b–53 comprise a series of elements each containing two parallel clauses; in vss. 52–53, the clauses are antithetical and the order changes from a–b to b–a. Praise is followed by its occasion in the first two strophes, the occasion by reference to the Old Testament in the second and third. The expression "his handmaiden" (48a) is reflected in "his servant" (54); between them, "he has done" (49a) is reflected by the identical Greek word in vs. 51.

In vs. 48b there is no trace of terminology corresponding to vss. 68–75 (q.v.); instead, we find a typically Lukan expression ("henceforth") and the only clause that uses the future tense and does not speak of God's actions. The mention of "all generations" goes far beyond the parallel in Genesis 30:13 and is inappropriate to the idea that John is the last prophet before the imminent judgment of God (vs. 50 is formulaic). Without this verse, the hymn could originally have been Elizabeth's (see the introduction to 1:5—2:52). This theory is supported by vs. 48*a* and the parallelism with the Song of Hannah (1 Sam. 2:1–10), as well as by vs. 41 (Elizabeth's being filled with the Holy Spirit) and vs. 56 ("her" referring to Elizabeth, while Mary is named explicitly). Was the conclusion of vs. 41 together with vss. 46–55 circulated as a hymn of Elizabeth, like vs. 67 with the hymn of Zechariah? Was it Luke who placed the song in the mouth of Mary, adding vs. 48*b*, to make Elizabeth more clearly subordinate to her (cf. Gen. 30:11)?

[39–40] Recently betrothed, Mary was probably twelve to fourteen years old. She sets forth on a journey taking three or four days (cf. the discussion of 2:16) and stays for three months (vs. 56). She accepts the sign offered by God (vs. 36) even though she has already said "yes" to the way of God's purpose. We are told only of the women in the "house of Zechariah." For the narrator, they constitute a kind of first community, at one in the praise of God.

[41] Not only is Elizabeth's "heart glad, leaping like a child that leaps in its mother's womb" (Odes of Sol. 28:2), but something like a first encounter takes place between John and Jesus. Genesis 25:22–23 does not furnish any parallel—closer is the hymn of the unborn passing through the Red Sea (rabbinic; Bill.). [42] There is something uncanny about Elizabeth's response with its "loud cry." In any case, what takes place is not rational, reasonable, and orderly—it is more like an eruption of subconscious drives and emotions. Ultimately, then, it is not Elizabeth's own voice that emerges: it is God who speaks the praise of divine deeds and as creator "blesses" Mary (cf. 2:28). [43] Thus the very first recognition of Christ is a gift of the Spirit of God (1 Cor. 12:3). "Lord" (Jesus!) is understood personally as "my Lord." [44] This issues in joy, which often points to the eschaton, as does the coming of the Spirit upon Elizabeth. Malachi 4:2 likens it to the leaping of calves let out to pasture, John 3:29–30 to the rejoicing of the friend of the bridegroom.

[45] Mary is praised for her faith like Judith for her hope (Jth. 13:18–19); in Mary's case, however, the visible fulfillment of her faith still lies in the future. Thus the movement of the text leads back to the great act of God of which there is more to tell.

[46] Mary is not responding to Elizabeth in her song. Elizabeth's blessing places her in the presence of God, whose praise she sings (in the third person). "Spirit" and "soul" (see the discussion of 8:55) may recall that aspect of the human person that is open to the Spirit of God. [47] Again we hear of "eschatological" rejoicing (cf. Ps. 31:8; 35:9; Hab. 3:18). It is directed to God (not the Messiah, as in 2:11) as "Savior." [48] In God's presence, Mary, recalling the words of the angel (cf. 2:17), can only call herself a "handmaiden" chosen by the Lord (vs. 38).

"Low estate" may once have referred to Elizabeth's barrenness but now it describes the human situation in general. This is not false humility; it is a great amazement, childish in the best sense, at the goodness of God. This goodness looks (see the discussion of 9:38) even upon those who are not "remarkable." In its presence all individual merit and all individual failure pale into insignificance (cf. 18:9–14 and the Pauline justification of sinners). Therefore vs. 48*b* can follow immediately, almost like the exaltation of Christ alongside his humiliation in Philippians 2:6–11 (cf. the excursus following 2:52, c).

[49] God's great act must not be disdained. It is divine "might" (cf. Zeph. 3:17; Ps. 45:4–6) and the divine "name" that have done "great things" (Deut. 10:21; 1 Sam. 12:24; Ps. 126:2–3). God is not an abstract fate; God has a name that can be called upon. [50] Then divine might becomes mercy (Ps. 111:9; 103:1, 13, 17), arousing the human "fear" of taking far too little pleasure in God's mercy (see the discussion of vs. 29). Once again the song opens upon an unlimited future.

[51] Here it shifts to God's work throughout the world, which has social consequences (Isa. 57:15; 61:1–3; En. 92–104). Expectation of a reversal of the social order is a widespread phenomenon (Test. Jud. 25:4; Test. Sol. 10:12 [C]; Greek: Xenophon *Hell*. 6. 4. 23; Euripides *Troj*. 612–13). Here, however, it takes the form of praising God for what the future will bring rather than admonition or indictment of God in the light of capricious fate. [52] The exaltation of the lowly, already visible in Elizabeth and Mary, will achieve its goal in Jesus himself, and through him among those who stand poor be-

fore God. Empty bowls are filled. The eyes of God do not see high and low as human eyes do. But there is also mention of concrete social consequences, of "the mighty" and "the rich"—though not of "Gentiles"! None of this was eliminated when the psalm was inserted into the destiny of an individual woman. It praises the equalizing work of God, which treats all alike (cf. 1 Sam. 2:5–7), rather than threatening judgment and calling for repentance (like Luke 6:20–21, 24–25; 12:13–21; 16:19–26).

[54] Although vs. 51 comes from a Davidic messianic psalm (89:11), there is no mention of the Messiah even here: the "servant of God" is Israel (cf. Isa. 41:8–9). The community of Jesus is incorporated into Israel, wherever God's mercy and election are at work.

[55] Abraham is mentioned twenty-two times in Luke-Acts; the "fathers" are of the utmost importance (see the discussion of vs. 72).

[56] The long stay and the mention of "her" home assume that Mary was still single. Despite the association with 2 Samuel 7 (vss. 32–33!), there is no allusion to 2 Samuel 6:11, where the ark, in which the Lord is present, remains outside Jerusalem for three months.

The entire section focuses on two women, one of whom has no husband, the other a husband struck dumb. They are the first to greet the coming Lord in the power of the Spirit. Therefore joy permeates everything. Overpowering as is the personal miracle they both experience, however, they do not stop there but see a revolutionary vision of God who seeks to reach beyond their small personal lives and restore all those who are humbled and lost. Thus Mary has been the hope and focus of faith of millions of poor women. In her it is made clear that not only is the promise God's own work but also the human response of praise which extends to the concrete shape of society. The hymn, which has no counterpart in the corresponding Jesus section (see the introduction to 1:5—2:52), emphasizes this like the chorus in a Greek drama. God is not a capricious Lord, setting out to do first one thing, then another. From the first election of Israel to final deliverance, God's work is the single whole into which even the tiny fate of the individual is incorporated.

# C. BIRTH—NAMING—PRAISE OF GOD
## (1:57—2:40)

A quick survey will exhibit the parallelism. Birth: 1:57–58/2:6–7; circumcision and naming: 1:59–63/2:21; work of the Holy Spirit: 1:67/2:25d–27a; praise of God: 1:64/2:27b–28; hymn: 1:68–79/2:29–32; human reaction: 1:65–66/2:33; growth: 1:80/2:40. This arrangement omits 2:1–5, 8–20, 22–25c, 34–39 (q.v.).

### Fulfillment of the Promise: Birth and Naming (1:57–66)

[57]Now for Elizabeth the period for childbirth was fulfilled, and she gave birth to a son. [58]And her neighbors and kinsfolk heard that the Lord had made his mercy great with her, and they rejoiced with her. [59]And it happened on the eighth day that they came to circumcise the child, and they named him after the name of his father Zechariah. [60]And his mother answered and said, "No, rather he shall be called John." [61]And they said to her, "There is none among your kindred who is called by this name." [62]Then they made signs to his father, inquiring what he wished to have him called. [63]And he asked for a writing tablet, and wrote: "John is his name." And they all marveled. [64]And immediately his mouth was opened and his tongue, and he spoke, blessing God. [65]And fear came upon all who lived in their neighborhood, and through all the hill country of Judea these things were talked about, [66]and all who heard them laid them up in their hearts, saying, "What kind of a child will this be?" And the hand of the Lord was with him.

The gift of Holy Spirit and the hymn that follows belong directly after the miracle (vss. 63–64). Clearly the hymn and its introduction (vs. 67) were already extant—otherwise Zechariah would not be reintroduced as "his father." Thus the hymn was added at the end. The naming (vss. 59–64a) is developed extensively and constitutes the focus of the narrative because in it the faith of both parents overcomes resistance of friends and neighbors, leading up to the restoration of Zechariah's power of speech as a sign from God. True to style, the section concludes with the praise to God by the father and the inquiring amazement of all present (vss. 64*b*–66).

[57] The term of childbirth (1:24, without reference to vss. 26–56!) is "fulfilled" (as in the case of the previously childless Rebecca, Gen. 25:24). The solemn expression (also found in 1:23; 2:6, 21, 22) may have overtones of the fulfillment of God's promise. [58] God makes his (ever present) mercy "great" in a special act of help (also Gen. 19:19).

[59] This is the first attestation of naming at the time of circumcision (as later in Christian baptism; in the Hellenistic world a child was named on the seventh or tenth day after birth). The choice of the father's name is not unusual (appearing elsewhere only in Tob. 1:1, 9; Qumran; Josephus); the suggestion only serves to introduce the mother's response, [60] which is a sign of gratitude from a human heart that attaches more importance to God's promise than to family considerations. Neither parents nor kinsfolk have the final claim to this child but God, who has already marked him for service (vs. 13). Whether and how Zechariah had communicated this name to his wife is not said, but their agreement can hardly be taken as a miracle.

[61] The other members of the family have some idea of the divine event but are not yet initiated into the secret. [62] The signs (is Zechariah also deaf?) and [63] the tablet (wood covered with wax) give a vivid picture of Zechariah's infirmities before they are removed by God's miracle.

[64] His following of the angel's instructions shows, obvious as it may be, that he, too, now believes. Therefore the first sound he is able to make is praise to God (see the discussion of 17:15), not an explanation of the mystery and an illuminating account of why the name was chosen.

[65] Fear comes upon all those in the surrounding region (see the discussion of vss. 12, 29). On "Judea" (not "Judah," as in the transitional vs. 39) see the discussion of 1:5. The term does not refer (as it does elsewhere in Luke) to the entire land but only to its southern portion. The final short sentence can hardly represent the words of the people; it is probably a concluding comment by the narrator.

"The hand of God," guiding providence, is revealed in this section in the concrete fulfillment of God's promise through the birth of a child, in the ability of others to see in this birth something of the "greatness" of God's mercy, and in the way those directly concerned learn to accept God's gift and witness to it before others through their obedience. Elizabeth begins by holding fast to the message of the angel. Zechariah experiences the miracle that puts him to shame and breaks forth in praise of God. The sign given by God does not render faith unnecessary; the question of its meaning imposes itself upon the eyewitnesses, for whom what had been purely human sharing of a happy occasion is turned into fear and amazement. For the time being there is only "talk"—serious, reflective, thankfully informative, but also garrulous, exaggerated, trivial. Everywhere, though, there are those who in one way or another lay it up in their hearts (like David in 1 Sam. 21:13). And so it all issues in a question that ultimately concerns God. Even in the very first days of John, the living hand of God is at work.

## Benedictus (1:67-80)

[67] And Zechariah his father was filled with Holy Spirit and prophesized:
[68] "'Blessed be the Lord, the God of Israel,'
for he has visited and made redemption for his people,
[69] and has raised up 'a horn of salvation' for us
in the house of David his servant,
[70] as he spoke by the mouth of his holy prophets from of old,
[71] salvation from our enemies
and from the hand of all who hate us;
[72] to show mercy 'to our fathers
and to remember his holy covenant'—
[73] 'the oath which he swore to Abraham our father'—
[74] and 'to grant' us, without fear,
'delivered from the hand of our enemies,'
[75] to serve him in holiness and righteousness before him all our days.
[76] And you, child, will be called prophet of the Most High;
for you will go before the Lord to prepare his ways
[77] and to grant knowledge of salvation to his people
in forgiveness of their sins

[78] through the tender mercy of our God,
  in which 'the rising' from on high has visited us,
[79] to appear to those 'who sit in darkness and in the shadow of death,'
  to guide our feet into the way of peace."
[80] But the child grew and became strong in spirit and was in the wilderness till the day of his manifestation to Israel.

(Vs. 69—1 Sam. 2:10; Ps. 89:25. Vs. 72—Exod. 2:24. Vs. 73—Gen. 26:3. Vs. 74—Jer. 11:5; Mic. 7:20. Vs. 76—Mal. 3:1; Isa. 14:3. Vs. 78—Isa. 60:1-2; Zech. 3:8. Vs. 79—Ps. 107:10; Isa. 9:1; 42:7.)

In this hymn certain words appear in chiastic order: (a) visit (68*b*), (b) people (68*b*), (c) salvation (69), (d) prophet (70), (e) enemies (71), (f) hand (71), (g) our fathers (72), then in reverse: (g') our father (73), (f') hand (74), (e') enemies (75), (d') prophet (76), (c') salvation (77*a*), (b') people (77*a*), (a') visit (78*b*). In the middle stands a reference to the covenant and oath of God (72*b*, 73*a*). In a second chiastic series we find (a) mercy (72), (b) grant (74), (c) before him (75), and in reverse: (c') before the Lord (76*b*), (b') grant (77), (a') mercy (78). Here the midpoint is the "prophet" spoken of in vs. 76a. The future tense is used in vss. 76–79; it is a birth hymn prophesying the future significance for the newborn child, not a hymn of praise for what God has already done.

In vss. 68–75 there are many words that are also used in the song of Mary; from vs. 76 on, this is true only of words repeated from vss. 68–75. The first section closely resembles Jewish prayers; like vss. 46–55, it is full of Old Testament expressions (in both cases associated with the Davidic tradition). In vss. 76–79, on the contrary, as in the (Christian) hymn 2:29–32, we find only expressions that appear elsewhere in Christian (usually Lukan) tradition: 1:76 = Mark 1:2 = Luke 7:27; 3:4; 1:79 = Matthew 4:16 (on the relationship of this passage to Luke, see the discussion of Matt. 4:13); 2:30 = 3:6; 2:31 = Acts 13:47. Finally, vs. 75 is based on a common concluding formula (Isa. 38:20; Ps. 16:11; 18:51; 23:6; 28:9; 29:10; 30:13; cf. 35:28; 71:24; but also 27:4; 90:14; 128:5. In short, an existing (Jewish) Psalm has been expanded topically by the addition of vss. 76–79 and adapted to the narrative (cf. especially 1:14–17).

The key words of the psalm, "mercy . . . grant . . . before him" and "visit . . . people . . . salvation," have been incorporated into vss. 76–78 in reverse order.

It is unlikely that vss. 68–75 were inserted into a unit originally comprising vss. 67, 76–79; such an insertion is in fact conceivable only if vss. 68–75 were already extant as a traditional psalm. The original hymn can be divided into three sections: vss. 68–69, 71; 72–73; 74–75. In the first two, a key word is repeated at the end in a loosely appended clause ("salvation," 69a, 71a; "our fathers, our father," 72a, 73), while vs. 74 incorporates the terminology of vs. 71 in reverse order ("salvation from our enemies and from the hand . . ."; "delivered from the hand of our enemies"). Vs. 70 is the only true subordinate clause (almost identical with Acts 3:21; cf. 3:25). It was probably added by Luke.

Does the addition in vss. 76–79 derive from a disciple of John or from a Jewish Christian? If the former, the "Lord" would be God, as in 1:16–17. But since vs. 69 already speaks of the Davidic Messiah, this can hardly have been applied to John, who is not of Davidic lineage. The quotations in vss. 76 and 79 also appear in Christian tradition (see the discussion). The visitation of the "rising" obviously means more than the appearance of any prophet, however great. Thus vss. 76–79 understand the relationship between the Baptist and Jesus in the same way as whoever linked the two figures and defined their relationship, i.e., from the perspective of a Jewish Christian. These verses automatically identify the "we" of Israel's hymn with the community of Jesus.

The phrase "forgiveness of their" (not "our") "sins" is noteworthy. Is it a Lukan addition (Luke 24:47; Acts 2:38; 5:31; 10:43; 13:38; 26:18) or a standard Jewish Christian idiom (Mark 1:4 = Luke 3:3; Matt. 26:28; cf. Col. 1:14; not in the LXX)?

[67] The expected celebration (and disagreement, vss. 58, 61) is followed by the hymn. "Filled with Holy Spirit" (also in vss. 15 and 41; cf. 2:27; possibly absent from 1:46 on account of 1:35) also describes Elisha (Ecclus. 48:12; elsewhere only Prov. 15:4 LXX). God's presence is conceived in realistic terms, like the cloud that

fills the tent of meeting or the temple. What follows is "prophecy" with respect to Jesus.

[68] The hymn begins with the traditional blessing formula praising the God of Israel (Ps. 41:14; 72:18; 89:53; 106:48; 1QM 14:4 [end]). The reason is God's gracious visitation. In the Old Testament, the Hebrew word for "visit" refers to God's coming in wrath (e.g., Exod. 20:5) as well as in mercy (Ps. 106:4). Most often in the Greek translation and always in the New Testament (besides here, only Luke 1:78; 7:16; 19:44; Acts 15:14) it refers to God's *gracious* visitation. The Greek word means literally that God fixes his gaze on someone, making the divine universal presence felt in a special way and marking out a special course.

[69] That is the meaning of "liberation." It comes when God "raises up" something (a prophet or king: Deut. 18:15, 18; 1 Sam. 2:35; 2 Sam. 23:1; Acts 3:22, 26; cf. 13:22), in this case the "horn" in which an animal's strength is thought to be concentrated. In 1 Samuel 2:10 we find "the horn of his anointed," which was interpreted by Jewish scholars as referring to the Messiah (Bill.). In the Eighteenth Benedictions of the Jewish liturgy, the fifteenth (albeit in a late version) prays: "May the scion of David spring forth quickly, and may his horn be raised up through thy aid" (Bill. 4, 213). For God to set up power "in the house of David" must have messianic implications (cf. the discussion of 1:31). In Acts 4:25–27, Jesus (the "Lord and Christ of God"), like David, is God's "servant" (a concept that appears only in Jewish and Christian prayers).

[70] While vss. 69 and 72–73 describe the continued course of God's saving history begun in David and Abraham, the reference in vs. 70 is to Luke's view of Jesus as the fulfillment of all the prophets. [71] "Salvation from enemies" was originally meant politically; Luke probably has in mind temptations (cf. "sins," vs. 77). [72] "Mercy to our fathers" may assume that the fathers in heaven share in the fate of their people (16:23, 27; John 8:56; Bill. 1, 892). There are frequent references to them (vs. 55; cf. Mic. 7:20; 1 Macc. 4:10). [73] God's "remembering" an "oath" is remarkably appropriate with respect to the names of John's parents (see the discussion of 1:5). Centuries of silence in which Israel had only the record of God's

word from the past therefore do not mean that God had forgotten Israel.

[74] The ultimate purpose of God's salvation presupposes deliverance from the enemy [75] but is in fact undisturbed worship. The only other passage that speaks in these terms is Isaiah 24:14, in the context of God's instruction to the chosen people. Here we have a spirituality for which worship (probably engaged in by the entire community, not just by the representative priesthood) is the utmost joy. Freedom of worship is the ultimate, unsurpassable goal. This is underlined by the hope for its eternal duration—or does "our" refer only to the present generation?

[76] "And you" marks the transition from general praise to God to the concrete situation. On the basis of Deuteronomy 18:18–19, Israel expected an eschatological messianic prophet (4QTest 5; 1QS 9:11; cf. the discussion of Luke 1:17). Like Mark 1:2–3; Luke 3:4–6; and 7:27, however, vs. 76 interprets John as the forerunner of Jesus, against the background of the expected return of Elijah (Mal. 3:1, influenced by Exod. 23:20 and Isa. 40:3). [77] According to Mark 1:4 (q.v.) = Luke 3:3, John's baptism of repentance results in the forgiveness of sins (see the discussion of 24:47). This passage, too, can hardly mean that John announces the forgiveness to come but rather that in his preaching Israel already encounters the coming Jesus, [78] in whom God's "mercy," God's entire loving favor, becomes reality. "Rising" can refer to the rising of the sun and also to the appearance of a new scion or branch (as in Jer. 23:5 LXX; Zech. 3:8; 6:12; 1QFlor 1:11; 4QPatr 3), as Judaism called the Davidic Messiah. The author probably has these passages in mind, but what follows shows that he is picturing the rising of a heavenly body, the "great light" of Isaiah 9:1, the "sun of righteousness" of Malachi 4:2, or the "star out of Jacob" of Numbers 24:17. But this luminary does not appear above the horizon, rising from the depths (like the son of Man rising from the sea, 2 Esd. 13), but "from on high," like the sudden appearance of a meteor. Furthermore, it is not a general illumination but a light that visits "us," that looks upon "us" (see the discussion of vs. 68), lifting the shadow of death and showing the right way. Here, too, Christ is seen as the one in whom God enters

into the life or mankind, giving light in the darkness in which mankind has lost the way, in whom peace is found (cf. Matt. 4:16, with
the same root meaning "rise").

[80] Only here do we learn that John lived in the wilderness until
his public appearance (see the discussion of 3:2–3). He was certainly
not at Qumran, for his father was a priest of the temple (against
which the monks of Qumran directed their polemic); his dress was
that of a prophet, not a monk; his baptism was singular, not repeated
daily; his message was addressed to the populace, not to a monastic
community; and his ideal was not the rigorous legalism of Qumran.
In addition, vs. 80 stresses his independence from human ideas and
beliefs. "Spirit" refers to the Spirit of God, but it is vouchsafed to
him and thus also becomes his spirit (see the discussion of vss. 46–
47). The verse leads into 3:1–20, forming part of the "biography" of
the Baptist.


Unlike vss. 46–55, this hymn begins with God's actions on behalf
of all Israel; only in vs. 76 does it address the personal life of an
individual—albeit one who, as prophet of the Most High, will bring
salvation to the whole people. This people is not further identified;
in any case there is no mention of the Gentiles. The visitation of the
God of Israel means (positively) salvation for the entire nation through
the scion of David, as well as (negatively) deliverance from enemies. This deliverance (negatively) makes it possible (positively) to
worship God in peace. In the center stands the fulfillment of the
covenant with Abraham: God has brought to its culmination divine
historical involvement with Israel.

The mention of David (emphasized by Luke in vs. 70) shows that
a messianic king is meant. The language is that of nationalistic hopes,
motivated religiously by the goal of free worship. This theme is taken
up by a Jewish Christian and applied to the preaching of John, who
paves the way for the "Lord" Jesus and thus for God's final gracious
visitation (vss. 76–79). God's great act is so central that nothing is
said of repentance and baptism, only of deliverance from enemies,
interpreted as forgiveness of sins. The crucial point is the shining
forth of God's presence in Jesus, his "epiphany" (from the Greek

word) in darkness and the shadow of death. This epiphany makes worship possible or, as the author puts it, brings peace.

When the community turns to God directly in its hymn of praise, the subject of the hymn must be God's actions and boundless mercy. This does not mean the solution of every problem, as the stress on forgiveness of sins indicates. But the fact that Jesus' coming brings new ways of peace that could not be seen before applies also to human society and its problems. The circumstance (emphasized by Paul) that only those who have been granted forgiveness and peace by God are able to worship in peace appears here in the hymns of praise prefixed to the preaching of the Baptist.

## God's Visitation of His People (2:1–20)

[1]It happened in those days that a decree went out from Caesar Augustus that all the world should be enrolled. [2]This was the first enrollment, when Quirinius was governor of Syria. [3]And all went to be enrolled, each to his own city. [4]So Joseph also went up from Galilee, from the city of Nazareth, to Judea, to the city of David, which is called Bethlehem, because he was of the house and lineage of David, [5]to be enrolled with Mary, his betrothed, who was pregnant. [6]And it happened while they were there that the days were fulfilled for her to give birth, [7]and she bore her first son, and wrapped him in swaddling cloths, and laid him in a manger, because there was no place for them in the dwelling.

[8]And there were shepherds in this region out in the field, and they were keeping watch over their flock by night. [9]And an angel of the Lord came to them, and glory of the Lord shone around them, and they were filled with great fear. [10]And the angel said to them, "Do not be afraid; for behold, I proclaim good news to you, a great joy, which will come to all the people; [11]for to you was born today a Savior, who is Christ, the Lord, in the city of David. [12]And this will be a sign to you: you will find the babe wrapped in swaddling cloths and lying in a manger." [13]And suddenly there was a multitude of the heavenly host with the angel, praising God and saying,

[14]"Glory in the highest to God,
and on earth peace among those of the [divine] pleasure."

[15]And it happened, when the angels went away from them into heaven, the shepherds said to one another, "Let us go over to Bethlehem and see this thing that has happened, which the Lord has made known to

us." [16]And they went with haste, and found Mary and Joseph, and the babe lying in the manger. [17]When they saw it, they made known the saying that had been told them concerning this child. [18]And all who heard it wondered at what was told them by the shepherds. [19]But Mary kept all these words and pondered them in her heart. [20]And the shepherds returned, glorifying and praising God for all they had heard and seen, as it had been told them.

As a counterpart to 1:57–58 and an introduction to 2:21, a short statement of Jesus' birth such as 2:6–7 would have been enough. The shepherd episode is a self-contained unit. Vs. 8 clearly marks a new beginning, and vs. 20 closes with the stylistically correct praise of God. The structure is transparent: the watch of the shepherds and the coming of the angel (vss. 8–9a) are matched in reverse order by the departure of the angels and the leaving of the shepherds (vs. 15); the fear of the witnesses and the proclamation of the angel with the manger as a sign (vss. 9b–12) are matched by the proclamation of the shepherds at the manger and the astonishment of the witnesses (vss. 16–18); the praises sung by the angels (vss. 13–14) are matched by those sung by the shepherds (vs. 20). Vs. 19, like vs. 51b, is typical of Luke's style; he probably added it.

The origin and growth of the Christmas story are hard to trace. There are three basic points: (1) The shepherd episode is so clearly a self-contained unit that it must have been extant in finished form at least orally before being incorporated into Luke 1—2. Its Christology is also very different from that of 1:32–35 ("Savior," "Christ the Lord"; see the discussion of vs. 11). But it could easily have originated in Palestine, where shepherds have played their part since the time of the patriarchs, David, and the prophets, and where the "people [of God]" and "those of [God's] pleasure" (vss. 10, 14) live. (2) Vss. 4–7 make no reference to the annunciation of the virgin birth; Joseph and Mary are introduced afresh. These verses, however, provide a good introduction to 2:22–38; Jerusalem is easy to get to from Bethlehem. Despite Acts 5:37, did the occasion of the census form part of this account, connecting Nazareth, Jesus' residence, with Bethlehem, his place of birth? (3) If Mary was termed the "betrothed" of Joseph (vs. 5, where some ancient versions read instead "his wife") when the account was connected with chapter 1, at the same time the catchwords "city of David" and "manger" (vss. 4, 7) were probably added in vss. 11 and 16, and vs. 12 was rephrased. Luke himself may be responsible for the information in vss. 1–2 (or 5), the comment about Mary in vs. 19, and overall stylistic revision.

Did the Christmas story take place in this fashion? Luke's account cannot be reconciled with Matthew's (see the discussion of Matt. 1:18, 23) except for the mention of Bethlehem and Herod (Luke 1:5). But even within Luke 1—2 we find distinct traditions that cannot easily be harmonized. The census is historically dubious (see the discussion of vs. 2), and Mary would have had to travel along at most if she also owned property in Bethlehem. Furthermore, it is hardly conceivable that an unmarried couple would have traveled together. But the Christmas story does use vivid imagery to describe what really took place: in the birth of this child, God came to an encounter with the world; there was rejoicing in heaven; and humankind was given the possibility of God's peace.

Of course this is known only to faith, and faith must interpret what transcends all human understanding in the images of this account. We do not know to what extent the details of the narratives represent later elaboration, in which faith attempts to flesh out the dimensions of the event. But there are two crucial points: first, this birth, wherever and whenever, really took place; and second, that is indeed true which only faith can see and express in a wealth of stories—that in this birth God came to the world in a unique way. Compare what was said about the question of truth in section 5 of the Introduction to *The Good News According to Mark.*

[1] The abrupt transition is typically Lukan in style. The "going out" of an imperial decree to the whole inhabited world (Greek *oecumene*) sets events in motion, not an angelic message. [2] According to Josephus, Quirinius was not governor of Syria between 9 and 4 B.C. (when Herod died), and the tax census came after Palestine was incorporated into the province of Syria (A.D. 6) (*Ant.* 17. 27, 89; 18. 2). Such a census is hard to imagine before then since Herod was legally an independent king; it is not impossible, though, as an

example from Asia Minor shows. Also attested are a census of Roman citizens (but not "all the world") in 8/7 B.C. and a census of Palestine in A.D. 74/75 (just before the time Luke wrote). [3] During an Egyptian census in 104 B.C. those living abroad had to return "to their homeland" (but cf. 2:39!). It is possible, but not likely, that the tax rolls were compiled under Herod, but the tax was not collected until A.D. 6, when Quirinius really was governor of Syria. Or if Josephus confused two similar events (which is most unlikely), Quirinius, who had been posted to the Near East in 12 B.C., may have collected a tax as special emissary rather than governor. Or there may be confusion between Quirinius and Quintilius (Varus), who was governor of Syria from 4 B.C. on.

Probably Luke made a mistake, such as we would be apt to make about events almost a century in the past. But the question is totally irrelevant since Luke's purpose is not to cast light on the history of taxation in Palestine but to show how God speaks in an earthly historical event (whether it was a Roman census or something else), rather than in a philosophical system explaining the world or in a myth embodying a universal truth that would be true apart from its mythic presentation. And there is more. God's act does not invade our history like a meteor shower. It begins in the context of a totally secular event, a tax edict, whose meaning can be seen only from the perspective of what emerges from it. There are no angels, no signs of glory, only Roman officials and more or less unhappy taxpayers—but God is nonetheless the agent of an earthshaking event.

[4–5] The expectant excitement surrounding Augustus had long vanished by the time of Luke, but the pagan emperor is still for him the one to whom the Son of David gave allegiance, unlike the revolutionaries of his age. In 2 Samuel 5:7, etc., Zion is the "city of David"; here, following Micah 5:1, it is Bethlehem. Joseph's Davidic lineage (see the discussion of 1:32) is emphasized. The point is not to bear witness to the continuity of saving history—for almost a thousand years, nothing more than hope for a saving son of David had been maintained—but to God's faithfulness, which is not arbitrary but stands by the history begun in Israel.

[6] The days "are fulfilled" (see the discussion of 1:57). Nothing is said of thoughts, emotions, words; the fact of birth is presented

with utmost simplicity. **[7]** Mary's bearing of "her first son" suggests subsequent births (see the discussion of Mark 6:3), but the expression may only recall the fact that the first-born belongs to God (see the discussion of 2:23–24). The midwife's discovery that Mary's virginity was still intact belongs to a later legend (Protev. James 19:3). The fact that Mary wraps the baby in swaddling cloths is not a sign of a painless birth, abrogating Genesis 3:16, but of the total humanness of this birth.

Later Christians read in Isaiah 1:3 that the ox and ass "know the manger of their master/lord" and interpreted this as referring to Jesus. There is nothing unusual about the manger. It is a container used for fodder or a kind of trough in a bench, which protects the baby from the hooves of the animals that in Palestine often spend the night in the same room as their owners.

Nothing is said about Jesus' parents' seeking shelter and being turned away. The Greek word is used in 22:11 (also 1 Sam. 1:18 LXX?) for a guest room or guest house; a different word is used for "inn" in 10:34. Does this mean that while staying at the house of one of Joseph's friends or family members, they withdrew for the actual birth to an adjacent structure used for animals (or to a cave beneath the house?) because there was not enough room in the dwelling? The later "cave" may derive from a reading of Isaiah 33:16 LXX ("he dwells in a high cave in the rocks") (Justin *Dial.* 70; 78. 5–6). We really have no information because all that matters to Luke is that there was a normal human birth in the unromantic and unappealing context of the way the poor commonly lived, if not in extreme poverty.

**[8]** Shepherds play a role in Hellenistic birth narratives, but David was also a shepherd in the vicinity of Bethlehem (1 Sam. 17:15; 16:4, 11; cf. Ps. 78:70–72). Later rabbis looked for the birth of the Messiah, the Shepherd of Israel, at the "tower of the flock" (Mic. 4:8) near Bethlehem (Mic. 5:1–2; cf. "feed his flock," vs. 4). This notion may be in the background here rather than the later rabbinic attitude that looked down on shepherds (Bill.). The flocks are let out in March or April and brought back in in November, but camping out near a settlement as late as 24 December (see the discussion of 1:26) is conceivable. "Night" is mentioned only in the context of the shepherds (cf. the discussion of 9:28). The story depicts the appearance of the first "congregation" or "community" of those who "hear the word of God and praise him."

[9] The immediate "coming" of the angel (not named, in contrast to 1:11, 26) suddenly makes God's presence a reality. [10] Once more fear is the natural reaction, and deliverance from fear is the first concern of the word from God (see the discussion of 1:12, 29). God's intrusion into the human world becomes outwardly visible in "glory." God's word counters "great" fear with "great joy." As in 1:19 (q.v.), this joy is proclaimed as "good news." The form recalls Hellenistic proclamations, but the word for "people" always refers to Israel (more than eighty occurrences) except in Acts 15:14 and 18:10. Israel is probably also meant here; extension to include the Gentiles comes later (cf. the discussion of 2:31).

[11] In the Old Testament, "Savior" (cf. Luke 1:47; Jude 25; 1 Tim. 1:1; etc.) is a term referring to God but also to a "judge" sent by God to deliver Israel (Judg. 3:9, 15). This point is crucial for Philippians 3:20, which speaks of Christ's return as "Savior" of his community, and later for Acts 5:31; 13:23; Ephesians 5:23; John 4:42; 1 John 4:14; etc. The title makes sense in a Hellenistic context, where it designates the souls that have become demigods (Plutarch *Is. et Os.* 376*d*) and also emperors (see the excursus on 2:38) and such "deliverers" as physicians, philosophers, and statesmen. In contrast to this extended use, we find here a characterization of Jesus as "Christ, the Lord," a reference to the Davidic Messiah (cf. 1:32–33, 69). The phrase is unique; only in Acts 2:36 ("Lord and Christ," referring to the exalted Jesus) do we find anything comparable. Was the original reading "the Christ of the Lord," as in 2:26 (see the discussion of 9:20); Lamentations 4:20 (where copyists have also changed the text to read "Christ the Lord); and Psalms of Solomon 17:32? In vs. 9, "Lord" refers to God!

"Today" refers to an earthly event, located in time and history, not understandable without the message from God but also not reducible to a general principle. The Egyptian statement "Today Kore [a female deity] has given birth to the Aion" (Epiphanius *Haer*. 51. 22. 10) may be only an interpretation by Epiphanius and has nothing to do with Luke 2:11 because it merely connects the annual rebirth of spring with the dawn of a new age. Luke 2:11, on the contrary, emphasizes the unique act of God that makes all things new as irreducible and inexplicable without God's word as the crucifixion of Jesus (cf. the discussion of 4:21).

[12] "This will be a sign to you" appears also in Qumran texts (1Q27 1:5; cf. Exod. 3:12). It is astonishingly unpretentious since there is no echo of Isaiah 7:14 (virgin birth). Perhaps the point is the very discrepancy between what can be seen and what can be understood only on the basis of God's word.

[13] For a moment, however, the curtain is pulled back so that we can see God's world from which all things come, even what still lies in the future for humankind. This is what we call the transcendence of God. The essential point is that it takes form in the hymn of the angels which is addressed to God but promises salvation to humankind. [14] The message is bipartite (with reversal of the order of subject and place), as in 19:38, except that in the latter both members refer to God alone. The angels (see the discussion of 1:11) represent the earthward movement of God and therefore ascribe glory to God and God's peace to humankind. The two are not confused: the earth does not become heaven but is bound up with heaven so that it bears the mark of God's heaven and does not remain heavenless.

"Those of [God's] pleasure" (cf. 10:21) are God's elect (1QH 4:32–33; 8:6; 11:9: "those of pleasure"); this merely emphasizes the absolute need of God's grace rather than limiting salvation (for "all the people," vs. 10). More is meant than peace among humankind (Isa. 2:4; 9:7; 11:6–9): "the dwelling of God" will be with humankind (Rev. 21:3), bringing ultimate peace. In tone the formula recalls the glowing expectations that were associated with the rule of Augustus (see the excursus following 2:38), but how differently they are fulfilled in the mind of Luke! Luke 19:38 repeats the key words "peace" and "glory" (going beyond Mark 11:10) at the beginning of the Passion. It is Jesus' Passion that brings the peace of God.

[15] The angels' departure sets the shepherds in motion. They want to see the "word" (see the discussion of 1:37) that was made known to them. God's word is so trustworthy that it takes on visible form. [16] Their "hasty" reaction to God's call (cf. 1:39; 19:5–6; Acts 20:16; 22:18) exhibits what Paul calls "faith." It is part of the

Christmas story. [17] Mary is mentioned before Joseph (cf. the discussion of vs. 19). Thus God's word leads to setting forth in faith, to seeing (also stressed in vss. 15 and 20 although there is nothing extraordinary to see), and finally to proclamation. The word without the experience of God remains empty, but conversely it is the word "that had been told them" (also vs. 20) and that they in turn proclaim that interprets what they see as an act of God.

[18] Those present are amazed; they do not neutralize what they have heard by incorporating it into the familiar order. "The more firmly one believes in something, the more he wonders at it and the more he rejoices at it" (Luther). "To walk rightly in the Word of God is never to cease to be amazed" (Calvin). [19] But Mary is "moved." The word does not vanish from her when the shepherds vanish. She continues to ask what it means and remains open to anything new that it might bring her—hardly in the sense that she "connects" (a possible meaning of the term) it with earlier events in order to figure out God's plan.

[20] The end and goal of the whole story is the praise of God which now resounds upon earth, this time not from the tongues of angels but from the tongues of very human shepherds. Those who utter this praise do not constitute a new messianic group. Like most readers, they go once more about their work, but their praise is joined with that of the angels.

The text should overcome any trace of sentimentality in the Christmas story. There is no mention of winter, and the parents are not turned away when they seek shelter. They are not desperately poor but most likely belong to the lower middle class. The "manger" is a kneading bowl or a trough along the wall; there is no ox or ass standing alongside. The shepherds can see heavenly glory but not the parents. To them the word of God is brought by a shabby bunch of witnesses. The insignificant sign from God, which is no sign at all to human eyes, the manger, is mentioned in each of the three sections. A trivial everyday object becomes a sign of God's great act and shows that the kingship of the Son of God will have a different appearance than expected and will demand rethinking on our part.

But to some witnesses, oddly chosen to human eyes, God grants a special experience which gives them ears for the word that is entrusted to them. Not only do they hear the message, they also deliver it. It is possible to be present as a contemporary and see nothing, like Augustus. Or one can hear the word and be open to it. One can be amazed and ask what it means. Such amazement can fade away, or it can be so moving that the word does not vanish but can live on and finally achieve its ultimate goal.

Whoever heeds this call to faith will see the trajectory of the text: it begins in the capitol of the empire with an imperial edict meant to affect "all the world," causes two of the humblest citizens of this empire to go forth, leads to a tiny provincial village (albeit one already set apart by God, Gen. 35:19; Ruth 1:1, 19, 22; 4:11; 1 Sam. 16:1; Mic. 5:1; Matt. 2:5–6), and there to an obscure birth.

But this chain of events evokes a countermovement, the coming of the hosts of heaven to proclaim to "all the people" the "Lord" anointed by God, who in turn cause a band of shepherds to set forth. This leads to the formation of a first community, praising God and proclaiming his mighty acts, from which there will then arise a movement back to Rome (Acts 28:14–31) and into the entire world. Little is said about the birth itself. Only the proclamation in heaven and on earth reveals the significance of the event, as is also true of the cross and resurrection.

## The Presentation: Nunc Dimittis (2:21–40)

[21]And when the eight days for his circumcision were fulfilled, his name was called Jesus, the name given by the angel before he was conceived in the womb. [22]And when 'the days of their purification were fulfilled' according to the law of Moses, they went up to Jerusalem to present him to the Lord, [23]as it is written in the law of the Lord, that 'every male that opens the womb' shall be called holy to the Lord, [24]and to offer a sacrifice according to what is said in the law of the Lord, 'a pair of turtledoves or two young pigeons.' [25]Now behold, there was a person in Jerusalem named Simeon, and this person was righteous and devout, looking for the consolation of Israel, and the Holy Spirit was upon him. [26]And it had been promised to him by the Holy Spirit that he should not see death before he had seen the Christ of the Lord. [27]And he came in the Spirit into the temple. And when the parents brought in

the child Jesus, to do for him as was the custom of the law, [28]he took him up in his arms and blessed God and said:

[29]"Now thou mayest dismiss thy servant, Lord,
    according to thy word in peace;
[30]for my eyes have seen thy salvation,
[31]which thou hast prepared in the presence of all peoples,
[32]a light for revelation to the Gentiles,
    and for the glory of thy people Israel."

[33]And his father and his mother marveled at what was said about him. [34]And Simeon blessed them and said to Mary his mother:

"Behold, he is set for the fall and rising of many in Israel,
    and for a sign of contradiction,
[35]and through your own soul also a sword will pierce,
    that thoughts out of many hearts may be revealed."

[36]And there was a prophetess, Anna, the daughter of Phanuel, of the tribe of Asher; she was of a great age, having lived with a man seven years from her virginity, [37]and she was a widow of some eighty-four years. She did not depart from the temple, and served the Lord night and day with fasting and prayer. [38]And at that very hour she came up, gave thanks to God, and spoke of him to all who were looking for the redemption of Jerusalem.

[39]And when they had performed everything according to the law of the Lord, they returned into Galilee, to their own city, Nazareth. [40]But the child grew and became strong, filled with wisdom; and the favor of God was upon him.

(Vss. 22–24—Lev. 12:4–8; Exod. 13:2; 34:19–20. Vss. 30–32—Isa. 52:10; 42:6; 49:6.)

Like 1:59–66, 2:21 emphasizes the naming by referring to the command of the angel. The circumcision serves only as an indication of time. Vss. 22–24 have no equivalent in the John narrative. Like 1:5–7 (and unlike 1:26–38; 2:1–20), they and vs. 27b stress the parents' obedience to the law. Did Luke use them to transfer the scene to Jerusalem, assimilating the Jesus tradition to the John tradition (cf. the discussion of 4:16)? In any event, he does not speak of a return to Nazareth until afterward (vs. 39), i.e., after forty days (Lev. 12:24—but is Luke aware of this requirement?). Is he even implying that both parents are purified ("their")? The expression "the days were fulfilled" and the use of "Lord" for God in vs. 22 are borrowed from vss. 21/15, 26. "The law of the Lord" is found only here and in the concluding verse 39 (Lukan?). In Acts 22:12, also, Luke praises Ananias as "devout according to the law," and in Luke 2:25 he calls Simeon "righteous and devout." Was vs. 22*b*, the Greek text of which uses the un-Lukan form for "Jerusalem" (see section 2.a of the Introduction), the original introduction of what was once an independent narrative, which, like vss. 4–5, speaks of Joseph and Mary as the parents (vss. 27, 33) and links the clauses with "and" (even in vss. 21 and 28)? Vss. 34–35 could be a separate saying inserted by Luke. The story may possibly contain an echo of the Essene Simeon, who according to Josephus (*Ant.* 17. 3, 146; *De bello jud.* 2. 113) interpreted the future for Archelaus on the basis of a dream during the taxation of A.D. 6 (on the temple, see the discussion of vs. 27).

[21] According to vs. 21, obedience to the angel's message is more important than obedience to the law (vss. 22–24). The name "Jesus" is not uncommon; it is not interpreted as in Matthew 1:21. Everything takes place as it would for any other Jewish child—except that, as the reader knows, it all stands under God's special promise. [22] Devotion to the temple and the law are important (the requirements are cited in detail); there is nothing analogous for John, the son of a priest. It is hardly likely that there is any reference to Malachi 3:1 ("the Lord will come to his temple," the verse cited in 1:17, 76). [23–24] The narrative associates the purification of the mother after seven days with the offering prescribed for the first-born, normally carried out through payment to a local priest (cf. the excursus following vs. 52). Nothing is said here of such a "redemption" of Jesus; instead he is received into the service of God (in which he will redeem others: Mark 10:45, not used by Luke). Perhaps there is also an echo of 1 Samuel 1:11, 22–28. There, however, the mother dedicates her child to God, whereas here God sets the child apart for service through the agency of a prophet. Thus a prescribed ritual takes on new meaning as a kind of "presentation" of the newborn child.

[25] Israel appears in Simeon as blessed by God. He is "righteous" (see the discussion of 1:6) and "devout" (also Acts 2:5; 8:2;

22:12). The Old Testament rarely speaks of someone possessing the Spirit continuously (Gen. 41:38; Dan. 4:5; also Num. 11:17; Isa. 59:21?). Nevertheless, the Spirit's coming ever anew is necessary. It brings Simeon to the temple. He is totally concerned for the future, the "consolation" of Israel (cf. Isa. 40:1–2; 49:13; Apoc. Bar. 44:7; Bill.; Talmud Y. Ber. 8d: the subject of the last conversation between Elijah and Elisha [end of the fourth century A.D.!]). He is not the kind of person who lives backward (3:8); he lives forward. The Holy Spirit does not bring religious satiety but hunger and thirst for the consummation (Rom. 8:23–27). [26] This is not just a pious notion. The imminence of the fulfillment dominates Simeon's life and that of those who hear him (on "Christ of the Lord," see the discussion of 9:20).

[27] After the annunciation to his parents in the temple, John is brought into hiding (1:24) and then into the wilderness (1:80); after the annunciation to Mary in a small Galilean town, Jesus is brought to the royal city of Bethlehem and to the Jerusalem temple. [28] The presentation itself is not described. The crucial point is not that the human parents bring Jesus into God's presence but that God reaches out to Jesus through a prophet.

[29] Vss. 29–32 have been used as a prayer of thanksgiving in evening worship since the fifth century C.E. Simeon addresses "his Lord" in the terminology used by a slave (also Acts 2:24; Rev. 6:10). He is ready to "depart in peace" (Acts 15:33). There may be an echo of Psalm 4:9 LXX ("In peace I will sleep . . . in hope, O Lord, thou makest me dwell"). This is not a personal longing for death, as in Genesis 46:30; Tobit 11:9, or an expression of despair, as in 1 Kings 19:4 (Josephus *De bello jud.* 1. 78–79; *Ant.* 13. 311–12). [30] Simeon has seen much in the course of his life, both good and evil. Now he can see God's salvation, which is intended for more than him alone. [31] In contrast to vs. 32a, the word is used that in the singular refers to the people of God (see the discussion of 2:10). But "all peoples" must mean the Gentiles (and Israel?), as in Isaiah 55:5; 60:5; 61:9 (cf. Acts 4:25, 27, where it refers to Israel). [32] As vs. 32 shows, the Gentiles are not mere onlookers (as in Isa. 52:10; Ps. 98:1–3), and are even mentioned before Israel. The "glory" of Israel consists in the fact that from it comes the light of the entire world

(Isa. 49:6; 42:6; 60:1–3; cf. Luke 3:6). Its special role as the first chosen people is maintained as fully as the unrestricted extension of salvation to all.

[33] Here, too, only the parents' amazement is recorded, with special emphasis on Mary (see the discussion of 2:19 and the introduction to this section). [34] Unlike the praise of God (vss. 28–33), Simeon's message is meant for her alone (vss. 34–55). Does it mean that some will fall and others will rise? Isaiah 8:14–15 and 28:16 are already associated and interpreted this way in Romans 9:33; 1 Peter 2:6–8 (cf. 1QH 2:8–9; 3:9–10; 4:34–36; 1QM 14:10–11): the cornerstone of the faithful is the stumblingstone of others (but see the discussion of 20:18). Of course the idea of "contradiction" and separation is involved. But only those who have fallen can be raised up; and in all the Old Testament passages that use both terms, it is always the same ones who fall and either rise or do not rise (negative: Amos 5:2; 8:14; Isa. 24:20; positive: Prov. 24:16, "A righteous man falls seven times, and rises again"; and especially Mic. 7:8: "When I fall, I shall rise; when I sit in darkness, Yahweh will be a light to me"; cf. Eccles. 4:10). Many, i.e., all who can really hear this, will fall and rise again, will experience judgment and grace (similarly Rom. 1:17–18).

[35] God's grace as judgment always reveals each one as he or she truly is (1 Cor. 14:25). Therefore the coming of "consolation" is also like the sword that passes through whole nations (Ezek. 14:17 LXX; Sib. Or. 3:316; cf. Job 20:25). It will cause pain, and perhaps also (as in Heb. 4:12) divide thoughts, so that Mary will be "two-minded" (James 1:8 = "doubting") (8:19–21; 11:27–28). Blessing is not the gift of amenities. It brings the receiver into the presence of God, into judgment and grace.

[36] Alongside the hymn of the man (vs. 28) comes the "corresponding" hymn of the woman (vs. 38, literally; see the discussion of 8:3). Like Judith, Anna has remained a widow. If we assume that she was fourteen when she married (the usual age), and if the 84 ( = 7 × 12) years refers to her widowhood, their ages are even the same (Jth. 16:23–24). Her ministry of intercession is also the prototype for the Christian widows (1 Tim. 5:5), who are not, however, forbidden to remarry (1 Cor. 7:7–9). [38] Again we see her openness to

the future, from which her message issues. A group of "Zion's watchmen" (Ps. 130:5–8; Isa. 52:8–10) is gathered about her.

**Israel and the Nations** (cf. the excursus following 21:24). According to 2:31–32, the nations do not take the place of Israel; when they come from all sides (13:29), Israel will enjoy the glory intended by God (2:32). The stories of John and Jesus are therefore rooted in the spirituality of Israel, in the law and the temple. This is not the spirituality of the rich. A childless couple, a prophet and a prophetess are waiting for their consolation and the consolation of Israel, for the deliverance of Jerusalem. Zechariah is speechless (1:20), and Jesus' parents do not understand (2:33, 50). Whoever linked the two traditions saw in the two women an openness to the immanent act of God (1:41–45; cf. 76–79); Luke brings this out even more (2:19, 51).

A division within Israel is attested by 2:34–35 and Q, with its call to repentance addressed to an Israel that feels secure but will be confounded by the nations (3:7–9; 13:28–29), as well as the tradition behind Luke 4:24–27 (cf. also the discussion of 7:1–10).

According to Acts 13:46; 18:6; 20:26; 28:28, Paul turns to the Gentiles after failing among the Jews, despite mass conversions of the Jews in Jerusalem itself (cf. the excursus following 21:24). But the Gentile mission is already mentioned in Luke 24:47 (cf. Acts 1:6, 8; 2:39; 3:25), and is commanded by the Lord in Acts 10:20. "Salvation" for the Gentiles is spoken of in Luke 2:30–32; 3:6; and Acts 28:28. It is therefore not true that Israel's hardness of heart leads to the Gentile mission, or vice versa (cf. also the discussion of 8:39). Luke accordingly never calls the community of Jesus the new or spiritual Israel (for Paul, cf. the discussion of 1 Cor. 10:18; Gal. 6:16) and hardly ever the "people" (of God; see the discussion of 2:10).

Contrary, therefore, to Matthew 16:18, Jesus does not found a "church"; the word occurs for the first time in Acts 5:11, describing the Jews who believe in Jesus. Paul, too, is a teacher of Israel: educated as a Pharisee, familiar with the law and faithful to the Bible, he preaches only the hope of Israel, which has begun to be fulfilled in the resurrection of Jesus (Acts 22:3; 23:6; 26:5–7; 28:20; cf. Peter in 4:2). The Christian communities are rooted in the synagogues (Acts 15:21) and are made up of Jews and Gentile "God-fearers" who understand Moses correctly (13:14–43, etc.; cf. the discussion of Luke 4:44). The tradition behind Luke 2:35 and 13:28–29 thus remains active in Luke himself (cf. the discussion of 4:23). The messengers of Christ go forth to the Gentiles from Jerusalem (Luke 24:47; Acts 1:8; 3:25–26; Rom. 15:19–20).

On the other hand, the Christmas story also bears the mark of contemporary Hellenistic expectations that are rooted in turn in ancient hopes found throughout the Near East (see Wildberger's commentary on Isa. 8:23—9:6 and 11:1–10). After four hundred years of Greek, Egyptian, Syrian, and Roman rule in Palestine, the two cultures are hard to distinguish.

Following Daniel 9:24, deliverance was expected after seventy "weeks," i.e., seventy times seven "days" (cf. also the discussion of Luke 3:23–38; Matt. 1:1–17). With three and a half periods the half-way point is reached (Dan. 7:25; Rev. 12:14 = 1,260 days; 11:3, 6; cf. the discussion of Luke 4:25). Other calculations were based on ten weeks (En. 93; 91:12–17). Expectation of an imminent end is attested by numerous messianic figures (see the discussion of Acts 5:36–37) and the biblical interpretation of Qumran, which relates the prophecies to the present age.

The Greek world, too, was filled with an almost unimaginable hope, which had centered on Augustus and was therefore already waning during the period of Jesus' ministry. Augustus ruled as autocrat from 31 B.C. to A.D. 14; in 29 B.C. he closed the Temple of War, and in 14 B.C. consecrated the Altar of Peace. He is hailed by Virgil with expectations similar to those in Isaiah 11:1–10 and in ancient Near Eastern texts (*NTD*, Ergänzungsreihe, 1:161–62). Inscriptions refer to him as "savior" (conjectured in the inscription cited *ibid.*, p. 148) of "the entire human race," who "fulfills and surpasses all prayers" and transforms the world with his "good news" (Halicarnassus and Priene).

There was, then, a widespread conviction that the world was approaching the goal of God's entire history with Israel, or, in Hellenistic terms, the dawn of a new golden age in the "cycle" of history. Therefore Luke sees the fulfillment of the Old Testament in the fate of Jesus taken as a whole, not in isolated scriptural proofs (see the excursus following Matt. 1:18–25).

[39] As in 2:4, Nazareth is the home of Jesus' parents (Lukan redaction?; cf. Matt. 2:23). [40] Jesus' growth and development is described in parallel to 1:80, though without mention of growth in spirit. Created by the Spirit, he is totally filled with the Spirit from the beginning (see the discussion of 4:1).

As an institution, the temple is as dubious as the church. But an Israel that does not live in the past and put its faith in what has gone before, being open instead to God's new and astonishing act, will see this act as the fulfillment of what has gone before; it therefore begins appropriately in the temple (1:8–9; 2:22, 27, 37). The two prophet figures, like the parents of Jesus, represent a good but "unfulfilled" life. Such a life does not give up its yearning in resignation or heal it with some "religious" patent medicine but holds fast to the experience of God's grace, thereby truly hungering for God's presence to be realized and looking for it in the future.

Its coming, however, is totally different from what was expected. Anna and Simeon, therefore, have a sense of the sword of judgment without which God's good coming is impossible. Only those who allow themselves to be delivered from all perversion and extenuation know the meaning of grace and peace. That is the "consolation" of Israel. Here all that Israel had learned through the centuries from experiencing the word of its God becomes visible as a ministry to the nations, a ministry that gives Israel, too, its meaning and identity as "light to the nations" (Isa. 49:6). Simeon shows that peace can also consist in retreating to the rank and file and letting God work.

In Galatians 3:23 and 4:4–5, Paul meditated on the meaning of Jesus' being born "under the law." His answer is totally different from Luke's. He sees the law as a means by which human beings would render their own lives secure and assert their claims before God (also Luke 18:11–12!); the Lukan infancy narrative sees in the law the joy of worship and a hope that is open to God's act of grace.

For both Paul and Luke, therefore, humankind is set free from itself for God's great act—otherwise there can be no peace for the

"Gentiles" among the "devout." But this must be interpreted in different ways, depending on who is being addressed: different dangers threaten, and different messages are needed. Paul is thinking of the "devout," who seek their own religious security. The Lukan infancy narrative thinks of those already overcome by God, who already know what it is to be "raised up" through their "fall" (cf. the excursus following 21:24, b).

# D. JESUS, AT HOME WITH GOD AND HUMANITY (2:41–52)

[41]And his parents went to Jerusalem every year at the feast of the Passover. [42]And when he was twelve years old, they went up according to the custom of the feast; [43]and when the days were fulfilled, as they were returning, the child Jesus stayed behind in Jerusalem, and his parents did not know it [44]since they supposed he was in the company. So they went a day's journey, and sought him among their kinsfolk and acquaintances; [45]and when they did not find him, they returned to Jerusalem to seek him. [46]And it happened after three days they found him in the temple, sitting among the teachers and listening to them and asking them questions. [47]But all who heard him were amazed at his understanding and answers. [48]And when they saw him they were astonished, and his mother said to him, "Child, why have you treated us so? Behold, your father and I have been seeking you anxiously." [49]And he said to them, "Why did you seek me? Did you not know that I must be in [the world] of my Father?" [50]And they did not understand the saying that he spoke to them. [51]And he went with them and came down to Nazareth, and was obedient to them. And his mother kept all these words in her heart.

[52]And Jesus progressed in wisdom and age and "favor with God and people."

(Vs. 52—1 Sam. 2:26.)

This section links the prophecies concerning Jesus with the narrative of his ministry beginning in chapter 3. It can be analyzed in various ways. Correspondences can be seen between the journey to

Jerusalem and the return (41–42/51a), Jesus' staying behind without his parents' knowledge and his reply, which they cannot understand (43/49–50), the parents' successful search and their reproachful question (44–46a/48). The overall structure would then be abc/cba, with Jesus' presence among the teachers of Israel as the midpoint (46b–47). But vs. 47 is really intrusive: in it the onlookers are suddenly the subject rather than Jesus' parents (vss. 46, 48), and Jesus is described as answering, in contradiction to vs. 46b (q.v.).

If vs. 47 is omitted, the structure becomes clearer. An introduction (vs. 42) names the persons, the place, and the time; then follows the problem occasioned by Jesus' action (staying behind), with the consequent reaction of his parents (43–46a). Next comes a preliminary solution in an action of Jesus (his devotion to learning), which again evokes a reaction (his parents' reproaches) in vss. 46b, 48, and finally the definitive solution brought about by Jesus' action (his word) and the parents' reaction (not understanding him) in vss. 49–50. The return constitutes the conclusion; Jesus is again the subject as in the introduction (vs. 51a). Now the focus is on Jesus' words, which emphasize his exalted nature, and his conduct, which emphasizes his subordination.

Because divine sonship and wisdom go together (Wisd. 2:13, 18) and Jesus is more than an ambitious student, Luke (?) has added vs. 47. Vs. 51a is the normal end of the story (cf. the return in 1:23, 38, 56; 2:20, 39). Vs. 51b is clearly meant to correct vs. 50; in addition, "all these words" cannot refer to "the saying" (vs. 50). The verse is intended to be taken with vs. 52 as the (Lukan) conclusion to the infancy narrative as a whole; it is identical almost word-for-word with 2:19. This observation, like the non-Lukan use of Jewish "teachers" rather than "scribes, teachers of the law," shows that Luke was making use of a story that was already extant.


[41] In theory all males—later women and children as well—were required to go up to Jerusalem for the three major festivals (Exod. 34:23). In fact, depending on distance, the journey might be possible only once a year or once in a lifetime. Passover (see the excursus on Mark 14:12—16) began as a nomadic festival in the

spring in which blood was used to ward off demons. The Egyptian experience gave it new meaning: it was celebrated henceforth as the "feast of unreadiness," with bread that was not yet salted and leavened; in Samaria it was even celebrated standing, staff in hand. For centuries it was a major festival, keeping Israel open to the coming act of God. Luke 22:15-18 (q.v.), 28-30 take it once more as a sign of the pilgrim community.

[42] The age of twelve as an early beginning of wisdom is associated with Cyrus (Xenophon *Cyrop*. 13. 1), Epicurus (Diogenes 50. 10 .14), Samuel (Josephus *Ant*. 5. 348; cf. Moses in 2. 231 and Philo *Vit. Mos*. 1. 18–25), Solomon (1 Kings 2:12 LXX), Daniel and David (Ignatius interpol. *Magn*. 3. 2, 4), and others. At the age of thirteen a Jewish boy becomes a "son of the law," i.e., personally responsible for keeping the commandments. The text may possibly therefore suggest that Jesus' parents wanted to introduce him to the festival. On the other hand, children were supposed to be brought along as soon as they could walk or even be carried although this probably applies only to those who lived in Jerusalem.

[43] From Jerusalem to the border of Galilee is about sixty-five miles. [44] Since entire villages might travel together, the confusion is easily imaginable. [45] We can already glimpse something of Mary's suffering (vs. 35).

[46] Three days are a round number; nothing is said about the starting point for counting. The "temple" is not the building proper, which was open only to the priests, but the outer court, open even to women. For Luke it is not the locus of the cult but a place of instruction (Luke 19:47; 21:37-38; Acts 2—5). In contrast to the examples cited, Jesus appears as a pupil, squatting on the ground and asking questions of the experts, something not expected of a twelve-year-old but certainly in accord with the usual school practice.

[47] Vs. 47 interprets the situation differently, possibly contrasting the wisdom of Jesus' answers to the scholarly conclusions of the scribes. [48] But the parents take no pleasure in such wisdom. This is not the point of the story. The unusual expression "your father and I" paves the way for Jesus to speak of his other father who is totally different (cf. Targ. Jon. on Exod. 15:2, where the babes in arms cry out to "our God" [or Father?] after the deliverance at the Red Sea).

**[49]** In Luke the first word spoken by Jesus is a reference to the God who is above him yet with whom he is associated as with no other. Jesus "must" be in what belongs to his Father. This refers not only to the house which he is about to leave but to everything that belongs to God. Earthly rules and regulations cannot keep him out. This "must" (cf. 4:43; 9:22; 22:37) separates Jesus from his parents. **[50]** He is astonished that they do not realize this. Mary is pictured very differently in 2:19 (q.v.).

**[51]** Human beings are so alienated from God that they will think of anything rather than the real and active presence of God in their lives. Only on isolated occasions does this presence appear, for instance in the life of prayer. The strangeness of what Jesus says is increased by the fact that he does not underline his words with miracles but rather through participation in the everyday life of his family in which he lives for thirty years in the almost unimaginably narrow and primitive environment of a small Near Eastern town, with no variety except for sabbath worship, instruction in the synagogue, and an annual pilgrimage. **[52]** This is growth in "wisdom and grace" (or: "favor"; see the discussion of 2:40). Clearly such growth is possible without special education and activity when God gives time for his work.

The only New Testament story about Jesus' youth is not the story of a juvenile. It says nothing about his development, the roots of his ministry in his early experience, the beginnings of his later gifts (vs. 47 at most). On the contrary, Jesus knows from the very beginning who his Father is. The real Jesus is therefore not "our" Jesus, the Jesus whom we can explain and understand. At most his appearance as a student in Jerusalem might characterize him as an early achiever, but its real meaning becomes apparent only in his words. Remarkably enough he demonstrates this in a way of life in which he integrates himself in the household of his parents, but also in the history of Israel and its temple—in no way apart from others. That this will go beyond all power of human imagination will be shown by the Passion (which is not to suggest that "Passover," "seeking" in the wrong place, and "three days" refer proleptically to 22:15; 24:5, 7).

**The Christology of the Infancy Narrative.** (a) The structure of Luke 1—2 exhibits a kind of forward progress. It begins with the spirituality of Israel and the announcement of John's birth as the unexpected act of God and goes on to the more important annunciation of Jesus. Again surpassing the story of John, there follow the birth of Jesus and the message of the angels, the shepherds, and the prophets, who interpret Jesus' birth as a divine eschatological event. A transitional section hints at the mystery of Jesus' divine sonship, thus leading up to his ministry. It is possible to count seventy weeks (six plus nine months plus forty days) for 1:5—2:39, which would agree with Daniel 9:24 (see the excursus following 2:38). But since this is never stated explicitly, and since the forty days before the purification (but not before the "redemption" of the first-born; Exod. 22:29; 34:20; Num. 18:15–16) have to be calculated from Leviticus 12, this is probably accidental.

(b) The use made of the tradition concerning the Baptist is itself unprecedented: the forerunner of God (1:16–17) becomes the forerunner of Jesus. The eschatological coming of God is thus identified with the coming of Jesus. Not only are texts interpreted as applying to Jesus but so is an earthly human life, coinciding in time with that of Jesus and still a matter of living memory. The prophets, too, are not texts but contemporaries dwelling in Jerusalem. It is God's act in the story of an earthly human life that culminates in Jesus and announces the eschaton (cf. the excursus following 4:30). What is astonishing is that—in contrast to Mark, John, all the Epistles, and all the summaries of the faith (even in Acts)—infancy stories are recounted. The crucial salvation is identified with the birth of Jesus itself (and its proclamation). Of course his subsequent ministry is presupposed but it is only important because in it the fate of Israel and of the nations will be decided. This notion is related to Isaiah 9:6; 11:1 and Hellenistic expectations (see the excursus following 2:38). But salvation does not wait for this ministry. The human race is so alienated from God that the very fact of God's present reality means salvation. That is the message of the angel. Therefore the focus here is not on the adult Jesus with his active faith and approach to life but on the child who is primarily a passive recipient of the action. The only saying of Jesus that is recorded is his mention of the Father in whose world he belongs. Salvation comes through judgment, rising up through falling, as is shown by the failure of Jesus' own parents to understand. There is no hint of an atoning act of God, unless atonement is understood so broadly that every righteous act of the devout is interpreted as atonement. But even this would hold at most for Jesus' parents, the parents of the Baptist, and the prophets in Jerusalem, not for the child Jesus himself. And so atonement consists in God's turning once more to his people out of unmotivated love, making them once more his people through judgment and grace.

(c) Luke will take up this theme (see the excursus following 22:30). In contrast to John 1:11–14; Galatians 4:4–5 (see the conclusion following 1:26–38), Luke 1—2 emphasizes not Jesus' coming from a heavenly realm but the restoration of God's covenant with Israel, which is brought to its culmination, far surpassing everything that has gone before.

At the annunciation of Jesus' birth nothing is said of human righteousness and spirituality—only of God's grace, which may then be accepted in faith (1:38; cf. 2:19). The parents of the Baptist are still cast entirely in the mold of the Old Testament, but the light of the New Testament already shines in the angel's words to Mary (see the discussion of 1:48) and what is said of Jesus.

Jesus is therefore not unique in the sense that, like a meteor, he falls into a totally alien world. The life of God, the Holy Spirit, already shapes the lives of thousands in Israel, and the influence of the Spirit is concentrated once more in John. What makes Jesus unique is the fact that in him this act of God finds its culmination, that without him none of this can be understood because he alone gives meaning to it all (cf. the discussion of 24:27). To Luke this holds not only for Israel but even for the political decisions of the Roman emperor (2:1–5).

This can be seen only by faith. God brings forth this faith in Zechariah, Elizabeth, and Mary, in the shepherds and in the Jerusalem prophets. The Gospel and Acts will have more to say of it. But the faithful in Israel have known from the beginning that Israel's entire history draws its meaning only from God's future; the exodus and journey through the desert can be understood only from the entry into the promised land, persecution and suffering only from the coming kingdom of God. It is possible that the non-Christian Judaism of today is more aware of this through its experience than is a self-satisfied Christendom, which often ignores its origin in this divine history and God's purpose for it in the future.

# II

## THE GROWTH OF THE COMMUNITY
### (3:1—9:50)

---

## A. PREPARATION: APPEARANCE AND MESSAGE
## OF THE BAPTIST AND JESUS
### (3:1—4:30)

The public ministries of John and Jesus as adults begin in 3:1/23*a*. Again the story of the Baptist is intertwined with that of Jesus. Skipping 2:1–52, 1:80 continues in 3:3; skipping 3:1–20, 2:40 continues in 3:21–22. (cf. the discussion of 3:19–20). The call, preaching, and arrest of the Baptist stand in parallel to 3:21–22; 4:16–27, 28–30; it is better therefore to include 4:14–30 with the preparatory section. This makes clear the parallel between the use of Isaiah 40:3–5 to introduce the Baptist and Isaiah 61:1–2 to introduce Jesus, as well as the emphasis on the Spirit in 3:22; 4:1, 14, 18.

The break could also be made at the shift to Judea (4:44; cf. 23:5; Acts 10:37), especially since 4:31–43 is a counterpart to 16–30 and takes up vs. 18 once more in 4:43. In this case, Galilee would be represented by Nazareth (vss. 16–30) and Capernaum (31–43). But 4:38–39 clearly leads up to 5:1–11, and 4:31*b* marks the beginning of Jesus' public ministry. In addition, 4:31–43 clearly follows the structure of Mark 1:21–39, whereas 3:1—4:30 follows Q with additional material from L (3:10–14, 23–38; 4:16–30), while showing the influence of Mark (3:3, 16, [19–20], 21–22, 4:16–30).

Luke himself was probably responsible for the introduction (3:1–2), an additional quotation (3:5–6), and framework (3:15, 18–20). The section 4:14–31*a* probably comprises a special tradition. The gift of the Spirit in 3:22 is a theme taken up again in 4:1, 14, 18.

If Luke had added chapters 1—2 as an afterthought, 3:1–2 would have been an impressive beginning, corresponding to Acts 1:1 and

10:37, and the genealogy of Jesus would follow the first mention of him. But it is more likely that 3:1–2 is meant to describe the situation in Palestine that was important as the background to Jesus' ministry and that the genealogy follows the words from heaven "Thou art my Son" so that both sections emphasize the humanity and divinity of Jesus.

## The Forerunner (3:1–6)
Cf. Mark 1:2–6; Matthew 3:1–6

[1]In the fifteenth year of the reign of the emperor Tiberius, when Pontius Pilate was governor of Judea and Herod was tetrarch of Galilee, and his brother Philip tetrarch of of Ituraea and Trachonitis, and Lysanias tetrarch of Abilene, [2]under the high priest Annas and Caiaphas, the word of God came to John, the son of Zechariah, in the wilderness. [3]And he went into all the region about the Jordan, preaching a baptism of repentance for the forgiveness of sins, [4]as it is written in the book of the words of Isaiah the prophet:
"The voice of one crying in the wilderness:
Prepare the way of the Lord,
make his paths straight.
[5]Every valley shall be filled,
and every mountain and hill shall be brought low,
and the crooked shall be made straight,
and the rough ways smooth,
[6]and all flesh shall see the salvation of God."

(Vss. 4–6—Isa. 40:3–6.)

[1] The section begins with the historical background. Depending on whether one counts the reign of Tiberius together with Augustus and chooses the Roman or Eastern system of determining the year, the date falls between the end of 26 and the beginning of A.D. 29. Judea and Samaria have been under Roman rule since A.D. 6; the other three of what had originally been four tetrarchs rule more or less independently under the hegemony of Rome. [2] Annas was deposed in A.D. 14/15 but continued to play an important role and may have retained the title (cf. Josephus *Vita* 38). Luke knows there is only one high priest and therefore uses the singular, "the high

priest." According to Acts 4:6, he seems to consider Annas the actual holder of this office, not Caiaphas, who was its legal occupant. Augustus, once hailed as bringer of paradise, was succeeded by the sullen and paranoid Tiberius, and Roman troops occupied the Holy Land. The sacred status of the high priesthood vanished; the Romans appointed and deposed high priests according to their political desires.

At this point there took place an event described with the utmost brevity after the long introduction: "A word of God happened," concretely, "to [or: 'upon'] John" (to render the Greek as literally as possible). More is therefore involved than a teaching to be shared with others.

[3–4] A description of John's preaching, again very brief, is followed by a long quotation from Isaiah. Like Matthew 3:3, Luke introduces the quotation only after mentioning John's message, and does not use the passage cited in Mark 1:2 until 7:27 (Matt. 11:10). He also speaks of "all the region about the Jordan" (Matt. 3:5), possibly on the basis of Q (cf. the discussion of Matt. 3:11–12 and the introduction to Matt. 4:1–11).

[2] Theologically, he underlines God's sudden coming into the history of the world and the fulfillment of God's promises. "Came" may indicate divine origin, as in 7:33. God's word comes to one who had been called while he was still in his mother's womb (1:15), as it did to Jeremiah (Jer. 1:1–5; cf. Hos. 1:1, with date and patronymic). The details of how this took place are not described. Neither is anything more said of John's ascetic way of life (presupposed in 1:15 and 7:25). [3] Indeed, according to Luke John leaves the wilderness where he had been and enters the region of the Jordan (cf. the similar account in John 1:28; 3:22–23; a different version appears in Matt. 3:5; 11:7). [4] The "voice . . . in the wilderness" is thus God's call to (and then through) him.

[5] Luke may understand the "leveling" or "lowering" in a spiritual sense (in 18:14 the same form of the word occurs; cf. 1:51–53 and Acts 2:40): in the time of salvation, no one can be exalted before God, but neither will anyone remain in the depths (cf. the discussion of 6:20–26). [6] The last clause promises salvation (only LXX) to "all flesh," thus including the nations (Acts 28:28).

## The Gospel of the Baptist (3:7–20)
Cf. Matthew 3:7–12; 14:3–4; Mark 1:7–8; 6:17–18

[7]He said therefore to the crowd that came out to be baptized by him, "You brood of vipers, who warned you to flee from the wrath to come? [8]Bear fruits that befit repentance. And do not begin to say to yourselves, 'We have Abraham as our father'; for I tell you, God is able from these stones to raise up children to Abraham. [9]Even now the ax is laid to the root of the trees; now every tree that does not bear good fruit is cut down and thrown into the fire."

[10]And the crowd asked him, "What shall we do?" [11]He answered and said to them, "Whoever has two undergarments should share with whoever has none, and whoever has food should do likewise." [12]Tax collectors also came to be baptized, and said to him, "Teacher, what shall we do?" [13]And he said to them, "Demand no more than is appointed you." [14]Soldiers also asked him and said, "And we, what shall we do?" And he said to them, "Mistreat no one, and extort from no one, and be content with your wages."

[15]As the people were all wondering in their hearts about John, whether he were not perhaps the Messiah, [16]John answered and said to all of them, "I baptize you with water; but he is coming who is mightier than I, the thong of whose sandals I am not worthy to untie. He will baptize you with Holy Spirit and fire. [17]He has his winnowing fork in his hand, to clear his threshing floor and to gather the wheat into his granary; but the chaff he will burn with unquenchable fire."

[18]So, with many other exhortations, he preached good news to the people. [19]But Herod the tetrarch, reproved by him on account of Herodias, his brother's wife, and all the evil that Herod had done, [20]added this to all the rest, that he shut up John in prison.

From the warning against complacency contained in Q (vss. 7–9), a special tradition of instructions for various groups (vss. 10–14), and the announcement of the one to come, found also in Mark and Q (vss. 15–18), Luke has fashioned a comprehensive presentation of the Baptist's preaching, introducing it with an account of his call (vss. 1–6) and concluding it with an account of his imprisonment (vss. 19–20). In comparison with Mark and Q, he has expanded vss. 15–20 by adding a comment on the mistaken messianic expectations of the people (vs. 15) and a statement about the good news preached by the Baptist (vs. 18), followed by the concluding report of his arrest. The result is to separate the announcement of Jesus more markedly from the threat of judgment in vss. 7–9. Like Matthew 3:11–12, the statement in vs. 16 distinguishes John from Jesus in such a way that the description of John baptizing with water at the beginning corresponds to that of Jesus baptizing with the Spirit at the end (vs. 16*a/d*), while in between these descriptions the mightier Jesus to come is spoken of before his unworthy servant John (vs. 16*b/c*).

For Luke, John's preaching is his most important act. He is the embodiment of Old Testament prophecy, which knows that there can be no grace without judgment, no salvation without repentance, no forgiveness without a divine claim on the human will. The Baptist is not hampered by any sense of inferiority vis-à-vis the official troop of theologians and the regent, or by any sense of spiritual superiority that would shut him off from tax collectors and soldiers with their needs.

[7] Vss. 7–9 agree almost verbatim with Matthew 3:7–10 but are addressed to all the people (cf. 1:17, 77; Acts 13:24) rather than the Pharisees and Sadducees (Matt. 3:7). They are not meant to soften the hardhearted and bring them to baptism but are addressed to those who are already pressing forward to be baptized: they are warned not to delude themselves with the illusion of security through membership in the company of "believers" and participation in the sacrament (vss. 7–9), they are called on to live the practical consequences (vss. 10–14), and they are told about the one to come who will give the Holy Spirit (vss. 15–18). On the one hand, Luke does not see a "holy remnant" such as would not need to be warned; on the other, he does not exclude the Pharisees (cf. the discussion of 13:31). He proclaims Christ for "all flesh" (vss. 4–6).

[8] "I have Abraham as my father" is not enough—neither in its strict Pharisaic sense nor in its superficial popular sense. "Stones" certainly do not attend synagogue or church, but God can raise up even stones. The notion that Israel is the wheat and the nations the chaff (Bill. 1. 122) could turn out to be a deadly error (cf. the image

in Mal. 4:1). **[10–14]** Luke illustrates this point in the instructions that are unique to his tradition (vss. 10–14). The "fruits" (plural in vs. 8, contrary to Matthew) are found among tax collectors and soldiers, whom the devout have written off.

John is questioned three times (in formal resemblance to Apoc. Moses 9; Vita Adami 35; Apoc. Ezra 7:4). **[11]** The first answer establishes the basic principle; the second and third go into more detail regarding specific situations. **[12]** Only the middle group, the tax collectors, are described explicitly as coming to be baptized and recognizing John as "teacher"; this is because they were the most controversial (Mark 2:14–17; Matt. 11:19; 21:31–32; Luke 7:29; 15:1–2). Those who have begun to have doubts about what they do, mounting questions, and clear answers—all are part of the "good news" or "gospel" (vs. 18).

**[11]** The first answer recalls the radicalism of the Sermon on the Mount although it does not suggest the giving away of everything (cf. 6:29). In fact, what is proposed is not even "giving away" but rather "sharing" of what is enough for two. Property is not attacked as an institution as long as it is not clung to but made available to those who need it as well as to the owner. In contrast to Qumran (1QS 1:12; and the equivalent modern economic systems), it is important that this take place by free choice. To live by this principle despite experiences that are not all comforting is of course radical enough!

**[12]** But there is also the special question of conduct within a particular vocation and its regulations. **[13]** In this period taxes were farmed out to the highest bidder, who had to raise this sum through his factors, the "tax collectors," plus something for himself to live on. For this reason there could hardly be such a thing as an honest tax collector. About the time of Jesus' ministry, Vespasian's father was even honored by a statue in Asia Minor, with the inscription: "To the one who collected the tax well" (for the taxpayers or for the state?). The fact that he did not end up personally out of pocket is shown by the fact that he later founded a bank in Switzerland (Suetonius *Vitae* 8. 1. 2–3)! The tax collectors in Galilee, however, were more likely small independent contractors. Change is expected to come through an individual change of heart, not through an alteration of the tax system, which would in that period have remained an unrealizable utopia.

For modern tax collectors, cheating is not a great temptation if only because of the supervising bureaucracy. In the light of vs. 11, therefore, it is worth considering whether "what the regulations require" is still just, or whether the system must be changed. Such a change could not be accomplished without laws and compulsion; but the initiative and persistence of individuals would still be crucial: their change of heart would aim at changing the hearts of others. For this reason it is not enough to reform the secular law or the ecclesiastical cult (e.g., 1QS 3:5–6). The aim of the gospel is a change of heart leading to specific changes in the conduct of office, such as lobbying for new tax systems—without allowing such changes to be confused with the salvation promised by the gospel (cf. the excursus following Matthew 5—7).

[14] Is Luke thinking of non-Jewish soldiers, of Jewish mercenaries employed by Herod, or primarily of problems in his own community? The Baptist's reply does not confront them with the ultimate question, which in practice they are not in a position to judge, whether what they are ordered to do is just; it does, however, impose a distinct limitation. Here, too, vs. 11 raises the question of whether an offensive or defensive war tramples the rights of others underfoot and therefore demands conscientious objection while vs. 14 also raises the question of whether total rejection of military service does not open the doors wide to injustice in its most terrible forms of totalitarianism and terrorism. (For vs. 15 see the conclusion below.)

[16–17] The words of the Baptist are almost identical with Matthew 3:11–12, except that Luke distinguishes baptism "by means of" water from baptism "in" the Holy Spirit (cf. the discussion of vs. 22). In contrast to Matthew 3:12, vs. 17 seems to suggest that the harvest is being winnowed and gathered in at that very moment; only the burning of the chaff remains in the future. As in 3:7, therefore, the "people" are addressed, and John preaches to "all." The separation is yet to come. The "mightier one" (the same root appears in 2 Thess. 1:9; Rev. 5:12) who is yet to come was, for the Baptist, the bringer of the last judgment. For Luke he is the one who will baptize in the Holy Spirit (above all at Pentecost; Acts 1:5, also 19:1–7). But he also brings judgment. Luke omits the additional phrase "and with fire" in Acts 1:5; 11:16, so that it does not refer to the flames of the Holy Spirit (Acts 2:3). But when the Spirit makes it possible for a person to accept God's judgment, judgment becomes blessing.

[19-20] Luke anticipates John's arrest (Mark 6:17-18), perhaps in order to distinguish his role from that of Jesus. Herod is mentioned first and his crime, as the last straw, at the end; he also appears prominently in 13:31-32; 23:6-12; Acts 4:27.

Luke does not stress the fact that Jesus' ministry did not begin until John's had ended (cf. also Mark 1:14 = Matt. 4:12). Jesus' coming "after him" (Mark 1:7 = Matt. 3:11) is omitted entirely in vs. 16, perhaps because the expression often designates a successor. Nothing is said in 7:18 about the Baptist's imprisonment and 7:29-30 even suggests that he continued to baptize. One of Luke's favorite techniques is to bring an episode to a close only to go back (here even with a new statement of time) to something that went before (8:37/38; 1:80/2:1; 21:12; 23:54/55-56; 24:51b/Acts 1:9; Acts 11:18/19; cf. Luke 9:51 and the introduction to 3:1—4:30). And so he mentions John's imprisonment here because he is not going to tell of his execution (presupposed in 9:7, 9; see the conclusion to 20:9-19). Furthermore, this arrangement emphasizes the preliminary nature not only of his preaching but also of his life and death. This may have been welcome to Luke because it leaves up in the air the question of who actually performed the baptism of Jesus, mentioned only in a subordinate clause in vs. 21.

[7-9] Luke's sources (Mark 1:4 and Q) already spoke of a baptism of repentance and penitential exhortation. He uses vss. 5-6 to emphasize the fact that this message is already a harbinger of salvation.

[10-14] Even vss. 10-14 are not concerned with onerous demands in the domain of religion which many *cannot* fulfil (cf. 18:12; Acts 15:10); neither do they represent a moral law. In Acts 2:37-38; 16:30-31; 22:10-16, the answer to the same question "What shall we do?" (here given by Jesus) is equally concrete but very different from John's answer. This shows that even the clearest response never relieves anyone of the responsibility of asking again and struggling for an answer. Simple obedience to the instructions of Luke 3:13-

14, for example, would be guaranteed in a well-administered system of taxation and a disciplined army. This is not to be despised; it is probably much more a fruit of the gospel than we realize. But it is not identical with the gospel. Only hearts that have been deeply affected by the gospel are always open to what God expects as the next concrete requirement after the present one.

More important to our text, therefore, than the practical instructions is the fact that tax collectors and soldiers are brought back into communion with God by being expected to do the will of God. What the educated Jew considered association with bad company (Origen *Contra Celsum* 1. 62) is in fact God's love for the despised. In his pastoral dialogue John anticipates what will find fulfillment in Jesus (7:29–30; 15:1–2): no vocation must be allowed to corrupt, however much it can be corrupted. Something similar takes place in the *Haustafeln* (Col. 3:18—4:1, etc.): in contrast to their Greek prototypes, the Christian guidelines address not only the free adult males concerning their conduct toward women, children, and slaves, but impose responsibilities on the latter and thus take them seriously as human beings. The gospel and God's salvation often come in the form of new responsibilities which give a life its meaning.

[15–20] Luke goes to some pains to distinguish the Baptist from Jesus because certain groups have been formed that worshiped John (as the Messiah?) (vs. 15; Acts 11:16; 13:25; 19:4; John 1:20). Despite his function as forerunner (1:17; 7:27), he is not even compared to Elijah, possibly because the returning Elijah was identified with the Messiah (see the discussion of 1:17, 76). Mark 1:6; 9:11–13; Matthew 11:14 are lacking; contrariwise, Jesus is presented in the image of Elijah in Luke 4:25–27; 7:12–16; 9:61 (see also 8:55; 9:54; 10:46; Acts 1:11*b*). Luke, therefore, no longer juxtaposes the two figures as messengers of wisdom, as is done by Q (7:33–35) and perhaps by an ancient Jewish Christian tradition also appearing in Revelation 11:13–14, which saw in them the return of the prophets Elijah and Moses (cf. Acts 3:22; 7:38).

On the other hand, Luke also relates Jesus especially closely with John (cf. 11:1). The birth of both is "gospel" (1:19; 2:10) and both in turn proclaim the "gospel" (see the discussion of Mark 1:1 and the beginning of the excursus following Luke 4:30) to the people (accusative, 3:18; 20:1; also Acts 8:25; 14:21; etc.), John as preacher of repentance (3:3, 8; Acts 13:24; 19:4), Jesus as preacher of the kingdom of God (Luke 4:43; cf. Mark 1:14–15). The preaching of John as forerunner is part of the Christian confession (Acts 10:38; 13:24). His baptism is the beginning of the Christian baptism: there is no further command to baptize like Matthew 28:19. Just as John gives the possibility of repentance that brings forgiveness (3:3; 7:29–30), so too does Jesus (15:1–2; Acts 5:31; 11:18 [life]; 20:21 [faith]). Jesus is also considered a prophet like John (4:24; 7:16, 39; 13:33; 24:19; *the* prophet: Acts 3:22–23; 7:35–37). Luke 7:28, therefore, cannot mean that John is excluded from the kindgom of God (13:28 already to the contrary). Above all, Luke describes those who have been baptized with the baptism of John, who probably are in a kind of competition with the Christian community, as Christians without full knowledge and therefore still in need of a further baptism in the name of Jesus (Acts 19:1–7; cf. 18:25). To Luke's mind, therefore, John belongs to the dawn of the age of salvation (see the discussion of 16:16).

## The Son of God Is Proclaimed: Jesus' Baptism and Genealogy (3:21–38)
Cf. Mark 1:9–11; Matthew 3:13–17; 1:1–17

[21]And it happened at the baptism of all the people, when Jesus had been baptized and was praying, the heaven was opened [22]and the Holy Spirit descended upon him in bodily form as a dove, and a voice came from heaven, "Thou art my beloved Son; in thee I have taken pleasure."

[23]And he, Jesus, was about thirty years old when he began—the son (as was supposed) of Joseph, of Heli, [24]of Matthat, of Levi, of Melchi, of Jannai, of Joseph, [25]of Mattathias, of Amos, of Nahum,of Esli, of Naggai, [26]of Maath, of Mattathias, of Semein, of Josech, of Joda, [27]of Joanan, of Rhesa, of Zerubbabel, of Shealtiel, of Neri, [28]of Melchi, of Addi, of Cosam, of Elmadam, of Er, [29]of Jesus, of Eliezer, of Jorim, of Matthat, of Levi, [30]of Simeon, of Judah, of Joseph, of Jonam, of Eliakim, [31]of Melea, of Menna, of Mattatha, of Nathan, of David, [32]of Jesse, of Obed, of Boaz, of Sala, of Nahshon, [33]of Amminadab, of Admin, of Arni, of Hezron, of Perez, of Judah, [34]of Jacob, of Isaac, of Abraham, of Terah, of Nahor, [35]of Serug, of Reu, of Peleg, of Eber, of Shelah,

³⁶of Cainan, of Arphaxad, of Shem, of Noah, of Lamech, ³⁷of Methuselah, of Enoch, of Jared, of Mahalaleel, of Cainan, ³⁸of Enos, of Seth, of Adam, of God.

(Vs. 22—Ps. 2:7; Isa. 42:1.)

A substantial introduction, in which the syntax distinguishes Jesus' baptism from that of the people (see the discussion of vs. 20), is followed by three key verbs describing the opening of heaven, the descent of the Spirit, and the sound of God's voice. These are described "objectively" (no longer in terms of what Jesus sees; see the discussion of Mark 1:9–11) and conclude with a proclamation: "Thou art my Son. . . ."

Like Matthew 3:16, Luke 3:21 speaks of the heaven "opening" (not "splitting," as in Mark 1:10); this is an expression associated with eschatological expectations (Ezek. 1:1; Isa. 64:1; Test. Levi 18:6; see the introduction to Mark 1:9–11). Whether this term and the mention of the coming of the "Holy" (not in Mark) Spirit "upon" him (= Matt. 3:16) derive, like vss. 16–17, from Q is uncertain, although Q (4:3) does presuppose the title "Son of God." A small group of manuscripts reads, "Thou art my Son; today I have begotten thee" (as in Acts 13:33, where the "today," however, is Easter!). Was this form in Q, and was the passage assimilated to Mark 1:11 because of the conflict with 1:35? No other group of manuscripts exhibits any trace of this reading. It is therefore more likely that (Jewish Christian) copyists assimilated the passage to Psalm 2:7 (a royal psalm) in order to emphasize Jesus' kingship; the Gospel according to the Hebrews 4 (Jewish Christian) has the two readings side by side.

The genealogy is totally different from that in Matthew 1:1–17 (q.v.). Only from David to Adam does it follow the Old Testament in a reasonably clear way; the Greek versions must have been used since only there does "Cainan" appear (vs. 36). Almost all the individuals from Jesus to David are unknown; some bear the names of the patriarchs. Even the name of Joseph's father differs from that recorded in Matthew 1:16. The sequence "Jesus—(two names)—Matthat—Levi (absent in an African manuscript)—(two names)—Joseph" in vss. 23–24 is repeated in vss. 29–30. In addition, vss. 25

and 26 mention a Mattathias, vs. 31 a Mattatha. Were vss. 23–26 and 29–31 at one time different versions of the same generations, here placed in temporal sequence? This would explain why Luke counts fourteen more generations than Matthew from Joseph back to Abraham.

[22] The Spirit appears "in bodily form." The comparison to a dove ("as"!) refers to this form, not just to the act of "hovering." The corporeal reality of the event is important to Luke—of course not the details, which may well have been elaborated by addition of legendary features, but the beginning of Jesus' ministry on the basis of unity with God. The word of God comes to Jesus here in a way that contrasts sharply with vs. 2, proclaiming him "Son of God" in the presence of "all the people" (vs. 21). The reality of the coming of the Spirit is depicted graphically in the image of the dove descending from the Father to the Son, just as it is later by the flames of fire (Acts 2:3), the special language of the Spirit (2:4; 10:44–46; 19:6; probably also 8:17–19), and the earthquake (4:31). But the words from God clearly distinguish the relationship of the "Son" to God from that of the community. What matters to Luke is not exorcisms and the like but the witness given by the Spirit (see the discussion of 12:10–12 and 4:23; also Acts 1:8; 4:8, 31; 6:10; etc.). Jesus himself is clearly set apart from prophets and miracle workers who simply open themselves to the operation of the Spirit; he consciously occasions the work of the Spirit (see the discussion of 4:1 and 12:10; 21:15; cf. 4:14; also the discussion of 1:35; 2:40), and after his exaltation imparts the Spirit to the community (24:49). Therefore the Spirit is *the* gift of God (see the discussion of Luke 11:13), given, in contrast to Judaism (and 1:15, 41, 67; 2:25, 27), to the entire community (see the discussion of 3:16; 20:42; cf. Acts 2:38–39; 15:8–9; 19:2; etc.). Contrary to Paul, however, the Spirit does not give the knowledge of faith (1 Cor. 2:10–16) but rather gives to those who already believe and obey the power to live accordingly (Acts 2:38; 5:32; etc.). Therefore prayer often precedes receiving of the Spirit (Acts 4:31; 9:9, 11–12; 13:1–3), as it does here in the case of Jesus (not in Mark 1:9; Matt. 3:15; cf. the discussion of Luke 6:12). Luke 3:21–22 is not in fact an account of Jesus' baptism but

of what God says and does in the context of the prayer that follows. The Greek speaks of completed baptism and continuing prayer. The first report of Jesus' adult ministry shows how he opens himself to receive the grace and power of God (cf. Acts 10:37–38).

**[23–38]** The genealogy begins: "And he, Jesus, was the son . . . " and ends: "of Adam, [the son] of God." This shows what Luke considers the important point. In this man, described in human terms as being of a certain age and descent, who fulfills God's history with Israel, the divine sonship of Adam comes to its perfection through God's Spirit in a totally new way, bringing all humanity back to God.

The age of thirty is also mentioned in Numbers 4:3; Genesis 41:46; 2 Samuel 5:4; (Ezek. 1:1); it need not be biographically accurate. From Jesus to Shealtiel, the first man from the Exile, is three times seven generations; likewise from Neri, the last man from the time of freedom, to David. Jesus thus begins the seventh series of seven generations, starting with David. In addition, there are twice seven names from David to Abraham and three times seven from Abraham to God, the creator of Adam. There are thus seventy-seven names altogether, so that Jesus begins the twelfth series of generations: according to 2 Esdras 14:11, the last in the history of the world (cf. the end of the excursus following 2:38).

Luke, however, is no longer aware of this regular pattern in divine history. All that matters to him is the line that runs from God, the father of Adam and thus of all humanity (Acts 17:28–29), to Jesus, suggesting the solidarity of Jesus with all humankind. For Paul, Christ is the "last Adam" (Rom. 5:14; 1 Cor. 15:22, 45–49; cf. Heb. 2:6–7, 17–18); the new person created by the Spirit is spoken of in Colossians 3:10 (= Christ?; cf. Gal. 3:27) and Ephesians 4:24 (cf. Rom. 6:4 and Acts 17:26, 31).

The mention of the baptismal movement that affects "all the people" shows that it is not just individuals who must be prepared for the Christ event but all Israel. Mark already speaks of the beginning of the new age of God, when the heaven opens and the Spirit descends to proclaim the Son of God and call him into service. This is lent even greater importance by what Luke associates with the gift of the Spirit and by what the genealogy says with its notion of the new

Adam (also in Mark 1:12–13 [q.v.], but no longer in Luke 4:1–13 Q).

## The Temptation of Jesus (4:1–13)
Cf. Matthew 4:1–11; Mark 1:12–13

¹And Jesus, full of Holy Spirit, returned from the Jordan and was led by the Spirit in the wilderness ²for forty days, tempted by the devil. And he ate nothing in those days, and when they were ended, he was hungry. ³Then the devil said to him, "If you are God's Son, speak to this stone that it may become bread." ⁴And Jesus answered him, "It is written, 'Not by bread alone shall one live.'" ⁵And he took him up and showed him all the kingdoms of the world in a moment of time. ⁶And the devil said to him, "To you I will give all this authority and their glory; for it has been given to me and I give it to whom I will. ⁷If you, then, will fall down before me in worship, it shall all be yours." ⁸And Jesus answered and said to him,

"You shall fall down in worship before the Lord your God,
  and him only shall you serve."
⁹And he took him to Jerusalem and set him on the pinnacle of the temple, and said to him, "If you are God's Son, throw yourself down from here; ¹⁰for it is written,

'He will command his angels concerning you, to guard you'
¹¹and
'on their hands they will bear you up,
  lest you strike your foot against a stone.'"
¹²And Jesus answered and said to him, "It is said, 'You shall not tempt the Lord your God.'" ¹³And when he had ended every temptation, the devil stood aside from him until an opportune time.

(Vss. 4, 8, 12—Deut. 8:3; 6:13–14, 16. Vss. 10–11—Ps. 91:11–12.)

Vss. 1–2a are formulated by Luke on the basis of Mark 1:12–13; everything else follows Matthew (q.v.), except that the second and third temptations have been interchanged. At Qumran, a messianic prophet, king, and priest were awaited; the last of the three was the most exalted (1QS 9:11; 4QTest 5–8; 1QSa 2:11–22). Did Luke interpret the temptation according to this schema? Vss. 2–4, however, do not suggest a prophetic act; Luke even omits the reference to the word (Matt. 4:4). Neither does vs. 9 speak of any priestly function although it mentions the temple. All that remains is vs. 6, which is clearly concerned with royal messianism (cf. Bill. 3. 675: "I [God] will give you [the messianic king] the goods of the nations for your property, and for your possession the rulers of the ends of the earth"). Neither do we receive any help from the Jewish legend of Balaam, who flew to heaven as God's eschatological opponent but was outdone by the high priest (Targum Jon. on Num. 31:8), for nothing suggests that Luke saw in the last miracle an overcoming of the antichrist. Most likely he moved the leap from the temple to last position because Jesus is at home there (2:49) and because vs. 12 can be understood as a definitive rejection of Satan or because Jerusalem is the goal and end of Jesus' ministry.

[1] Jesus' return from the Jordan is hardly meant to underline his separation from the Baptist; it merely provides a transition from the baptism to the temptation. The other Gospels, too, even John 3:23, do not mention the Jordan again, only the land "beyond the Jordan." In contrast to Mark 1:12 (Matt. 4:1), Jesus is the subject in vs. 1 (as in 4:14; 10:21) and the Spirit is called "Holy" (as in 3:22, q.v.). Jesus determines his own course; he lives "in" the Spirit, who descended upon him (3:22), fills him completely (4:1), anoints him for his work, and rests upon him (4:18). The Spirit also leads Jesus "in the wilderness," as God led the people of Israel (Deut. 8:2). Mark 1:12 (but cf. vs. 13) and Matthew 4:1 read "into the wilderness."

Although "anointing" with the Spirit can bring about the healing of "all those oppressed by the devil" (Acts 10:38), possession of the Spirit and temptation are closely related. According to Scripture, it is precisely those who are called by God that are tempted because they are torn between their God, who will not set them free, and the world, whose suffering they share.

[2] Like Exodus 34:28 and Deuteronomy 9:9, Luke speaks of "not eating" (Matt. 4:2: "fasting"). In contrast to Matthew 4:3, he probably thinks of the devil as tempting Jesus throughout the entire forty days. [3] But he avoids the statement that the devil "came" to him and (vs. 7) the command to "fall down" before him (Matt. 4:3, 9). Luke is aware of the now more than human dimension of this en-

counter. The transformation of a single stone into bread is not a repetition of the manna miracle (Matt. 4:3) or a miracle of the antichrist (Apoc. Ezra 4:27); it is meant to still Jesus' hunger.

[5] The devil varies his attack. In the first and third temptations he questions Jesus' divine sonship in a conditional clause, demanding proof and looking for a successful demonstration, in vss. 10–11 even in the form of a biblical quotation. In the second temptation, the promise comes first and (in contrast to Matt. 4:9) the devil's power is explicitly stated. Only then comes the condition, once more followed by the promise of success. In each case Jesus merely replies by citing the words of Scripture; he does not need diplomacy.

Not from a high mountain (spatially; Matt. 4:8) but "in a moment" (temporally) the devil shows Jesus all the kingdoms, probably including those of the past and future. [6] Luke thus emphasizes the element of the superhuman and miraculous and has the devil state that the world has been given to him (Jer. 27:6), a claim that seems superficially accurate (cf. Rev. 13:2). Not only are the kingdoms mentioned (Matt. 4:9), i.e., political sovereignty, but also their "authority and glory," which may suggest the danger of both political and ecclesiastical authority and dignity. But even Luke's devil does not paint the earth in so bad a light as to pretend to be its creator, as later Gnostics claimed.

[9] The last temptation takes place in the temple. But shortly after Jesus determines finally to go to Jerusalem (9:51), Satan is to fall (10:18, q.v.). What looks like his triumph—Jesus' failure to save himself from the cross by an outward miracle—will be his final defeat. And so Jesus will go to the temple, the community of his followers will tarry there, and the mission into the world of the nations will begin there (19:47; 21:37–38; 24:53; Acts 2:46; 5:42; 22:17–21; 26:20–21). As in these passages (and Luke 2:46; 18:10), the temple stands here at the conclusion of a section as a reference to something that God is planning.

[10–13] The fact that Satan, whose misuse of the Bible does not prevent Jesus from using it correctly, departs from Jesus "until an opportune time" (typically Lukan) does not mean that Jesus' life is the kingdom of God without temptation until the time of his Passion. Luke 22:3, where Satan (see the discussion of 8:12) enters into Judas, is traditional (see the discussion) and therefore hardly represents the Lukan perspective, and according to 22:28 the disciples shared the "temptations" (plural, as in Acts 20:29) of Jesus (e.g., in struggles with demons: 9:41; 10:17; 11:14–22; 13:11–17). Temptation in the singular, though, comes only to those who fall away (8:13), not to disciples (cf. 22:40, 46; 11:4).

Here, too, the temptation narrative stands at the beginning of Jesus' ministry. But Luke is thinking less of messianic demonstrations than of demonstrations in which Jesus proves his true humanity (cf. the preceding baptism and genealogy, and the reference to Jerusalem and the Passion at the end). Of course he alone could change a stone into bread, but he bases his conduct on commandments that apply to all, and Luke omits the miracle of the angels who wait upon him (Mark 1:13; Matt. 4:11). At the same time, it is not "wicked" deeds that the devil proposes, but good deeds—which are intended to multiply Jesus' own glory rather than the glory of God. Two points are made. Jesus overcomes temptation on behalf of all humankind—this will culminate on the cross—but also as a model for the conduct of his followers in (infinitely lesser) temptations of everyday life—this will culminate in the history of the Apostles and the Christian community. Thus the answers of the gospel to the central questions are already hinted at: Who is Jesus with respect to us? Who are we with respect to him? How can we live through him and how should we live after him (cf. the excursus following 22:30)?

### Jesus' Programmatic Sermon (4:14–30)
Cf. Mark 6:1–6; 1:14, 28, 39; Matthew 4:12; 9:26; 13:54–58

14And Jesus returned in the power of the Spirit to Galilee, and a report concerning him went out through all the surrounding country, 15and he taught in their synagogues, being glorified by all.

16And he came to Nazareth, where he had been brought up, and went as was his custom on the sabbath day to the synagogue and rose up to read. 17And there was given to him the book of the prophet Isaiah. And when he opened it, he found the place where it was written:
18"The Spirit of the Lord is upon me,

because he has anointed me.
To preach good news to the poor he has sent me,
to proclaim release to captives
and recovering of sight to the blind,
to set at liberty the oppressed
¹⁹to proclaim a year acceptable to the Lord."
²⁰And he rolled up the book, gave it to the attendant, and sat down. And the eyes of all in the synagogue were fixed on him. ²¹And he began to say to them, "Today this Scripture has been fulfilled in your ears." ²²And all testified concerning him and wondered at the words full of grace that came out of his mouth, and said, "Is this not Joseph's son?" ²³And he said to them, "Doubtless you will quote this proverb to me, 'Physician, heal yourself! What we have heard, what took place at Capernaum, do the same here also in your home town.'" ²⁴But he said, "Amen, I say to you, no prophet is acceptable in his home town. ²⁵But in truth I tell you, there were many widows in Israel in the days of Elijah, when the heaven was shut up three years and six months, when there came a great famine over all the land, ²⁶and to none of them was Elijah sent but only to Zarephath in the land of Sidon, to a widowed woman. ²⁷And there were many lepers in Israel under the prophet Elisha, and none of them was cleansed but only Naaman the Syrian." ²⁸And all in the synagogue were filled with wrath when they heard this, ²⁹and they rose up and put him out of the city and led him to the brow of the hill on which their city was built in order to throw him down. ³⁰But he passed through the midst of them and went away.

The structure of vss. 16–22 is clear: "And he stood up, and there was given to him . . . , and he opened" (vss. 16–17) at the beginning and "he rolled up . . . , gave it . . . , and sat down" (vs. 20a, in reverse order) frame the text from the Old Testament (18–19); the reaction of "all" (vss. 20b, 22) encloses the words of Jesus (vs. 21). Jesus' actions are described as punctiliar in aorist clauses, the reaction of the people as continued, in imperfect clauses. In vss. 16–17 and 20a the subject is Jesus, the book, or the text; that there was a synagogue attendant we learn only in passing from vs. 20. In vss. 20b and 22 it is Jesus on whom the people's attention is focused. In these verses, then, everything centers on him and the words of Scripture.

The situation is less clear in vss. 23–30. The protest of the people (vs. 23) is followed by Jesus' answer (vs. 24) and two Old Testament examples (vss. 25–27). The wrath of all (vs. 28) leads to an assault on Jesus (vs. 29) and his deliverance (vs. 30). Here, too, Jesus dominates as subject. He provocatively formulates the people's objection. But in vss. 25 and 27*a* the subject is the unhelped Israelites, in vs. 27*b* the Gentile, and in vss. 28–29 the listeners. In both cases the emphasis is on opposition to Jesus. These dramatic events, narrated in the aorist, contrast with Jesus' withdrawal, reported in vs. 30*b* as a continuous act.

Luke must have known vs. 24 (= Mark 6:4; but also John 4:44!) in fixed form; elsewhere he avoids the word "amen." Vss. 25–27 are out of place in this context because they deal with the home*land*, not the home town. These verses may derive from a scribal Christian argument for the mission to the Gentiles.

Vss. 28–30 are written totally in Luke's style. Jesus' departure in vs. 30 matches his entrance in vs. 16. Vs. 31*a* marks a new beginning, explaining the shift to Capernaum (Mark 1:21) as a consequence of rejection at Nazareth (cf. 2:39, 51). Matthew 4:13 (q.v.) suggests a pre-Lukan narrative in which Jesus turned from "Nazareth" to the "Gentiles" at Capernaum (vss. 16, 24, 31*a*) because both use the unique form "Nazara" for Jesus' home town. This version may have begun with vss. 14–15 since Luke would hardly have written "their synagogues" (see the discussion of vs. 44). The pre-Lukan narrative would then have developed Jesus' "teaching" (Mark 6:2) in vss. (14–15)16–22, interpreting the question "Is this not Joseph's son?" as expressing amazed agreement or neutrality, followed in vss. 25–27 by the critical question of real faith. Or could "testify" and "wonder" have been taken at one time in a hostile sense, as in Matthew 23:31 and John 7:15?

Vs. 23, Lukan in its language, is quite unexpected. This "proverb" was current among both Jews and Greeks (Bill.; Euripides *Fr.* 1071; Cicero *Fam.* 4. 5. 5). That the promise of salvation to the poor should be fulfilled in miracles is typical of Luke (see the introduction to 4:31–44 and the discussion of 7:21). Luke thus makes the transition to vss. 25–27, which he borrowed from tradition and introduced with "in truth" (his translation of "amen"). Of course these verses contrast Mark 6:5, which tells of healing miracles in Nazareth. For

Luke, the real conflict is provoked by the positive estimate of the Gentiles, already found in Matthew 4:15. It is presumably pre-Lukan (cf. the discussion of 8:39). In the Gospel of Thomas 31 we read: "A prophet is not acceptable [as in Luke 4:19, 24] in his homeland, nor can a physician heal those who know him." This is an illogical secondary assimilation already dependent on Luke.

Luke omitted Mark 6:1–6, thus deliberately prefacing this other version to Jesus' ministry. Like the Baptist in 3:4–9, Jesus is introduced with a long quotation from Isaiah. John's preaching of the judgment to come is matched by the experience of grace here (cf. also the discussion of 3:1—4:30). Luke incorporates a tradition (vss. 18, 24, 25–27, 29; cf. the conclusion to 3:15–20) that enshrines Jesus' ministry as an eschatological prophet (1QS 9:11) but in such a way that the eschatological fulfillment in which everything will be changed is highlighted by Jesus' preaching, his reference to the Gentiles, the attack on him, and his miraculous deliverance. He is attacked because he has already hinted at his departure (contrast Mark 6:1–6).

Just as the narrative begins with Jesus' "rising up" (the same word as "resurrection"), it ends with the "rising up" of the people against him. This is an allusion to the fate of Jesus but also to that of the Apostles, for whom positive response, rejection, turning to the Gentiles, and banishment will likewise follow (Acts 13:45–50; cf. 40–41; also the discussion of Luke 11:49 and the excursus following 22:30, b.2). In neither case does failure mean that God is impotent. Sacred history includes both human rebellion and God's gracious guidance. The positive interpretation of Isaiah 61:1–2 (Heb. without the healing of the blind) and the promises to the Gentiles (cf. the discussion of 8:26) are both important to Luke.

[14 -15] The Spirit, who had led Jesus into the wilderness, now leads him back to the world of human habitation. Each has its season, and each can reflect God's guidance. Unlike the Baptist, Jesus does not wait for people to come to him. "In the power of the Spirit" (see the discussion of 4:1) he returns to Galilee (2:51!). He and his "teaching" are on everyone's lips, not the announcement that the kingdom of God is at hand (Mark 1:15).

[16] As vs. 16 shows, Luke is thinking in terms of worship, not of scriptural study in a special room of the synagogue. Since sacrifice could be offered only in the Jerusalem temple, the synagogue with its liturgy of the word became an accepted institution, possibly as early as the end of the Babylonian Exile, in any case by the third or second century B.C. It was the synagogue that enabled Judaism to survive the destruction of the temple. Synagogue worship begins and ends with prayers and benedictions; its core is the reading of the law, as a rule by several lectors. This reading was probably fixed by the time of Jesus, while the reading from the prophets was still chosen freely. The Hebrew text was translated into the Aramaic vernacular and usually explained by one or more individuals. Any man—women were excluded—could announce his intention to read by standing up (cf. also 1 Cor. 14:30); as a rule, however, there was generally prior agreement on who would be asked to perform this function (Acts 13:15). The reader would sit to begin his explanation (vs. 20).

Jesus' private initiative shows how unusual this incident was. In Luke all six sabbath narratives (see the discussion of 13:10–17) lead to dissension; for this very reason, he uses an expression from the LXX (also found in Acts 17:2) to emphasize that it was Jesus' custom to participate in worship, thus rejecting any tendency to look down on the regular routine of preaching. This is in harmony with the spirituality of both sets of parents as described in 1:5–7 and 2:22–24, 27b. God begins his new message at the point where the divine word is to be expected, however imperfect and dubious the business of synagogue and church may be. God remains faithful to himself and to his covenant, and it is the ancient word of Israel that lays the groundwork for the new. But the discontinuity is visible. The question is whether Israel has understood this ancient word.

[17] The selection of the scroll and presumably also of the text was not up to Jesus. Luke does not use "Christ" only as a name; it also means "the anointed one," as is here explained (cf. the discussion of 4:1 and Acts 4:27; 10:38).

[18–19] Luke 4:43 and Acts 10:38 support the translation above although a different division is possible: ". . . has anointed me to . . . , has sent me to . . ." The release spoken of in Isaiah 61:1–2 (also cited in 1QH 18:14 and A. Barn. 14:9) is already associated with the jubilee years of Leviticus 25:10 and Deuteronomy 15:2 (in 11QMelch). "Melchizedek" is expected to proclaim the year of release; he can hardly be a heavenly being (11QMelch 10–11 speaks of *God's* judgment) but is probably an eschatological figure (1. 4) superior to the king (11. 15–6), anointed with the Spirit (1. 18), supported by angels (1. 14), like the high priest. Eschatological and messianic interpretation of Isaiah 61:1–2 was therefore already current. But to conclude that A.D. 26/27 was observed as a year of release, alluded to here by Jesus, requires a good measure of fantasy.

The first element is the preaching of good news to the poor, which is in harmony with 6:20 and the view that Jesus is a prophet (see the introduction above). Next comes an interpolation from Isaiah 58:6: "To proclaim release [the same word also means 'forgiveness'] to captives," which Jesus could not have found in the text of Isaiah 61:1–2. This addition is very important for Luke: Jesus not only announced forgiveness and freedom (like the Baptist in 1:77 and 3:3) but brought them (see the discussion of 24:47).

[21] The first word we hear from the adult Jesus is "today." In Mark 1:15 the "time" is fulfilled, i.e., the eschaton has begun; in Luke 4:21 it is Scripture that is fulfilled, and on a specific day that can be recalled. Is God's special act therefore limited to the years of Jesus' lifetime, marking not the "end time" but the "middle time"? But it is fulfilled "in your ears," in such a way that the *words* of Jesus can be experienced as salvation. This is far from obvious. The speaker seems totally mismatched with his message and is not even prepared to demonstrate his own uniqueness. "Today" is thus also the day of unpostponable decision for God (cf. the excursus following vs. 30, a).

That Scripture is fulfilled in the life and death of Jesus is the common belief of all Christians. It is natural to tell the story of the Passion in the terminology of the Psalms (see the introduction to Mark 15:22–24), and Christian scribes are continually finding new passages that refer to Jesus (see the excursus following Matt. 7:13–23 [3]). That the kingdom of God is present in the ministry of Jesus is already stated in Matthew 12:28 (Q), less directly in Matthew 11:2–6 and Jesus' parables. But this always presumes that people will allow the actions and words of Jesus to confront them with the question of his significance (see the conclusion to Mark 4:35–41) until they can receive the answer given by Jesus himself—without simply achieving intellectual comprehension of God's mystery (see the excursus following Mark 4:1–9). Like John, Luke here connects this directly with the person and words of Jesus. But for him, too, such understanding in human ears is still a miracle of God.

[22] The very fact that people praise Jesus' "words of grace" (or "pleasing words") and thus interpret him in familiar terms prevents their understanding. The same word for "grace," but with the addition of "God's," appears in Acts 14:3; 20:24, 32; more precisely, it means God's "pleasure" graciously bestowed on human beings (cf. 2:40, 52). Jesus' words are thus "pleasing" to God and his hearers but for different reasons: the Nazarenes see only rhetorical skill. Deuteronomy 8:3 speaks similarly for the word "that proceeds out of the mouth of the LORD" (cf. Matt. 4:4; not cited in Luke 4:4).

Luke omits the clear rejection described in Mark 6:3 and describes something like noncommital or even mistaken agreement (as in Acts 13:42; 14:11–13; 17:11, 19–21). There is no suggestion that the congregation would rather have heard about the "day of vengeance" (against the Gentiles) mentioned in Isaiah 61:2 but not read by Jesus. [23] Even so, this conduct embodies rejection before it is stated explicitly (cf. the future "you will quote"). Jesus does not go to Capernaum until vs. 31a, but Luke can hardly be thinking of a later reaction following 4:31–41, of which nothing is said; he even omits the plan of Jesus' friends to bring him back to Nazareth (Mark 3:21; see the discussion of Luke 8:19–21). Vs. 23a merely serves to introduce the traditional sayings in vss. 24 and 25–27 (see the discussion of 3:1—4:30). Only Jesus' response reveals the insufficiency of mere wonderment at him. He rejects any proof that would make faith unnecessary (see the discussion of Mark 8:11–13), but Deuteronomy 13:1–3 is already aware that it is not signs and wonders that determine whether a prophet is from the Lord but the content of the prophet's message.

[25] The three and a half years (also in James 5:17–18, in contrast to 1 Kings 18:1; cf. Bill. 3. 760–61) may include the normally rainless summer (but see the end of the excursus following 2:38). [27] The warning is addressed to "Israel," as it was by the Baptist (3:8).

Luther described the word of God in similar terms as a shower that passes over the land, watering the earth here and there. As will happen later in Pisidian Antioch and in Rome (Acts 13:14–52; 28:23–31), the continuity is emphasized between God's work in Israel and among the Gentiles. The listeners' faith or lack of faith determines whether it bears fruit.

[28] Approval turns to rage, not because Jesus wanted to suppress messianic enthusiasm—the text says nothing of this— or claimed to be a prophet—the protest would have had to follow vs. 21. It is the protest of the "devout," who think they have a claim on God and cannot understand unconditional grace (see the discussion of 15:1–2). [29] They react like Jeremiah's fellow citizens (Jer. 11:21; 38:4). Stories of prophetic martyrdom were popular in those days.

Nazareth is not built on a rock; a mile or two away are cliffs some 20 and 160 feet high. According to a collection of laws ascribed to Rabbi Meir (middle of the second century C.E.), blasphemers were stoned by being thrown from a height of ten to fifteen feet and if necessary pelted with rocks (Bill. 2. 521, 685–86). This can hardly be what Luke has in mind; when he mentions stoning in Acts 7:58 (cf. John 8:7, 59; 10:31, 39), he describes it in totally different terms. Execution by being thrown from a cliff is also described in 2 Chronicles 25:12. All that matters to Luke is the mortal opposition to Jesus.

[30] Jesus' mysteriously majestic departure is not to be explained psychologically; for Luke it is a sign pointing already to Easter. Human beings have no power over him; when he dies at their hands, it is because that is God's will. They cannot stand in the way of his work but must even advance it: he goes on to Capernaum.

The first words from the mouth of the adult Jesus are not his own words but the words of the prophet. What he preaches is not something new. What is new is the "today" in which God seeks to become reality, to aid all those who are oppressed (cf. the discussion of 14:21), the Gentiles (4:25–27), prostitutes (7:36–50), tax collectors (15:1–2), and criminals (23:40–43). This is where the interpretation of Jesus begins. Ever since that day in Nazareth it is true for anyone who reads or hears this message. Happy assent to such preaching of grace must not deceive anyone: grace for the poor is always judgment for the rich. This programmatic narrative also censures a religious luxury so certain of the divine that it has ceased to realize that God could come "today," to judge and to transform. The second part of Jesus' sermon follows because the message of God's grace cannot be heard without this possibility. It provokes the hostility that introduces Jesus' ministry in Galilee, as well as his journey to (9:53) and stay in Jerusalem (19:39). This hostility will bring him the death that in this sense he will die "for us."

**Sacred History.** (a) Chapters 1—2 link the story of John with that of Jesus in such a way that the latter surpasses and fulfills the former, giving it meaning (see the excursus after 2:52, c). But what is this meaning? Can we answer with Bultmann and say: the kerygma (preaching)? Or must we follow Teilhard de Chardin and Rahner: insight into a sacred history that moves toward the good goal of God's purpose? Neither is the answer of Luke. He does not use the word "gospel" (except in Acts 15:7; 20:24). In an eternally valid "kerygmatic" formula, human beings would have mastered Jesus Christ, would have shown how to deal with him. But in Jesus God appeared in such an astonishing way that the appearance seemed scandalous and foolish to the entire world (1 Cor. 1:23). The later Gnostic movement took what Paul said about the cross and resurrection of Jesus and the justification of the sinner, to whom is given "life out of death" (Rom. 14:17), and made of it an eternally valid doctrine. It then ceased to matter whether the doctrine was illustrated in Jesus or through other myths of dying and rising gods. All that mattered was that those who heard the message were brought to "die" to everything earthly and thus discover the authentic divine life within themselves. Here Jesus Christ was dealt with so thoroughly that he could be dispensed with. In this case, God's acts in the Old Testament also ceased to matter. Now people possessed the new knowledge that all they had to do was find the way to the inner divine self.

But Luke himself does not have a real schema of sacred history. It is important to him that God does in fact act within history, uses it as the path to humankind, and stands by this path faithfully (see c and d below); but behind the way God acts there is no law accessible to human knowledge and therefore at human disposal. Like Mark, Luke tells stories, but even more than Mark he avoids concentrating everything on one focal point (e.g., the cross and resurrection).

According to Matthew 1:1–17, there is a plan of history that runs from Abraham to Jesus. Luke knows nothing of such a plan (see the discussion of 3:23–38). His purpose is to unfold the full richness of God's action, which culminated so astonishingly in Jesus, contrary to any human schema. God's love is not abstract; it takes on concrete form in many unforeseen and varied actions. Therefore Luke cannot get a firm hold on it; he must tell his story so as to illuminate this love from many different sides.

Are we then saved by knowledge of the miraculous events of the time of Jesus, to be historically verified, handed on, and considered true? We could be misled to this conclusion by 1:4 and also by the "today" in 4:21 if it is interpreted as referring strictly to that specific day in contrast to the "now" of the preaching of the gospel in 2 Corinthians 6:2. But it is appointment to the ministry of the word that makes such tradition possible (1:2), and 4:21 speaks of fulfillment "in their ears," that is, where Jesus' appearance becomes the word of God to those who truly hear. It is the "today" of worship! In 19:9, therefore, it refers to the decision of Zacchaeus (similarly in 23:43); it is therefore understood in the sense of Hebrews 3:7, 15; 4:7 (see the discussion of vs. 21). "Today salvation has come" to Zacchaeus because he believed; similarly, according to Acts 13:26, "the message of salvation has been sent to us." According to Acts 4:12, in the word comes the salvation that becomes present in his "name," i.e., "in him" (Jesus Christ; cf. the discussion of Luke 10:17). Thus also the "today" of Deuteronomy 26:16–19 (cf. Ps. 95:7–8), which refers historically to the time of Moses, refers actually to the day on which the community hears these words (cf. the transition of the historical account to the first person plural of the community in Deut. 26:5/6–9 and 6:21–25). In this fashion the stories of Jesus have also been accomplished "among us" (Luke 1:1). Similarly, Luke 17:11–19 shows that it is not the historically factual event of healing that brings salvation but its proper understanding.

(b) Chapters 1—2 speak of people who, in their law- and temple-centered spirituality, were open to God's new act even before Jesus.

But they are clearly described as expectant, not yet possessing that which would give meaning to their conduct and thus to the entire history of Israel. Paul's use of Abraham (Rom. 4:18–22; Gal. 3:18) is paralleled by Luke's use of Zechariah and Elizabeth, Joseph and Mary. The same spirituality of the law becomes a stumbling block when people think they can use it to take firm possession of God (7:39; 15:1–2; 18:10–14). God really encounters only those who allow him to take them by surprise.

The same holds true for people after Easter (cf. the excursus following 21:38, e). Precisely because Luke knows that the gospel cannot be reduced to a religious idea (or at least to an idea that would be evident to Christians), he must tell about them and their experiences. Half a century later it was impossible to act as though everything that had taken place after Easter had not happened, and the people listening in the year 80 were the same as those standing in Jesus' presence in the year 30. Luke must therefore reflect on what the history of the community means. For the time of Israel and Jesus, this is done in Luke 11:49–51 Q and Mark 12:1–9; for the time after Easter it is done in Matthew 10:17–25; 23:34–36; and Mark 13, but also in 1 Corinthians 15:3–11 and above all Romans 11:11–26. In a certain sense, Luke sees the work of Jesus before and after Easter even more as a unity. Both are "God's word" (see the discussion of 5:1): the deliverance of Jesus at Nazareth and his going to Capernaum (alluded to in vss. 24–27), signs of the resurrection and the mission to the Gentiles. Acts 1:1 probably means that after Easter Jesus *continued* "to do and teach." The "departure" in Jerusalem (9:31) points beyond Easter, and the goal of Jesus' journey includes his ascension into heaven and his continued work on earth afterwards (see the discussion of 9:51). The Passion, resurrection, and preaching to all nations are a unified event (24:46–47; cf. Acts 5:30–32; 10:41–42; 13:31; 17:3). It is the crucified Jesus himself who was made Lord and Christ and continues his work even more mightily after Easter (Acts 2:32–36), even proclaiming himself on his own behalf (Acts 26:23).

(c) For Luke, this means more than that an already formulated message must still be made known to the world and that the Lord must help. He understood that faith in this message is itself God's doing, not merely in the sense that in all ages God must in like manner overcome the resistance of the wise and self-righteous, but also in the sense that there is a history of faith, with defeats and victories, which put their stamp in turn on the history that follows. What matters is not the intellectual appropriation of some (kerygmatic or theological-historical) principles in which God can be captured but a life in which God bears self-witness. In Jesus' earthly life, astonishing and unforeseeable events repeatedly took place; in like manner God continues to astonish the community (e.g., Acts 10:19-20, 44-46; 16:6-10). The Jesus who is proclaimed comes to life in countless unforeseeable and inexplicable events, apparently quite random. The faith that lives after Easter therefore is still fundamentally the faith that waits for God to act and thus for the living presence of Jesus. This holds true for more than the individual. The living Lord accompanies God's word on its trajectory through history, reawakens it in new languages and new situations, and exerts divine influence even in the decisions of international politics (Luke 2:1-3; also Acts 23—26, e.g., 23:11-24; 24:26). Neither the imposition of a new tax nor the venality of a Roman official is God's will, but God can use both to create faith.

(d) Luke saw how history, with its civilization and tradition, puts its stamp on human beings, often more noticeably than carefully formulated and consciously adopted teachings. Therefore the Christian community in Corinth is different from that in Jerusalem, and the Christian message there takes on a form different from that of its early years in Jerusalem; Acts 2:44-45, for example, is not repeated there. Therefore the working of the Lord after Easter cannot be described except in narrative; there are no universally valid laws. The "name" of Jesus is the power of God's act that came to pass in the life, death, and resurrection of Jesus of Nazareth as salvation for the world but in such a way that it becomes reality here and now, once more astonishing everyone, not reducible to any schema. Of course it is important for Luke (as for Paul in Romans 9—11) that there is continuity in the way God acts. But this continuity consists solely in God's faithfulness, which human beings can rightly hope for and expect. Thus we can see in the way of Israel that, even when humankind has forsaken God, God is still present for them, waiting for them although no one knows in advance how this act of God will look or what God's own positive or negative response will be (Rom. 11:25–26 also describes it as "mystery").

The community therefore cannot conceptualize this development either as constant progress or as constant apostasy to be countered only by return to the beginning. On the one hand, the ideal of Acts 2:44–47 and 4:32–35 (and also 9:31) is not attained later (20:29–30!); on the other, the presbyters are to remember Paul and do as he has already done (Acts 20:31–35), and the community must not forget the new knowledge it has received (Acts 10:1–11, 18; 15; 28:28). There is no trace, however, of a continuous development that preserves the identity of the community throughout generations (2 Tim. 2:2). Even less is it possible for the community, as Christ's "body" (1 Cor. 12:27), to dream of simply being one with him. Jesus himself sees to this through his exhortations and warnings. In a certain sense, Luke stresses even more than Paul that we are always dependent on the unique act of God in Jesus of Nazareth. Paul can speak of Christ in the Old Testament (1 Cor. 10:4) because for him every act of God's pure grace is fundamentally an act of Christ. Luke cannot do so because it is so important to him that God encountered us once and for all in Jesus, in the confusion of events, words, deeds, and experiences of a concrete human life in Palestine in the first decades of our era.

## B. "Throughout All Judea, Beginning from Galilee" (Acts 10:37) (4:31—5:11)

In the large section from 4:31 to 9:50, with a preliminary conclusion in 6:49, we find the first statement of how the good news of the kingdom of God (4:43) is offered in the teaching and acts of Jesus. It culminates in the appointment of the first disciples (5:1–11). As early as 4:44 (q.v.) Jēsus' work extends to Judea. But there is no clear sense of geography: in the next verse Jesus is standing by the lake of Gennesaret, and in 5:12 he is back "in one of the cities" (mentioned in 4:43–44?). Place names are borrowed from tradition (4:31; 5:1; 7:1; 8:26); a "lake" appears only when it is indispensable (5:1; 8:22), being dropped in other passages (5:27; 6:17; 8:4, 40; 9:10). This shows that the geographical information is intended only to illustrate the expansion of Jesus' ministry. In 5:12—6:11 there will follow the separation of the community from Israel and in 6:12–49 its first instruction.

## The Good News of the Kingdom of God (4:31—44)
Cf. Mark 1:21–38; Matthew 8:14–17

[31]And he went down to Capernaum, a city of Galilee, and was teaching them on the sabbaths. [32]And they were astonished at his teaching, for his word was with authority. [33]And in the synagogue there was a person who had a spirit of an unclean demon. And he cried out with a loud voice, [34]"Let alone! What have we to do with you, Jesus of Nazareth? You have come to destroy us. I know you, who you are, the Holy One of God." [35]And Jesus threatened him and said, "Be silent and come out of him." And the demon tore him in the midst and came out of him, without doing him harm. [36]And terror came upon all, and they spoke to one another and said, "What is this word? For with authority and power does he command the unclean spirits and they come out?" [37]And the report of him went out into every place in the surrounding region.

[38]And he arose and left the synagogue and entered the house of Simon. Now Simon's mother-in-law was afflicted with a high fever, and they besought him for her. [39]And he stood over her and threatened the fever, and it left her. Immediately she arose and served them.

[40]After sundown all those who had any that were sick with various diseases brought them to him. And he laid his hands on every single one of them and healed them. [41]And demons also came out of many, who cried and said, "You are the Son of God!" But he threatened them and would not allow them to speak because they knew that he was the Christ.

[42]And after daybreak he went out and wandered to a lonely place, and the crowd sought him and came to him and would have kept him from leaving them. [43]But he said to them, "To the other cities also I must preach the good news of the kingdom of God, for I was sent for this purpose." [44]And he was preaching in the synagogues of Judea.

Luke follows the outline of Mark. Jesus' coming to Capernaum (vs. 31a) is matched by his departure (vs. 42a); the general description of his teaching (vs. 31b) and people's reaction to it (vs. 32) by his healings (vss. 40–41) and the reaction to them (vs. 42b). In the middle stand two examples: an exorcism (vss. 33–37) and a healing (vss. 38–39). The first reaction (vss. 36, 38a) is described in the aorist ("he arose"), the continuing success (vss. 37, 39b) in the imperfect ("she served"). Like the narrative (vss. 33–39), vss. 31a and 42a are in the aorist; vss. 31b, 32 and 40–41, 42b are in the imperfect. Vss. 31–32, 43 emphasize the teaching of Jesus, which forms the framework around his miracles (cf. the discussion of 6:19 and 7:1–9, 50); vs. 36 therefore speaks only of the miracles without any mention of "new teaching" (Mark 1:27). Miracles are in general important to Luke (quite crassly in Acts 5:15; 19:12) but always interpreted through the preaching of Jesus and therefore able to bring forth faith (cf. 4:23, 38–39 before 5:1–11; 5:16, 17; 7:21–22; 17:18–19). Like vs. 31a, vs. 44 serves as a transition to Jesus' extended activity (imperfect tense).

[31] In the middle of the second century C.E. Marcion published a New Testament in Rome consisting of Luke and the (expurgated) Epistles of Paul. It was meant to show that the creator of the material world (which Marcion considered evil) and God of the Old Testament was in fact a demon, in contrast to the God of the New Testament. He began his Gospel with Luke 3:1a and 4:31a, understood as describing a descent from heaven. In vs. 31b (in contrast to Mark 1:21), Luke probably is thinking of several sabbaths (cf. the discussion of 13:10). [32] As in 4:36 and 5:1, Luke speaks not only of Jesus' "teaching" (Mark 1:22, 27; 4:1) but also of the "word" (of God) which then continues on through Acts. This astonishing "word" is the subject of people's questions, not the person of Jesus himself. The people in vs. 36 asks the same question although the identical Greek expression in 2 Samuel 1:4 shows that it can be interpreted more generally ("What is that?"). But since Mark 1:27 also speaks of Jesus' "new teaching," Luke, too, is probably emphasizing the verbal nature of the event. Such questioning stands under the sign of God's promise (cf. the conclusion to Mark 4:35–41). What Jesus

says is new neither in content nor in rhetorical form but probably in its "authority." The contrast with the scribes (Mark 1:22), who were no longer so important in the time of Luke, is omitted (see the discussion of Luke 3:7).

[33–34] Jesus' word is effectual and represents an event. Therefore the word is accompanied by an act. "The Holy One of God" (as in Mark 1:24) is "the Son of God," "the Messiah" (vs. 41); the two expressions already appeared together in 1:35 (cf. 1:32). [35] The demon tears the sick man "in the midst" of the assemblage, making the healing all the more conspicuous.

[38] As in Matthew 8:14, the names of Andrew, James, and John (Mark 1:29) are omitted, and the house is referred to only as Simon's; his identity is assumed. [39] Jesus' authority is emphasized. His mere spoken "threat" to the fever suffices; he does not have to lift the sick woman up (Mark 1:31). [40] Luke goes beyond Mark in stressing that Jesus "laid his hands on every single one of them" (for healing; in Jewish texts only 1QGenApoc 20:21; 22:29; cf. the discussion of Luke 13:13) [41] and that this is a sign that he is Son of God (not until 3:11 in Mark) and Messiah (cf. the discussion of 22:67).

[42] Of course there is no mention of the disciples, whom Jesus has not yet called (contrast Mark 1:36). [43] The narrative focuses on the crowd and above all the "preaching of the good news of the kingdom of God" (see the discussion of 1:19; 3:15–20 [conclusion]; 16:16); this is probably why Luke shifts the statement about Jesus' praying to 5:16. A similar statement appears in Matthew 4:23 (par. Luke 4:44), where verse 25 likewise mentions the crowd.

Only Luke connects "kingdom of God" (see the excursus following 21:38, b) with a verb meaning "preach" or "proclaim" (8:1; 9:2, 11, 60; 16:16). This is the way Acts begins and ends; Paul refers to it before his death (Acts 1:3; 20:25; 28:31; cf. 8:12; 28:23). But preaching the gospel is not antithetical to the healings; the text does not suggest that the people were interested only in the latter. This preaching addresses human life in its entirety. Therefore ethical exhortation can also be good news (3:18). This is clearly something different from a mere theory, which even the demons could understand—perhaps even better than human beings, as vs. 41 shows.

Jesus appears with authority, but he is not authoritarian; therefore his word and his deed belong together (9:6).

[44] Instead of "towns" (Mark 1:38), Luke says "cities" (see the discussion of 8:1); instead of Galilee (Mark 1:39), "Judea" (cf. the discussion of 24:6), which includes the entire land as in the Old Testament before David. For Luke, Galilee is most decidedly only the beginning (Acts 10:37; 13:31); it is not mentioned later as the site of Jesus' ministry although some of the towns mentioned lie within it. As in vss. 33 (Mark 1:23) and 12:11 (Matt. 10:17), Luke does not use the phrase "their synagogues" (Mark 1:39), as though they belonged only to the Jews (see the excursus following 2:38; but cf. Acts 13:5, etc.).

The two healings and their summarization in vss. 40–41 thus depict the authority of Jesus, which, as the beginning and end of the episode show (vss. 31–32, 43–44), reveals itself fundamentally in his preaching of the kingdom of God. "Deeds of power" or "deeds of authority" are thus better terms than "miracles."

## God's Call to Discipleship (5:1–11)

¹It happened, while the crowd pressed upon him and heard the word of God, he was standing by the lake of Gennesaret ²and saw two boats standing by the shore; but the fishermen had gone out of them and were washing their nets. ³Getting into one of the boats, which belonged to Simon, he asked him to put out a little from the land. And he sat down and taught the crowd from the boat. ⁴And when he had ceased speaking, he said to Simon, "Put out upon the deep and let down your nets for a catch." ⁵And Simon answered and said, "Master, we toiled all night and took nothing; but at your word I will let down the nets." ⁶And having done this, they caught a great multitude of fish, and their nets were at the point of breaking. ⁷And they beckoned to their comrades in the other boat to come and help them. And they came and filled both the boats, so that they were at the point of sinking. ⁸But when Simon Peter saw it, he fell down at Jesus' feet, saying, "Depart from me, for I am a sinful man, Lord." ⁹For he and all that were with him were struck with amazement at the catch of fish that they had taken, ¹⁰as also were James and John, the sons of Zebedee, who were Simon's partners. And

Jesus said to Simon, "Do not be afraid; henceforth you will be catching people." [11]And having brought their boats to land, they left everything and followed him.

The narrative in 5:1–11 follows the strong emphasis on the necessity of preaching in 4:42–44. Before and after this section (4:38–41; 5:12–16) healings are described and there are general references to Jesus' miracles. Preaching and miracles are also intertwined in 5:1–11. The wordplay about "catching people" (vs. 10*b*) also appears in Mark 1:17, but there the call is described quite differently, and the healing of Peter's mother-in-law comes after it (Mark 1:29–31; Luke 4:38–39). The Lukan sequence (cf. the change in 4:42) is meant to make Peter's obedience more comprehensible; he had already witnessed a healing. The preaching in 5:1–3 corresponds to the preaching in Mark 1:14–15; here, however, Peter also hears the preaching of Jesus. The account of Jesus' use of a boat to teach from, which introduces his parables in Mark 4:1 (omitted in Luke 8:4!), has been shifted here by Luke.

Vss. 4–11 are in fact a miracle story, subordinated here to the story of the call. The miracle leads up to the saying about "catching people" (vs. 10). Also typical of the call narrative is Jesus' initiative (vs. 4), the confirming sign (vs. 6), which lays bare the problem, namely the sinfulness of the one who is called (vs. 8), and the overcoming of this problem through the alleviation of fear, a commission, and a promise (vs. 10*b*), which in turn make it possible to obey the call (vs. 11). Within the Lukan corpus, the call of Peter thus stands in parallel with that of Paul (Acts 9:1–19), whose work is described in Acts as being parallel to that of Peter, and in contrast to the rejection of Jesus in Nazareth.

Both the miracle and the call center entirely on Peter (cf. the discussion of 8:45). The only direct dialogue is between him and Jesus. The change from singular to plural in vss. 4–6 is understandable because Peter needs partners for fishing. But the second boat (vs. 2) appears unexpectedly in vs. 7, and above all James and John are introduced almost as an afterthought in vs. 10, alongside "all" that were with Peter (vs. 9). In addition, vs. 11 says in conclusion that "they" followed Jesus although only Peter is called in vs. 10.

These tensions are explained most easily on the basis of the following hypotheses: (1) The saying about "catching people" was associated on the one hand with the call of the first disciples (cf. Mark 1:16–20), and on the other was developed in the story of Simon's miraculous catch of fish, to which his partners were witnesses; the latter probably included Simon's confession of sinfulness and Jesus' promise. The story could not exist without these words; Jesus is never depicted as performing miracles that simply provide material assistance. The name "Simon Peter" is pre-Lukan; before 6:14 Luke calls him "Simon" and afterward "Peter," except in the traditional sayings 22:31 and 24:34 (cf. the periphrastic expression in Acts 10:5, 18, 32; 11:13). (2) Before the time of Luke, this incident was linked with the tradition of Jesus' three companions (Mark 5:37; 9:2; 14:33). This matched the account in Mark 1:16–20, except that in the latter passage (as in 1:29 and 13:3, neither of which appears in Luke) Andrew is also included although in the list of the Apostles in Mark 3:17 and Acts 1:13 he is mentioned fourth rather than with his brother. In addition, in Mark 1 the call of the sons of Zebedee is recounted separately from that of Peter, which may explain the second boat in Luke 5:2, 7. Also pre-Lukan is the mention of James before John (as in Mark 1:19); elsewhere Luke reserves the order (8:51; 9:28; cf. the discussion of 22:8; also Acts 1:13 in contrast to the traditional order in Luke 6:14). (3) Luke added the introduction (vss. 1–3) and perhaps also "all that were with him" (vs. 9) because that was not yet possible in 4:42(= Mark 1:36). The discipleship of all (vs. 11) is important to him (cf. 6:13). Luke was also responsible for the emphasis on the "word" of Jesus (vs. 5).

The story has many points of contact with John 21:1–14. There, too, Peter was probably the focus of the narrative (cf. vs. 11a following vs. 9, as well as vss. 15–17). As in Luke 5:4–11, the two sons of Zebedee were added in John, along with other witnesses but not Andrew (21:2). As in Luke 5:4–11, they fished throughout the night without catching anything but at Jesus' word took an abundance of fish. In John, too, after a kind of confession of sin, Peter, here too called Simon (Peter), receives an appointment, albeit as shepherd rather than as fisherman, and follows Jesus (vss. 15–17, 22). If the 153 fishes (21:11, q.v.) symbolized the nations, there would be a clear echo of the saying about catching people. Peter's falling to his knees and beseeching Jesus to leave him (Luke 5:8) would also be more appropriate if he were already on the shore, as in John 21:11.

Is it possible, then, that an Easter narrative has been shifted back into the story of Jesus' life? The fact that the miracle is witnessed only by the disciples rather than by the people suggests an Easter narrative, but the accounts of Jesus' post-Easter appearances make no mention of miracles that would compete with the miracle of the resurrection. And several elements are lacking in Luke 5:4–11: the disciples' doubt and its conquest, their mission, and the vanishing of the risen Lord. In John 21:7 the motif of recognizing Jesus is clearly a late addition; vs. 12b at best might be original. Furthermore, John 21:11 ("the net was not torn") suggests rather that a statement in the call narrative, Luke 5:6 (literally: "their nets tore"), has undergone correction, and "following" is very understandable in Luke 5:11 but not in John 21:20, 22 since it is impossible in the literal sense to follow after the risen Lord. It is therefore more likely that the core of Luke 5:4–11 was transformed later into an Easter narrative because the earthly Jesus is the same person as the risen Lord.

This analysis suggests the following conclusions. The tension between the introductory scene, in which (despite 4:38–39) only the people really figure, and the narrative of the fishes, between the concentration on Simon alone and the inclusion of the sons of Zebedee and even a second boat, and the intertwining of the miracle story and call story forms can be explained from the way the account developed. As a result, call and discipleship are even more clearly the point of the present text. They are a gift of grace (see already the conclusion to Mark 1:16–20), as is underlined by the experience of the miracle, Simon's confession of sinfulness, and the promise of Jesus, which abolishes this and every fear. This clearly distinguishes what happens here from the reaction of the people to Jesus' miracles (4:42; 5:15). Certain inconsistencies reveal what was so important to the evangelist and the traditionist before him that they were willing to put up with the tensions. This point will be pursued in the discussion to follow. The truth that they wished to proclaim in the form of such a story is not dependent on the historicity of the details but on whether what is recounted sets forth the crucial nature of Jesus and characterizes him as he truly was—and is for us—in his life and ministry (see section 5 of the Introduction to *The Good News According to Mark*).

[1] The account begins with the "people," but the main clause begins with "he" (Jesus). With him something new and different enters the middle-class world of fishermen and farmers. Luke always uses the correct term "lake" rather than "sea." There is no mention of "Galilee" (Mark 1:16), possibly on account of 4:44. With "the word of God" Luke emphasizes the continuity with the preaching of the community (8:11; 21;11:28; Acts *passim*; Epistles; Revelation; elsewhere only in the sense of the Old Testament: Mark 7:13 = Matt. 15:6; John 10:35).

[2] As in Mark 1:16 (q.v.), Jesus "sees" the disciples; this marks a new beginning (see the discussion of 9:38). While the people, eager to hear, press toward Jesus, the important movement is taking place from Jesus toward the fishermen, of whom we are only told that they have just finished their work without result. [3] Jesus' purpose appears to be merely a small way in which Simon can be of use to him; but Luke nevertheless speaks of the protracted (imperfect tense) teaching of Jesus, which Peter hears.

[4] Jesus' real purpose appears when he has finished, when what had been a small distance from the crowd has increased to real separation on the "deep." Do we already see here the expansion of the mission in Acts 10? Simon alone is called although naturally his partners are needed as well to lower the nets. Like all the disciples in Luke (and the lepers in 17:13, of whom one is "saved"), he calls Jesus "master," not "teacher" like all the others (cf. 9:33, 49, where Mark 9:5, 38 has "rabbi" or "teacher"). This shows that Peter is already open to Jesus as "Lord" (vs. 8, cf. section 2, c of the Introduction).

[5] The statement describing the unproductiveness of human efforts heightens the significance of what Jesus is about to do and emphasizes once more the movement of the text, which emanates from Jesus alone. Simon unhesitatingly expresses his doubts and reservations, thus learning to attach even greater importance to Je-

sus' word. This describes the situation in which one has nothing except the word—which must then be "done" (as Q already emphasizes: 6:46; 8:21; cf. 11:28).

[6–8] Vss. 6–7 describe the miraculous result. It is hard to picture Simon's falling at Jesus' feet in a boat already full to the gunwales with fish, but the action merely underlines his recognition of Jesus' incomparable greatness. It is equally hard to picture other than a divine being "departing," as Simon asks Jesus to do, but again this merely emphasizes the infinite distance between them. "Sin" (Greek and Hebrew = "miss the mark") is not moral inferiority but human distance from God. Therefore Simon recognizes his sinfulness only after experiencing the unimaginable grace of God. No more than in Isaiah 6:5 is a particular lapse involved (contrast John 21:15–18). At most, Luke might be thinking of 22:32*b*, where the sinner is singled out for the promise to "catch people."

[9] "Amazement" also comes over those for whom it does not lead to confession (see the discussion of 2:33). [10] This is the first we hear of the sons of Zebedee (in the second boat?), Simon's "partners," in contrast to the "comrades" making up the crew (vs. 7). Like God in the Old Testament or the angel (cf. 1:13; 2:10), Jesus frees Simon of fear. What follows is not really a call in the imperative but a statement in the indicative. Nothing is said of forgiveness; sin is overcome through service (as in Mark 2:14 with the tax collector). Service brings close to God those who are distant. Luke does not speak of "fishing" (Mark 1:17; see introduction) which kills but of "catching people" (alive) to save them from death (Num. 31:15, 18; Josh. 2:13; 6:25; 9:20; etc.). The "catch" in vss. 4 and 9 makes the image come alive.

[11] The statement that the disciples left "everything" (also in 5:28) had already been inserted into Mark 1:18 by copyists whose readers hardly needed to leave nets, boats, or tax stations. Luke's purpose is to emphasize the special demands made on the inner circle of those who were disciples of the earthly Jesus (14:33; cf. the discussion of 6:20*a* and 18:28). As a result, however, it becomes less clear that renunciation in itself is not of primary importance to Jesus but rather that people should renounce whatever hinders them in their specific service. Nothing is said of any response—hesistant, enthusiastic, or

humbly declining. We read only that they returned from their experience changed and—now that they were on dry land—"followed" Jesus. The last word is "him"; from now on, he determines their lives. But his goal is "people." Thus the experience of individuals transcends its subjects and becomes a matter to move the world.

There is a double truth about the text: it focuses entirely on Simon (originally probably on him alone); at the same time it begins with Jesus' preaching to all the people and leads up to the saying about "catching people." In the divine encounter experienced by the individual there takes place something that has all humanity as its goals and must be viewed in the larger context. But it is not enough that Jesus' preaching to the people must continue through those who follow after him. Between vss. 1 and 11, those who are set apart for this task have experienced personally God's act that heals sin. Therefore they will not merely proclaim salvation *like* Jesus; they will proclaim him and what they have encountered through him *as* salvation.

The word "salvation," it is true, is not used, and only Simon himself speaks of "sin." The narrative recounts God's invasion of a human life, expanding on what Mark 1:16–20, like a woodcut, reduces to essentials. It is a highly concrete experience, told almost without religious vocabulary. God's way to Simon is sketched step by step. In 4:38–39 he experiences the power of Jesus. Through a small service he is asked to perform, he comes under the word of God. Nothing is said of any desire on his part, nor or resistance, nor of the impression it makes on him. Everything happens quite normally. The decisive experience begins with a failure in the purely secular realm. Faith does not come as assent to the statements previously preached but as trust in Jesus' call to try once more, contrary to all the dictates of reason. In a practical problem, not in itself of earthshaking importance, and in the experience of help that surpasses all expectations, Simon learns to see Jesus as who he really is but learns also to see himself as a "sinner." This is not a moral judgment but rather the knowledge that God has not had in his life the place that rightfully belongs to deity, which God has now occupied on divine initiative. Therefore it is not necessary for Jesus to speak of sin and forgiveness but rather of Simon's future service. Salvation comes when God wins a place in the life of Simon. But it would represent a total misunderstanding if Simon, in faith and thanksgiving, were to stop there. The meaning of what has happened to him does not lie within him but with the "people" whom he is to "catch." The experience of a single individual is enormously important but only in the light of God's will to reach all people.

# C. THE GROWTH OF THE COMMUNITY (5:12—6:11)

## Conflict (5:12—6:11)
Cf. Mark 1:40—3:6; Matthew 8:1–4; 9:1–17; 12:1–14

¹²And it happened when he was in one of the cities, and behold, there was a man full of leprosy. And when he saw Jesus, he fell on his face and besought him, "Lord, if you will, you can make me clean." ¹³And he stretched out his hand, touched him, and said, "I will; be clean." And immediately the leprosy left him. ¹⁴And he charged him to tell no one, but "Go, show yourself to the priest, and make an offering for your cleansing, as Moses commanded, for a witness to them." ¹⁵But so much the more the report went abroad concerning him, and great multitudes gathered to hear and to be healed of their infirmities. ¹⁶But he withdrew to the wilderness and prayed.

¹⁷And it happened on one of the days when he was teaching, Pharisees and experts in the law were sitting by, who had come from every village of Galilee and Judea and from Jerusalem. And the power of the Lord was present so that he could heal. ¹⁸And behold, there were men bringing on a litter a person who was paralyzed, and they sought to bring him in and lay him before him. ¹⁹And not finding a way to bring him in because of the crowd, they went up on the roof and let him down with his bed through the tiles into the midst right in front of Jesus. ²⁰And when he saw their faith, he said, "You, forgiven are your sins."

²¹And the scribes and the Pharisees began to think, saying, "Who is this that speaks blasphemies? Who can forgive sins but God only?" ²²But Jesus, perceiving their thoughts, answered and said to them, "What are you thinking in your hearts? ²³Which is easier to say, 'Forgiven are your sins,' or to say, 'Rise and walk'? ²⁴But that you may know that the Son of Man has authority to forgive sins on earth"—he said to the paralytic—"I say to you, rise, take up your bed, and go home." ²⁵And immediately he rose before them, took up what he had been lying on, and went home, glorifying God. ²⁶And amazement seized them all, and they glorified God and were filled with fear, and said, "We have seen strange things today."

²⁷And after this he went out and saw a tax collector named Levi sitting at the tax office, and said to him, "Follow me." ²⁸And leaving everything he rose and followed him.

²⁹And Levi made him a great feast in his house, and there was a large crowd of tax collectors and others who were reclining with them at table. ³⁰And the Pharisees and their scribes murmured and said to the disciples, "Why do you eat and drink with tax collectors and sinners?" ³¹And Jesus answered and said to them, "Those who are well have no need of a physician but those who suffer. ³²I did not come to call the righteous to repentance but sinners."

³³But they said to him, "The disciples of John fast often and offer prayers, and so do the disciples of the Pharisees, but yours eat and drink." ³⁴And Jesus said to them, "You cannot make the wedding guests fast while the bridegroom is with them. ³⁵There will come days when the bridegroom is taken away from them; then they will fast in those days." ³⁶He also told them a parable: "No one tears a piece from a new garment and puts it on an old garment; else one will tear the new garment and the piece from the new will not match the old. ³⁷And no one puts new wine into old wineskins; otherwise the new wine will burst the skins, and it will be spilled, and the skins will be destroyed; ³⁸but new wine must be put in new wineskins. ³⁹And no one having drunk old wine desires new, for one says, 'The old is good.'"

6. ¹Now it happened that on the sabbath he was going through the grain, and his disciples plucked ears and ate them, rubbing them with their hands. ²But some of the Pharisees said, "Why are you doing what is not lawful on the sabbath?" ³And Jesus answered and said to them, "Have you not read also what David did when he was hungry, he and those with him? ⁴How he entered the house of God, how he took the bread of the Presence and ate it and gave it to those with him, which it

is not lawful for any but the priests to eat?" ⁵And he said to them, "The Son of Man is lord of the sabbath."

⁶It happened on another sabbath that he entered the synagogue and taught. And there was a person there whose right hand was withered. ⁷And the scribes and Pharisees watched him, whether he would heal on the sabbath, so that they might find an accusation against him. ⁸But he knew their thoughts and said to the man with the withered hand, "Stand up and come into the midst." And he rose and stood there. ⁹And Jesus said to them, "I ask you whether it is lawful on the sabbath to do good or evil, to save life or destroy it?" ¹⁰And he looked around on them all and said to him, "Stretch out your hand." And he did so, and his hand was restored. ¹¹But they were filled with fury and discussed with one another what they might do to Jesus.

Luke writes in "biblical" style: "And it happened . . . and behold . . . immediately" (5:12–13/17, 18, 25; cf. 8:40–56; 18:35–43; and the introduction to 9:28–36). He carefully organizes the controversies of Mark into a fundamental disagreement between Jesus and the Pharisaic scribes (5:17, 21, 30, 33; 6:2, 7; cf. the discussion of 4:31—5:11). Mark separated the healing of the leper from the conflict stories by means of a new introduction in 2:1; Luke places it before them, following 5:1–11, in order to demonstrate Jesus' faithfulness to the law (5:14) and thus represent what is to follow as true obedience to the will of God. This has the additional effect of bringing the cleansing closer to the forgiveness of sins (5:13, 20). This episode is also alluded to in 7:22.

The healing of the paralytic demonstrates Jesus' authority to forgive sins, as though he stood in the place of God. His eating with the tax collectors illustrates God's love for those who are offered repentance. Repentance cannot be achieved through fasting or prayer exercises; it demands the radical turn to a new life that Jesus brings.

Sabbath legalism can actually stand in the way of doing the good that God demands. The final story is thus the climax: it is not the letter of the law that matters but obedience to the will of God, who wants to forgive the sinner (5:17–26), invite the erring to repentance (5:27–32), proclaim the joy of the wedding feast (5:33–39), and do good (6:6–11).

Something can be seen of Jesus' unpredictability. He is scrupulous in observing the law but breaks the sabbath. To one is given healing, to another forgiveness. Now it is the sick person, now Jesus, who seizes the initiative; on one occasion the healing is to be kept secret, on another it is to be demonstrated to all by the carrying home of a bed. Faith is never knowledge but readiness to learn afresh from each new encounter with God. Thus Jesus in his authority (5:17, 24) shows himself to be the eschatological "bridegroom" (5:34) and "lord of the sabbath" (6:5).

[12–16] The typically Lukan introduction, in biblical language, leaves both place (vs. 12) and time (vs. 17) vague. What takes place here is of universal import. As in Matthew 8:1–4, there is no reference to Jesus' emotions (Mark 1:41, 43) or the disobedience of the healed leper. Jesus' praying is mentioned (appearing already in Mark 1:35; cf. the discussion of Luke 4:43; 6:12), perhaps in order to emphasize his intimate relationship with God at the very beginning of the conflict that follows. [15] Luke interprets the crowds (Mark 1:45; cf. the discussion of Luke 14:25) as a desire for the word and for healing.

[17–26] "Pharisees and experts in the law" come to Jesus, even from Jerusalem, [17] which here appears for the first time in a negative role. Luke distinguishes them from the very beginning (Mark not until 2:6, "some of the scribes"). Before the Passion he always associates the scribes with the Pharisees, during the Passion with the high priests (see the discussion of 3:7). The theologians, then, begin to take note of Jesus.

Inward (vss. 20–21) and outward (vss. 24–25) healing are linked. The "power of the Lord" (cf. 6:19; 8:46; also 4:14, 36; 24:49; Acts) to heal is mentioned programmatically at the beginning of the conflict, rather than Jesus' teaching, as in Mark 2:2.

[19] Luke pictures a tile roof (cf. the discussion of Mark 2:4) and has the paralytic brought "before Jesus." Like Matthew 9:5, 7 (see the discussion of Matt. 4:17—11:30, chapters 8—9), he shortens vs. 23, but adds in vs. 25 the statement that the healed paralytic "went home," obeying Jesus' command (vs. 24). [25] At the same time he draws a sharper distinction: the one who was cured glorifies

God freely (cf. the discussion of 17:15); **[26]** the others are struck with fear because they have seen a "paradox" (the literal sense of the Greek), i.e., something that goes beyond all familiar knowledge and thus points to the one who acts contrary to all expectations: God.

**[27–32]** Here, too, Luke intensifies the conflict, leaving out the people (Mark 2:13) and having only the Pharisees and scribes (vs. 30) appear as witnesses. They "murmur" (not in Mark 1:16), which in Luke is always related to Jesus' conduct toward sinners (15:2; 19:7). **[28]** Levi leaves "everything" (see the discussion of 5:11) **[29]** but can still be host to many "tax collectors and others" (Mark 2:15: "and sinners"), which is left unclear in Mark 2:15–17 (q.v., introduction; cf. also the discussion of Luke 8:20; 15:2).

Luke speaks of "following" only in the case of Levi (contrary to Mark 2:15); he is the classic instance of "repentance," as vs. 32 adds to Mark 2:17 (cf. Luke 24:27; Acts 11:18; 20:21). Repentance leads to forgiveness of sins (Mark 1:4; Acts 2:38; 3:19; 5:31; 8:22). For Luke it is not just the act of faith (Mark 1:15) but rather the associated turning from "everything" old, "conversion" or "turning" from wicked works to good (17:3–4; Acts 3:19; 26:20; cf. the discussion of Luke 3:8).

**[30]** In Luke when the disciples are asked why "they" eat and drink with tax collectors and sinners (similarly 6:2; Mark 2:16 refers the question to Jesus), Luke probably is already thinking of the Lord's Supper celebrated by the community (cf. Gal. 2:12 and the discussion of this problem in Acts 15:19–20, as well as 10:13–14).

**[33–39]** No occasion is mentioned (cf. Mark 2:18); the discussion at Levi's feast (see the discussion of 14:1) continues without interruption. **[33]** According to vs. 30, Pharisees and scribes are asking the questions; but vs. 33*b* speaks of them in the third person. Are others asking questions as well? In comparison to Mark 2:18, there is more emphasis on the disciples of John (see the discussion of 11:1). **[34]** As in Matthew 9:15, Mark 2:19*b* is omitted. New is the question (of the Lukan community?) about regular prayer, which is not addressed in Jesus' answer. Or is it merely being stressed that fasting is preparation for prayer? Fasting is represented as a Pharisaic requirement ("you cannot make . . . fast"; expressed differently in Mark 2:19). **[35]** Vs. 35, too, is expressed rather differently; "those days" (singular in Mark 2:20*b*) probably refers to the time after the "departure" of Jesus (cf. 19:12; Acts 13:2–3)—or perhaps only the days until Jesus' resurrection is confirmed?

[36] A Lukan parenthesis ("he told," a frequent expression in this context) describes the metaphors that follow as a "parable" (see the discussion of 6:33–39). [36–39] Vss. 36–39 are obscure. Luke clarifies vs. 36 in comparison to Mark 2:21, as he does elsewhere (11:18; 20:26, 38; etc.). But vs. 39 argues for the old on the grounds that "old wine" tastes better. Is the whole passage therefore to be understood as a warning against innovations? Such a reading would not fit vss. 33–35 unless vs. 35 were considered in isolation. Above all, Luke has inserted in vs. 36 the comment that under such circumstances the new garment will be torn. The "new" must therefore be the message of Jesus (as in Mark 2:22). In this case, the "old" fasting of John's disciples and Judaism, adopted once more by the Christian community, cannot be viewed with approval. Is vs. 39, then, only meant to state that discrimination is necessary, without any implicit evaluation of the old? In 16:1 and 18:2, also, the unjust rich man and judge are not held up as models; no estimate of their conduct is implied. There, however, the conclusion is simpler: if they can act in this way, how much the more will God! More likely Luke is trying to say that unfortunately it is natural for people (including the speakers of vs. 33) to stick with the old than to be open to the new call of Jesus (cf. 18:8*b*).

[6:1–5] As in Matthew 12:1–8 (q.v.), the fact that the disciples ate the grain (see the discussion of 5:30) is mentioned (vs. 1), but the erroneous dating (Mark 2:26) and the statement that the sabbath was made for people (Mark 2:27) are omitted—the latter possibly because it might have served to legitimate Christian observance of the sabbath (which is still attested around A.D. 200 by Tertullian; *Jej.* 14.3) or because its elimination brings the Son of Man in conjunction with David. The "rubbing" of the ears may count as preparation of a meal which was forbidden on the sabbath (cf. the discussion of 13:10 and the conclusion; also Bk. Jub. 2:29; 50:3, 8–9; preparation should even be made for guests on the day before, cf. Bill. 2. 202–203).

According to some manuscripts, this took place on the "second first" sabbath. Does this mean "next but one," so that, 4:31, 44 notwithstanding, 4:16 was counted as the first and 4:33 as the second? Is it the second sabbath after the beginning of the harvest, or in Passover week, or in the first month? Or does "first sabbath" refer to the Jewish sabbath, "second" to the Christian (= Sunday)? Later copyists add in vs. 5: "On this day he saw someone working on the sabbath, and said to him, "If you know what you are doing, good for you, but if you do not know, you are accursed and a transgressor of the law." In the background there is lurking the problem of Romans 14:1–6, 22–23: only faith can understand freedom from the law in such a way that it becomes not an easy excuse but a call to love. The law is annulled only in a fulfillment that looks for the will of God expressed in the law, not for the letter, attaching no importance to the fence but only to the garden it protects.

[6–11] In contrast to Mark 3:1 and Matthew 12:9, the story, parallel to vs. 1, is transferred to "another" sabbath, and Jesus' "teaching" in "the" synagogue (cf. Matthew) is emphasized (also in 13:10; cf. 4:15–16). [7] Only Luke mentions "scribes and Pharisees" (but cf. Mark 3:6), [8] whose "thoughts" (as in 9:46) Jesus "knows" and challenges with his questions. [9] Vs. 9 possibly speaks of "destruction" (instead of "killing," Mark 3:4) because the word "life" also means "soul," which cannot be killed (see the discussion of 8:55) but can be destroyed through failure to do good. "You have gained wealth but destroyed souls" is also a rabbic saying from around A.D. 140 (Bill. 1. 588; cf. the conclusion to 13:10–17).

[11] The fury of Jesus' enemies (also in 11:53–54) has not yet reached the point of a desire to kill him as in Mark 3:6 (but cf. 4:29). Neither is it the Pharisees who take him (see the discussion of 13:31) but the high priests and the scribes (19:47–48; 20:19–20; 22:2). The hostility of Herod and his supporters (Mark 3:6) is not seen until later (9:7–9; 13:31–32; 23:6–16; Acts 4:27).

# D. CALL AND INSTRUCTION
## (6:12–49)

The climax of the conflict (see the discussion of 4:31—5:11) leads directly to the selection of the Twelve and a discourse in which Jesus prepares those who hear him (vss. 20–49).

## Call to Disciples and People (6:12–19)
Cf. Mark 3:7–18; Matthew 4:24—5:1; 10:1–4

¹²It happened in those days that he went out upon the mountain to pray. And all night he continued in prayer to God. ¹³And when it was day, he called his disciples and chose twelve of them, whom he named Apostles: ¹⁴Simon, whom he also named Peter, and Andrew his brother, and James and John and Philip and Bartholomew ¹⁵and Matthew and Thomas and James the son of Alphaeus and Simon the so-called Zealot ¹⁶and Judas the son of James and Judas Iscariot, who became a traitor.

¹⁷And he came down with them and stopped at a level place, with a great crowd of his disciples and a great multitude of people from all Judea and Jerusalem and the seacoast of Tyre and Sidon, who came to hear him and to be healed of their diseases; ¹⁸and those who were troubled with unclean spirits were healed. ¹⁹And all the crowd sought to touch him, for a power came forth from him and healed them all.

Luke reverses the order of Mark 3:7–19. The crowd does not gather until vss. 17–19, thus becoming Jesus' audience. [12] Jesus' praying is also mentioned in 3:21; 5:16; 9:18, 28–29; 11:1; 22:41 (kneeling); 23:34, 46 (words quoted). As in 9:28, Jesus prays "at night" on "the" mountain (omitted in 4:5 and 21:7) before the choice of the Twelve, which must be given by God (similarly Acts 1:24; 6:6; 13:2–3; 14:23; cf. 4:24–31). The mountain remains the site of Jesus' companionship with his closest followers while the plain to which he descends is the site of the everyday life of the world which is addressed by Jesus' preaching. Despite Exodus 24:1, 9, and 34:29, it is unlikely that we have here an echo of Sinai, the mountain where God is worshiped (Exod. 3:12; 24:1; cf. 19:3, 20; 24:9–18). According to Mark 6:46, Jesus also prays on "the mountain" (before walking on the lake; similarly John 6:15); the mountain symbolizes God's nearness.

[13] Luke has described the call of only four disciples (5:10–11, 27) but assumes the existence of a substantial number (vs. 17), from among whom Jesus "chooses" twelve (as God chooses the patriarchs of Israel, Acts 13:17). The election of the Twelve is important to Luke and John (Acts 1:2, 24; 15:7; John 6:70; 13:18; 15:16, 19) while Mark 13:20; 1 Corinthians 1:27–28 and Ephesians 1:4 empha-

size the election of the community. Luke says nothing about their staying with Jesus or being sent out to preach and heal (Mark 3:14–15). In contrast to Matthew 10:1–2 (and Mark 6:30), Jesus himself designates the Twelve "Apostles" as well as "disciples." Luke is the first to restrict the title "Apostles" clearly to the Twelve (cf. the excursus before Mark 6:7–13). Only in Acts 14:4, 14 are Paul and Barnabas also called "Apostles," probably in borrowed missionary terminology, as "ambassadors" of the Christian community in Antioch. For Paul, the circle of the Apostles is larger (1 Cor. 15:5, 7) and probably includes a woman: Junias (Rom. 16:7) is attested only as a woman's name; it is hardly likely to be an otherwise unknown short form of the masculine name Junianus (cf. also Rev. 2:2). For Paul, too, the circle of the Apostles is still limited to those who have seen the risen Lord (1 Cor. 9:1; 15:8). Luke uses Acts 1:21 to defend against the assertion on the part of later individuals that they were called by the Spirit to be Apostles.

Those chosen here are initially not those who are sent forth but rather Jesus' companions on the way who hear his teachings; later they become missionaries, having become witnesses to his resurrection (Acts 1:21–22 [q.v.]; 4:33), having been eyewitnesses to his life and the first to receive the Holy Spirit.

"Cephas" (John 1:42; Gal. 2:7–9; etc.), in Greek "Petros," English "Peter" (= "rock") is a descriptive epithet, not a double name like Saul/Paul, for "Paul" is not a second name bestowed when he was chosen to be an Apostle but simply the form of the name that was used in Greek (from Acts 13:9).

[14] In contrast to Mark 3:16, 18, the two pairs of brothers are brought together (see the end of the introduction to 5:1–11; for discussion of the other discrepancies see the introduction to Mark 3:13–19); there is still no fixed list of sacred persons. The emphasis is wholly on Jesus' call to service. The group, which comprises fishermen and tax collectors (roughly lower middle-class individuals), exhibits a breadth that can encompass the revolutionary Simon (see the discussion of Mark 3:18) and the "traitor" (more strongly expressed than Mark 3:19).

[17–18] Nothing is said about a lake or boat (Mark 3:7, 9; see the discussion of 4:31—5:11). Those who have come to "hear" (con-

trast Mark 3:8) do not include "Galileans" because "Judea" designates the entire land. The audience consists of the Twelve, surrounded
by "a great crowd of his disciples" (also in 19:37) and a multitude
of people. The picture resembles that of the Lukan community. All
are addressed although some things are addressed specifically to the
disciples (see the discussion of vs. 20a). Jesus' sense of mission to
all the twelve tribes (see the excursus following Mark 6:7–13), not
to a special community, is depicted here; Luke is probably thinking
already of the Gentiles (Tyre and Sidon being Gentile territory).

[18–19] Once again word and act stand side by side, and the
"power" that heals "all" (Mark 3:10: "many") is emphasized (cf. the
discussion of 5:17). Jesus' acts provide a framework (6:18–19; 7:1–
17) for the Sermon on the Plain, looking ahead to 7:21–23. Vs. 19
may reflect superstitious beliefs (cf. Acts 5:15; 19:12), but it is certainly better to harass Jesus than simply to stand in awe of him.
God's helping and healing initiative precedes Jesus' sermon in vss.
20–49.

### The Sermon on the Plain (6:20–49)

The Sermon on the Plain is significantly shorter than the Sermon
on the Mount and has remained unfairly in the shade of the latter.
Fundamentally it follows Q, the basic source of its Matthean parallel
(see the discussion of Matt. 4:7—11:30; 5:21–48, and the individual
sections). It probably comes very close to representing Jesus' own
words. Its concentrated form does more to emphasize the fundamental commandment to love one's enemies, with the motivation provided by God's eschatological act (vss. 35–36). It is developed in
the interpolated command not to resist evil and in the golden rule
given a more radical interpretation than in Matthew by the appended
statements and outdone in turn by the commandment not to judge.
We thus have two series of four positive commands (vss. 27–28, 29–
30) and three somewhat artificially parallel motivations (vss. 32–
34), with vs. 31 in the middle and vss. 35–36 as the goal. This
central section is surrounded by macarisms and woes preceding it
and the parables of the tree and the building of the house afterward,

which underline the choice between the two possibilities. The traditional references to the "kingdom of God" and the "day of Jesus" (vss. 20, 23) are connected by Luke with the decision that must be made at once (see the discussion of vs. 48). The sequence of prophetic promise (vss. 20–26), ethical exhortation (vss. 27–38), and parable (vss. 39–49) appears in similar fashion in the visions, commandments, and parables of Hermas. The sequence of exhortations (beginning with love for one's enemy, vss. 27–28), community order (vss. 39–45), and anticipated judgment (vss. 46–49) appears in the Didache. But echoes of the Sermon on the Plain appear only in Didache 1 (see the excursus following Matt. 7:28–29, b.7), so that it is hardly possible to speak this early of a fixed tradition for baptismal instruction.

The Sermon on the Plain is a call to action. The promise of salvation is followed by the series of woes, and the concluding parables present the two possibilities. God's grace appears in the category of a model. But comparison with the Didache shows the distance between them. The Didache begins immediately with the choice between the two ways; the commandments (love your enemies, do not resist evil, be generous) are presented as rational rules of conduct that promise success, followed by a long series of commandments and prohibitions. The community rule is designed merely to insure that baptism, prayer, fasting, and the Lord's Supper are carried out correctly; only in the liturgical prayers do we catch a glimpse of God's great goodness. The eschatological perspective is primarily a warning against false doctrine.

The Sermon on the Plain, in contrast, begins with a promise of salvation—originally without the woes—addressed to the "poor" (cf. 4:18). It is precisely those who have nothing to offer who can hear the promise of the coming salvation. The ethical instructions following this promise also refer to God's mercy even toward the unworthy. Even more than in the Sermon on the Mount there is emphasis on the salvation to come, without any matching threat, and on the "master" who does not look after his own interests (see the discussion of vss. 35, 38, 40). Other stronger emphases include renunciation of the right to pass judgment, refusal to cultivate a sense of superiority or inferiority, and the image of the fruit that can only grow and cannot be forced. The concluding parable of the house built on a rock, the only foundation that can survive the judgment, is also more clearly etched.

The crucial motifs of Jesus' teaching are thus preserved, presented in quite different form by Paul as the precedence of God's actions over human actions (Gal. 5:25, etc.), the warning against "boasting" (2 Cor. 10:17–18, etc.), and the one sure foundation of righteousness that has already been laid (1 Cor. 3:11). The Sermon on the Plain is not a theologically conceived attempt to summarize the Christian message in its entirety. It is a call to the life of discipleship—originally interpreted through the total ministry of Jesus, interpreted by Luke through the rest of his Gospel. Paul undertakes this interpretation through a concentrated reference to the cross, resurrection, and parousia. The Sermon on the Plain stands in relation to the totality of the Gospel as the ethical exhortations stand in the totality of Paul's epistles. It is the offer of salvation in the form of exhortation.

### (1) God's Partisanship on Behalf of the Poor (6:20–26)
Cf. Matt. 5:3–12

[20]And he lifted up his eyes on his disciples and said, "Blessed are you poor, for yours is the kingdom of God.

[21]"Blessed are you that hunger now, for you shall be satisfied.

"Blessed are you that weep now, for you shall laugh.

[22]"Blessed are you when people hate you and when they exclude you and revile you and cast out your name as evil on account of the Son of Man. [23]Rejoice in that day and dance, for behold, your reward is great in heaven. For so their fathers did to the prophets.

[24]"But woe to you that are rich, for you have already received your consolation.

[25]"Woe to you that are full now, for you shall hunger. Woe to you that laugh now, for you shall mourn and weep.

[26]"Woe to you when all speak well of you, for so their fathers did to the false prophets."

[20a] When speaking of the hearers of Jesus' words, Luke is fond of distinguishing between the disciples and the outsiders: 17:20/22;

18:1/9. The people are present, however, when the disciples are addressed: 6:17–19; 7:1/6:20 (cf. 12:1; 16:1/14; and the discussion of Matt. 5:1–2). Conversely, Jesus spells out for the people (14:25) the conditions for discipleship (in the narrower sense of following the earthly Jesus: 14:33 [q.v.]). Thus the promise of salvation to the poor is addressed to the disciples in the narrower sense, who have given up everything and suffer persecution (6:20), the woes in vss. 24–26 to the outsiders (not false teachers although Luke is fond of castigating their love of riches and pleasure [cf. the discussion of vs. 39]), and the commandment to love one's enemies to all who are willing to hear. Chapter 12 also distinguishes exhortations addressed to all who are willing to hear (vss. 13–15) from those addressed to the disciples in the narrower sense, who are not in danger of greed but of hypocrisy and anxiety (vss. 1, 4, 22). The question of whom Jesus' words are addressed to is therefore raised explicitly in 12:41. Only disciples in the narrower sense, not the "great crowd of disciples" (6:17) have to give up "everything" (only Luke: 5:11 [q.v.], 28; 14:33; 18:22; see the discussion of 18:18–30). Even Luke says that the community obeyed this command only in the earliest period at best (Acts 2:44–45; 4:32–35; but singled out as a special deed in 4:36–37; similarly 5:4). A narrower circle of the disciples of the earthly Jesus is called to a special witness that is intended to help all those who are rich to achieve freedom from possessions. It is to take whatever form is appropriate at any given moment (Luke 8:3; 10:38; 14:12–14; 19:8; Acts 20:33–35). It is therefore important that the people are already present in vs. 20.

[20b] The beatitudes are addressed to the poor, the hungry, those who weep (without further specification). The use of the second person is unusual: in the Old Testament, only a land or a people is so addressed. Not until apocalyptic literature are those set apart for the age of salvation distinguished by having a promise addressed directly to them (En. 58:2; otherwise only in Test. Isaac 8:12, which could be a Christian text).

The promise is not formulated in such spiritual terms that it glosses over the concrete sufferings to be faced. In Palestine, the poor thought of themselves largely as the humble, whose only hope was in God (Matt. 5:3); in the Hellenistic cities of the Lukan communities there was social oppression on the part of the rich (James 5:1–6). Faced with this situation Jesus preaches not Stoic renunciation of externals but God's shocking partisanship on the side of those who suffer (see the discussion of Matt. 5:3).

But who is right, Matthew or Luke? Is Jesus talking about spiritual poverty or real poverty? Jesus addressed himself unconditionally to the poor and never allowed fanaticism to ignore earthly suffering as though the believer were already dwelling in heaven. He expected his promise to be fulfilled in the future of the kingdom of God. Of course his word can help only those who can hear and receive it, so that something of the reality to come is already made present. This is Luke's understanding of the promise. In vs. 21 he has twice introduced the word "now" in order to set the coming fulfillment clearly apart. But this fulfillment is already on the way. Therefore a special message is addressed to the disciples who have already accepted Jesus' word into their lives. With their radical renunciation, they are intended to move others to make their possessions available to the poor. Luke is therefore especially fond of telling about the rich and respected who respond to this call (19:1–10; Acts 4:36–37; 10; 16:14–15, 27–34; 18:8).

And so what took place in Jesus continues in the Christian community: the good news that is fulfilled "today" (4:21; 7:22; cf. the present tense in 6:20) is made visible in Jesus' healings (4:23–27; 6:18–19; 7:21) and in his call to invite the hungry (cf. 14:13, 21). This is stated in 6:20 not as a condition but as a promise. In everyone who truly hears, God will work to show forth in a sign something of the kingdom that he will one day bring to pass. At the same time, total poverty gives the disciples the chance to understand the word of Jesus especially well in their need.

This aspect of the truth, well known to contemporary Judaism, entered into the composition of Matthew 5:3 (q.v.). It goes beyond the narrower circle of disciples, holding true for all who know their poverty (in whatever form!); compare 2 Corinthians 6:10: ". . . as sorrowful, yet always rejoicing." Two things are therefore being said: Jesus promises to those who are economically poor that their fate will change in the kingdom of God, and, in anticipation, in the

Christian community. But this can be heard only by those who allow themselves to be moved by it (vs. 22 assumes that Jesus' call is being followed)—to this extent, Matthew's interpretation coincides with Luke's. Whoever hears in this spirit is free to give and to receive, and this in a very practical way. Giving or receiving, all will be open to the coming kingdom because they are no longer content with the situation of this world (cf. Isa. 55:1; Amos 8:11; Ecclus. 24:21).

[21] Hearing the promise of Jesus leads to both the espousal of the cause of the poor, the hungry, and those who mourn, together with unlimited hope for the world to come that is contrasted explicitly to the "now." Without this hope, the result would be an outbreak of religious fanaticism that would see everything fulfilled in faith, being blind to the suffering that will never be overcome totally by human efforts. But without the attempt to overcome it, as far as humanly possible, there would be no real hearing of the promise. [22] That is why Luke speaks so unreligiously about the concrete details of "being full" and "laughing," of hate, exclusion, reviling, and calumny (possibly formulated awkwardly because of an error in translation; cf. the introduction to Matt. 5:11).

[23] "That day" probably refers to the day on which they are "excluded" (cf. Acts 8:1). Originally this probably meant exclusion from the synagogue, which made life almost impossible in a Jewish environment. In this very setting they are to "dance" with joy like children. It is unlikely that the reference is to the day of the last judgment (Luke 10:12; 17:31, where the context makes this clear). In this case the future tense would have been used: "You will rejoice in that day." The next clause speaks of the promise, the heavenly "reward."

[24–26] Four "woes" were added to the beatitudes at a later date. This is shown by the (pre-Lukan) new beginning with "but," the different formulation ("woe to *you* . . ."), and the use of the catchword "hate," which originally linked vss. 22–23 with vs. 27. At one time, "persecute" in Matthew 5:11 and 5:44 were probably juxtaposed in a similar fashion. Not only is vs. 26 longer, it is also formulated without an apodosis, a clause giving a conclusion.

The woes are addressed to those who stand outside the group of disciples and make up the dark background—the "rich," the "full," those who "laugh" (cf. Eccles. 8:14; Ps. 126:1–2; 137:1; Rev. 19:7; 21:4), of whom "all speak well," not simply those who have enough to live on and can be content. The target is the superfluity that has no need of anyone or anything, not even God.

Isaiah 61:1–2 has influenced both the Matthean beatitudes and the Lukan woes (see the discussion of Matt. 5:4); now, however, there is an echo of the contrast between the salvation and the vengeance of God (also Isa. 57:15–21; 65:13–14). Isaiah 56—66 (Trito-Isaiah) appears to have had an increasing influence on the Sermon on the Plain (cf. the introduction to vs. 38).

[24] Like vs. 20 (q.v.), vs. 24 is stated in the present: God's promise of the future is already at hand, but when it is not heard, the "woe" has already come to pass.

[26] False prophets who say what they are expected to say (Jer. 28:8–9), genial, popular preachers can be more dangerous than those who owe their failure to their own boorishness.

## (2) The Central Commandment of Love (6:27–36)
Cf. Matt. 5:38–48; 7:12

[27]"But I say to you that hear: Love your enemies, do good to those who hate you, [28]bless those who curse you, pray for those who abuse you. [29]To one who strikes you on the cheek, offer the other also, and from one who takes away your outer garment do not withhold your undergarment as well. [30]Give to everyone who asks you, and from one who takes away your goods do not ask them again. [31]And as you wish that people would do to you, do so to them.

[32]"If you love those who love you, what grace is that to you? For even sinners love those who love them. [33]And if you do good to those who do good to you, what grace is that to you? For even sinners do the same. [34]And if you lend to those from whom you hope to receive, what grace is that to you? Even sinners lend to sinners, to receive as much again. [35]But love your enemies and do good and lend, expecting nothing in return, and your reward will be great, and you will be sons of the Most High, for he is kind to the ungrateful and wicked. [36]Be merciful, as your Father is merciful."

**[27-28]** This central commandment of Jesus has been preserved in many versions (see the discussion of Matt. 5:21-48 [38-48 and 43-48] and of 1 Cor. 4:12). It is addressed to all who "hear" (see the discussion of vs. 20*a*; most likely not in the sense of 8:8). Luke goes beyond Matthew 5:44 in emphasizing the concrete expression of doing good and blessing. The word "abuse" (verbally) can also mean "abuse" (physically) and thus covers a broad range of experiences. The primary call is not for prayer or action but for a fundamental attitude of love—which of course issues in action (vss. 32–35). "Doing good" (vs. 27) is taken up with slight variations in vss. 33 and 35 (cf. 1 Macc. 11:33). What is given in return for such love, which is itself the gift of God, Luke calls "grace" (vss. 32–34; contrast vs. 35*b*), not "reward" (Matt. 5:46–47; see also the discussion in the introduction to 5:21–48).

**[29-31]** Into this passage has been interpolated the prohibition of resistance, formulated in the singular (see the discussion of Matt. 5:21-48 [38–48]; on assimilation to the Hellenistic situation, see the discussion of vss. 39–42, *ibid.*). Didache 1:4–5 (cf. Justin *Apol.* 1. 16. 1) presupposes the form in Luke 6:29–30 and therefore was probably familiar with its *Vorlage* (most likely not with the Lukan passage itself).

**[31]** The golden rule follows as a summary (see the discussion of Matt. 7:12). It is obviously not meant merely as good advice because one would then expect equivalent treatment (as in Ecclus. 12:1–6; Epictetus 2. 14. 18; Dio Chrysostom 7. 88–89). It follows vs. 30 naturally since both Luke's source and Matthew 5:42 spoke of lending, not asking for the return of stolen property, as Luke formulates the verse on the basis of vs. 29. **[34]** This is also shown by vs. 34, which refers back to the form involving lending. Despite its assimilation to vss. 32–33, its formulation does not parallel theirs (not: "from those who lend to you"), which means that it was present in Luke's source.

Did the prohibition of resistance (vss. 29–30), like Matthew 5:39–42, originally come at the beginning, together with the golden rule (in the singular?), followed by the command to love one's enemies (vss. 27–28, 32–33)? Were vss. 34 and 35*a* added before Luke, summarizing and repeating both elements? Vs. 35*b* might have been shifted here in recollection of Matthew 5:45, and rephrased in more general terms.

[35] Vs. 35 calls for generosity in lending even without prospect of returned service. Does the verse have to do with interest or repayment? Or is it perhaps even based on a misunderstanding of an Aramaic expression that simply meant "without refusing"? In any case, Luke is thinking in practical terms: the reader is more apt to be asked for a loan than beaten and robbed. Therefore Luke attaches greater weight to the directive concerning lending. Love of enemies is not an emotional high to be stimulated but good deeds done for those we find unattractive, money loaned to those who are not dependable. The future "reward" is that one day they will perfectly be what they practice to be now: sons of the Most High, who is kind to the "ungrateful and wicked." This goes beyond Ecclus. 4:10, LXX: "Be a father to orphans and as a husband to their mother, and you will be as a son of the Most High, and he will love you more than your mother loves you." [36] Vs. 36 is stated in almost the same way by Jewish teachers (Bill.) but as instruction in the proper way of slaughtering. Here God's grace and mercy toward ungrateful receivers is emphasized, differently from Matthew 5:45 which stresses God's equal rule over the wicked and the good.

A person is therefore like a riverbed, through which flows the water of God's goodness. Therefore there is no immediate call to pray or to perform some other religious act. But even a riverbed is changed by the water that flows through it. Thus the life of God's goodness seeks to open us to prayer and to the actions demanded of us even in a hostile world, to a life that is carefree and therefore truly caring, not to patronizing "Christian love." God even creates for himself some who are disciples in the narrower sense, in whom there already shines forth something of the perfection that is God's will for all humanity. This goes beyond the golden rule.

## (3) Love That Does Not Judge (6:37–42)
Cf. Matthew 7:1–5; 15:14; 10:24–25

37"And do not judge, and you will not be judged; and do not condemn, and you will not be condemned; set free, and you will be set free. ³⁸Give, and it will be given to you: good measure, pressed down, shaken and running over will be put into your lap; for the measure you give will be the measure you get back."

³⁹He also told them a parable: "A blind person cannot lead another blind person; will they not both fall into the pit? ⁴⁰A disciple is not above the teacher. When he is fully instructed, he will be like the teacher. ⁴¹Why do you see the speck that is in your brother's eye but do not notice the log that is in your own eye? ⁴²How can you say to your brother, 'Brother, let me take out the speck that is in your eye,' when you yourself do not see the log that is in your own eye? You hypocrite, first take the log out of your own eye, and then you will see clearly to take out the speck that is in your brother's eye."

Here, too, Luke follows Q. Vss. 37b and 38, which are not found in Matthew 7:1–6 (q.v., introduction), contain un-Lukan terminology and therefore probably represent a pre-Lukan addition, or else were omitted from Q by Matthew. The change from passive to third person plural active in vs. 38 does not prove that vs. 38b was originally independent; the same change occurs in 12:48. Like Matthew 4:24 (end), vs. 38 reflects the overflowing fullness of God's gift, except that it makes use of an expression from Isaiah 65:6–7 (cf. the discussion of 6:24–26).

Should vss. 39–40 be combined with vss. 41–49 and understood as being addressed to the Twelve or as a warning against teachers of false doctrine? No change of audience is suggested, and vss. 41–42 continue vss. 37–38 (like Matt. 7:1–5). It is more likely that vss. 39–40 (par. Matt. 15:14; 10:24–25) were added by Luke or by his source, which also elaborated vss. 37–38 to go beyond Matthew 7:1 if they were not already in Q. The new introduction could signal a Lukan addition (but see the introduction to 21:10).

Except in 8:10 (q.v.), Luke always speaks of "parable" in the singular, even when several follow (5:36; 14:7; 15:3; 18:1) or Mark uses the plural (8:4, 9, [11]; 20:9). Thus he takes vss. 39–42 as a parabolic discourse on the blindness that illustrates what was said in vss. 37–38.

[37] The direct linkage with the reference to God's mercy and the promise of being sons of the Most High (vss. 35–36) motivates the

warning against judging and the promise of not being judged. Luke also interprets the command by adding "condemn" and "set free" (used of prisoners and in everyday society of forgiveness or the fulfillment of a request). **[38]** Just as Luke explained "love" in vs. 27 as meaning "do good," so now he adds the positive command to "give." The "measure" is now associated with giving rather than with judging, as in Matthew 7:2 (q.v.); it probably was found in Q (in the form of Luke 6:38, while Matt. 7:2 has been assimilated to Mark 4:24?). In rabbinic writings, the third person plural is often used periphrastically for God (Bill. 2. 221; CD 2:13), which also suggests association with Q. Thus the words of Jesus came repeatedly to be set in new contexts.

**[39]** Since Luke 6:17—8:1 never mentions Pharisees, Luke 6:39, which refers to the Pharisees in Matthew 15:14, can only refer to disciples of Jesus who claim to judge others and thus occupy a leadership role while they themselves have a "log in the eye" (vs. 41) and are therefore blind—probably leaders of the community (see the discussion of 12:42). The rabbinic example of the shepherd who blinds the bellwether when he is angry at his flock (Bill. 1. 721) emphasizes the judgment upon the leaders and its effect on the entire people; Luke 6:39 emphasizes their responsibility.

**[40]** In Matthew 10:24–25 the metaphor of teacher and student says that the disciples will be treated no better than Jesus (cf. John 15:20); in John 13:16 it is a call to humble service. In Luke 6:40, however, the second clause speaks not of slaves and masters but of one who is "fully instructed," i.e., the teacher in the community, who would set himself "above" Jesus by condemning others. The correct model is Stephen and his intercession (Acts 7:60). The reference could only be to "new teachings" (as in Acts 20:30) if the entire section dealt with false teachers, but in this case the continuity of vss. 41–42 with vs. 37 would be broken. **[42]** Perhaps the interpolated vocative "brother" also alludes to condescending forms of address used by community leaders, while Jesus' paradoxical image is meant to make them laugh at themselves and their ridiculous presumption.

## (4) Roots and Foundations (6:43–49)
Cf. Matthew 7:15–27; 12:33–35

43"For there is no good tree that bears bad fruit, and again there is no bad tree that bears good fruit; 44for each tree is known by its own fruit. For one does not gather figs from thorns, nor does one pick grapes from a bramble bush. 45Those who are good out of the good treasure of their heart produce good, and those who are evil out of their evil treasure produce evil; for out of the abundance of the heart the mouth speaks.

46"Why do you call me 'Lord, Lord' and do not do what I tell you? 47Everyone who comes to me and hears my words and does them, I will show you what he is like: 48He is like a person who built a house, who dug deep and laid the foundation upon rock. And when a flood arose, the stream broke against that house and could not shake it because it had been well built. 49But whoever hears and does not do is like a person who built a house on the ground without a foundation, against which the stream broke and immediately it fell, and the ruin of that house was great."

Vss. 43–49 also derive from Q (see the discussion of Matt. 7:16–18; 12:33–35, introduction). The passage uses the singular throughout: "fruit" (also 20:10), "good," "evil." Life is a single whole. With all its bright spots and shadows, it is either totally centered on God or it is not.

[44] The fact that vs. 44b (Matt. 7:16) cites only negative examples is not to be taken as polemic; this is really the only way to illustrate the paradox, which summons those addressed to be good trees from the root up.

[45] Vs. 45a introduces the "heart" (not in Matt. 12:35), which determines every action in the same way as a tree determines its fruit. The Old Testament term refers to the self, including the will. Only at this point (not at the outset, as in Matt. 12:34) is speech (teaching?) mentioned as a special instance exemplifying the general truth.

[46] Vs. 46 and the concluding parable call once more for the "doing" that must result from true knowledge of the "Lord" and hearing his word. There may already be a hint of the contrast between the emotional sincerity of worship and the lamentable failures of everyday life.

[47–48] The double introduction to the concluding parable seems to be typical of Q (cf. 13:18–21 and the discussion of Matt. 7:24–27, introduction). "I will show you" has the immediacy of direct address. Luke reinterprets "hearing" as "coming to Jesus" (also in 14:26; is he thinking of baptism?) and emphasizes the human effort required to dig down to a rock foundation (see the discussion of Matt. 7:24–27; 16:18; and the introduction to Mark 12:1–12). The need for decision, stressed throughout the Sermon on the Plain, is reasserted (cf. Deut. 28:1–2, 15), whereas the images of Matthew 7:25, 27 that recall the last judgment are played down. Like Matthew 7:28, Luke 7:1 underlines the fact that Jesus' discourse is meant for all the people.

# E. CALL TO ASSEMBLE
## (7:1—9:50)

Chapters 7—8 describe Jesus' struggle on behalf of Israel. Jesus' mighty works in 7:1–17 and 8:26–56, each concluding with a resurrection, surround a central section (7:36—8:21) that deals with what it means to hear the word of God. This section is itself preceded by the question of who Jesus is (7:18–35) and a summons to decision (8:22–25). All this leads up to the sending forth of the Twelve (9:1–6) and the question "Who is this?" (9:9; cf. already 7:49), now clearly stated, which obviously looks forward to 9:20 (cf. vss. 8/19!). The question is answered in the feeding of the five thousand (9:12–17) and above all in Peter's confession (9:20), which is corrected by Jesus (9:22, 44) with a warning against wanting to be great (also vss. 46–50), and in the dialogue of Moses and Elijah with Jesus on his "departure" in Jerusalem, i.e., his Passion (9:31, cf. 9:41). More emphasis is put on Jesus' Passion here than in Mark (see the discussion of 9:31), but neither in the first nor in the second part of Jesus' ministry does it play the determinative structural role it plays there (see the retrospect in *The Good News According to Mark*).

The story of the centurion probably came at this point even in Q (cf. section 2 of the Introduction to *The Good News According to Matthew*) and probably the section dealing with John the Baptist as well (7:18–35; Matt. 11:2–19), for in Matthew 8:18–22 (q.v.) and 10, Matthew has consciously shifted Q material forward (see the discussion of Matt. 4:17—11:30, section 1).

Looking ahead to 7:22, Luke or his prototype inserted 7:11–17 as an instance of the dead being raised. The story of the sinful woman in 7:36–50 (cf. 8:1–3) is appended to vs. 34 as an example of how the gospel is offered to the poor.

Luke omits the entire passage Mark 3:20–35 because he is going to use Q's version of the discussion about Beelzebul in 11:14–23 (12:10). The associated saying (Mark 3:21, 31–35) concerning Jesus' family and those who "hear and do the word of God" he includes in 8:19–21. Typically Lukan is the stress on hearing and doing. Like Matthew, he omits the negative estimate of Jesus' family (Mark 3:21). By the shift to 8:19–21 and the reduction to a single parable in 8:1–15, he illustrates what it is to "hear" the "word of God" (8:11, 15, 18).

For the rest, Luke follows Mark up to the feeding of the five thousand, omitting what he has already introduced (Mark 6:1–6a, 17–29 [see the discussion of Luke 20:9–19]) or intends to use later (Mark 4:30–32), or what does not seem clear (Mark 4:26–29). Between 9:17 and 9:18 the entire section Mark 6:45—8:26 is missing. Did his copy of Mark lack, say, 6:47–8:27a? Such a possibility is conceivable; Mark 6:45–46 would then have concluded the story of the feeding (6:32–44) and 8:27b would have introduced the account of Peter's confession, while vs. 27a would have still constituted the conclusion of the missing episode of the healing of the blind man. In Luke's copy of Mark, then, Peter's confession would have followed directly upon the feeding and Jesus' solitary prayer (Mark 6:46). Bethsaida would have been mentioned immediately before (Mark 6:45; some texts omit "to the other side") as the destination of the boat trip. This could explain the strange statement in Luke 9:18 that Jesus was praying alone and yet the disciples were with him, as well as the choice of Bethsaida as the setting for Peter's confession (Luke 9:10). In this case, of course, Luke would also have read in Mark 6:46 that Jesus took his leave of his disciples.

The omission can also be understood as deliberate abbreviation since Luke is adding much new material elsewhere. Luke 11:16 recalls Mark 8:11; Luke 11:38, Mark 7:2, 4; and Luke 12:1, Mark 8:15 (q.v., introduction). But the passages involved are all introductions to Q material, so that dependence on the omitted Markan materials is no more proven than by the fact that the parable of the mustard seed, for example, in Q has much in common with its Markan form. There is no way to be certain. Apart from the question of the law (Mark 7:1–23; cf. 24–30), which was no longer a matter of concern (and for Luke had never been a matter of concern to Jesus), and the episode of Jesus' walking on the water, the omitted material resembles material already presented (cf. Mark 6:51 with Luke 8:24). The journey into Gentile territory can also be eliminated (cf. 8:26, 39) because it is not opened to the disciples until after Easter, and the question about Jesus' identity that Luke adds (9:9) is brought closer to its answer (see above, and the introduction to 9:18–27). Also omitted is the apocalyptically tinged identification of the Baptist with Elijah (Mark 9:9–13; see the conclusion to Luke 3:15–20). It is not he but the returning Christ who will restore all things (Acts 3:20–21).

The authority and weakness of the Apostles (9:1–17; 37–50) make a nice contrast. They are linked by Peter's confession and a call to follow Jesus on the way of the cross (9:18–36), framed by two miracles (9:10–17; 37–43) that demonstrate Jesus' power. The central mystery, therefore, is not Jesus' messiahship but his Passion. It is first mentioned in 9:22, and the way to it is prepared in 9:51. But it is a sign of God's power, not God's powerlessness.

### The Faith of the Centurion (7:1–10)
Cf. Matthew 8:5–13

[1]After he had ended all these sayings in the ears of the people, he entered Capernaum. [2]Now a centurion's slave, who was dear to him, was sick and at the point of death. [3]But when he heard of Jesus, he sent to him elders of the Jews, asking him to come and heal his slave. [4]And when they came to Jesus, they besought him earnestly and said, "He is worthy that you grant him this, [5]for he loves our people and built us

our synagogue." [6]And Jesus went with them. When he was not far from the house, the centurion sent friends and said to him, "Lord, do not trouble yourself, for I am not worthy to have you come under my roof; [7]therefore I did not presume to come to you. But say a single word, and my boy shall be healed. [8]For I, too, am a person placed under authority, and have soldiers under me, and say to one, 'Go,' and he goes, and to another, 'Come,' and he comes, and to my slave, 'Do this,' and he does it." [9]When Jesus heard this, he marvelled at him, and turned to the crowd that followed him, and said, "I tell you, not even in Israel have I found such faith." [10]And those that had been sent returned to the house and found the slave well.

There are several pre-Lukan features in the language of this episode: [2] the sick slave is at the point of death (so that he cannot be transported; also John 4:47); [6] the centurion sends his friends; Jesus and the centurion have a conversation that follows Matthew's account. Luke himself framed the introduction and conclusion. Originally, perhaps, there was just a delegation who told Jesus about the sickness of the slave and conveyed the message of vss. 6*b*, 7*b*, 8—almost precisely the words of the centurion according to Matthew 8:8–9. Then Luke, drawing on oral tradition or Acts 10:2, 5, 22, composed vss. 3–6*a* and linked them with his archetype by means of vs. 7*a* (in contrast to vs. 4*b*).

[7] The breakthrough of a *mission* to the Gentiles comes only after Israel's decision (cf. the discussion of 8:26, 39). Therefore Luke does not have the centurion appear in person, and his being a Gentile serves only to shame Israel. The statement in Matthew 8:11–12 about the influx of the Gentiles is also put by Luke 13:28–29 in the context of putting Israel to shame.

[9] At the same time we see Jesus' concern for Israel; he turns to the "crowd" (not in Matt. 8:10). Israelites (possibly intended as models for Luke's contemporaries) also open the way to Jesus for a God-fearing Gentile (in Herod's service?). While they praise the centurion's good works (cf. Acts 10:2), Jesus praises his faith. In this context the demonstration of Jesus' power is important: it is a call to faith. Whoever trusts him, especially in the light of his own unworthiness, has built upon a rock (6:48).

## Power over Death (7:11–17)

[11]And it happened soon afterward that he went to a city called Nain, and his disciples and a great crowd went with him. [12]But when he drew near to the gate of the city, behold, a man who had died was being carried out, the only son of his mother, and she was a widow, and a large crowd from the city was with her. [13]And when the Lord saw her, he had compassion on her and said to her, "Do not weep." [14]And coming up he touched the coffin, and the bearers stood still. And he said, "Young man, I say to you, arise." [15]And the dead man sat up and began to speak, and he gave him to his mother. [16]But fear seized them all, and they glorified God, saying, "A great prophet has risen among us," and "God has visited his people." [17]And this word concerning him spread through the whole of Judea and all the surrounding country.

The story begins with movement in opposite directions: Jesus is approaching the town with his train of followers while the funeral procession is coming out. Jesus' initiative prevents the two groups from simply passing by each other. The mercy Jesus shows the mother in both word and deed (vss. 13, 15*b*, each time with Jesus as subject) frames the central event: Jesus' gesture and his words spoken to the dead man, followed by the latter's reaction and demonstration of the miracle (vss. 14, 15*a*). The result is depicted through the fear of the people and their praise of what God has done in Jesus (16) as well as through the spread of Jesus' fame (17).

Only Luke tells this story, which he probably had before him in oral or (more likely) written form. His style appears only in vss. 11–12, 16*a* (see the discussion of 17:15), and 17. The story follows the model of Elijah, who likewise approaches a city and its gate, where he meets a widow whose (only?) son he later raises from death and "gives back to his mother" (identical wording), which proves that he is a man of God (prophet) (1 Kings 17:8–24). Vss. 13–16 contain un-Lukan material. In Mark 6:34, for example, Luke eliminates the statement that Jesus "had compassion"; Mark 8:2 and 9:22 are totally lacking, and the word never occurs in Acts. Furthermore, Jesus is referred to as "the Lord" (see section 2.c of the Introduction). "Do not weep" also appears in 8:52, where, however, Luke may have introduced it in imitation of 7:13.

[11–12] The helper and those who need help approach each other. Those who are helplessly exposed to the power of death find God's help in Jesus, who goes before his disciples as "author of life" (Acts 3:15). As "only" (cf. the discussion of 8:42) son "to his mother" (literally), the dead man was responsible for supporting her. [13] Jesus is "Lord" because he "sees" her need and responds to it (see the discussion of Mark 1:16; 6:34; Matt. 20:34).

[14] Coffins were used for burial (Bill. 1. 696, 1047–48, etc.); John 19:40–42; 20:6 (cf. Mark 15:46) is an exceptional situation. But the dead body was carried out (in an open coffin?) on a bier, wrapped in a cloth or cover. Unlike Elijah, Jesus neither calls upon God nor stretches himself out over the dead man. He orders him to arise. [15] The restored man neither cries aloud (1 Kings 17:22, LXX) nor sneezes seven times (2 Kings 4:35) to call attention to the miracle but sits up quite naturally and speaks. Like vs. 13, the returning of the son to his mother emphasizes Jesus' pity toward those who suffer and are despised (because misfortune was considered a punishment from God).

[16] As in 17:15 (q.v.), God is praised. John was already called a "great prophet" in 1:15, 17, but the present passage may have in mind the final messianic prophet (see the discussion of 3:15–20, conclusion). Luke may see in the statement that the prophet has "risen up" (i.e., appeared) an unconscious anticipation of Easter. God's "visitation," introduced by an additional "that" in Greek, is important to Luke (see the discussion of 1:68). [17] The fame of Jesus is now spreading even into the lands surrounding Judea (beyond 4:14, 37; 5:17; cf. 6:17).

For a discussion of fundamental issues, see the excursus following Mark 5:43. A pagan miracle worker of the first century C.E. is compared to Hercules: "A girl appeared to be dead at the hour of her marriage. The bridegroom was following the bier, lamenting. . . . Now when Apollonius arrived just at the time of the misfortune, he said, 'Set the bier down.' . . . But he merely touched her and said something under his breath and thus aroused the girl from her supposed death. The virgin made a sound, and returned to the house of her father" (Philostratus *Apollonius* 4. 45, about A.D. 200; for further discussion, see the excursus following Mark 4:35–41). But such accounts may have been influenced not only by the story of Hercules but also by competing Christian narratives.

Unlike the critical Philostratus, Luke is not thinking in terms of apparent death; the miracle that cures the slave at the point of death (vss. 1–10) is surpassed through the power of God, which transcends all human possibilities; this power works through Jesus and will be manifested in his resurrection (see the discussion of 9:31).

Luke inserted the story in anticipation of 7:22; its significance is therefore stated in 7:23. It is a call to faith in him in whom the promises of God are fulfilled. Luke knows that this is not plain to see; it is quite possible to "take offense" at Jesus. The very fact that restoration of the dead to life was also ascribed in this period to Greek miracle workers helps our understanding: for Luke, the story is not a clear proof but rather a sign from God that must not be overlooked. It is meant to point to the One whose will is not death but the perfect and authentic life that lies beyond death.


## God's Astonishing Work in the Baptist and in Jesus (7:18–35)
Cf. Matthew 11:2–19

[18]And John's disciples told him all these things. [19]And John, calling to him two of his disciples, sent them to the Lord, saying, "Are you the coming one, or shall we look for another?" [20]And when the men came to him, they said, "John the Baptist sent us to you, saying, 'Are you the coming one, or shall we look for another?'" [21]In that hour he cured many of diseases and plagues and evil spirits, and on many that were blind he bestowed sight. [22]And he answered and said to them, "Go and tell John what you have seen and heard: blind see, lame walk, lepers are cleansed, and deaf hear, dead are raised up, and poor have the good news preached to them. [23]And blessed is whoever takes no offense in me."

[24]When the messengers of John had gone, Jesus began to speak to the crowds concerning John: "What did you go out into the wilderness to see? A reed shaken by the wind? [25]But what did you go out to see? Someone clothed in soft clothing? Behold, those who are gorgeously appareled and live in luxury are in kings' courts. [26]But what did you go

out to see? A prophet? yes, I tell you, and more than a prophet. [27]This is he of whom it is written,

'Behold, I send my messenger before thy face,
who shall prepare thy way before thee.'

[28]I tell you, among those born of women none is greater than John. But the least in the kingdom of God is greater than he." [29]When they heard this, all the people and the tax collectors justified God and were baptized with the baptism of John. [30]But the Pharisees and the experts in the law rejected the [saving] purpose of God for themselves, and refused to be baptized.

[31]"To whom then shall I compare those of this generation, and whom are they like? [32] They are like children sitting in the market place and calling to one another,

'We piped to you and you did not dance,
we wailed and you did not weep.'

[33]For John the Baptist came eating no bread and drinking no wine, and you say, 'He has a demon.' [34]The Son of Man came eating and drinking, and you say, 'Behold, a glutton and a drunkard, a friend of tax collectors and sinners!' [35]And wisdom was justified by all her children."

Luke returns to Q, here in extensive agreement with Matthew 11:2–19. [18] He accounts for John's question as a historian: John is motivated by news of Jesus' miracles, not by his imprisonment and doubts concerning God's cause, which appears to be lost (Matt. 11:2, 12–13 are omitted). His question is taken up by others: 7:49; 9:9, 18. [21] The correct answer, not revealed precisely until 9:22 (cf. the discussion of 9:31), is found only by those who see in what Jesus "bestows" (end of vs. 21) an eschatological fulfillment (vss. 22–23, like 4:18–21). Matthew has collected Jesus' teaching in the Sermon on the Mount and his works in chapters 8—9, thus preparing for Jesus' response to the Baptist (see the beginning of the discussion of Matt. 4:17—11:30). Luke has added a resurrection narrative in 7:11–17 and a summary of Jesus' miracles in vs. 21, so that the disciples of John are actually made eyewitnesses. Therefore the blind, not mentioned previously, are singled out here although not the deaf. On the poor, see the discussion of 6:20*b*; on the significance of the miracles, see the discussion of 10:17 and 14:21; on "Lord" (vs. 19), see the discussion of vs. 13.

**[28]** In what Jesus has to say about the Baptist, Luke omits Matthew 11:12–13 as a doublet of 16:16 (q.v.), thus avoiding the statement about the present kingdom of God that suffers violence (cf. the excursus following 21:38, b), as well as the interpretation of the Baptist as Elijah (Matt. 11:14–15; cf. the conclusion to Luke 3:15–20).

**[29]** Vss. 29–30 are out of place in the response of Jesus. A very few manuscripts have Jesus begin speaking again in vs. 31. But if vss. 29–30 are taken as a narrative interpolation, it would mean that Jesus then bestowed the "baptism of John" unless the text is taken as referring to the past. Now in fact Matthew 21:31–32 contains a similar statement uttered by Jesus. The discourse is better preserved in Matthew, the form in Luke. Q may have had a similar saying at this point, since "justify" appears also in vs. 35.

The (saving) purpose of God appears also in the Qumran Manual of Discipline (1QS 1:8). It probably constituted the conclusion before vss. 31–35 were added. Possibly prostitutes were mentioned as well as tax collectors (Matt. 21:31; cf. Luke 7:37, albeit with reference to Jesus). Luke may be responsible for the reference to "all the people" (cf. the discussion of 14:21); this might explain why the tax collectors now appear as a kind of second thought as though they were not part of the people. Luke kept vss. 29–30 because he valued the positive effect of the Baptist and the faith of the tax collectors in contrast to the Pharisees and scribes (15:1–2). At the same time, Luke was enabled to interpret the parable that followed: it was not "all the people" but only a particular group that rejected the Baptist and the Son of Man. The "baptism of John" is already distinguished from Christian baptism. **[30]** The expression "for themselves" can refer in Greek to the verb "rejected" or to the noun "will."

**[31]** On the introduction to the parable, cf. the discussion of 13:18–21. The imprecise statement that John "neither ate nor drank" (Matt. 11:18; cf. the discussion of Luke 15:2) is defined more precisely by Luke as rejection of bread and wine (1:15; Luke omits Mark 1:6).

**[35]** Luke preserves the original wording of the concluding statement (see the discussion of Matt. 11:19c): the wisdom at work in both John and Jesus is recognized by "all her children" (Prov. 8:32; Ecclus. 4:11), those who resemble her, who are born (again) of her. It is totally untrue that "all the people" rejected John (and Jesus) and did violence to the kingdom of God. In contrast to what is said in Matthew 11:2–19, Jesus' acts brought the Baptist to the most crucial and salutary question concerning Jesus, and alongside him there are children of wisdom who justify God and listen to John, even if they have not yet understood who he realy is (vss. 27–28).

## The Friend of Sinners (7:36–50)
Cf. Mark 14:3–9; Matthew 26:6–13; John 12:1–8

³⁶One of the Pharisees asked him to eat with him. And when he went into the Pharisee's house, he reclined at table. ³⁷And behold, a woman who was in the city, a sinner, when she learned that he was reclining at table in the Pharisee's house, brought an alabaster flask of ointment; ³⁸and standing behind him at his feet, weeping, she began to wet his feet with her tears, and wiped them with the hair of her head, and kissed his feet, and anointed them with the ointment. ³⁹When the Pharisee who had invited him saw it, he said to himself, "If this one were a prophet, he would know who and what sort of woman this is who is touching him, for she is a sinner." ⁴⁰And Jesus answered and said to him, "Simon, I have something to say to you." And he said, "Speak, Teacher." ⁴¹"A creditor had two debtors. One owed him five hundred denarii, the other fifty denarii. ⁴²Since they could not pay, he gave it to them both. Now which of them will love him more?" ⁴³Simon answered and said, "The one, I assume, to whom he gave more." And he said to him, "You have judged rightly." ⁴⁴And turning toward the woman, he said to Simon, "Do you see this woman? I entered your house; you gave me no water for my feet, but she has wet my feet with her tears and wiped them with her hair. ⁴⁵You gave me no kiss, but from the time I came in she has not ceased to kiss my feet. ⁴⁶You did not anoint my head with oil, but she has anointed my feet with ointment. ⁴⁷Therefore, I tell you, her many sins are forgiven, for she loved much. But one to whom little is forgiven, loves little." ⁴⁸And he said to her, "Your sins are forgiven." ⁴⁹And the table companions began to say among themselves, "Who is this, who even forgives sins?" ⁵⁰And he said to the woman, "Your faith has saved you; go in peace."

"Your faith has saved you" (vs. 50) elsewhere concludes miracle stories, but what we have here is a description of the situation (vs. 36) and the appearance of the woman whose need is only indirectly visible (vss. 37–38) followed by a long account of the problem (vs. 39) and its solution (vss. 40–47). The parable is quite peripheral and misses the point since help does not come until vs. 48, bringing forth a new conflict (vss. 49–50). The passage must therefore be read as a controversy: a statement of the situation (vs. 36: place, circumstances, persons involved) is followed by a description of the conflict brought about by the appearance of a woman who is a sinner (vss. 37–39); the resolution is provided by a parable and its application (vss. 40–47). The more serious Christological question (vss. 48–50) is a (not necessarily needed) appendix which is totally in the style of Luke, who, following the model of Mark 2:5*b*–7, uses the entire passage to lead up to this question. Therefore the forgiveness that is already implicit in the social intercourse described in vss. 40–47 must be pronounced again in vs. 48. For Luke, what precedes is repentance and faithful gratitude, in response to which Jesus promises her salvation in words that elsewhere conclude healings (vs. 50).

Did vs. 50 originally end the story after vs. 47 or even vs. 43? Perhaps at one time vs. 47*a* read, "One to whom much is forgiven, loves much," and Luke adapted it to his purposes; otherwise vs. 47*a* would originally have indicated the criterion by which the grant of forgiveness can be recognized (see the discussion of vs. 47).

Strictly speaking, the parable tells Simon that he owes little and therefore has little obligation to love; but its purpose is only to describe the conduct of Jesus (and his community) without going into the question of others who are less sinful. Was the parable invented out of whole cloth on the basis of the story? If the value of the ointment had been set from the beginning at three hundred denarii, as in John 12:5, this could have suggested the image of the debtor. But without this image there would be no point to the narrative. On the other hand, the parable is incomprehensible without its setting. Some details may have been added secondarily (but before Luke), together with the interpretation of the parable in vss. 44–46 from the tradition on which Mark 14:3–9 is based. John 12:1–8 (oddly referred to by John 11:2) exhibits the same tradition with features that also occur in Luke (cf. vs. 3 with the end of Luke 7:38).

The name "Simon," not introduced until surprisingly late in Luke 7:40, is the same as in Mark 14:3. The anointing of feet (vss. 38,

46) is conceivable before going out (Bill. 1. 427, c) but hardly at other times (the "washing" with oil described by Bill. 1. 428 is exceptional). The deliberate bringing of a flask of ointment fits well with Mark 14:3–9 but is a bit out of place with the spontaneous tears that bathe Jesus' feet in Luke 7:38. On the other hand, the wiping of Jesus' feet makes sense here to dry the tears but not the wiping of Jesus' feet after anointing in John 12:3. Luke noticed the parallelism and therefore omitted Mark 14:3–9 in the Passion narrative.

[36] On Jesus' table conversation, see the discussion of 14:1; on the openness of the Pharisee, see the discussion of 3:7. [37] The name of the city is not mentioned; it could just as well be that of the reader. "Sinner" probably means "prostitute" (cf. Matt. 21:31–32, but not Luke 7:29). The doors are open and there are onlookers, but for a prostitute to invade a male gathering is scandalous. [38] Fearfully, clumsily, a bit frantically she tries to dab her flood of tears from the feet stretched out by Jesus as he reclines at table. Despite 1 Corinthians 11:5–6 (cf. vs. 15), it was probably not considered improper in Palestine for women to wear their hair uncovered (Bill. 3. 443), but Luke may have thought differently. Of course the scene has erotic overtones and may exhibit a touch of hysteria; the spiritual and the natural always occur in combination. Certainly the story is not about an angel—but precisely because the woman is not respectable, she can "justify God" (vs. 29).

[39] Nothing is said about Jesus, but Simon's politely apologetic thoughts, which also denigrate Jesus' authority ("prophet"; see the conclusion to 3:15–20) focus on Jesus' silent acquiescence, which Simon correctly interprets as social acceptance. While Jesus stakes his personal integrity on the encounter, Simon remains an outside observer, judging without becoming involved. [40] But the prophetic vision that he misses in Jesus is now turned on him, and in such a way that he is not simply put to shame, but is instead invited in the parable to see himself. His way of addressing Jesus exhibits a kind of recognition but a recognition that is still tentative and uncommitted (see the discussion of 5:5).

[41–42] For a creditor simply to forgive a debt is conspicuously unlikely; God, who comes to life in the parable, bursts the bounds of human probability (see the end of the excursus following Mark 4:1–9). **[43]** The parable does not deny the difference so stressed by Simon between him and the prostitute (any more than 18:11–12), nor is he expected to ᵫreak down in tears. But both are guilty; and, because the Pharisee (as in 18:11) for theological reasons cannot admit this in his cautiously formulated answer, he (as in 18:14) becomes the truly guilty party, being incapable even of "lesser love" (vss. 44, 46). At best he has behaved properly while the improper actions of the woman show that she understands what has happened to her.

**[45]** "From the time" could also be translated "from whom," suggesting that Jesus had been with her and come to Simon from her. But to read all this out of a single word requires an exercise of fantasy; "from the time I came in" makes good sense, and is meant to emphasize the duration of her ministrations in contrast to a hospitality expected only on first entering.

**[47]** In the context of the parable, vs. 47 can only be understood as meaning "much must have been forgiven her [perfect] since she shows so much love." This is like saying, "It must be cold outside since the thermometer is so low." But Luke has a different interpretation; he is probably intending to stress the act of love (cf. the discussion of 10:37), which is not only the consequence but the basis of forgiveness. **[48]** He takes the same form of the perfect ("are forgiven," vs. 48) also as a present in 5:20, 23 (cf. John 20:23), and thus parallel to vs. 47*b*.

**[49]**On the basis of the love that has been shown toward *him*, Jesus declares the forgiveness of *God*. This leads to what is for Luke the all-important question, going far beyond 5:21, of Jesus' own person, a question already touched on in vs. 39. The woman may be incapable of expressing her more or less clear self-knowledge intellectually; in all that she does, however, she finds her way to Jesus. **[50]** For him that is the faith that brings salvation (Acts 16:30–31) and sends forth in peace.

The parable describes Jesus' openness to those who stand on or beyond the fringes of the people of God, the "friend of tax collectors and sinners" (vs. 34), and is thus an invitation to joy. The scene uses the extreme case of a prostitute as an illustration. The antagonist resembles the elder brother in 15:25–32. An additional element is the warning against self-sufficiency that thinks it stands in need of nothing. Simon's answer, which inculpates Simon himself, asks the readers whether they are also addressed. Finally, Luke focuses the entire narrative on the Christological question. Unlike Mark 14:3–9, however, he emphasizes not Jesus' majesty but his love for the poor.

Luke's use of the declaration that appears also in 8:48; 17:19; and 18:42 shows that faith can find expression in acts even without confession of sins or confession of faith, without even a request for help. It also shows that "salvation" and "healing" are very close together (see the discussion of 17:19). What was given to the woman is something more than an amazing healing of the body; there is also a sickness that suffers from the meaninglessness of life, which leads to self-rejection and an attempt to find meaning in self-pity or obstinate resignation, in alcohol or drugs, in chronic sickness or prostitution.

Later the woman's life will make visible what has happened to her here invisibly. Another time the visible healing will come first, and whether it will become a sign that leads to salvation remains an open question (17:19). But salvation always strives to take visible form.

## Women Follow Jesus (8:1–3)

[1]And it happened soon afterward that he went on from city to city and from village to village, preaching and proclaiming the kingdom of God as good news, and the Twelve were with him [2]and some women who had been healed of evil spirits and infirmities: Mary, called the woman of Magdala, from whom seven demons had gone out, and Joanna, the wife of Chuza, Herod's steward, and Susanna, and many others, who provided for him out of their means.

[1] Vs. 1 recalls Matthew 9:35 but can hardly be based on Q since, like vss. 2–3, it is made up of idioms that are clearly Lukan. In any case, there follows in 9:51–56 and 9:57—10:16, after passages from Mark (8:4—9:50), material deriving from L and Q on the theme of mission. Did Luke consciously bring together narra-

tives involving women (7:11–17, 36–50) and use 8:1–3 to show that they, too, as witnesses to the resurrection (23:55; 24:1, 6–8) like the Apostles (Acts 1:21–22), were already present during Jesus' earthly ministry? Or did 8:1–3 originally introduce 9:51 ff.? The preaching of the kingdom of God (cf. the discussion of 4:43) looks ahead to 8:10. In the time of Luke, "cities" are the centers of the Christian community (cf. also Matt. 9:35).

[2] Mary of Magdala was later identified with the sinful woman of 7:37 because the two texts stood close together and perhaps even because Magdala was infamous for its lewdness (but this was a different town of the same name; cf. Bill. 1. 1047). If the identification were correct, 7:37 should have mentioned that she had been healed of possession (8:2; cf. 11:26). In addition, if all the "anointing" narratives were identified—which the variety of setting and content does not permit—Mary of Magdala would be the woman of Mark 14:3, according to John 11:1–2 the sister of Lazarus and Martha, who "served at table," like the woman in Luke 10:40, i.e., the "Mary" mentioned in Luke 10:39, 42. In this case Jesus would be near Jerusalem in Luke 10:38, which Luke at least does not assume. This is pure speculation, but she does appear clearly in all the Easter stories, where she is always (except for John 19:25; but cf. 20:1) the first of the women mentioned, usually three.

[3] Joanna (who also appears in 24:10), from the upper circles of society, and Susanna appear only in Luke. They all "provide for" Jesus out of their means. This might suggest provision of food and sleeping quarters, but that is difficult to imagine as Jesus travels since they obviously accompany him. In that period women could hardly have taken money and provisions with them. In composing this passage, Luke was probably thinking of the services provided by women in the communities with which he was familiar. This emphasis on women undoubtedly goes back to Jesus himself, particularly as he is depicted in Luke's special material, but the groundwork is laid by such figures as Sarah, Miriam, Deborah, Hannah, Ruth, Judith, and Esther, and the mention of women, for example, in Deuteronomy 29:11, 18; 31:12. Luke realized how unprecedented was the change from the low status usually accorded women (John 4:27!). Jesus did not develop a program, but he initiated changes that were to have far

greater effects. Therefore together with Zecharias we find Mary (1:11–12/27–29 and 46/67); with Simeon, Anna (2:25/36); with the mother of a dead son, the father of a dead daughter (7:12/8:41); with the scribe, the two sisters (10:25–37/38–42); with the insistent man, the insistent widow (11:5–7/18:1–8); with the woman healed on the sabbath, the man healed on the sabbath (13:10–17/14:1–6); with the daughter of Abraham, the son of Abraham (13:16/19:9); with the parable of the shepherd, the parable of the woman (15:3–7/8–10); with men who are witnesses, women who are witnesses (8:1/2–3; 24:22/24); with the man who sows the mustard seed, the woman who hides the leaven (13:19/21 Q); with the two men, the two women at Jesus' return (17:34–35 Q); see also 4:33–37/38–39 (= Mark).

## The Parable of Those Who Hear the Word (8:4–21)
Cf. Mark 3:31—4:25; Matthew 12:46—13:23

[4]And when a great crowd came together and people from town after town came to him, he said in a parable: [5]"A sower went out to sow his seed, and when he sowed, some fell along the path and was trodden underfoot, and the birds of heaven devoured it. [6]And some fell on the rock and, when it grew up, withered away because it had no moisture. [7]And some fell among thorns, and the thorns grew with it and choked it. [8]And some fell into good soil and, when it grew, yielded fruit a hundredfold." When he said this, he called out, "Whoever has ears to hear, let him hear."

[9]But his disciples asked him what this parable meant. [10]He said, "To you it has been given to know the secrets of the kingdom of God, but to the others [it is given] in parables. [11]Now the parable is this: The seed is the word of God. [12]The ones along the path are those who have heard; then the devil comes and takes the word away from their hearts, that they may not come to faith and be saved. [13]And the ones on the rock are those who, when they have heard, receive the word with joy, and these have no root; they believe for a little while and in time of temptation fall away. [14]But as for what fell among the thorns, they are those who hear, and as they go on their way, they are choked by the cares and riches and pleasures of life and their fruit does not mature. [15]But as for that in the good soil, they are those who hold fast in an honest and good heart the word that they have heard and bring forth fruit with patience.

[16]"But no one takes a lamp and hides it with a vessel or puts it under a bed, but puts it on a stand, that those who enter may see the light. [17]For nothing is hid that shall not be made manifest, and nothing is secret that shall not be known and come to light. [18]Take heed then how you hear, for whoever has, to him more will be given, and whoever does not have, even what he thinks he has will be taken away."

[19]Then his mother and his brothers came to him and could not reach him on account of the crowd. [20]And it was told him, "Your mother and your brothers are standing outside desiring to see you." [21]But he answered and said to them, "My mother and my brothers are these, who hear and do the word of God."

[4] Beginning with 8:4, Luke goes back to following Mark but initially records only a single parable (singular, vs. 4; see the discussion of 7:1—9:50). He emphasizes the cities (see vs. 1) and omits the motif of the boat (already used in 5:1–3; see the discussion of 4:31—5:11). The parable is quite similar to the one in Mark; in details (through oral tradition or Q?) it resembles Matthew's version. Mark makes a fine distinction between the "one" and the "other" that is lost (Greek singular) and the (much!) "other" that bears fruit (plural in Mark 4:8), whereas Matthew uses the plural throughout and Luke the singular. Jubilees 11:11 forms a good parallel to vs. 5 and shows that ploughing took place *after* sowing in Palestine. Luke 8:6 also omits the sun, so that the opposing forces are mentioned twice rather than three times. In compensation, he elaborates his account, [5] adds the danger of being trampled under foot and [6] the lack of moisture (cf. Jer. 17:8), neither of which is incorporated into the interpretation. The important difference in tense in the interpretation (see the discussion of Mark 4:20) is also not included. Instead, Luke emphasizes the "seed" (vss. 5, 11), omits (like Matthew) the special reference to failure (Mark 4:7), [8] and magnifies the success (vs. 8a: only a hundredfold). Or is his intention to avoid the idea that there are several classes of success (see the discussion of 19:13)? The call to hear is emphasized by Luke's introduction: the very use of parables (see the excursus following Mark 4:1–9, a) invites the kind of hearing that issues in decisions (cf. vss. 19–21).

[9] Luke reinterprets the question in Mark 4:10–12 about speaking in parables in general so that it becomes a question of the interpre-

tation of this particular parable. **[10]** The response opens to the "disciples" (not the Twelve) the secrets (plural, as in Matt. 13:11) of the kingdom of God, which remain mysteries to others. Only in this formula does Luke keep the plural "parables" (see the discussion of Mark 4:11). He neither says that the rest (here the crowd) remain "outside" nor that the opportunity for repentance and forgiveness is denied them (Mark 4:11–12; but cf. the end of Luke 8:12; Acts 28:26–27). He also omits Mark 4:34, which states that Jesus explained his parables to his disciples (cf. the discussion of Mark 8:18–20), pointing instead in vss. 16–17 to the open availability of the message. In 20:9, too, the parable is addressed explicitly to the "people" (cf. the discussion of 19:48 and 21:5). On the other hand, Luke also says nothing of the disciples' lack of understanding (Mark 4:13); Jesus answers their question in vss. 11–15.

**[11]** The sower is no longer mentioned, and so is not identified directly with Jesus. The seed is both "the word of God" and, in vss. 12–15, humankind as sown by God. In 2 Esdras 9:31, similarly, the law is sown in the heart, and in 2 Esdras 8:41 the human race is sown in the world although not all are saved.

**[12]** The "devil" actually means the "slanderer," who causes confusion and thus seeks to alienate human beings from God. Mark always uses the term "Satan," which Luke uses only in his special material (see the discussion of 22:3) and in 11:18 (Q?). The rabbis think primarily of material damage caused by Satan and evil spirits; the New Testament almost always has in mind sin and temptation.

**[12–15]** The situation of the community receives greater emphasis in Luke. He goes beyond Mark in speaking of "faith" and "being saved" (vs. 12), of temptation (vs. 13; see the discussion of 4:13), and of the "heart" (as in Matthew) that should be "honest" (literally: "beautiful") "and good" (vss. 12, 15)—the Greek ideal, found also in Tobit 5:14; 2 Maccabees 15:12. Does he omit "in themselves" (Mark 4:17) in vs. 13 because the roots derive nourishment from the earth in which they are planted (cf. Mark 4:28)? The concluding statement is a call for "patience," literally "remaining under" something when others run away (cf. the verb in 2:43), the confident perseverance, trusting in God (cf. 21:18–19), that brings salvation. Luke thus places greater emphasis on human conduct but does not forget that it is the word that bears this fruit. Even in Luke's time, then, the parable and its interpretation were still undergoing development.

**[16–17]** Vss. 16–17 have been assimilated in form to 11:33; 12:2 (Q). The "bushel" and the phrase "on the lampstand," which copies Mark 4:21 precisely, do not appear until 11:33; the phraseology here is un-Lukan (see the discussion of 11:33). The verses have been joined to the parable without an introduction. In contrast to Mark 4:21–22, they speak of "taking" a lamp instead of its "coming," of "those who enter" who are to see the light, and of the secret that is "known." Does this refer to Jesus, who cannot remain hidden (see the discussion of Mark 4:21–22 and Luke 11:33)? The differences between Luke and Mark suggest rather that the disciples are being exhorted to "take" the lamp (the message of Jesus) in order to bring it to those who are coming (the nations?).

**[17]** Vs. 17 could describe knowledge of the gospel but is more likely a warning to the disciples concerning the judgment (future tense, as in Matt. 10:26) that would reveal any failure (see the discussion of 12:2–3). **[18]** That is also the subject of vs. 18 (Mark 4:25). The saying about the measure one gives (Mark 4:24b), which no longer fits in the Lukan context, is omitted; it has also appeared already in Luke 6:38. The judgment will determine "how" (Mark 4:24a: "what") they have heard, whether they have taken seriously their missionary responsibility in their lives and preaching (19:11–27, where 8:18 is repeated). Those who do not do so merely "think" (only in Luke 8:18) they possess faith. In any case, it is clear that the community must not remain a small, reclusive sect: the sowing must continue.

**[20]** On the place of vss. 20–21, see the discussion of 7:1—9:50. The term "outside" suggests a house (as in Mark 3:20). But Luke omits or alters Mark 2:1, 15; 3:20; 7:17(24); 9:28, 33; and 10:10, according to which Jesus has the use of a house "in Capernaum." For Luke Jesus is a wanderer who "has left his house" (18:29) and cannot return to it with his disciples (cf. the discussion of 8:9–10). The negative description of Jesus' family is omitted (Mark 3:21); nevertheless, they remain "outside." **[21]** "These" (vs. 21) can hardly refer to them; in the context of 8:11, 15, 18, it can only mean those who hear Jesus' word as the "word of God" and also do it. (The expression has already been used in 6:47 [Q]; if Jesus' mother and brothers were the subject, they would have to have the article in the original text, as in vs. 20.) Vs. 21 not only includes all those listening, as in Mark 3:34, but leaves open the question of who fulfills these conditions (e.g., later on even Jesus' family [Acts 1:14]).

## Jesus' Authority over Storm, Demons, and Death (8:22–56)
Cf. Mark 4:35—5:43; Matthew 8:23–34; 9:18–26

[22]It happened on one of these days that he got into a boat with his disciples. And he said to them, "Let us go across to the other side of the lake." And they began the trip. [23]But as they sailed, he fell asleep, and a storm of wind came down on the lake, and water poured in, and they were in danger. [24]And they went to him and woke him and said, "Master, Master, we are perishing!" But he awoke and rebuked the wind and the raging waves, and they ceased, and there was a calm. [25]And he said to them, "Where is your faith?" But they were full of fear, and they marveled and said to one another, "Who then is this, that he commands even wind and water, and they obey him?"

[26]And they went to the country of the Gerasenes, which is opposite Galilee. [27]Then, when he stepped out on land, there ran to him a man from the city who had demons, and for a long time he had worn no clothes and he lived not in a house but among the tombs. [28]When he saw Jesus, he cried out, fell down before him, and said with a loud voice, "What have I to do with you, Jesus, Son of the Most High God? I beseech you, do not torment me." [29]For he had commanded the unclean spirit to come out of the man. For a long time it had seized him, and he was bound, secured with chains and fetters, but he was driven by the demon into the desert with broken bonds. [30]But Jesus asked him, "What is your name?" And he said, "Legion," because many demons had entered him. [31]And they begged him not to command them to depart into the abyss. [32]But there was a substantial herd of swine there, feeding on the hillside. And they begged him to let them enter these, and he permitted them. [33]So when the demons had come out of the man, they entered the swine, and the herd rushed down the cliff into the lake and drowned.

[34]When the herdsmen saw what had happened, they fled and told

it in the city and in the country. ³⁵And they came out to see what had happened, and they came to Jesus and found the man from whom the demons had gone, clothed and in his right mind, sitting at the feet of Jesus, and they were afraid. ³⁶But those who had seen it told them how the demoniac had been saved. ³⁷The great crowd from the surrounding country of the Gerasenes asked him to depart from them because they were seized with great fear. So he got into the boat and returned. ³⁸The man from whom the demons had gone out begged that he might be with him. But he sent him away, and said, ³⁹"Return to your home and declare how much God has done for you." And he went away and proclaimed throughout the whole city what Jesus had done for him.

⁴⁰Now when Jesus returned, the crowd welcomed him, for they were all waiting for him. ⁴¹And behold, there came a man whose name was Jairus, and he was a ruler of the synagogue. And falling at Jesus' feet he besought him to come to his house, ⁴²for he had an only daughter, about twelve years of age, and she was dying.

When he went, the crowd pressed around him. ⁴³And a woman who had had a flow of blood for twelve years, who could not be healed by anyone, ⁴⁴came up and touched the fringe of his garment from behind, and immediately the flow of her blood ceased. ⁴⁵And Jesus said, "Who is it that touched me?" But when all denied it, Peter said, "Master, the crowd surrounds you and presses upon you!" ⁴⁶But Jesus said, "Some one touched me; for I knew that a power had gone forth from me." ⁴⁷When the woman saw that she could not remain hidden, she came trembling, and falling down before him declared in the presence of all the people why she had touched him and how she had been immediately healed. ⁴⁸And he said to her, "Daughter, your faith has saved you; go in peace."

⁴⁹While he was still speaking, there came someone from the home of the ruler of the synagogue, and said, "Your daughter is dead; do not trouble the teacher any more." ⁵⁰But Jesus on hearing this answered him, "Do not fear; only have faith, and she will be saved." ⁵¹And he went into the house and let no one come in with him except Peter and John and James and the father of the child and the mother. ⁵²And all were weeping and bewailing her. But he said, "Do not weep; she is not dead, but sleeping." ⁵³And they laughed at him,

knowing that she had died. <sup>54</sup>But taking her hand, he called and said, "Child, arise!" <sup>55</sup>And her spirit returned and she got up at once, and he directed that something should be given her to eat. <sup>56</sup>And her parents were beside themselves. But he charged them to tell no one what had happened.

[22] The interpolation of vss. 19–21 has broken the connection with the parable (Mark 4:35: on the same "evening"). [23] Jesus' being asleep is essential to the story but not the fact that it was night (vss. 26–27 suggest the contrary). Luke reshapes and abbreviates the material much like Matthew 8:23–27 (see the discussion of this passage in the introduction to Matt. 4:17—11:30; [24] also the discussion of Matt. 8:25 ["they went"] and Luke 5:5 ["Master"]). [25] To "do" the word that has been heard (vs. 21) means primarily to have "faith," which has confidence in Jesus and takes him more seriously than threatening storms and waves. Luke does not say directly that the disciples have no faith (Mark 4:40; cf. the discussion of Matt. 13:16–17).

[26] This is the only mention of a (partially) Gentile region—but is Luke aware of this? He does add that it is "opposite Galilee" on the basis of Mark 5:1, and in vs. 32 (Mark 5:11) speaks of swine. Nothing is said, however, about the "Decapolis" or the "amazement" of the populace (Mark 5:20). [37] Indeed, the rejection of Jesus is underlined by the addition of the "surrounding countryside" (vs. 37). Nor is special mention made in 8:40 of Jesus' return across the lake to Jewish territory (Mark 5:21). The hour of the Gentiles has not yet come. Luke therefore also omits the suspension of dietary laws and the conversation with the Syrophoenician woman (Mark 7:20, 27–29). The Gentile centurion is described as a God-fearer in 7:3–6 (q.v.), enjoying close relations with Judaism. Neither magi from the East (Matt. 2:1–12) nor Greeks (John 12:20–21) come to Jesus, and the confession of the Roman officer (Mark 15:39) is much toned down in 23:47. The promise that the temple will be a house of prayer for all peoples (Mark 11:17) is omitted. The spread of the gospel throughout all the world (Mark 13:10; 14:9) is not mentioned until 24:47. Thus the historical situation is maintained. The Gentile mission, hinted at in 2:31–32; 4:24–27, does not come until after Pen-

tecost. At the same time, its close association with the eschaton (Mark 13:10) is broken.

[27] The statement that the man is naked is based on vs. 35 (Mark 5:15). [28] The demon "beseeches" Jesus, being unable to "adjure" him (Mark 5:7). [29] The bonds and fetters of the demoniac (Mark 5:4–5) are mentioned at a later point, probably because Jesus' help provides such a strong contrast. [35] "Sitting at the feet of Jesus" (cf. 10:39; Acts 22:3) shows the man's openness to being instructed.

[40] Nothing is said about a boat trip or shore (Mark 5:21; cf. the discussion of 4:31—5:11); instead, we are told that the crowd "waited" for Jesus and "welcomed" him. [42] The distress of the petitioner has been heightened: the child is his "only" daughter (as in 7:12; 9:38), and she is "twelve years of age," just old enough to be married. But he says nothing about Jesus' laying his hands on her (Mark 5:23); he does not prescribe the form Jesus' help should take. The girl is "dying" (like Mark 5:23; in Matt. 9:18 she is already dead).

[43] Some of the earliest manuscripts omit the statement that the woman had spent all her living upon physicians; it was presumably added on the basis of Mark 5:26. [44] The "fringe" of Jesus' garment (also Matt. 9:20; not in Mark until 6:56; see the discussion of Matt. 23:5) indicates his obedience to the Jewish law. [45] In contrast to Mark 5:31, Peter acts as spokesman for the disciples, as he does in 12:41, a redactional transition. In 22:8, the two unnamed disciples (Mark 14:13) are identified with Peter and John (cf. Acts 3:1–11; 4:19; 8:14; and the discussion of Luke 24:12). In 9:32 (many manuscripts also here), we find "Peter and those with him" (cf. 5:9 and Mark 1:36). Above all, Luke 5:1–11 (q.v.) and Acts 1—15 emphasize the importance of Peter (on "Master," cf. the discussion of 5:5).

[46] Luke 8:46 has Jesus state explicitly that a power went forth from him, thus emphasizing the fact (cf.Mark 5:30). Jesus does not look around for the woman (as in Mark 5:32); it is entirely up to her to decide whether to step forward. [47] She does so in a public confession, doing nothing to conceal her sickness (in that time a disgrace which made her always unclean) and her cure. Faith reveals itself as a confidence that dares to break through the boundaries of convention, and yet has an element of timidity (cf. the conclusion to 7:36–50).

**[51]** Vs. 51 speaks of entering the house (unlike Mark 5:37), and so the parents have to be mentioned (Mark 5:40). **[52]** We must therefore assume that the rest were weeping outside (contrast Mark 5:39). **[53]** The fact of the girl's death is reconfirmed. **[54]** Like vs. 8, vs. 54 emphasizes Jesus' loud cry but omits the Aramaic words, as does Matthew 9:25 (Mark 5:41; cf. the discussion of Luke 19:38); they would have sounded like a magical formula in an alien tongue.

**[55]** Vs. 55 is not evidence for immortality of the soul. Luke does say that the girl's "spirit" returns (like 1 Kings 17:21, which uses "soul"); but in Acts 20:10 he speaks of the "soul" or "life," and in Acts 9:40 merely reports that the dead woman opened her eyes. In Luke 9:25, he says "himself" instead of "his soul" (Mark 8:36), possibly because a "soul" cannot be forfeited (Mark 8:36). But the statement of Matthew 10:28 that the soul cannot be killed is not found in Luke (cf. also the discussion of 6:9). According to Acts 2:31, it is not the "soul" but the "flesh" that survives death (contrast vs. 27 = Ps. 16:10!); according to Luke 16:22–23, it is the whole person. This shows that Jesus' words to the crucified thief in 23:43 are not referring to a disembodied existence, like that envisioned by Seneca (*Heracles Oet.* 1703–1704, 1725–1726: "Take my spirit, I beseech you, up to the stars. . . . Behold, my father calls me and opens the heaven; I come, father, I come"). It is true that usage is not uniform; in Ethiopian Enoch 22:3, 5 (as well as in the Aramaic and Greek versions), too, "souls" and "spirits" are mentioned side by side, in the Book of Jubilees 23:31, "spirits." Nevertheless, Luke 24:39 (q.v.) shows in any case that the "spirit" is certainly not the resurrected self but a kind of shade.

**[56]** Jesus' instructions to give the child something to eat comes at the right place (later in Mark 5:43), so that the story ends with the amazement of the parents and the admonition of Jesus, who does not want to see the miracle turned into propaganda.

## The Sending of the Twelve (9:1–6)
Cf. Mark 6:7–13; Matthew 10:1, 7–14

[1]And he called the Twelve together and gave them power and authority over all demons and to cure diseases, [2]and he sent them out to preach

the kingdom of God and to heal. ³And he said to them, "Taking nothing for your journey, neither staff, nor bag, nor bread, nor silver; and do not have two tunics apiece. ⁴And whatever house you enter, stay there, and from there depart. ⁵And all who do not receive you, leave the city and shake off the dust from your feet as a testimony against them." And they departed and went through the villages, preaching good news and healing everywhere.

[1] The sermon at Nazareth (Mark 6:1–16) has already been recounted in 4:16–30 (q.v.); there follows now the sending of the Twelve (see the introduction to Matt. 10:1–16), albeit not "two by two" as in 10:1 and Mark 6:7. Does this mean that Luke pictures the Twelve as staying together? Beyond Mark 6:7, they are commissioned to preach (Mark 3:14) and to heal (vss. 1–2, 6; not until vs. 13 in Mark); nothing is said, however, about exorcism and anointing (Mark 6:13). Like Jesus (vs. 11), they are to proclaim the "kingdom of God" (cf. 10:9; see the conclusion of 3:15–20), not just "repentance" (Mark 6:12). Important as the latter is to Luke (see the discussion of 5:32), here he emphasizes the fundamental good news (vs. 6; also in Acts 8:12).

[3] The command not to take a staff (or sandals, 10:4) does not appear in Mark 6:8 but is found in Matthew 10:10 (q.v.; cf. also "silver," like Luke 9:3). Luke stresses that only disciples who concretely live their trust in God by renouncing all forms of security are credible, [4] but he realizes that literal obedience to this principle is possible only where hospitality (vs. 4) is an accepted social norm, as in Palestine (see the discussion of 22:36a).

[5] The prophetic sign directed against a whole "city" comes from the other version of the same discourse (10:8–11). Perhaps this statement, [6] which stands in contrast to the small beginning in Palestinian "villages," is meant to emphasize the eschatological salvation brought by the good news, which must be announced "everywhere" (cf. also Mark 16:20; Acts 17:30; 28:22; 1 Cor. 4:17). In the good news, the kingdom of God is already at hand. Whoever rejects it, rejects salvation. [1] In the Greek text, therefore, the authority given the messengers is described more clearly than in Mark 6:7 as a single definitive event (aorist).

## Who Is This? (9:7–9)
Cf. Mark 6:14–16; Matthew 14:1–2

[7]But Herod the tetrarch heard of all that was done, and he was perplexed because it was said by some that John had been raised from the dead, [8]but by others that Elijah had appeared, and by others that a prophet, one of the old ones, had risen. [9]But Herod said, "John I beheaded, but who is this about whom I hear such things?" And he sought to see him.

[7] Herod is an enlightened "tetrarch" (also Matt. 14:1, q.v.); unlike the populace, he does not believe in the resurrection of someone who has been executed (contra Mark 6:14–16), but Jesus' activity embarrasses him into making inquiry (cf. vs. 9 with 23:8). The question of who Jesus is has already been introduced by Luke in 7:49 (cf. vs. 16), 7:19–20 (repeated) from Q, and 8:25, 28 from Mark. It points ahead to 9:18–20, where we also find "a prophet, one of the old ones [contra Mark 6:15!], has risen." The terms "raised . . . appeared . . . risen" both describe God's eschatological miracle and at the same time compare Jesus to events of the past. Elijah will in fact appear but only to bear witness to Jesus as the one who is to be heard (9:31).

There is no evidence for Jewish belief in a resurrection before the end of the world; only those who, like Elijah, had "ascended" and therefore not died were expected to return (see the discussion of 1:17). It is highly dubious whether anyone ever really believed that Jesus was the risen John. As long as people still knew that John had baptized Jesus, such a notion was inconceivable. Herod might have thought so (Mark 6:14) if he had known nothing of the beginning of Jesus' ministry. It is more likely, however, that Mark derived such a belief from a figurative expression intended only to suggest that the Baptist, who was thought to be safely out of the way, had returned in Jesus with his message of repentance (Mark 6:16). For Luke in any case the idea expressed in vs. 7 is nonsense alongside chapters 1—2. [8] But he does presuppose that such expectations were current among the people, even with respect to the prophets, if he did not take vs. 8 merely in the sense of Acts 3:22; 7:37 (cf. CD 6:10–

11, Qumran) as meaning "appear." [9] He omits the execution of the Baptist (see the discussion of 3:20 and the conclusion of 20:9–19).

Such a question is good when it remains open to hearing the correct answer rather than providing its own hasty answer. But it is perilous when the questioner does not admit his "perplexity" (vs. 7) and will not hear the call to repentance. Then it leads to removal of the source of this unpleasant question, with or without violence (13:31; 23:11–12).

## Jesus' Authority in the Feeding of the Five Thousand (9:10–17)
Cf. Mark 6:30–44; Matthew 14:13–21

¹⁰And the Apostles returned and told him what they had done. And he took them and withdrew apart to a city called Bethsaida. ¹¹But the crowd noticed and followed him. And he welcomed them and spoke to them of the kingdom of God, and he cured those who had need of healing. ¹²Now the day began to wear away. And the Twelve came to him and said to him, "Send the crowd away, to go into the villages and country round about, to find lodging and provisions, for we are here in a lonely place." ¹³But he said to them, "You give them something to eat." But they said, "We have no more than five loaves and two fish, unless we are supposed to go and buy food for all these people." ¹⁴For there were about five thousand men. And he said to his disciples, "Make them sit down in companies of fifty each." ¹⁵And they did so and made them all sit down. ¹⁶And taking the five loaves and two fish, he looked up to heaven, said the blessing over them and broke them, and gave them to the disciples to set before the crowd. ¹⁷And all ate and were satisfied. And the leftover bread was taken up, twelve baskets full.

As in Mark 6:30, the return of the "Apostles" (see the discussion of Luke 6:13) leads into the feeding narrative. Strangely, Jesus withdraws (not in a boat, as in Mark 6:32) "apart" into the city (!) of Bethsaida (see the discussion of 7:1—9:50). Then, however, as we are to learn in vs.12, he finds himself in a "lonely place" (as in Mark 6:32). Matthew 14:13–16 and Luke 9:11–13 agree against Mark in the following: "the crowd followed him" (similarly John 6:2); there is no mention of the shepherd motif (also absent in John 6:5) or the two hundred denarii (John 6:7 and Mark 6:37); use of the same word for "eat" (cf. the term for the "leftovers" in Matt. 14:20; Luke 9:17; John 6:12). Oral (or even written?) tradition before and contemporary with Mark probably continued to influence the text.

[10] Bethsaida, according to John 1:44 the home or at least the birthplace of Peter, Andrew, and Philip, lies outside Herod's territory. [11] The "following" of the crowd may merely indicate curiosity (9:7-9; cf. John 6:2, with reference to the "signs" done by Jesus), in contrast to the Apostles (vs. 10). [12] Luke 9:12 calls them the "Twelve"—on account of their role in the community (Acts 2:14) or on account of the twelve baskets (vs. 17)? [13] The emphatic "you," which concludes the command in Greek, may emphasize their helplessness. The disciples' suggestion that they go to purchase food (not in Matt. 14:17) is placed here by Luke after it has been determined that there are only five loaves and two fish for provisions. [14] On the other hand, he introduces the number five thousand earlier, in order to make it immediately clear that Jesus is performing a miracle. [16–17] The account of Jesus' actions agrees almost verbatim with Mark 6:41–43 (without the end of vs. 41). This is the nucleus that first coalesced in the narrative. The fact that Jesus blesses "them" emphasizes the creative miracle of Jesus' word of blessing. This statement appears only in Mark in the second feeding (Mark 8:7); it does not occur in Luke 22:19 in the context of the Last Supper.

The period of calm that forms part of missionary work here includes readiness to be disturbed by people in need. To the ministry of the word is joined concrete earthly help in which creative power makes itself known. Then, however, there follows once more withdrawal for solitary prayer and conversation in an intimate group (9:18).

## Who Is This?—The Answer (9:18–27)
Cf. Mark 8:27—9:1; Matthew 16:13–28

[18]And it happened when he was praying alone that his disciples were with him. And he asked them and said, "Who does the crowd say that I am?" [19]And they answered and said, "John the Baptist; but others say,

Elijah; and others, that a prophet, one of the old ones, has risen." [20]And he said to them, "But you, who do you say that I am?" And Peter answered and said, "The Christ of God." [21]But he threatened them and commanded them to tell this to no one, [22]saying, "The Son of Man must suffer many things, and be rejected by the elders and high priests and scribes, and be killed, and on the third day be raised."

[23]And he said to all, "If any one would come after me, let him deny himself and take up his cross daily and follow me; [24]for whoever would save his life will lose it. But whoever loses his life for my sake will save it; [25]for what does it profit a person if he gains the whole world but destroys or forfeits himself? [26]For whoever is ashamed of me and of my words, of him will the Son of Man be ashamed when he comes in his glory and the glory of the Father and of the holy angels. [27]But I tell you truly, there are some among those standing here who will not taste death until they see the kingdom of God."

Like John 6, Luke knows of only one feeding, which is followed by Peter's confession (cf. the introduction to Mark 6:32–44). John 6:16–21 also tells of Jesus' walking on the water (Mark 6:45–52). The story is set not near the northern border of the country (Mark 8:27*a*) but in the region of Bethsaida (see the discussion of 7:1–9:50), near Capernaum, where John 6:59 says he had been dwelling. **[18]** The reference to Jesus' praying is a new element (see *ibid.* and the discussion of 6:12). Is the "crowd" (instead of "people," Mark 8:27) the same as in vs. 11, still remaining in the vicinity (also vs. 23)?

**[19]** The response of the disciples agrees almost verbatim with the formulation in vss. 7–8 (q.v.). **[20]** The title "the Christ of God" used by Simeon, Peter, and Israel (cf. 2:26; 23:35; Acts 3:18; 4:26; Rev. 11:15; 12:10) understands the Messiah in the sense of the Old Testament and Judaism as the representative of the one and only God. Of course Jesus is more than the king of Israel, ruling vicariously for God; therefore angels, demons, and Jesus himself omit the qualifier "of God" (2:11; 4:41; 20:41; 24:26, 46). On the other hand, the qualifier does guard against confusion with God himself or with a nationalistic revolutionary (and is therefore omitted in 22:67 and 23:2). It also clearly makes the way of suffering God's will. Until it has been traveled, the nature of the Christ cannot be understood, not even by the disciples (see the discussion of 18:34). **[21]** This is the sense in which Luke understands Jesus' warning in vs. 21, **[22]** which he therefore associates closely with the prediction of the Passion in vs. 22. The harsh attack on Peter found in between in Mark 8:32–33 he is happy to omit in any case, so as not to speak ill of Peter. "Be raised" (see the discussion of Matt. 17:9) emphasizes, more than "rise" (Mark 8:31; Luke 18:33; 24:7, 46), that it is God's act ("on the third day," as in Matt. 16:21).

**[23]** It is emphasized that "all" are called to discipleship. Suffering is the necessary road to glory, both for Jesus (24:26) and for the community (Acts 14:22). Luke has in mind the "everyday" realization of a life that no longer has only itself as its purpose (see the discussion of 14:33 and Mark 8:34).

**[24]** Luke omits "for the gospel's sake" (Mark 8:35, q.v. introduction) like Matthew 16:25. Vss. 23–24 are repeated in 14:27; 17:33 in their Q form. The Apostles themselves exemplify this way of life (Acts 15:26). **[25]** "Himself" (instead of "his soul, his life," Mark 8:36) makes it clear to the Greek that more is involved than just psychic experiences or physical life; therefore Mark 8:37 is also left out (see the discussion of Luke 8:55).

**[26]** According to Luke, the Son of Man will come in his own "glory" (not merely in that of the Father, Mark 8:38). The same glory is shared by the angels, who no longer accompany Jesus as in Mark 8:38 (likewise 21:27, q.v.). A portion of the early community saw Christ and the angels together as representatives of the heavenly world, without making a point of the differences. Wisdom of Solomon 18:15–16 already represents God's word (*logos*) as an angel, and the Son of God is the greatest of the seven (arch)angels in Hermas *Similitudes* 9. 12. 7–8 and Pseudo-Cyprian *Centesima* 25 (218). This notion is echoed here as well as in 1 Timothy 5:21; 1 Thessalonians 3:13 (if "his holy ones" are angels); and especially Revelation 1:4–5 ("spirits" is often a term for "angels"; cf. Rev. 4:5 with 8:2). It therefore makes hardly any difference whether the Lord, the Spirit, or an angel shows the way to the messengers (Acts 18:9; 16:6–7; 8:26, 29; 10:3, 7, 13–14, 19). Jesus is subordinate to God. God alone is Creator. God determines the plan of salvation, of which Jesus is the instrument and "prophet" (see the conclusion of 3:20–

25). Jesus repeatedly prays to God. God chose him (Luke 9:35; 23:35) and made him Lord and Christ (Acts 2:36). But at the same time it is appropriate to say of Jesus what otherwise can be said only of God precisely because Jesus is God's perfect instrument.

[27] The promise that some will see the kingdom of God follows directly without introduction but also without the further statement "coming in power" (Mark 9:1). According to 19:11-12, however, the kingdom of God comes only upon Jesus' "return" at the last day (section b of the excursus following 21:38). One might, therefore, translate: "some of those standing there" (at Jesus' return)—but who would understand this meaning? The natural interpretation is that "standing" refers to the listeners (cf. also the discussion of vs. 31). Either Luke really expected the world to end in the next twenty to thirty years, or the "seeing" (cf. 8:10) of the kingdom must be distinguished from its definitive "coming," and refer to an anticipatory presence as in passages like 10:9, 11, 23-24; 11:20; 17:21. The transfiguration should also be kept in mind, when the disciples "saw his glory" (vs. 26; vs. 32 is a Lukan addition; cf. vs. 36 and Acts 7:56).

Luke attaches the call to discipleship directly to the prediction of Jesus' death and resurrection. He emphasizes readiness to suffer and daily renunciation of a purely self-centered life; therefore there is no preaching of Christ before Good Friday and Easter. But whoever does not lose his own self may see something of God's kingdom and Jesus' ministry even before the end of the world.

## God's Affirmation of Jesus' Suffering (9:28–36)
Cf. Mark 9:2–8; Matthew 17:1–8

28And it happened about eight days after these words that he took Peter and John and James with him and went up on the mountain to pray. 29And it happened, while he was praying, that the appearance of his countenance was altered and his raiment became dazzling white. 30And behold, two men talked with him, who were Moses and Elijah. 31They appeared in glory and spoke of his departure, which he was to fulfill in Jerusalem. 32Now Peter and those who were with him were heavy with sleep. But while they kept awake, they saw his glory and the two men standing with him. [33]And it happened, as they parted from him, Peter said to Jesus, "Master, it is good that we are here, and we will make three booths, one for you and one for Moses and one for Elijah." He did not know what he was saying. [34]As he said this, a cloud came and overshadowed them. And they were afraid as they entered the cloud, [35]and a voice came out of the cloud, saying. "This is my chosen Son, listen to him." [36]And when the voice came, Jesus was found alone [once more]. And they kept silence and told no one in those days anything of what they had seen.

The story takes on a different value than in Mark because it is God's response to the confession of Peter, which is not censured in Luke as it is in Mark 8:30, and to Jesus' call to discipleship. It is the high point of the first half of Jesus' ministry and also looks ahead to the second half, Jesus' road to his Passion in Jerusalem (vss. 31, 44–45). Biblical language is particularly in evidence here. Three times we read "and it happened," once "and behold." The same is true of vss. 37–39. In both cases the Markan "immediately" or "suddenly" is omitted (Mark 9:8, 20; cf. the introduction to Luke 5:12— 6:11). The present tense in vs. 33 (see the introduction to 16:23) underlines the biblical style. For Luke, it suggests the mystery of the event, inaccessible to human mind and tongue.

Does this style derive from a source? In any event, the addition of the names in vs. 30*b* is remarkably clumsy (based on Mark 9:4?). Luke dates the episode "eight days" after the prediction of the Passion, not six like Mark 9:2. He is also thinking in terms of night, as vss. 32 and 37 show. Does this derive from a special source, which also accounts for the peculiar construction that gives the date?

Twice we are told of Jesus' praying on "*the* mountain." In 6:12, also, he prayed at night "on the mountain." "*The* mountain" is also mentioned in Mark 3:13 (q.v.) and 6:46, while for the transfiguration Mark 9:2 speaks more generally of "a high mountain." The mountain symbolizes the sphere of the divine, set apart from the common world of human experience. The variant dating could come from oral tradition or even a Christian liturgical calendar; but vss. 31–33*a*, too, where the reference to the Passion reappears, are special material and therefore also suggest a source.

[29–30] As in Matthew 17:2 (q.v.), Luke speaks of the change in Jesus' countenance and places Moses before Elijah (cf. "Moses and the prophets," Luke 16:29, 31; 24:27). He speaks of the brilliant whiteness of Jesus' raiment (cf. Dan. 12:3) because he must use human words to describe the fundamental otherness of God, which nevertheless shines through in the human person of Jesus, just as a painter might use luminescent color or a halo or a symbol (cf. also 24:36–37). [31] Moses and Elijah also appear in heavenly glory; having ascended, they have "not tasted death" (2 Esd. 6:26; of believers, John 8:52). The "departure" of Jesus to which they refer corresponds to his "coming" at his baptism in the Jordan (Acts 13:24; cf. 1:21–22); it therefore means his death, not his departure from the tomb or his ascension. The same is true in Acts 1:21, which states that the Apostle to be chosen must be a witness to Jesus' "coming in and going out," for he was not present either at Jesus' "departure" from the tomb or at his ascension. It is the cross of Jesus that is confirmed by the Old Testament.

The true secret is not that Jesus is the Messiah but that "the Son of Man is delivered into the hands of men" (see the discussion of 18:34), as vs. 44 states in contrast to Mark 9:31, which speaks of the resurrection as well as the Passion. In 9:51; 12:49–50; 13:31–35; 17:25; 22:15, 37, Luke adds statements about the Passion that are not in Mark, and it is mentioned again in the context of Easter (24:7, 20, 25–27, 46–47; cf. Acts 3:13–15). But Luke probably looks on Jesus' death as an "entrance into glory" (24:26; cf. Acts 14:22), and, like John, takes Jesus' exaltation and death together as a single event, emphasizing his death while John emphasizes his exaltation. The reference to Jerusalem is new; it is there that all will be decided (vs. 51).

[32] Jesus' praying and the disciples' sleepiness recall Gethsemane. Matthew 26:43 describes the disciples' eyes as "heavy" there, like Mark 14:40; while Luke 22:45 says that they are asleep. Again the condition of the disciples suggests the mysterious and incomprehensible (vs. 45) aspect of Jesus' "glory," which they "see" (see the discussion of vs. 27). In John 12:24–30, the discourse about discipleship, Jesus' temptation, the voice from God, and Jesus' transfiguration occur together.

[33] Peter appears as the primary figure (see the discussion of 8:45); the others are only "with him." But no attempt is made to conceal his foolish words (see the discussion of vs. 21; on "master" as a form of address, see the discussion of 5:5). Peter's insistence on making booths is more understandable because, according to Luke, Moses and Elijah are on the point of vanishing. [34] But the cloud, God's own dwelling place, shows how unnecessary earthly booths are. It is obscure whether only Moses and Elijah "enter" the cloud, or whether Jesus and the disciples do also—in other words, whether the latter are afraid that the glory is coming to an end or even that Jesus is about to leave them. [35] Since the voice of God "from the cloud" refers to Jesus, the former is more likely. The cloud also recalls Exodus 24:15–18; 40:34; and 1 Kings 8:11, where God's presence fills the tent of meeting or the temple; according to 2 Maccabees 2:8, it is the eschatological sign of God's glory. The description of Jesus as God's "chosen" Son is new (cf. Isa. 42:1, of the servant of God; see the discussion of vs. 26). Luke omits Jesus' demand for silence; the disciples are silent of their own accord. They have "seen" the ineffable (see the discussion of vs. 27).

In Luke, the episode points forward to 9:51 and thus to Jesus' journey to his cross and resurrection. Luke sees the problem posed by Jesus' departure which will leave the disciples dependent wholly on his word. Because for a brief moment the curtain, as it were, is drawn aside, they have been allowed to see in Jesus something of the glory of God and his kingdom, of that other life to which human eyes are otherwise blind. They are so overwhelmed that they cannot speak. And yet they know that in Jesus the glory of the future kingdom of God has already taken form, and that it is proclaimed in his word.

## The Incomprehension of the Disciples (9:37–50)
Cf. Mark 9:14–41; Matthew 17:14–23; 18:1–5

[37]And it happened on the next day, when they had come down from the mountain, a great crowd met him. [38]And behold, a man from the crowd cried out and said, "Teacher, I beg you to look upon my son, for

he is my only child, [39]and behold, a spirit seizes him and he suddenly cries out and it convulses him till he foams, and hardly leaves him and shatters him. [40]And I begged your disciples to cast it out, and they could not." [41]Jesus answered and said, "O faithless and perverse generation, how long am I to be with you and bear with you? Bring your son here." [42]When he was coming, the demon tore him and convulsed him. But Jesus threatened the unclean spirit and healed the boy and gave him back to his father. [43]And all were beside themselves at the greatness of God.

But while all were marveling at everything he did, he said to his disciples, [44]"Let these words sink into your ears; for the Son of Man is to be delivered into human hands." [45]But they did not understand this saying, and it was concealed from them, so that they did not comprehend it, and they were afraid to ask him about this saying.

[46]And there arose a thought among them as to which of them was the greatest. [47]But Jesus knew the thought of their hearts, and took a child, put it by his side, [48]and said to them, "Whoever receives this child for my name's sake receives me, and whoever receives me receives him who sent me. For he who is least among you all is the one who is great."

[49]John answered and said, "Master, we saw someone casting out demons in your name, and we wanted to forbid him because he does not follow with us." [50]But Jesus said to them, "Do not forbid it; for whoever is not against you is for you."

Even more noticeably than in Mark, the end of the first portion of Jesus' ministry is marked by the disciples' incomprehension (vss. 37–45), desire to be great (vss. 46–48), and egoism (vss. 49–50) in the face of Jesus' authority. These give a premonition of his path of suffering, signaled in 9:51. Like Matthew 17:14–21 (q.v.), Luke 9:37–43 provides a shorter variant. [41] As in Matthew, Jesus' plaint has been influenced by Deuteronomy 32:5 (also cited in Phil. 2:15) and 32:20, but the discussion of the disciples' lack of faith (Mark 9:28–29) is left out entirely since Matthew 17:20 (Q) does not appear until Luke 17:6. This lack of faith is not the theme but rather the miraculous power of Jesus, which is met by incomprehension (on the part of the crowd or the disciples?). The omission of the conversation on the way down from the mountain (Mark 9:11–13; cf. the conclusion of Luke 3:15–20) contrasts this incomprehensibility more directly with the glory of the transfiguration and the miraculous power of Jesus in vs. 42–43 with his prediction of the Passion in vs. 31 (see the discussion of vs. 43*b* and especially the end of the comments on 7:1—9:50).

[40] Is Luke trying to tell his community that only their "perversity" prevents miracles, not the absence of the miracle worker? [38] The father begs Jesus to "look" with mercy (likewise Luke 1:48; Lev. 26:9; 1 Sam. 1:11; 9:16; 1 Kings 8:29; Ps. 13:4; etc. with respect to God) on his "only" (see the discussion of 8:42) son. [42] Jesus "gives" the cured child back to him (as in 7:15). The point of the narrative is to bear witness to "the greatness of God," which is at work in Jesus (cf. Acts 10:38). [44] But the second prediction of the Passion is linked directly with the amazement of the people (contrast Mark 9:30); it is also underlined by Luke's use of a biblical idiom to introduce it. Because Luke connects the prediction of the Passion with the introductory statement by means of the conjunction "for," and because "these" usually refers to what has preceded, it has been suggested that the reference is to the amazement of the crowd, which the disciples should take to heart in view of the coming Passion. But vs. 43 does not even mention the "words" of the crowd; the reference is therefore to the words that follow, which, in contrast to Mark 8:31 (q.v.), predict only the rejection of Jesus, not his resurrection. His Passion is a continual topic of conversation (see the discussion of vs. 31), not limited as in Mark to the three explicit predictions. [45] On the other hand, Luke emphasizes that it remained "concealed" from the disciples (according to God's will?). A similar statement appears in 18:34 (q.v.). It is in fact the very revelation of God's "secrets" (8:10) that leaves them perplexed before the incomprehensible way of God.

[46] The quarrel among the disciples also follows directly (contrast Mark 9:33). It reveals their incomprehension, which they share with all the others. Even outwardly they are not set apart from the others by withdrawing into a house (as in Mark 9:33; cf. the discussion of Luke 8:20). [47] As in 6:8, Luke adds that Jesus sees their thoughts, and he shifts the symbolic act to its place before the saying about true greatness (contrast Mark 9:36). [48] Thus Jesus' statement refers to "this" child, understood as an exemplary figure. It does not simply commend care for one such child in general terms

(Mark 9:37; similarly Matt. 18:5), but states that whoever receives someone who is weak and insignificant receives Jesus himself and thus receives God. This is underlined by the next statement. It is less an exhortation to the disciples to be "small" through service (like Mark 9:35) than a statement about those who are least, who must be the most important in the eyes of the community because they are "great" in the eyes of God. Since Luke adds "among you all," he is thinking of members of the community.

[49] John's statement is also appended directly to Jesus' admonition as a "response" (on the "name" of Jesus, cf. the discussion of 10:17). Here we are dealing with someone who is not following "with" the disciples of Jesus (Luke 9:49 is more correctly formulated than Mark 9:38, q.v.). [50] But again Jesus disapproves all narrow-mindedness; Matthew 12:30 deals with a different question (q.v.). A similar statement is attributed to Caesar by Cicero (*Ligarius* 33), albeit in a document that is meant to curry his favor.

Mark 9:14–29 focuses on the question of what faith is. The confession of Peter (Mark 8:29) defines the end of the first portion of Jesus' ministry; no real miracle comes afterward (see the conclusion to Mark 9:14–29). In Luke, however, the new section does not begin until 9:51. For him, God's great power is visible one final time in the healing of the boy. The human mind, which is set only on its own aggrandizement and is thus blind to all else, makes even the disciples incapable of understanding the way of the Son of Man. Therefore he will fall into the hands of those who are blind to God's way (vs. 44). This shows the direction Jesus will take from 9:51 on. Just as the weakest and most insignificant are great and important to him, just as he renounces all the fever of competition, so only those will understand his way who follow him in it.

Mark 9:41—10:12 is lacking. Parallel sayings appear in Luke 17:1–2; 14:34–35; 16:18; and Mark 10:1 may be echoed in Luke 9:51.

# III

## THE ROAD TO JERUSALEM
## 9:51—19:27

This section is usually called the journey narrative, but Jesus has been on the road previously and dependent on hospitality (5:29; 7:36; 8:1–3). Jesus is also described as "going" in 4:30, 42; 7:11; 22:22. What is new is the destination, Jerusalem (9:51; 13:22, 33; 17:11; 18:31), which marks conscious acceptance of God's mandate (9:31). Jesus' baptism introduces the first period of his ministry (3:21–22); the parallel transfiguration narrative (9:28–36) introduces his journey to Jerusalem. The former begins with his rejection in Nazareth, the latter with his rejection in Samaria. In both cases Jesus is led to go on (4:31a; 9:56). It is therefore better not to conclude this section at 18:14 but rather at 19:27 (or even 19:44; see below).

No place names are indicated before 18:35 and 19:1 (Jericho) except for the puzzling reference in 17:11. As in Mark 10:32–33, Jesus' journey is less geographical than an expression of his readiness to travel his appointed way (to the cross; 12:50; 17:25; 22:22). He does not even have the relative security of a home. His only source of stability is the dedication of his life to God, on whose instructions and gifts he must depend each day. If the first section explained Jesus' consciousness of himself as Messiah, the second explains his consciousness of his Passion. Of course this includes each step of the way to his being "received up" (see the discussion of vs. 51) by the Father, which is central to John (as early as John 3:14). Both themes are already announced in 9:22, 29–31, and Jesus' post-Easter ministry is now more clearly in view. In contrast to Mark 9:2— 10:52, Luke depicts Jesus as instructing both the crowd and his disciples. The motif of discipleship and mission is especially strong at the beginning (9:52, 57–62; 10:1; 14:25–33).

The structure of the section is difficult. The journey narrative has been called a "Christian Deuteronomy" on the basis of the following parallels: Deuteronomy 1:22–25/Luke 10:1, sending of messengers; 5:6–21; 6:4–5/10:27, ten commandments and the commandment to love God; 8:3/10:38–42," ". . . not by bread alone"; 9:10–13/11:14–26, obstinacy despite (the ten commandments written by) the finger of God; 12:1–16/11:37–44, purity before God; 12:17–28/12:13–34, responsible use of possessions; 13:6–11/12:51–53, division of families; 13:12–18/13:1–5, destruction of the wicked city and "all its inhabitants"; 15:1–18/13:10–17, release of debts in the seventh year/release of a sick woman on the seventh day; 18:15/13:31–35, a prophet (like Moses); 20:5–7/14:18–20, excuses (military service/banquet); 21:15—22:4/15:1–32, lost and found; 24:1—25:3/16:18–31, divorce and oppression of the poor; 26:12–18/18:12, tithes. But often these parallels are only associations, and many passages are not accounted for. Since the parallel Lukan passages derive in part from Q and in part from L, a prototype of the journey narrative more or less following the structure of Deuteronomy is also ruled out.

Similar themes are repeated, and a chiastic sequence can even be found: (A) 9:51–56, Jerusalem and God's judgment; (B) 9:57—10:24, discipleship; (C) 19:25–42, what must be done to inherit eternal life? (D) 11:1–13, prayer; (E) 11:14–36, signs of the present and coming kingdom; (F) 11:37—12:1, conflict with the Pharisees, true discipleship; (G) 12:2–34, faithful discipleship, use of money; (H) 12:35–59, readiness for the coming kingdom; (I) 13:1–9, call to Israel; (J) 13:10–21, healing on the sabbath, nature of the kingdom of God; (K) 13:22–35, God's judgment and Jerusalem; (J') 14:1–14, healing on the sabbath, nature of the Kingdom of God; (I') 14:15—15:32, call to Israel and outsiders; (H') 16:1–8, readiness for the coming kingdom; (G') 16:9–13, use of money, faithful discipleship; (F') 16:14—17:10, conflict with the Pharisees, true discipleship; (E') 17:11–37, signs of the present and coming kingdom; (D') 18:1–14, prayer; (C') 18:15–30, what must be done to inherit eternal life? (B') 18:31—19:10, discipleship; (A') 19:11–27 (or through 44?), Jerusalem and God's judgment. In this arrangement, too, some parallels are convincing, others less so. Other sayings are often interpolated or appended that do not strictly belong to the theme. Perhaps we may recognize that the middle (K) is framed by J and J', and that the theme BCD, D'C'B' is appropriate after the first and before the last mention of the journey to Jerusalem. In between come disputes with the Pharisees, instruction of the disciples, and eschatological discourses (F–H, H'–F'). The very long section I' differs from I in being expanded to include outsiders. The new beginning in 17:11 is left out of account; but Jerusalem is inserted by Luke in 17:11 before the first eschatological discourse and in 19:11 before the second. In both cases, too, the theme of the eschaton is taken up again in connection with that of faith and knowledge (18:8, 14; 19:41–44).

Starting with 18:15, the Markan outline determines the sequence but in such a way that the new life expected of the disciples is presented. For the story of Zacchaeus, the theme of discipleship and the localization in Jericho determine the place where it is interpolated. The journey of Jesus to Jerusalem is illuminated by its end in 19:10, and vs. 11 connects the story with vss. 12–27, a parable that protects Jesus' traveling from apocalyptic misinterpretation. Then 19:28 begins over again with its reference to the journey to Jerusalem. And so only a gross structuring is possible. This shows that Luke is primarily a traditionist and only as such also a narrator with a theological purpose.

# A. THE COMING KINGDOM
## CALL TO DISCIPLESHIP
## (9:51—11:36)

The refusal of hospitality and Jesus' awareness of God's patience in judgment (9:51–56) set the tone. Vss. 57–62 include the disciples in Jesus' fate. There is a corresponding passage (10:21–24) in praise of the God who calls the lowly. The sending of the seventy (10:1–12) is matched by their return (10:17–20). Their mission—after Herod's questions, the confession of Peter, the transfiguration, and the departure for Jerusalem—goes beyond that of the Twelve. The woes between sending and return (vss. 13–16) underline the seriousness of the impending decision. In 10:25–37, Jesus, in conversation with a Jewish lawyer who is open to the double command of love, stresses the importance of doing; in vss. 38–42, he stresses the importance of hearing his words. The manner of the disciples' prayer is distinguished in 11:1–13 from that of John's followers; the brevity of Jesus' prayer does not detract from its urgency. In 11:14–36, accusations against Jesus (vss. 14–26), mere enthusiasm (vss. 27–28), and misunderstanding of his saving work (vss. 29–36) are rejected. On the question of sources, see section 2 of the introduction to Matthew 11:21–24. The Q material was probably combined with L (9:52–56, 61–62; 10:29–42) even before Luke.

### To Jerusalem (9:51–56)
Cf. Mark 10:1; Matthew 19:1–2

⁵¹It happened, when the days of his death were fulfilled, he set his face to journey to Jerusalem. ⁵²And he sent messengers before him [his face], and they journeyed and entered a village of the Samaritans to prepare shelter for him. ⁵³And they would not receive him, because he [his face] was journeying toward Jerusalem. ⁵⁴And when his disciples James and John saw it, they said, "Lord, do you want us to bid fire come down from heaven and consume them?" ⁵⁵But he turned and threatened them. ⁵⁶And they journeyed to another village.

Vs. 51 constitutes the superscription for all that follows. It concentrates entirely on what Jesus does. In vs. 52a, Jesus sends forth his disciples, and in vs. 55 he rebukes them. In between we are told of their carrying out their commission (vs. 52b) and the suggestion made by two of them (vs. 54). Vs. 53, however, is in the singular and refers only to Jesus because his road to Jerusalem determines everything else. It is his decision to journey on. In vs. 56, Jesus and his disciples are combined for the first time as the subject of the sentence. Luke probably composed 9:51 as his equivalent to Mark 10:1; Mark 9:41–50 is replaced by Luke 17:1–2; 14:34–35 (q.v.). Vss. 52–53, 56, with their four "and" clauses, were probably in his sources (cf. also the end of the introduction to 5:1–11) although vs. 53b exhibits Lukan style.

[51] In biblical style, the "fulfillment" of the time appointed by God is emphasized (also Acts 2:1; cf. 7:23, 30; 9:23, 31; 24:27;

Luke 9:31; a different word is used in 1:23, 57; 2:6, 21–22). The Greek word translated "death" is ambiguous. Etymologically it means "taking up," and the corresponding verb is used for the ascension of Jesus or Elijah (Acts 1:11; 2 Kings 2:11; Ecclus. 48:9 [cf. 49:14]; 1 Macc. 2:58). Similar terminology appears also in chapter 24, albeit corrected by clear emphasis on the Passion (vss. 26, [39?], 46). But the noun means "death" (Ps. Sol. 4:18; Pseudo-Clement *Hom.* 3. 47). His death is also predicted in 9:31 (q.v.) and is the focus of the narrative (cf. the excursus following 22:30, a). But Luke is aware that the Passion leads to the ascension, and therefore uses a word that has overtones of both.

[53] It is not that the fate determined by God simply befalls Jesus. The statement that "his face" is journeying to Jerusalem emphasizes the conscious act of will with which he makes the goal his own. A similar expression is used of Absalom in 2 Samuel 17:11: "may your face go to battle with them." [51] In biblical usage, to "set one's face" toward someone or something means to "decide against" (Ezek. 6:2; 13:17; 14:8; 15:7; Jer. 3:12; 21:10); only once in the Hebrew text does it mean "decide" (2 Kings 12:18). But this usage is not sufficient to interpret Jesus' journey as a threat of judgment against Jerusalem. More to the point are the words of the servant of God in Isaiah 50:6–7, LXX: "I did not turn my face away from shame. . . . I set my face like a firm rock [upon God, my helper]." Ultimate security comes not from a fortress built upon a rock, but from rock-hard devotion to God. This is what makes Jesus so mobile, so open to all and to everything that he encounters, including changes of course (already in vs. 56). Jesus' "face" is mentioned three times in vss. 51–56; the verb "journey" appears four times, and is used also in 9:57; 10:38; 13:33; 17:11; 19:28, 36; 22:39; 24:28.

[52] On the Samaritans, see the discussion of Matthew 10:5. Ever since the destruction of their temple on Mount Gerizim in 128 B.C., their hostility toward Israel and their friendship with the Romans had been growing. Militarily impotent, they were able at least to play tricks on their enemies, as when they scattered bones of the dead throughout the Jerusalem temple to desecrate it (Josephus *Ant.* 18. 30).

[54] On James and John, see the discussion of Mark 3:17. Their suggestion immediately recalls 2 Kings 1:10, 12 and shows an as-

tonishing trust in the power of God, but Jesus is not Elijah. [55] Luke does include a story that describes Jesus' miracles as resembling those of Elisha (7:15; cf. 4:25–27) but never takes up this theme on his own. The rebuke of the disciples is as sharp as in 9:21, 42 (against a demon!) and Mark 8:33. The temptation to impose one's own will must be firmly rejected at the beginning of the road to the Passion. The question, "Do you not know what manner of spirit you are of?" and the words taken from Luke 19:10 are not found in the earliest manuscripts, but are highly appropriate as interpretations of Jesus' spirit.

It is easy to see why Jews would not be welcomed with open arms. They look on Samaritans as marginal believers at best, for whom there is no resurrection. No daughter of a Jewish house would ever marry one of them. But accepting their hospitality is something else again. Jesus, however, instead of attacking this "fringe group" with its borderline theology, turns upon two in his own group who exhibit an extraordinary faith in miracles but expect judgment upon others from Jesus. Just as he does not remain in the relative security of his house but sets forth instead on his journey, so too he cannot impose recognition on the part of others, thus remaining true to himself. He maintains the integrity of his own nature by *not* staying where he was yesterday and the day before. He maintains the integrity of his own worth by *not* caring what others think of him, but only God. He maintains the integrity of his own life by risking it and losing it in Jerusalem in order truly to gain it in the resurrection. His will to powerlessness stands in contrast to even the most "religious" (and admirable) sense of strength. This will of Jesus will triumph on the cross, where Jesus is wronged in a much more serious way. The Nazarenes prefigure the attitude of Jerusalem (4:28–30) although the Galileans are otherwise friendly toward Jesus; the Samaritans play the same role here, despite 10:33–35 and 17:16. There is no place for Jesus on either side—neither where the devout look down on the rest, nor where people are so convinced they are living as they ought that there is no need for the sanctimonious. In 9:54, as in 4:23, the emphasis is on what Jesus says and does, in contrast to the expectation of a miracle to fulfill one's own hopes.

**Discipleship (9:57–62)**
Cf. Matthew 8:18–22

[57]And as they were journeying along the road, someone said to him, "I will follow you wherever you go." [58]And Jesus said to him, "Foxes have holes, and birds of the air have nests, but the Son of Man has nowhere to lay his head." [59]But to another he said, "Follow me." But he said, "Let me first go and bury my father." [60]But he said to him, "Let the dead bury their dead; but as for you, go and proclaim the kingdom of God." [61]Yet another said, "I will follow you, Lord; but let me first say farewell to those in my house." [62]Jesus said, "No one who has put his hand to the plow and looks back is fit for the kingdom of God."

Readiness to follow Jesus as his disciple is met by his warning, in the third person with the Son of Man as subject (vss. 57–58); Jesus' call is met by a desire to compromise, which Jesus refuses in direct address (vss. 59–60); finally, the third potential disciple joins readiness with the desire to compromise, to which Jesus responds with a general rejection of all lukewarmness, stated in the third person with any potential disciple as subject. Vss. 57–60 derive from Q and also appear in Matthew 8:18–22 before the mission of the Twelve in 9:35—10:16 (see the discussion of Matthew 4:17—11:30). Vs. 61 exhibits Lukan style. The offer repeats vs. 57, the condition vs. 59*b*. The farewell to the family corresponds to Elisha's expressed desire; the call of Elisha (1 Kings 19:19–21) is suggested by the words "but let me first," which are already used by Q, and by the mention of the plow (vs. 62). The style of vs. 62 is not Luke's; the verse was undoubtedly already part of the tradition. In content it resembles certain Greek principles, perhaps already influenced by Jewish Christian thought: "When you go in to the sanctuary, do not turn back; . . . whoever sets out for God must not be held back by any internal conflict or human attitude" (Simplicius to Epictetus 74. 322). In contrast to vss. 57–60, metaphor and direct statement are intertwined at the end of the verse. Did Luke himself use vs. 61 to introduce this saying as a bridge to 10:1–12; or, since this is the only passage in which Jesus is likened to Elijah, did he merely rephrase this introduction, like those in vss. 57 and 59? The suggestion that

his purpose was to link prophetic solitude (vs. 58) and priestly proclamation (vs. 60*b*) with kingly authority (vs. 62) is unlikely.

[57–58] For the fifth time since vs. 51, Jesus' journeying is mentioned, lending topicality to his warning, which is identical with
Matthew 8:20 but not addressed to a scribe. [39] In contrast to Matthew 8:21 (q.v.), Jesus here calls someone to follow him. This is the
only instance in which the success of Jesus' authoritative call is not
reported (see the discussion of Mark 1:17, 20). Here, too, the wish
and Jesus' refusal correspond to Matthew 8:21–22. [60] But they
take on added weight in the light of Jesus' death (vs. 51) and the
call to preach the kingdom of God (10:9, 11!; see the discussion of
4:43).

It is human to yearn for the security of home, where the door can
be shut against all the demands of others, but Jesus is on his way to
Jerusalem to die. His only security is in God, his only home is God's
future. Therefore a house, to which it would be nice to retreat as a
fox retreats to its hole, makes discipleship impossible. Only a person
who is open to whatever comes can proclaim the kingdom of God.
Thus Jesus' journeying will live on in his disciples (cf. 23:26). [62]
The fact that God can heal the failure of a disciple and sow his seed
in very crooked furrows (22:32) does not cancel the radical nature
of the demand but rather keeps it from being honored—and written
off—as an unrealistic ideal (cf. also the discussion of Matt. 14:31;
5:48).

## Mission of the Seventy (10:1–16)
Cf. Matthew 9:37–38; 10:7–16, 40; 11:20–24

¹After this the Lord appointed seventy[-two] others and sent them
two by two ahead of him [before his face] into every city and to every
place where he himself intended to come. ²And he said to them, "The
harvest is plentiful, but the laborers are few. Pray therefore the Lord of
harvest to send out laborers into his harvest. ³Go; behold, I send you
out as lambs in the midst of wolves. ⁴Carry no purse, no bag, no sandals, and salute no one on the road. ⁵Whatever house you enter, first
say, 'Peace be to this house.' ⁶And if a son of peace is there, your peace

shall rest upon it. But if not, it shall return to you. ⁷Remain in that house; eat and drink whatever [is set before] you by them. For the laborer deserves his wages. Do not go from house to house. ⁸And whatever city you enter, if they receive you, eat what is set before you ⁹and heal the sick in it and say to them, 'The Kingdom of God has come near to you.' ¹⁰But whatever city you enter, if they do not receive you, go out into its streets and say, ¹¹'Even the dust of your town that clings to our feet, we shake off against you; but know this, that the kingdom of God has come near." ¹²I tell you, it shall be more tolerable on that day for Sodom that for that town.

¹³"Woe to you, Chorazin, woe to you, Bethsaida! For if the mighty works done in you had been done in Tyre and Sidon, they would have repented long ago, sitting in sackcloth and ashes. ¹⁴But it shall be more tolerable in the judgment for Tyre and Sidon than for you. ¹⁵And you, Capernaum, will you be exalted to heaven? You shall be brought down to Hades.

¹⁶"Whoever hears you, hears me, and whoever rejects you, rejects me, but whoever rejects me, rejects the one who sent me."

(Vs. 15—Isa. 14:13, 15.)

Cf. the introduction to Matthew 10:1–16, 40; 11:20–24; and Mark 6:7–13. Vs. 1 is a typically Lukan setting of the situation. "Two by two" and "places" recall Mark 6:7, 11. It is unclear whether the number seventy (or seventy-two) and the title "Lord" appeared in Luke's prototype; 22:35 (L) presupposes that the instructions in 10:4 were addressed to the Twelve. The programmatic statement in vs. 2 is followed by the sending (vss. 3–4), with directions for what to take (vs. 4) and how to act in house (vss. 6–7) and city (vss. 8–11). In the former, acceptance or rejection follow the greeting of peace (vss. 5–6); the right to receive hospitality comes afterward (vs. 7). In the latter, acceptance, the right to receive hospitality, and statement of salvation (vss. 8–9) are contrasted to rejection and statement of judgment (vss. 10–11). Vs. 12 threatens the rejecting city with judgment, illustrated by examples in vss. 13–15. Vs. 16 concludes the discourse with a fundamental statement concerning the authority of the messengers.

Was it Luke who introduced the "city" in vss. 8, 10–11 (cf. vs. 1) since there is substantial repetition? But the prophetic sign (vs. 11) makes sense only with reference to an entire locality. This means that house and city must have been distinguished already in Q, a distinction not made really clear in Mark 6:11 ("places"; cf. the discussion of Luke 9:5). Vss. 13–15 did not originally belong here; while the disciples are addressed in vss. 12 and 16, in 13–15 it is the three towns. Furthermore, these verses probably refer to the work of Jesus (as in Matt. 11:20), not that of the disciples (vs. 10). The parallel between vss. 12 and 14 probably led to the inclusion of these verses here even in Q. Luke may be responsible for adding the single saying in vs. 16 at this point. Mark 9:37 (Matt. 18:5; Luke 9:48) and Matthew 10:40 refer to the provision of food and lodging, Luke 10:16 to preaching (Lukan redaction, like vs. 17?). In other words, Luke incorporated the versions of Q and Mark separately in 9:1–6 and 10:1–11, as he did in 17:22–37/21:6–36 and 11:37–54/20:45–47.

[1] Jesus' magisterial act is emphasized: his own coming is announced by his messengers. They are nothing more than representatives of Jesus himself. Acts 9:4–5; 22:7–8; 26:14–15 similarly presuppose that whoever persecutes the disciples is battling against Jesus himself; and 18:10 states that he is himself at work in his people. Seventy is the number of the nations according to Genesis 10, Deuteronomy 32:8, and the rabbis (Israel a sheep among seventy wolves: Bill. 1. 754). The LXX, like many manuscripts of Luke 10:1, gives the number as seventy-two. Also possible are allusions to the seventy Israelites who went to Egypt (Exod. 1:5), the seventy elders (Exod. 24:1; Num. 11:16), or the seventy who translated the Old Testament in seventy days (Arist. 50, 307). Whether Luke had this in mind and, if so, whether he was thinking of the nations or Israel or the elders of Israel is hard to say. In addition, sending "two by two" would suggest thirty-five (or thirty-six) destinations, not the seventy places that might symbolize the nations. It is hard to conceive Jesus' really visiting so many sites.

[2–3] On vs. 2, compare the discussion of Matthew 9:37; on vs. 3, the discussion of Matthew 10:16a. The command to the disciples ("go") and their freedom from the burden of final responsibility ("pray the Lord") are closely intertwined. [4] As in Matthew 10:10 (q.v.) and in contrast to Mark 6:8–9 (q.v.), purse and sandals are also prohibited; in contrast to both passages, the reason is that whatever is not absolutely necessary merely gets in the way (cf. the discussion of 22:36). Only in Luke, as in 2 Kings 4:29, are the messengers forbidden even to greet others, so pressing is their errand. Luke, at least, is not suggesting that the kingdom of God is so close that a greeting on the way—which would be time-consuming in the Near East—might keep the disciples from arriving at their goal first. Probably the disciples are being distinguished by this conduct from other messengers: their commission from Jesus is so urgent that their language must not be reduced to polite formulas. In Acts 18:22, 20:1, 21:7, 19; 25:13, the word for "salute" that is used here means something like "visit" although in Luke 1:40 it clearly means "greet." The danger of stopping for a visit on the way would explain the warning but can hardly be accepted as the meaning of the text in the context of this discourse. **[5]** In any case, vs. 5 not only speaks of "greeting" (Matt. 10:12) but also describes the content of the disciples' proclamation. **[6]** The promise of the ultimate "peace" (2:14!) that brings salvation is conceived in such concrete terms (like the spirit in Num. 11:25 and 2 Kings 2:15) that it can rest upon a house or return to the disciples.

One must learn to see and evaluate the reality of peace or absence of peace upon a house, not just its visible advantages or disadvantages. Because such decisions are necessary, the preaching begins with a single house, indeed with a single "son of peace," a single individual who has been captured by the peace of God (cf. "those of the [divine] pleasure" in 2:14). The expression is without parallel (except Ps. 41:9, literally "man of my peace"). Did Jesus coin it, and as a Jew understand "peace" in the sense of all-embracing welfare? This says that all new life is ultimately God's act although without compulsion (see the discussion of Matt. 10:13). That the peace of an individual, his faith and his baptism, can also involve his house in salvation is shown by Acts 16:31.

**[7]** The missionary experience has shaped vs. 7. The basic principle of a right to "wages" (1 Tim. 5:18; contrast Matt. 10:10, "food") is hedged about with a warning against moving into more comfortable quarters (naturally not against preaching in other houses, vss. 5–6) and an exhortation to eat everything. The missionaries are therefore not to worry about food that is cultically unclean, which was forbidden the Jews. [8] Luke repeats the instructions in vs. 8, possibly because he is thinking already of non-Jewish cities. This became of incalculable importance later because it made possible the visible unity of the Christian community at meals and at the Lord's Supper (Gal. 2:12). Ecclesiastical traditions, customs, interpretations, racial segregation, which make this unity impossible, have no place in the body of Jesus' disciples. Preaching begins with the individual, but it cannot deny its claim to publicity. [9] Neither can a distinction be made between the welfare of the soul and the welfare of the body. The nearness of God's sovereignty that is proclaimed is now no longer temporal (as in Matt. 10:7) but spatial. In Jesus' acts it impinges on the bodies ("you") of those who allow themselves to be called to faith, to whom it is then "given" (12:32, with reference to the disciples [12:22]), and those who refuse it (cf. 11:20; 17:21). [10–11] In Jesus it is objectively present for both (end of vs. 11). Therefore the prophetic sign (see the discussion of Mark 6:11) is not only to be performed but to be pronounced publicly. Sign and word must go together. Thus the invitation to salvation becomes serious, and the possibility of repentance is kept open for those who have been warned. [12] Therefore a warning of judgment concludes the commission to the disciples. As in Matthew 11:24 (contra 10:15); Bill. 1. 574; 4. 1197); and Josephus *De bello judaico* 5. 566, "Gomorrah" is not mentioned.

[13] With vs. 13, Jesus turns to the towns that represent the three key locations of his ministry. Does Luke assume that he has returned from Samaria? But Luke rarely worries about geography. The verses agree almost verbatim with Matthew 11:21–23 (q.v.). Matthew 11:23b–24 is unnecessary in light of Luke's placing of them immediately after vs. 12. Their function in the Lukan context is probably to console the disciples for failures. Possibly the desire of the Gentiles to repent is also important to Luke (cf. 4:25–27).

[16] The summary conclusion clearly refers to the mission of the disciples (John 12:48; 1 Thess. 4:8; Jude 8 [cf. "Sodom" in vs. 7]; Hermas *Prayer* 3. 2). Vs. 16b is stated in strictly negative terms. Justin (*Apol.* 1. 63. 5; similarly, in combination with Matthew 7:21, 16:9–10) continues: "Whoever hears me, hears him who sent me"

(cf. Matt. 10:40). Perhaps there was a certain hesitation about identifying the word of the messengers so directly not only with the voice of Jesus but with the very word of God.

Of course Jesus, and thus God, speaks in the word of the messenger; it is therefore absolutely true that whoever totally rejects it rejects Jesus and with Jesus God, whose will it is to come in Jesus. But there are in fact no human words that can comprehend entirely what God says. Therefore the Spirit must speak at times in languages that are not humanly understandable, in the "tongues of angels" (Acts. 10:46; 19:6; 1 Cor. 13:1; 14:16, 23). This is a warning against the arrogance that finds the fault only in the hearer and not in one's own impure language, open far too little to the work of God. It is perhaps questionable whether people today can understand prophetic language at all. In any event, such language would necessarily be rooted in prayer, that is, in an awareness of constant dependence on God. The prophetic messengers are not meant to find a market for their own theories or ideas but to prepare the way for the coming of Jesus himself, the nature of which remains largely unknown to the envoys.

In Luke, Jesus is clearly journeying on the road to death. The important thing, therefore, is not triumphant missionary success but the chance to open others to *this* road, which often enough foregoes visible victories. In addition there is the sending "two by two," as a corrective to all self-aggrandizement and fixation on favorite notions, and the renunciation of all forms of security, including trust in advertizing, management, rhetoric, and mass enthusiasm.

At the same time, word and sign must go together. Of course an entire house can live in the blessing that flows from the faith of a single individual, as infant baptism is intended to express. But a church that ceases (in its baptismal practice, for example) to take seriously the fact of unbelief, whatever its basis, can itself no longer be taken seriously in its proclamation of belief and faith. It is not a church's job to decide who belongs here, who there, but healings and warnings against ignoring the kingdom of God, now coming, must illustrate what is at stake.

## The Fall of Satan (10:17–20)

[17]The seventy[-two] returned with joy and said, "Lord, even the demons are subject to us in your name." [18]And he said to them, "I saw Satan fall like lightning from heaven. [19]Behold, I have given you authority to tread upon serpents and scorpions, and over all the power of the enemy, and nothing shall hurt you. [20]Nevertheless do not rejoice in this, that the spirits are subject to you; but rejoice that your names are written in heaven."

Vs. 17a refers back to the preceding mission, not described (past tense), which has resulted in a discovery that remains still true (vs. 17b, present tense). Jesus speaks of the event that made this possible (vs. 19, past tense, subject = Jesus), which is based in turn on an even more fundamental event brought about by God (vs. 18, past tense). Vs. 20 returns to the subject of 17b (present tense) but surpassing it. Vss. 19a, 19c, 20b speak of benefits to the disciples, vss. 17b, 19b (and 20a in the present context) speak of the result that benefits others. The source of these statements is hard to determine. According to Luke, they now account for Jesus' rejoicing: "in that hour" (vs. 21) is a Lukan expression. In this case, vs. 17 is probably also his statement of the situation, constructed on the basis of the traditional saying in vs. 20, with "demons" replacing "spirits" (like 9:1, 42a; cf. 4:33 in contrast to Mark).

Deliverance from the fangs of serpents and scorpions is promised the righteous in Psalm 91:13 (Bill. 2. 168–69: Noah). A Jewish document speaks of serpents, scorpions, and evil spirits as a combination from which the redeemer will one day free the human race (Sifre Deut. 193), and according to the Testament of Levi 18:12, the "children" of the messianic high priest will have power to "tread" upon evil spirits. Originally, therefore vss. 19–20 say that the eschaton has come, the power of the evil one is broken, but God's election is more important than miraculous adventures. This fits well with vs. 18. Luke took these verses (together with vs. 16) and applied them to the missionary work of the disciples, probably interpolating in vs. 19 the disruptive phrase "and over all the power of the enemy" on the basis of 9:1 because the authority of the disciples to heal was more important to him than the fact that nothing could hurt them. It is easy to combine the two notions, as the Jewish citations and above all Mark 16:17–18 show.

Where does the vision of the fall of Satan come from? It could have been placed here even before Luke because vss. 15 and 18 are both based on Isaiah 14:12–15, where the story of Lucifer's fall is applied to the king of Babylon. That is why this section was not inserted earlier, at 9:10. If this is true, was it absent from Q or did Matthew 11:20–27 omit it? Does vs. 18, like Revelation 12:9, derive from the vision of a Christian prophet that was later put in the mouth of Jesus? But vs. 19 clearly refers to Jesus. Above all, the fall of Satan comes neither from Jewish tradition, which could make such a statement only with reference to the still future eschaton, nor from the Christian community, which would have to associate it with Jesus' descent from and ascent to heaven (Rev. 12:5!). Is the passage then based on something Jesus experienced, similar to the visions of the Old Testament prophets and above all the account in Mark 1:10 ("he saw the heavens open"), in which the presence of the eschatological kingdom of God (11:20; 17:21) finds expression in vivid imagery (cf. vss. 23–24)? It is characteristic of Jesus to echo Old Testament passages with a totally new interpretation (vss. 15 and 18). If so, Jesus had a vision of creation newly set free from Satan and placed under the sovereign authority of God, and experienced its reality in his ministry. This could even explain the juxtaposition of "eschatological" statements about the kingdom of God with "wisdom" aphorisms about trust in God's good creation (e.g., 12:6–7).

[17] The return of the messengers is described as joyful. Nothing is said about preaching or healing but only the experience of the reality of God. Exorcisms are mentioned in Matthew 10:8 but not in Luke's missionary discourse (or only in 9:1). The "name" of Jesus is important to Luke. When it is called upon in faith, Jesus' power is present. This is like an act done "in the king's name", but above all it is in line with the Old Testament conviction that the name of God describes divine presence among humankind (1 Kings 8:16–20). Whoever acts in the name of someone else so represents the other party that he is present in all matters of interest. Therefore Acts

4:12 (cf. 3:16) treats the "name" of Jesus and Jesus himself as equivalent. For Luke, miracle and teaching always go hand in hand (4:23–
27; 5:15, 17). They issue in the praise of God (see the discussion of
17:15) and faith (17:19; 4:23 before 5:1–11) and bear witness to
Jesus (7:21) because they go beyond what the prophets did (see the
discussion of 9:55; both 7:16 and 24:19 are statements from the mouths
of others).

[18] But it is Jesus' words that tell what actually happened. That
Satan originally dwelt in heaven, albeit as a messenger in the service
of God, is stated by writers from Job 1:6; 2:1 (cf. 1 Kings 22:21–22)
to John 12:31 and Revelation 12:7. Jesus sees the end of this state of
affairs. The Greek verb expresses a repeated act of seeing but the
form indicating a single isolated act had become rare, and an equivalent form did not exist in Aramaic. A battle between light and darkness is described in the Qumran documents and also in Jewish
apocalyptic (Sib. Or. 3:796–807; Asc. Moses 10:1–3). But here more
than hope is expressed: Jesus' eyes have opened to the reality of God
and already see Satan fallen. God is once again enthroned alone in
heaven (Ps. 33:14–15; 103:19). The part of God's work that had
seemed impenetrably dark and evil to human eyes has now come
basically to an end; God is shown unambiguously to act for good.
Of course Luke is not thinking of the fall described in Genesis 6:1–
4 but of what takes place in the ministry of Jesus. What has already
taken place in "heaven," i.e., in God's decision on behalf of human
salvation, is now to take effect on earth. The whole creation is re-
claimed for God's sovereignty, and there are those on earth who live
without care, like the flowers and birds (12:6–7, 24–27), who, like
God the creator, can encounter both the wicked and the good with
love (Matt. 5:45–47; Luke 6:35–36). Jewish wisdom had already
called for openness to the welfare of all on the grounds that the
world had been created for all; in Jesus, this call receives a totally
new foundation in God's absolute decision in favor of love, which
has dethroned Satan and thus directed all that takes place on earth
toward God's ultimate salvation.

[19] There are signs of such newness in the experience of those
who obey the call of Jesus. Of course it is only through the eyes of
Jesus that one can see something of this decision, which failure often

hides (vss. 13–15!). For Luke, such signs of the kingdom of God, as it breaks through and comes to people in the present, are more important than the temporal imminence of the end of the world.

[20] But vs. 20 also states a limit; signs of God's incursion merely point to the decisive fact. They are always ambiguous. The fact that they are "supernatural" proves nothing; only faith can see how God can use all the forces of creation, normal and totally abnormal, to effect salvation (Acts 28:3–6; also Gospel of Thomas 17; Acts of Thomas 33; cf. Lucian Pseudolog. 12). Therefore only one fact is crucial: that God has determined salvation for humankind. "It is not the expulsion of the devil but the presence of God that makes them rejoice" (Schlatter). The heavenly book is a common image (Dan. 12:1; Bk. Jub. 19:9; En. 47:3; 104:1, 3–4); Philippians 4:3 likewise speaks of Jesus' messengers being inscribed in it (cf. Rev. 3:5; 13:8; 20:15).

In the material incorporated by Luke we find the great joy over the salvation that has already begun in the ministry of Jesus (vss. 21–24). Luke has made this refer more clearly to the disciples' experiences rather than to their mission. He never mentions "preaching" (the noun *kerygma*) or "preachers." The speeches in Acts 2—5 are rather testimony to counter accusations than mission. The progress of the gospel to the nations is promised in 24:4; Acts 1:8, but not explicitly commanded: the Apostles remain in Jerusalem. But the Twelve, Paul, and Stephen are indeed "witnesses." The actual missionary period, which begins with Acts 9:15; 10:1–48, appears to be over for Luke (cf. the excursus following Luke 21:38, a). Nevertheless, 9:1–6 and 10:1–16 also have a present significance for Luke, in the responsibility of faith toward neighbors and friends, and in healings that show forth the power of Jesus. In any event, vs. 18 must not simply harden into a dogma that is believed but not experienced. On the other hand, vs. 20 warns against putting too much value on experience, which is always ambiguous. Jesus wants open eyes, which can see the reality of God at work behind outward events, without simply identifying this reality with outward success. This implies an amazing openness to creation, the dark and oppressive aspects of which are no longer demonic. There is still incomprehensible evil, but the disciple who has shared Jesus' experience of temptation and persecution can bear witness that even here can be seen the fall of Satan, enraged because his time is short (Rev. 12:12–13, 17). Luke—and the modern reader—can echo his words.

## The Presence of Salvation (10:21–24)
Cf. Matthew 11:25–27; 13:16–17

[21]In that hour Jesus rejoiced in the Holy Spirit and said, "I bless thee, Father, Lord of heaven and earth, that thou hast hidden these things from the wise and understanding and revealed them to babes. Yea, Father, for so it pleased thee. [22]All things have been delivered to me by my Father, and no one knows who the Son is except the Father, and who the Father is except the Son and anyone to whom the Son chooses to reveal him."

[23]And turning to his disciples in particular he said, "Blessed are the eyes which see what you see; [24]for I tell you, many prophets and kings desired to see what you see, and did not see it, and to hear what you hear, and did not hear it."

A Lukan introduction (vs. 21a) is followed by praise of God, with the motivation given in two antithetical parallel clauses introduced by "that" or "for" (the same word in Greek), and a concluding summary (vs. 21). The work of Jesus is not spoken of until vs. 22, with a reference to what God has done in the past and the resulting unity of Father and Son (present tense). The closing phrase opens this circle to the disciples, to whom vs. 23 accords the blessing whose grounds are given in vs. 24. The sayings were probably already placed here in Q; taken as a whole, they express Jesus' knowledge that the time of God is at hand (see the discussion of Matt. 11:20–24 and 25–27 [introduction], and 13:16).

[21] If "these things" in Q referred originally to the miracles mentioned in vss. 13–15, in the Lukan prototype the reference was to the fall of Satan, which Luke sees in the healings performed by the disciples (vs. 17). On the Holy Spirit, compare the discussions of 3:21–22; 4:1. The wordplay "hide/reveal" is clearer in the Greek of Luke than in Matthew 11:25. Marcion (see the discussion of 4:31)

omitted "and earth" because he distinguished the evil creator-god from the good redeemer-god.

[22] Vs. 22 uses the phrase "who the Son/Father is" instead of just "the Son/Father," thus putting more emphasis on revealed knowledge than on personal association (see the discussion of Matt. 11:27 and cf. 1QH 7:26). Luke 2:49 lends a special accent to this statement. Otherwise the verses agree verbatim with Matthew 11:25–27 (q.v.). [23] The transition to vs. 23 is un-Lukan, and so was probably already present in his sources (cf. 22:61). In contrast to Matthew 13:16–17, Luke 10:23 speaks only of seeing although "hearing" appears also in vs. 24. He does not say "*your* eyes," probably thinking also of later "disciples" (cf. the discussion of 10:17), even though he attached great importance to being an eyewitness (Acts 1:22) to Jesus' miracles. [24] Kings are mentioned together with the prophets (Isa. 52:15; 60:3; Matthew: "righteous")—those in whom God's acts became visible though they received only preliminary revelation.

The rejoicing of Jesus is here motivated directly by the power of God experienced by his disciples, the "babes." What took place can find expression only as praise of God, indeed according to Luke only "in the Holy Spirit," in God's own language. There are experiences that cannot be formulated with mathematical precision without falsifying them. But they can be expressed as prayer to God because God can understand what we want to say despite the insufficiency of human words. Someone who does not know that there is mystery, that there are immense areas of life closed to our knowledge and power of expression, may see what the disciples saw and yet not really see what has taken place. The disciples saw God himself in the work of Jesus, and understood Jesus' life to be the model and the measure for such divine activity. Therefore on their journey as messengers, separated from Jesus, they were allowed to recognize this same working of God (see Retrospect, especially section 3). Jesus rejoices at such "revelation." The term is therefore not limited to Jesus' contemporaries. On the problem of Father, Son, and Spirit, see the discussion of Matthew 28:19. In the context of Matthew 11—12, more emphasis is put on the proper recognition of Jesus as the Christ; Luke stresses above all God's incursion into the human world. The Lord's Prayer (Luke 11:2–4) was placed at this point in Q; in it the disciples are incorporated into the relationship between Jesus and his Father.

## The Chance to Love (10:25–37)
Cf. Mark 12:28–34; Matthew 22:34–40

²⁵And behold, a lawyer stood up to put him to the test, saying, "Teacher, what shall I do to inherit eternal life?" ²⁶He said to him, "What is written in the law? How do you read?" ²⁷And he answered and said, "You shall love the Lord your God with all your heart and with all your soul and with all your strength and with all your mind, and your neighbor as yourself." ²⁸And he said to him, "You have answered right; do this and you will live."

²⁹But he, desiring to justify himself, said to Jesus, "And who is my neighbor?" ³⁰Jesus took this up and said, "A certain person was going down from Jerusalem to Jericho and fell among robbers, who stripped him and beat him and departed, leaving him half dead. ³¹But by chance a priest was going down that road, and when he saw him he went by. ³²So likewise a Levite, when he came to the place and saw him, went by. ³³But a Samaritan, as he journeyed, came to where he was, and when he saw him he had compassion. ³⁴And he went to him, bound up his wounds, pouring on oil and wine, set him on his own beast, and brought him to an inn and took care of him. ³⁵And the next day he took out two denarii, gave them to the innkeeper, and said, 'Take care of him, and if you need anything more, I will repay you when I come back.' ³⁶Which of these three, do you think, proved neighbor to the one who fell among the robbers?" ³⁷And he said, "The one who showed mercy on him." And Jesus said to him, "You, too, go and do likewise."

(Vss. 27–28—Deut. 6:5; Lev. 19:18. Vs. 28—Lev. 18:5.)

The passage exhibits parallel structure. The lawyer's question (see the discussion of Matt. 22:35) is followed by Jesus' counterquestion (vss. 25/6 and 29/30–36); each is followed in turn by the lawyer's answer (27/37*a*) and Jesus' instruction (vss. 28/37*b*). The two sections formed a unit before Luke, as linguistic features show. Both lead up to Jesus' repeated command: "do" (vss. 28, 37*b*). Luke emphasizes this command through his redaction of vss. 25*b* ( = 18:18!)

and 37a (?). "Likewise" (vs. 37b) is un-Lukan but repeats the terminology of 6:31 and 10:32. Vss. 29–37 have been heavily edited by Luke but still exhibit un-Lukan features.

The narrative would speak for itself even without vss. 25–28, 36–37, for example in a situation where great importance was attached to cultic fulfillment of the law so that people like the Samaritans were excluded. Like 18:9–14 it is an extreme example, but compare 2 Chronicles 28:8–15. It starts with the person attacked by robbers (vs. 30) and tells of those who come upon him: three times someone comes, "sees" him, and "goes"—twice "by," the third time "to" him. The final encounter is developed in vss. 34–35 as full assistance. Vs. 33 is undoubtedly the turning point; but to take vss. 34a, 34b, and 35 as three states corresponding in reverse order to vss. 30, 31, and 32, so that vs. 33 becomes the central statement about Christ, is probably overreading. The story itself probably derives from Jesus although its form is different from that of the parables in Mark 4:1–32, etc.

The association of the story with the discussion about the greatest commandment (Mark 12:28–34) is pre-Lukan and emphasizes that God's love is expressed in love of others and therefore can know no limits; the question in vs. 29 is linguistically un-Lukan. Luke incorporates the entire unit but relates it more to the problem of knowing and doing. In Mark 12:32, the lawyer agrees with Jesus; Matthew eliminates this agreement; in Luke 10:27–28, Jesus agrees with the lawyer, who cites the double commandment himself.

[27] Luke assumes that the Jewish lawyer is familiar with this commandment, [25] and puts new emphasis on the lawyer's question about what must be "done" to inherit "eternal life." As in 18:18, it is for Luke a real, not academic, question. The statement that the lawyer was putting Jesus to the test was part of the tradition; Luke may have interpreted it in the sense of self-justification (vs. 29). The importance of the question accounts for the fact that love of God and love of neighbor now constitute a single commandment (cf. Mark 12:31; Matt. 22:39: two). The former is shown (only) in the latter. The affirmation of the uniqueness of God (Mark 12:29) is omitted because Jews, enlightened Gentiles, and Christians are agreed on

this point (cf. Acts 17:24–29 and the discussion of Matt. 22:40). [28] There is already theoretical agreement; what matters is how knowledge becomes practice. Instruction yields to story. [29] The counterquestion in vs. 29 could have been decisive: that is the heart of the matter, to see the place where the story that follows seeks to become true. But it is asked out of "self-justification" (see the discussion of 16:15 and 13:1–5). The questioner is concerned with the limits of the required love. He wants to stop where he is. He argues a lot to do a little. But Jesus wants to go forward with him, and the questioner once more becomes the questioned.

[30] The story Jesus tells is more of an exemplary narrative, aimed at producing conduct similar to what is described, but it cannot be distinguished strictly from a parable. It is as much a demand as a gift and an opening to free experience of reality. [31] The subject is "a certain person"; anyone may encounter this person. [32] The priest, God's professional servant, and the Levite, his subordinate, have fulfilled the law that defines their position; they have done what they have to do. They are impassioned fighters on behalf of God's honor, as are perhaps even the "robbers," the Zealots (see the discussion of Mark 3:18). And so they "see" the injured victim but not God, who waits within him, demanding and thus also giving.

[33] Next, in emphatic position at the beginning of the sentence, there appears "a Samaritan" (see the discussion of 9:52; 17:14), not a Jewish lay person, as one might expect. The Samaritan, who in the opinion of those listening to Jesus is ignorant of God's law, is as free to "have compassion" as Jesus himself (7:13; cf. 15:20). So love anticipates law. It is alive long before it might occur to its bearer that it is also demanded by the law (vs. 27). [34–35] It is not mere emotion but finds expression in the considered use of medical help. In addition to the direct ministrations of love, there is also room for indirect love through financial contributions—as long as help is really given. There is neither heroic accomplishment—the helper leaves and goes about his business—nor neglect of what is necessary. The one who needs help is the only law governing what is done. This should be obvious but it has been hidden from those who are under the power of the law by other "obvious facts"—for example, that Samaritans live outside the covenant of God. [36–37] And so even

in vs. 37*a* the lawyer will not mention the name. Therefore Jesus' question and command offer liberation. His story shows love to be the one necessary act, like faith in John 6:28-29.

The lawyer had asked, "Who is my neighbor?" As is true throughout the Old Testament, he sees his neighbor as the object of his actions. Jesus asks, "Who proved neighbor to the one who fell among the robbers?" A speculative question has been transformed: whoever is ready to prove neighbor to others will find those who need him and thus give to him everywhere. Therefore the victim is "a certain person," without further identification. The fact that a Samaritan finds him underlines the absence of limits. Who is a neighbor cannot, must not be defined; otherwise the neighbor would become an "object" of solicitude, and the door would be wide open for a humiliating "Christian charity" seeking a needy object for a good deed. Therefore the story forces the questioner to identify with one of the characters.

Other interpretations are less likely. It might be suggested that the parable is told from the standpoint of the victim; we are to identify with him. Even if this were correct, it would not be conclusive for the meaning of the story (see the end of the introduction to 15:11-32). Seen from this perspective, Jesus would be saying that non-Israelites who actually demonstrate love should be considered neighbors although the Old Testament limits this term to Israelites. Or one might stress that the priest came upon the victim "by chance" so that only God sends us our neighbors and we cannot define them ourselves. Or one might say that the questioner must think of himself as needing help and finding it where it was not expected: not in the temple cult but in Jesus.

Even more unlikely is the suggestion that the victim, rejected by Jews and accepted by Samaritans, represents the fate of Jesus. Certainly the religious boundary is broken through and the liberating gift of Jesus' message is central to the story but only in the sense that his invitation "do likewise" bestows both. "Grace" is not a theological concept to be acknowledged and accepted theoretically. It is something that happens—in Jesus' words, in such a way that his hearers are given a command to live by that frees them from fixed standards by which to judge themselves and compare themselves with the accomplishments of others. They may do what is obvious and thus become authentically human and find therein the meaning of their lives. They may accept themselves as they are and thus be set free for love of others. That this is not a burden but a liberation to live a meaningful life is the miracle of God's grace, which took form in Jesus' own ministry. This will be seen in the following section.

On Luke's understanding of the Law, compare the conclusion to 16:14–18 and the excursus after 21:24.

## The Chance to Have Faith (10:38–42)

38While they were journeying, he entered a village, and a woman named Martha received him into her house. 39And she had a sister called Mary, who also sat at the Lord's feet and listened to his word. 40But Martha was distracted with much serving. And she went to him and said, "Lord, do you not care that my sister has left me to serve alone? Tell her then to help me." 41But the Lord answered her and said, "Martha, Martha, you are anxious and troubled about many things, 42but one thing is needful; Mary has chosen the good portion, which shall not be taken away from her."

The episode, narrated in the aorist, is told entirely in terms of Jesus and Martha: Jesus came (vs. 38a); Martha received him (vs. 38b); she said, "Lord . . ." (vs. 41); he said, "Martha . . ." (vs. 42). In between and appended to the mention of Martha (vs. 39a), there is an account in the imperfect tense of Mary and her conduct (vs. 39b), contrasted once more with that of Martha (vs. 40a). Grammatically, Mary appears only as Martha's sister, with no part in the action, but she stands in the very center, and her focal position is declared by Jesus' concluding words. Here her conduct is described as an action (narrated in the aorist: "she has chosen"). Vs. 38 is thoroughly Lukan in style; the picture of Martha as mistress of a house inviting men to come in is almost inconceivable in Palestine (but see the discussion of 8:3). Vss. 39–41 contain un-Lukan elements, and the double form of address in vs. 41 is typically Palestinian (Luke 22:31; Acts 9:4; Bill. 1. 943; 2. 258). On Mary and Martha, see the discussion of 8:2.

[38] Journeying (see the discussion of 9:51) and visiting for a few hours go together (cf. the discussion of 14:1). The freedom Jesus gave women is reflected in this verse (see the discussion of 8:3). [39] It is appropriate to sit at the feet of a teacher (Acts 22:3; Bill.: "Let yourself be dusted with the dust of their feet"), but no real rabbi would teach a woman. But this does happen in the community of Jesus, where one speaks of "hearing the word of the Lord." [40] As Martha's use of "Lord" as a form of address shows, this refers not simply to the Lord of all but to one whom Martha and Mary look upon personally as *their* Lord. Nothing is said about whether Martha is thinking egoistically of herself or altruistically of seeing that Jesus and his companions finally get some supper. Is Luke still aware that there must have been nearly a hundred of them (cf. 10:1)? Martha's anxiety (cf. 12:22) is as culpable as her serving is laudable (4:39; 8:3; cf. Mark 10:43, 45!). [41] The "many things" that certainly have their place must be kept in proper relationship [42] to the "one thing" necessary, the event of the word of Jesus. This is the correct reading, attested by the earliest manuscripts. The reading "few things" means only that Jesus would be content with a simple supper, and the reading "few things, or [actually only] one" combines both ideas. In vs. 40, Martha's "much" serving is set in contrast to her being "alone"; here the "many things" are set in contrast to the one thing needful: hearing the word of Jesus, which provides a very different kind of nourishment. This is what Mary "has chosen" in contrast to Martha; only this interpretation explains the term "needful" (not: "sufficient").

Although Jesus is often served, it is ultimately always he who serves (12:37; 22:27). It is therefore not enough that love of God (vss. 38–42) be joined to love of neighbor (vss. 29–37). The one thing needful is Jesus' own service as the source of all action. To receive Jesus (cf. 19:6) means to receive his word (8:13; Mark 4:20) and allow oneself to be healed by it. Luke 19:1–10 shows that this has nothing to do with passive mysticism in contrast to active praxis but with a praxis that comes from hearing in which Jesus may be Lord.

## The Chance to Pray (11:1–13)
Cf. Matthew 6:9–13; 7:7–11

¹And it happened, when he was praying in a certain place and ceased, one of his disciples said to him, "Lord, teach us to pray, as John taught his disciples." ²And he said to them, "When you pray, say:
'Father, hallowed be thy name, thy kingdom come, ³give us each day our bread for the morrow, ⁴and forgive us our sins, for we ourselves forgive everyone who is indebted to us, and lead us not into temptation.'"
⁵And he said to them, "Which of you will have a friend and go to him at midnight and say to him, 'Friend, I need three loaves, ⁶for a friend of mine has arrived on a journey and I have nothing to offer him,' ⁷and he will answer from within and say, 'Do not bother me; the door is now shut, and my children are with me in bed; I cannot get up and give you anything'? ⁸I tell you, though he will not get up and give him anything because he is his friend, yet because of his importunity he will rise to give him whatever he needs. ⁹And I tell you: Ask, and it will be given you; seek, and you will find; knock, and it will be opened to you; ¹⁰for every one who asks receives, and he who seeks finds, and to him who knocks it will be opened. ¹¹Or what kind of a father among you, if his son asks for a fish, will instead of a fish give him a serpent? ¹²Or if he asks for an egg, will he give him a scorpion? ¹³Now if you, who are evil, know how to give good gifts to your children, how much more will the Father from heaven give the Holy Spirit to them who ask him?"

The attitude recommended in 10:42 is represented in 11:1–13 as instruction in prayer. The Q material in vss. 2–4 and the somewhat modified parable in vss. 9–13 were supplemented before Luke by the addition of vss. 5–8, a further parable providing a good illustration for vss. 9–10. Thus the specific instruction in prayer is followed by general instruction, set in the framework of two parables. For a discussion of the Lord's Prayer, see Matthew 6:7–13.

[1] The introduction in vs. 1 comes from Luke, for whom Jesus' own prayer is important as the source of all prayer on the part of his

disciples (see the discussion of 6:12). For "someone" from within or without the circle of disciples (9:57; 11:15; 21:5, 7, always contra Mark or Matthew; cf. 10:25; 20:27) to pose a question directly or indirectly through his conduct, and thus initiate Jesus' instruction, is typically Lukan (11:27, 45; 12:13, 41; 13:1, 23, 31; 14:15; 15:2; 16:14; 17:5, 20; 18:9; 19:11, 39; 22:24, 49; 23:27). This structure is based on the insight that, just as Paul writes his letters in response to practical problems, Jesus does not lecture about universal truths but rather seeks to help specific individuals to make sense of their lives in concrete situations. Apart from the situation, his truths can become falsehood: 10:37 is not addressed to Martha, and 10:42 is not addressed to the lawyer. At the same time, Luke recognizes the similarities and differences between the disciples of Jesus and the disciples of John (cf. the conclusion to 3:15–20 and 5:33), without turning the latter into heretics. Acts 18:25 and 19:1–3 also look upon them as potential Christians, while emphasizing that one must not stop there. This was obviously an important consideration in the time of Luke.

[2–4] In the Lukan form of the Lord's Prayer, the first three petitions (in reverse order) counter the three temptations of Jesus (4:1–12); the conclusion of the temptation narrative (4:13) corresponds to the last petition. The disciples of Jesus are to be protected from temptation (singular), however much they must stand by their faith in all kinds of temptations (plural; see the discussion of 4:13). It is important to Luke that the community lives by Jesus' instruction in prayer and that it shapes their entire life. Therefore prayer includes both the great purposes of God and the necessities of everyday life (cf. the discussion of 9:23).

[5–8] The parable (vss. 5–8) is conceived entirely as question (vss. 5–7; cf. the discussion of Matt. 12:11) and answer (vs. 8). The action of the petitioner (5a) has its counterpart in the answer in the action of his friend (vs. 8b), just as there is a correspondence between the words of the petitioner (vss. 5b–6) and the (unexpected) response of his friend (vs. 7). The frequent use of Semitic coordination with "and" (instead of subordinate, casual, and concessive constructions) can hardly be due to Luke. Like vss. 9–13 (13b explicitly), the parable emphasizes the confident expectation of the petitioner. [5] The question at the beginning underlines the naturalness of the expectation: the other person is a friend, not a neighbor picked at random; stores do not exist. Three loaves are the usual ration. The not-quite-accurate future tense "will have" in vs. 5, like that in vs. 8, may suggest future situations in which Jesus' disciples will be making similar requests. The question (vs. 5a) invites the hearer to identify with the petitioner; the translation "and he [the friend in need] comes to him . . ." would be very strange. [8] Nevertheless, the concluding sentence mentions only the friend, who provides "everything needed." The question in vs. 11 also points to the donor. It is this very knowledge that gives the petitioner confidence. God is present for those who know how much they need God. Vs. 8b, it is true, ascribes this to the importunity of the request (as in 18:1–8 [q.v.]; 21:36 = L?). The parable itself, however, says nothing about "repeated" knocking. Thus the tone shifts in vs. 8b to admonition, which would of course be pointless without confidence in the friend, unless one were to translate (referring to the friend): "so as not to stand there impudently." But that is hardly possible linguistically and out of place in meaning.

[9–13] Vss. 9–10 and 13 are preserved almost identically in Matthew 7:7–11 (q.v.). But the Lukan context is concerned entirely with prayer. In Matthew 6:1–18, almsgiving and fasting are also discussed, and in Matthew 7:7–11 other admonitions are included, which are summarized in the golden rule (Matt. 7:12). The anacoluthon (vs. 11a, first the son, then the father as subject) shows how important the introduction of the "father" was to the (pre-Lukan?) narrator. Luke mentions the Holy Spirit (vs. 13) because for him the Spirit represents the embodiment of all that is good (cf. Matt. 7:11 and the discussion of 3:21–22) and because he knows how ambiguous all "good things" are (12:18–19; 16:25; contrast 1:53). The gift of the Spirit sums up all that is given to the community of Jesus: joy, strength, courage for witness and therefore for life.

Prayer for the coming of God's kingdom (vs. 2), which, unlike the gift of the Holy Spirit, remains in the future, is thus more concerned with what the community will need in the temptations to come (cf. the discussion of 4:13; 22:28) than with the "Come, Lord" of 1 Corinthians 16:22 and Revelation 22:20 (cf. the discussion of Luke 18:8). Knowledge of parents (vs. 11) and knowledge of friends (vs. 5) are both cited; they encourage us to pray and to expect God's gracious response. Both parables appear to state the obvious—but only on the assumption that God is "friend" and "father" to humankind. For this very reason, they can come only from the mouth of Jesus. Like Jesus' own prayer (vs. 1), the prayer of the disciples can constantly accompany their new life (vs. 8; 18:1). God can use this prayer to open new paths (Acts 1:14, 24; 6:6, 8:15; 10:9; 13:3). And so this section involves the disciples—and thus also the readers—not only in Jesus' life with God but even in God's work on earth.

## The Chance to Encounter Jesus (11:14–36)
Cf. Mark 3:22–27; 4:21; Matthew 5:15; 6:22–23; 12:22–30, 38–45

[14]Now he was casting out a demon, and it was dumb. But it happened that the demon came out and the dumb man spoke. The crowd was astonished. [15]But some of them said, "He casts out demons by Beelzebul, the prince of demons"; [16]while others, tempting him, sought from him a sign from heaven. [17]But he, knowing their thoughts, said to them, "Every kingdom divided against itself is laid waste, and house falls upon house. [18]And if Satan also is divided against himself, how will his kingdom stand? For you say I cast out demons by Beelzebul. [19]But if I cast out demons by Beelzebul, by whom do your sons cast them out? Therefore they shall be your judges. [20]But if it is by the finger of God that I cast out demons, then the kingdom of God has come upon you. [21]When a strong man, fully armed, guards his own palace, his goods are in peace. [22]But when one comes who is stronger than he and overcomes him, he takes away his armor in which he trusted and divides his spoil. [23]Whoever is not with me is against me, and whoever does not gather with me scatters.

[24]When the unclean spirit goes out of a person, he passes through waterless places seeking rest and does not find it. He says, 'I will return to my house from which I came.' [25]And he comes and finds it swept and put in order. [26]Then he goes and brings seven other spirits more evil than himself; and they enter and dwell there; and the end of that person is worse than the beginning."

[27]Now it happened, when he said this, a woman in the crowd raised her voice and said to him, "Blessed is the womb that bore you and the

breasts that you sucked." 28But he said, "Blessed rather are those who hear the word of God and keep it!"

29But when the crowd gathered, he began to say, "This generation is an evil generation; it seeks a sign, and no sign shall be given to it except the sign of Jonah; 30for as Jonah became a sign to the inhabitants of Nineveh, so will the Son of Man be to this generation. 31The queen of the south will arise at the judgment with the men of this generation and condemn them; for she came from the ends of the earth to hear the wisdom of Solomon, and behold, something greater than Solomon is here. 32The men of Nineveh will arise at the judgment with this generation and condemn it; for they repented at the preaching of Jonah, and behold, something greater than Jonah is here.

33"No one takes a lamp and puts it in a cellar or under a bushel, but on a stand, that those who enter may see the light. 34Your eye is the lamp of your body. If your eye is clear, your whole body is light. But if it is evil, your body is dark. 35Look therefore lest the light in you be darkness. 36If then your whole body is light and has no dark part, it will be wholly light when the lamp illuminates you with its rays."

(Vs. 31—1 Kings 10:1–13. Vs. 32—Jonah 3.)

In contrast to the Holy Spirit (vs. 13), an unclean spirit is introduced (vs. 14), whom Jesus drives out with the finger (Matthew: spirit) of God. The occasion (vs. 14) leads to a corresponding charge (vs. 15) and a counterquestion addressed by Jesus to his opponents (vs. 19). There follow, as in Matthew 12:28–30, a positive answer (vs. 20), a cryptic reference to what is really happening in Jesus (vss. 21–22), and a warning (vs. 23). The saying about the return of the unclean spirit probably came at this point in Q (see the introduction to Matt. 12:43–45). Vss. 27–28 appear to be a Lukan interpolation, while vss. 29–32 and perhaps also vss. 33–36 belong to Q.

[16] Going beyond Matthew 12:22–28 (q.v.), Luke uses vs. 16 (Mark 8:11) to set the stage for vss. 29–32 (Q); he treats everything through vs. 36 as a unit. The basic attitude of the people (not the Pharisees, as in Matt. 12:24, 38) is important to him (cf. vs. 23). Or did Q already contain a similar statement, [17] perhaps together with the expression "against itself" in vs. 17, which is closer to Mark 3:24? The image is more compact than in Mark 3:24–25; Matthew

12:25; when the "kingdom" falls, so do the "houses." **[18]** Vs. 18*b*, with its good Greek construction, probably comes from Luke; **[20]** on vs. 20, see the discussion of Matthew 12:28. **[21]** In comparison with Mark 3:27 (q.v.), vss. 21–22 are substantially expanded, which probably goes back to Q (see the introduction to Matt. 12:29). **[22]** This is also suggested by the echoes of Isaiah 49:25; 53:12 toward the end of vs. 22; Luke generally omits such features (see the discussion of 23:35). Here it is no longer a householder but an armed man (a giant in Isa. 49:25) guarding a fortress who is captured and has his property divided. This places even more emphasis on the "someone" (no article!) who is stronger, who brings "peace" through his "victory" and vanquishes a false confidence based on possessions.

The crucial question is what one "trusts" in (vs. 22): that which appears to give security, or the "finger of God" seen by the psalmist in creation (Ps. 8:4) and by the historian in Israel's historic destiny (Exod. 8:19), which can only be prayed for (11:1–13) and to which eyes can be opened (10:23). The image makes its two points with almost perfect clarity: God really intervenes in the human world and is at the same time infinitely greater than anything we have eyes to see.

**[23–26]** Luke probably thinks of the gathering of the community in vs. 23 (12:32). Vss. 24–26 are almost identical to Matthew 12:43–45 (q.v.) and are hardly to be understood in a different sense, as referring to exorcisms (vs. 19). They are not meant to call into question Jesus' victory over the "strong man" (vss. 21–22) but to underline his warning to his listeners (vs. 23). Even personal experience of one of Jesus' miracles (vs. 20) is no guarantee (cf. 17:11–19). No one can remain neutral like an empty house; either the Holy Spirit (1 Cor. 6:19) or an unclean spirit will dwell there.

**[27–28]** But Luke also seeks to show in positive terms how the right decision is made, just as at the end of the parable of the sower, after warnings about the judgment (8:16–18; cf. 11:33), he emphasizes that even being a blood relative of Jesus is of no value but only hearing and keeping the word of God. In Mark 3:20–35, too, the discussion about Beelzebul is joined with the saying about the true family of those who hear God's word. The blessing of Jesus' mother's womb and breasts (also Jewish: Bill.; see Apoc. Bar. 54:10) is an indirect way of paying homage to Jesus himself; it can hardly be cited as evidence for incipient mariolatry (but cf. the discussion of Mark 3:33). The Greek word translated as "rather" can amend the previous statement or reinforce it. In any case, the point is that mere Jesus cult and Jesus enthusiasm are worthless (cf. 6:46); what matters is the readiness to hear in him the word of God and to hold fast to it (with Mary as a possible model: 2:19, 51).

[29–32] On the source and interpretation of vss. 29–32, see the discussion of Matthew 12:38–42 and the introduction to Mark 8:11–13. Just as Jonah became a sign through his proclamation of the word of God (cf. vs. 28) that called to repentance, so too does Jesus—albeit a "sign that is spoken against" (2:34!). There is no suggestion of a new offer after Easter; vs. 32 ends with a reference to the judgment upon "this generation." The purpose of the saying is nevertheless to call to repentance. The hopeless statement "So [like the man possessed by seven demons] shall it be with this evil generation" (Matt. 12:45) is omitted in vs. 26, and the urgent reference to Jesus ("Something greater than Jonah is here") leads up to [33] the image of the light that all are to see (vs. 33). It probably came here in Q. Luke presumably added the "cellar" of the Greco-Roman house, where a light would, in fact, be needed (or should the text be translated "into concealment"?). The verse refers to Jesus but in a different way from 8:16 (q.v.). Beginning with 10:25, Luke has been emphasizing that everyone must make a decision, enter (into the circle of disciples or the community?) and stand in the light of Jesus. [34–36] This is underlined by vss. 34–35 (Matt. 6:22–23, q.v.) and the additional vs. 36. Only clear and open eyes can see the light in such a way that it can permeate the entire person. Only the eyes determine whether one can see as a whole person. And so vss. 34–35 call for wholehearted openness to Jesus. In this context, it is not riches and possessions that could prevent this (as in Matt. 6:19–21, 24; cf. Luke 12:13–15) but the lack of faith described in vss. 14–32. [36] Vs. 36 appears to say only, "If you are light, you are light." Since the future tense appears only here (= Matt. 6:22!), the reference may be to the last judgment, in which the light (literally "lightning") of Jesus (17:24) fills with eternal glory those in whom the light of Jesus already dwells. [35] In any event, the "light in you" is emphasized once more. According to Proverbs 20:27 LXX, "the light of the Lord is the breath of life of humankind"; according to the Qumran Manual of Discipline (1QS 3:1, 7; 4:2) repentance and reconciliation allow the light of life to be seen, and the good spirit illuminates the heart. Philo (*Creation*, 53–54) teaches that light creates the power of human vision, using this as an image of God, who gives the power to think correctly. Here, however, Luke is not talking about knowing an idea but about the presence of God in Jesus and the illumination of the entire person reached by the light of Jesus. Therefore he uses the much more vivid image of the light that dwells within (in contrast to vss. 24–26).

The section closes, not with a warning about total darkness (Matt. 6:23), but with a promise. Even in its admonishing and warning sections, the text refers to the stronger person who has overcome the strong person (vss. 21–22), who is rightly understood only as God's direct word to all (vs. 28) and is therefore a sign above all kings and prophets (vss. 29–32), the light that permeates everything (vss. 33–36). The question is whether we will receive the gift of clear eyes or simply incorporate what happens in Jesus into our familiar categories (vs. 15) because we have forgotten how to be astonished (vs. 14) and no longer expect God's finger to enter this world and touch us (vs. 20).

# B. TRUE DISCIPLESHIP IN CONTRAST TO PHARISEES AND SCRIBES (11:37—12:59)

In 11:37—12:1, the battle is joined against Pharisees and scribes; 12:1, with its change of audience, points ahead to the instruction of the disciples in 12:2–34. Jesus calls all to be free from possessions (12:13–21, in response to an outsider's request). For the disciples (vss. 1, 4, 22, 32) this becomes a demand that they not be anxious even when their lives are at stake. This leads up to the eschatological discourse in vss. 35–59, which is addressed at first to the disciples (see the discussion of vss. 41 and 42) but ends with an appeal to all (vss. 54–59).

## Conflict with Pharisees and Scribes (11:37—12:1)
Cf. Matthew 23:1–36; Mark 7:1–5; 12:38–39

37While he was speaking, a Pharisee asks him to lunch with him. So he entered and reclined at table. 38Seeing this the Pharisee was astonished that he did not first wash before lunching. 39And the Lord said to him, "Now you Pharisees, you cleanse the outside of the cup and of the dish, but your inside is full of extortion and wickedness. 40You fools! Did not he who made the outside make the inside also? 41But give for alms those things that are within, and behold, everything will be clean to you.

42"But woe to you Pharisees, for you tithe mint and rue and every herb, and neglect justice and the love of God. These should be done and the others not neglected. 43Woe to you Pharisees, for you love the best seat in the synagogues and salutations in the market places. 44Woe to you, for you are like unseen graves, and the people who walk over them do not know it."

45One of the lawyers answered and said to him, "Teacher, in saying this you reproach us also." 46And he said, "Woe to you lawyers also, for you load people with burdens hard to bear, and you yourselves do not touch the burden with one of your fingers. 47Woe to you, for you build the tombs of the prophets, but your fathers killed them. 48So you are witnesses and take pleasure in the deeds of your fathers, for they killed them, but you build. 49Therefore the Wisdom of God said, 'I will send them prophets and Apostles, and some of them they will kill and persecute,' 50that the blood of all the prophets, shed from the foundation of the world, may be required of this generation, 51from the blood of Abel to the blood of Zechariah, who perished between the altar and the house [of the temple]. And I tell you, it shall be required of this generation. 52Woe to you lawyers, for you have taken away the key of knowledge. You yourselves will not enter, and you hindered those who wanted to enter."

53And when he went away from there, the scribes and the Pharisees began to press him hard, and to provoke him to speak of many things 54and to lie in wait for him to catch at something he might say. 1But since an enormous crowd, tens of thousands, was gathering, so that they were stepping on each other's feet, he began to say to his disciples, "Beware above all of the leaven, the hypocrisy of the Pharisees."

(Vs. 51—2 Chron. 24:20–22.)

The woes collected here appear also in Matthew 23 (q.v., especially the discussion of vss. 13–33). Luke found them in Q. The mealtime setting, with its striking use of the present tense (see the introduction to 16:23) in vs. 37, must also have been in Luke's sources as is indicated by some striking connections with Mark 7:4. It is possible that a saying like Luke 11:39 was, in one tradition, transformed at an early date into a woe (Matt. 23:25) and, in the other, incorporated into the way of life of Jesus and his disciples through the statement that they did not wash their hands (Mark 7:2; Luke 11:38; cf. the antithesis between inside and outside in Mark 7:14–23). At one time, vss. 49–51 in combination with the saying about Jerusalem in 13:34–35 constituted the conclusion of the woe discourse, as in Matthew 23:34–39 (q.v.). Luke had to move this to chapter 13 since in his account, in contrast to Matthew 23, Jesus is not yet in Jerusalem. Finally, 12:1 concludes the conflict with the Pharisees although it also introduces a new beginning. Echoes of Matthew 16:6, 11 suggest that the saying at one time appeared in Q, possibly at the end of the woe discourse (see the discussion of Luke 20:46).

[37] The invitation extended by the Pharisee (see the discussion of 14:1) exhibits a certain openness (see the discussion of 13:31). [40] Therefore Jesus does not begin with a "Woe . . . ," but with a reference to the Creator, which must have been especially appealing to the Pharisee. If cups are subject to the sovereignty of God, how much more so are hearts! This is so obvious that the Pharisee must agree if he is not to remain a "fool," a person blind to God (Ps. 14:1; 53:2; 92:7; 94:8; Bill. 1. 280; cf. 2. 102). To refuse to see a person as a whole, to separate the outward from the inward act, is in this broad sense foolish stupidity. Similar statements can be found in Jewish documents (Asc. Moses 7:7–10: "full of offenses and unrighteousness . . . hands and heart unclean . . ." and yet: ". . . do not touch me, lest you make me unclean"; cf. the "scribes" *ibid.*, 5:5).

This cuts the ground out from under any spirituality that relies on cultic fulfillment of all requirements. What Jesus expects is far more, and it is never possible to say that one has done everything required.

[41] Almsgiving (an un-Lukan term, like the Greek word for "but" used to begin the clause) was important to Luke's source as a way of giving the reader concrete assistance. Unless we adopt the rather forced translation "that which concerns what is within" (you), what is "within" can refer only to the contents of the cup; a person cannot give what is "within" as "alms." In Luke's source, therefore, vs. 39b (without "your") and vs. 41, like Matthew 23:25–26, referred to the contents of the cup which had been acquired dishonestly; Luke made it refer to the individual, who is to give himself, his heart. Luke is therefore probably also responsible for the summary abolishing every form of legalism, the statement that everything is clean to someone who is fundamentally clean (cf. Mark 7:15) because one practices love (cf. Rom. 14:14, 20, 23: because one has faith in God's justification; Tit. 1:15: because one is no longer under the law).

[42] With vs. 42 (Matt. 23:23, q.v., introduction and discussion) we leave the question of cleanness. "Neglect," literally "pass by," is a vivid image. In addition to "love" (and "alms") there is "justice" for others, which cannot be ignored. But our passage does not say that these are the weightier matters of the law (Matt. 23:23). And in contrast to Marcion (see the discussion of 4:31), who omits the final clause, conventional piety is not disparaged but called to see its implications.

[43] Vs. 43 (see the introduction above) would be more appropriately addressed to the lawyers (Mark 12:38–39 [q.v.], referring to them). Self-love, which is interested in superiority to others, makes real love impossible. [44] Vs. 44 is thinking of graves in the earth (contrast Matt. 23:27–28); the fact that they render those who come in contact with them unclean must be inferred from Matthew. It remains dubious whether there is an Aramaic word involved meaning "whitewashed" or "unknown."

[45] The lawyer may be introduced because vs. 46 will go on from ethical conduct to doctrine, in fact to that much more fundamental question of the authority of Scripture. After all, these precepts are in the Bible! [46] Therefore the saying in Matthew 23:4 is not in-

cluded in the woes. Luke solves the problem along the lines of Acts 15:10–11: as the lawyers interpret the Bible, no one can fulfill these commandments. Here, though, Luke does not mention the "grace of the Lord." It is found throughout the entire Gospel.

[47–48] The logic of vss. 47–48 is unclear. Are they boasting of their cult of the prophets instead of repenting? Or is the passage trying to say that they do not listen to the prophets or even that they are building the tombs of the prophets through their dead interpretation, or are paying homage to *dead* prophets in a religion that only worships the sacred past? Acts 2:29–31 calls in a similar way for those addressed to advance beyond the tomb of David to the message he prophesied: the raising of Jesus.

[49–51] This becomes clearer in vss. 49–51. Vss. 50–51 speak of the prophets within the period defined by the Old Testament canon. But Luke emphasizes that the persecution of Jesus (13:33) and his Apostles (11:49; cf. the discussion of 6:13), who are one with him, brings about the climactic judgment—for Luke the destruction of Jerusalem. What Matthew 23:34–39 predicts as an eschatological event has already taken place (see the discussion of 13:35). They will suffer the fate of the prophets (cf. the discussion of 13:33). Because Jesus is among the persecuted, not the persecutors, he speaks of "your" fathers (vs. 47).

[52] Vs. 52 concludes emphatically with the question of right knowledge (of Scripture) (cf. 1QH 4:11). Is the "key" that which opens the Scriptures or the key, given by the Scriptures, to the kingdom of God? More likely the latter (as in Matt. 23:13, q.v.), for the image of "entering into knowledge" would be odd although the saying is so abbreviated that it has become obscure.

[53–54] Luke brings this section to a close with a summary comment about the hostility of the scribes and Pharisees, which does not go as far as Mark 3:6 (see the discussion of Luke 6:11), whether one translates "press hard" or "aim at" (either is possible), and a warning against them.

[1] On the alternation between the disciples and the people, see the discussion of 6:20a. The word "above all," which can also mean "first," could belong to the previous clause. "Tens of thousands," as in Josephus (and Acts 21:20) is not to be taken literally. Originally

"hypocrisy" (cf. the discussion of Matt. 6:2) referred clearly to false doctrine (also in Mark 7:6 and 1 Tim. 4:2). This is included here and in 13:15, but 12:56 (and 6:42 Q; also 1 Pet. 2:1) does not limit hypocrisy to Jesus' Pharisaic opponents. Luke is thinking rather of an inconsistent life in which faith is not everywhere present (11:34–26), of an incongruity between knowledge and action that prevents people from living as whole human beings (cf. already Job 34:30; 36:13 LXX).

Against a life that involves a person totally, Luke sets a purely outward observance of specific regulations but without defending a purely inward disposition. It is to be a life that finds expression in almsgiving (vs. 41) and in renunciation of the trappings of success (vs. 43)—in sum, in standing up for the rights of others and loving them (vs. 42). The charge of "hypocrisy" (Matthew) is omitted but is added in 12:1; and vs. 44 describes the condition of a person whose evil is no longer visible, either to himself or others. Ultimately the question is how Scripture should be interpreted as a whole, as the shift to the lawyers shows. They prevent the right understanding of the commandments, which are intended not to oppress (vs. 46) but to open the kingdom of God (vs. 52). This understanding of Scripture is made possible only because Jesus and his messengers follow the road of the prophets, who were constantly persecuted and killed (vss. 47–51). There is nothing anti-Semitic about this statement. Luke is borrowing a Jewish proverb (see the introduction to Matt. 23:34–36 and the discussion of Matt. 23:29–30); the same charge appears in Nehemiah 9:26; the Book of Jubilees 1:12; and latter rabbinic passages (such as Pes. R. 138a: "We have killed our prophets and transgressed all the commandments. . . ."; 146a: "I [Zion] have killed the prophets . . ."; 153b: "How many messengers [the prophets] I have sent to you and you did not hear them"). It is a confession of sin on the part of Israel which calls to repentance because the climax has been reached, and God wishes to show mercy to repentant Israel. This makes a double statement with astonishing clarity: it is God's will to perfect salvation in Israel, and this is not because of any special devotion on Israel's part but rather, contrary to all logic, is granted to a people that has sinned repeatedly. The charge therefore emphasizes the special election of Israel and expects repentance and salvation (cf. already Deut. 4:25–31; also Zech. 1:2–4, the structure of Baruch in the LXX [prayer of confession—preaching of repentance—praise of the age of salvation], and 2 Esd. 7:127–31). The same thing happens in Acts 2:23–24, 36, 38; 3:15, 19; 4:10, 12; 5:30–31; 7:52 (speech interrupted); 10:39–40; 13:27–30. God-fearers and diaspora Jews are not explicitly called to repentance like Palestinian Jews and, in a different way, the Gentiles (14:15; 17:30), but for Luke there is no one who does not need to repent (cf. Retrospect 1). The crucifixion of Jesus by Israel coupled with God's love for Israel displayed in the raising of Jesus calls Israel and then all nations to repentance. Thus Jesus' journey to the cross, which brings God's history with the prophets to an end, takes on saving significance as a call to repentance (cf. the excursus following 22:30, b.2–3).

## Discipleship Without Anxiety (12:2–12)
Cf. Matthew 10:22–33; 12:31–32; 10:19–20; Mark 13:11

[2]"There is nothing covered up that will not be revealed, and nothing hidden that will not be known. [3]Therefore everything that you have said in the dark shall be heard in the light, and what has been whispered in private rooms shall be proclaimed upon the housetops.

[4]"I tell you, my friends: do not fear those who kill the body and after that have no more that they can do. [5]But I will show you whom to fear: fear the one who, after killing, has power to cast into hell. Yes, I tell you, fear that one. [6]Are not five sparrows sold for two pennies? And not one of them is forgotten before God. [7]But even the hairs of your head are all numbered. Fear not, you are of much more value than many sparrows.

[8]"I tell you, everyone who acknowledges me before others the Son of Man will acknowledge before the angels of God. [9]But whoever denies me before others will be denied before the angels of God. [10]And every one who speaks a word against the Son of Man will be forgiven. But whoever blasphemes against the Holy Spirit will not be forgiven. [11]When they bring you before the synagogues and the rulers and the authorities, do not be anxious how or what you are to say or speak in defense; [12]for the Holy Spirit will teach you in that very hour what you ought to say."

The warning imperative of vs. 1 (related in content to 11:37–54) precedes the motivation which follows in two pairs of parallel clauses, with a general statement (vs. 2) becoming direct address (vs. 3). A further warning imperative, developed in negative (vs. 4) and positive (vs. 5) terms, is again motivated by a general statement (vs. 6) and a statement in the second person (vs. 7). There follow four "legal maxims," two positive statements beginning "everyone who . . ." (vss. 8, 10a) and two negative statements using participial construction (vss. 9, 10b). A final warning imperative (vs. 11) is motivated by a statement addressed to the disciples (vs. 12).

Vss. 2–3 and 8–10 refer to the last judgment, whereas vss. 4–7 and 11–12 refer to the present age and are pure promise. Vss. 4 and 8 are introduced by "but I tell you"; vs. 11 is simply appended to vs. 10. Lukan redaction appears clearly in the reference to a fate after death in vss. 4b and 5. In vs. 8, however, Luke probably has preserved the earliest form of the saying. Vss. 8 and 10 are linked by the catchword "Son of Man" (also Mark 8:38 [q.v.]; and see the discussion of Matt. 10:32–33); vss. 10 and 11–12 are linked by the reference to the Holy Spirit, and are linked in turn with vs. 22 by the catchword "anxious." The alternation between subordinate clause ("everyone who"; vss. 8, 10a) and participle (vss. 9, 10b), which is not preserved in the parallels (Matt. 10:32/33 and 12:32), appears to be typical of Q (Matt. 5:32; 6:2/3, 16/17 [not in vss. 5/6]; 10:37–39, 40–42; cf. also the introduction to Luke 15:1–32). Since the parallel, Matthew 10:26–33 (q.v.), is contained in a discourse to the disciples that corresponds to Luke 12:1–9, vss. 10–12 together with vss. 8–9 were probably already part of such a discourse in Q. The passive form of vs. 9, omitted without apparent reason in an early papyrus, may be a later abbreviation. Vss. 11–12 also come from Q, as is shown by the agreement of the expression "do not be anxious how or what . . ." (vs. 11) with Matthew 10:19 against Mark 13:9–11 although the mention of synagogues may have come from Mark. In all passages, both Jewish and Roman courts are mentioned.

[2] Vs. 1 is suitable as an introduction to 2(–9) since mission is no longer under discussion in Luke. [3] Vs. 3 is therefore not a call

to the disciples to preach (as in Matt. 10:27). Is it intended as a promise that the gospel will be preached everywhere "from the rooftops," in contrast to being anxiously communicated in an inner circle? In contrast to Matthew 10:27, however, only the first of each pair of clauses speaks of human activity; the second is in the passive. Luke is thus probably thinking of God's judgment decree, as in vss. 8–9. The contrast then is not with the secret speech of the Pharisees but with the fainthearted speech of the disciples. The flat roofs of Palestine are the appropriate place for public proclamation (Isa. 15:3; 22:1). For God's judgment the idiom is probably somewhat strange, but it may be a proverbial expression.

[4] Vs. 4 mentions the disciples again although vs. 1 has already stated that they are being addressed. What follows speaks of persecution of the disciples to the point of death; in John 15:14–16, in the same context, Jesus speaks of his "friends" who will share his fate. Luke omits the formula about the soul, which cannot be killed (see the discussion of 8:55 and Matt. 10:28). [5] Life after death is an important subject for him, but he eschews, without actually attacking, the Greek notion of an immortal soul. In line with biblical tradition, he emphasizes death as a limit on everything that is human but not on God's actions. [7] Vs. 7a is repeated in 21:18; neither passage rules out the chance of violent death.

[8–9] In contrast to Mark 8:38, the stress is on the positive statement, which speaks of the "Son of Man" (see the excursus following Mark 8:27–33). It recalls 22:28; Matthew 19:28 and 2 Timothy 2:12 suggest that present fidelity to Jesus will be recognized eschatologically by the Son of Man. The transition to the third person is quite natural when the subject is God's mysterious dealings with a person (2 Cor. 12:2) and can be seen, for example, in the visions of Niklaus von Flües (1417–87).

[10] In the context of vss. 9–12, the sin against the Holy Spirit is no longer, as in the two earlier evangelists, the blindness that refuses to see God at work in Jesus' healings. Now the warning is addressed to the disciple who might be unfaithful to God's call, clearly the sense of the original Q passage. Since blasphemy against the Son of Man is forgiven, blasphemy against the Spirit is not just cowardice

or egoism (22:56–62; cf. Acts 8:18–22) but something like an attack on the work of the Spirit by virtue of a strength in which the blasphemer makes himself God (see the discussion of Mark 3:28–30).

[11] As in 21:12–14, Luke stresses the concrete act of being "brought" into court and the notion of defense. He makes a clearer distinction between what the Spirit (21:15: Jesus) will teach and the resulting ecstatic words of the disciples, not uttered unconsciously in an ecstatic way though determined by the Spirit's instruction (cf. Mark 13:11).

The whole section is a warning against the splitting of a person into an observable outward doing and an irrelevant inward being. Their knowledge of the last day will free the disciples from this danger. It will disclose the disunion that causes being and conduct to be at odds (however vs. 3 is interpreted). This also sets the disciples free from anxiety and for the fear of God, which is only anxious not to ignore the God who so loves creation that he is concerned for every sparrow, indeed for every single hair belonging to God's people. Vss. 9–10 are blunt warnings, but they are set in the context of God's great eschatological (vs. 8) and historical promise, which makes possible such a life, open to God.

## A Bad Investment (12:13–21)

[13]One of the crowd said to him, "Teacher, tell my brother to divide the inheritance with me." [14]But he said to him, "Man, who made me a judge or executor over you?" [15]And he said to them, "Take heed and beware of all covetousness; for a person's life does not consist in abundance and in what one possesses." [16]And he told them a parable and said, "A rich person's land had brought forth plentifully, [17]and he thought to himself, saying, 'What shall I do, for I have nowhere to store my crops?' [18]And he said, 'I will do this; I will pull down my barns and build larger ones, and there I will store all my grain and my goods [19]and I will say to my soul: Soul, you have ample goods laid up for many years. Take your ease, eat, drink, and be merry.' [20]But God said to him, 'Fool! This night they require your soul of you; the things you have prepared, whose will they be?' [21]So is he who lays up treasure for himself and is not rich toward God."

Between vss. 11–12 and 22 an exemplary story has been inserted. A request for adjudication (vs. 13) is refused by Jesus (vs. 14); there follows an admonition that is already a kind of summary (vs. 15). Like vs. 16a, this verse is Lukan and stresses that Jesus is speaking to everyone (cf. the discussion of 6:20a). Vs. 14, however, is un-Lukan in language. Were it and vs. 13b in Luke's prototype? It could, however, represent a proverbial expression deriving from Exodus 2:41 (Acts 7:27), so that only vss. 16b–21 were part of the tradition, as is suggested by the typically Lukan reintroduction in vs. 16a. The two parts also appear separately in the Gospel of Thomas (72 = vss. 13–15; 63 = vss. 16–21), but probably with dependence on Luke. The narrative comprises situation (vs. 16b), question (vs. 17) and answer (vss. 18–19) of the property owner, God's words (vs. 20), and application (vs. 21). Basically, the passage is an internal mono-logue in which God intervenes.

[13] A question brought before Jesus (see the discussion of 11:1) triggers Jesus' words. Scribes were asked for a decision in such mat-ters. [14] Without examining the rights and wrongs, Jesus refuses with remarkable acerbity. He is not a jurist and will not be turned into one. It is possible but not likely that the exchange reflects the ticklish questions confronting community leaders (1 Cor. 6:2–4). [15] Luke (cf. the discussion of 13:1–5) takes it as a warning against covetousness (Test. Jud. 18–19; Mark 7:22; Rom. 1:29; common in Christian catalogs of vices), which does not quite fit either the ques-tion or the narrative that follows. But the real point is the general statement about human life: possessions are not its source of strength, and abundance does not lend it meaning.
[16] In contrast to Jeremiah 17:11; Enoch 97:8–10; Ecclesiasticus 11:18–19 (Heb.), there is no suggestion of unjust gain, and certainly no hint as in Proverbs 11:26 that the person is trying to force prices up. [17–18] As it stands, his idea is straightforward. He is not even trapped in a compulsion to produce but is planning a rational breath-ing space. [19] Possibly he knows "no good thing under the sun but to eat, and drink, and enjoy himself." (Eccles. 8:15). [20] He is not criminal, only stupid. Stupid, because he has no one to share his thoughts with, neither God nor another person, and therefore he re-

volves around himself, as though he had control of his own destiny. But "they" can require his life (or "soul") at any moment. This hardly refers to the angel of death (Bill. 1. 144–49) but rather to God, for whom this periphrasis is common (see the discussion of 6:38). It is not stated that the rich farmer is being called to account to have his fate after death decided (cf. also vss. 22–23). What is said is that he will not keep his possessions; they do not constitute life, and therefore he has not really lived. That is the stupidity of the person who devotes himself to a course of life that actually misses (the real) life. [21] Surprisingly, the man fails himself precisely because he rakes in everything with himself in mind instead of God. It is not even stated that his possessions should be used (or given up) "for God" but only with an eye "toward" him. Or is the reference to riches in the sense of vss. 33–34?

To tear down old barns to make room for larger new ones is not a crime but a normal economic decision of the kind made all the time in every field. What is really questionable is the attitude behind it and the intended purpose. Whoever "makes flesh [i.e., anything of this world] his arm" (Jer. 17:5) discovers not only that what one had taken for security collapses but above all that there is no room left to exercise one's ultimate responsibility because one has "turned his heart aside from the Lord." Perhaps this is why vs. 14 is formulated in such strong terms. Any who is not rich "toward God" no longer sees how one's actions, proper in themselves, express an attitude that has ceased to reckon with the possibility of God's sudden intervention in life. As Paul puts it, one must possess all worldly goods as though one did not possess them (1 Cor. 7:29–31). He means that it is perfectly proper to enjoy and use them but never so as to be bound by them. Because a very different Lord has the final word, everything else that would exercise lordship over us must be given up when necessary.

This also establishes a totally different relationship with our neighbors. Much of their affliction is unavoidable. But anyone with open eyes will consider carefully before God what is needed and what is not, and in everyday decisions, large and small, will live a life that no longer stores up for itself alone. The point is made with special intensity because Luke sets the passage in the context of Jesus' journey to Jerusalem; there his serenity will become manifest, which, with total openness to God, can give up even life itself and finds no need to hold on frantically.

## Freedom from Anxiety (12:22–34)
Cf. Matthew 6:25–34, 19–21

[22]And he said to his disciples, "Therefore I tell you, do not be anxious about your life, what you shall eat, nor about your body, what you shall put on. [23]For life is more than food, and the body more than clothing. [24]Consider the ravens: they do not sow, they do not reap, they have no storehouse nor barn, and yet God feeds them. Of how much more value are you than the birds! [25]And which of you by being anxious can add a cubit to his length [of life]? [26]If then you are not able to do as small a thing as that, why be anxious about the rest? [27]Consider the lilies, how they grow; they neither toil nor spin; but I tell you, even Solomon in all his glory was not arrayed like one of these. [28]But if God so clothes the grass in the field, which is alive today and tomorrow is thrown into the oven, how much more will he clothe you, you of little faith? [29]And you, do not seek what you are to eat and what you are to drink, and do not be agitated; [30]For the Gentiles of the world seek all these things. But your Father knows that you need them. [31]Instead seek God's kingdom, and these things shall be given you as well.

[32]"Fear not, little flock, for it is your Father's good pleasure to give you the kingdom. [33]Sell your possessions and give alms. Provide yourselves purses that do not grow old, with a treasure in the heavens that does not fail, where no thief approaches and no moth destroys; [34]for where your treasure is, there will your heart be also."

In Q, 12:22–34 belonged with 12:11–12 and 39–46 (see the introduction to Matt. 6:19–34). Vss. 22–31 and 33b–34 are very similar to Matthew 6:25–34, 19–21 (q.v.). By means of vss. 22 and 32, Luke addresses the passage clearly to the disciples (see the discussion of 6:20a). Probably it was he who interpolated the saying (perhaps already familiar to him?) about the little flock. Jesus always addressed his demands to all Israel, not a special group; vs. 32 probably reflects the post-Easter situation. Or are the messengers in 10:3 intended? But in that case Jesus would hardly be speaking of a "flock."

[22] Following vss. 13–21, Luke underlines the special danger confronting the disciples—not covetousness, but a limiting of God to the realm of the soul, refusal to take the Redeemer seriously as Creator (cf. the discussion of 10:18). [27] Just as the lilies are a graphic image of great magnificence [28] even though they are short-lived "grass," [24] so the "ravens," which appear also in 1 Kings 17:6 (Elijah); Job 38:41; Psalm 147:9; and the Book of Jubilees 11:11, are more graphic than "birds" (Matt. 6:26; Luke 12:24 at the end). It is unlikely that they are mentioned because they were considered especially horrible and unclean (Bill.). [27] In vs. 27, the earliest manuscripts support the translation above.

[29] Vs. 29 ("seek," as in vs. 30, contra Matt. 6:31) refers to a total way of life that leaves no room for disquiet, for being torn between anxiety and hope. [31] In contrast to Matthew 6:33, vs. 31 does not mention God's righteousness (a Matthean addition); neither does it state that we need *all* these things (e.g., the "ample goods" of vs. 19). [32] Vs. 32 picks up the catchwords "kingdom" and "father"; behind all their endeavors stands God's decision on their behalf. The command follows from the fact of a salvation that has already been granted. They already enjoy the Father's pleasure (2:14). For discussion of the Old Testament image of a flock, see Mark 6:34; also John 10 and 21:17.

[33–34] In vs. 33a, Luke gives the practical application of vss. 33b–34. The disciples in the narrower sense (see the discussion of 6:20a) are called to an exemplary radical renunciation, not as an act of human supererogation but as a way of showing a heart devoted totally to the One who is their Creator and Redeemer, who "does not fail," as vs. 33 explains with a Greek idiom (also Wisd. 7:14; 8:18).

That almsgiving brings reward in heaven is stated by Tobit 4:8–11; Slavonic Enoch 50:5; Bill. 4. 552–57 (cf. the discussion of Matt. 6:2). The Stoics also (Seneca *Ep*. 17; Epictetus 2. 22:19) teach that human beings are unique among living creators contending for "me" and "mine" because they can become "free of spirit" and, like the gods, want nothing, because "where one's mind is, there is one's god." But Luke proclaims the God who, as Creator, seeks to care for people and, as Redeemer, to prepare a kingdom for them. That is where their hearts must beat, so that God may once again become a truly present reality. Therefore Luke sets the disciples before the community as a model to determine at least the direction of its members' lives; he wishes to keep them from the stupidity (vs. 20) of passing up the real life that God would give them.

## Openness to Whatever Comes (12:35–48)
Cf. Matthew 24:42–51

[35]"Let your loins be girded and your lamps burning, [36]and be like those who are waiting for their lord to set out from the marriage feast, so that you, when he comes and knocks, may open to him at once. [37]Blessed are those servants whom the master finds awake when he comes. Amen, I say to you, he will gird himself and have them recline at table, and he will come and serve them. [38]And if he comes in the second watch or in the third and finds them so, blessed are they! [39]But know this: if the householder had known at what hour the thief was coming, he would not have let his house be broken into. [40]You also must be ready; for at an hour you do not expect, the Son of Man is coming."

[41]Peter said, "Lord, are you telling this parable to us or to all?" [42]And the Lord said, "Who then is the faithful and wise steward, whom the lord will set over his household, to give them their portion at the proper time? [43]Blessed is that servant whom his lord when he comes will find so doing. [44]Truly I tell you, he will set him over all his possessions. [45]But if that servant says in his heart, 'My lord is delayed in coming,' and begins to beat the menservants and maidservants, and to eat and drink and get drunk, [46]the lord of that servant will come on a day when he does not expect it, and will cut him in two and give him his reward with the unfaithful. [47]And that servant who knows his lord's will but did not make ready or act according to his will shall receive a severe beating; [48]but whoever does not know and does what deserves a beating [will be beaten] only a little. From everyone to whom much has been given much will be required, and from him to whom they have committed much they will demand so much the more."

If vs. 39 once followed vs. 34 (see the introduction to Matt. 6:19–34), vss. 35–38 could be a Lukan interpolation. He did not make up the parable. Vss. 36–37a,(38) are the earliest form of Mark 13:34–

36 (q.v., introduction). It assumes the Jewish system of three watches during the night, not the Roman system of four, as in Acts 12:4. It could go back to Jesus himself and refer to the present or eschatological coming of the kingdom. The idea that all the servants should remain awake, not just the doorkeeper, is a later assimilation to the demand made of all the faithful.

Vs. 35 is an introduction, couched in popular imagery (see the discussion of 13:1–5). Vs. 38 expresses in a macarism what Mark 13:35 and Matthew 24:42 state as an admonition. The parable of the thief in Matthew includes the words "wake" and "watch (of the night)," like Luke 12:37–38. Does this show that the parable with its two catchwords came before Luke 12:39 in Q (even if not from the very outset) but was omitted by Matthew on account of 25:1–13? The "amen" in vs. 37*b* certainly does not come from Luke although the statement has been edited by him and contradicts 17:8 (= L?). It manifests so unexpected a hope that it might well derive from Jesus' proclamation of the kingdom of God. It is also more likely that Luke would have inserted vs. 41 between vss. 38 and 39 if vss. 37–38 had not already been linked to vss. 39–40.

All three parables have as their theme the unexpected coming of the Lord. The first is conceived as a promise for those who are expecting him, the second as a warning for those who are not prepared, and the third as an admonition to take the former, not the latter, as a model. All three emphasize conduct in the present, while the coming of Jesus can appear under the image of the master of a house or that of a thief. That the community has been waiting a considerable time can be sensed in vss. 38 and 45, but this is not the real theme. Vss. 39–46 agree with Matthew 24:43–51 (q.v.). Vss. 47–48 (q.v.) treat a different question, and probably, like vs. 42 (q.v.), presuppose a difference between community members and leaders.

The introductory admonition (vs. 35) is followed by a parable. Vs. 36 describes the situation in a complex of subordinate constructions, followed in turn by a macarism and a relative clause describing the proper conduct (vs. 37*a*). Together with another macarism (vs. 38) following the conditional clause, it provides the setting for vs. 37*b*. If the servants in the macarisms are still the subject (like those waiting for their lord in vs. 36), elsewhere they always become the object, and the lord the subject. The crucial point is vs. 37*b*, a promise authoritatively declared by Jesus. The parable form is treated freely. It is really not necessary for the servants all to remain awake or be ready for the arrival, or for all the lamps to be burning. In other words, the imagery of vs. 35 is already traditional (see below). The same is true of "knocking" and "opening" and the meal that follows, certainly not something to be expected around midnight or later (cf. Rev. 3:20). Neither do macarisms appear in other parables. Finally, vs. 39 really admits that it is impossible to stay awake all the time.

[35] The imagery of the introduction understands the Christian life as a pilgrimage, as a constant readiness to set out on new paths at uncertain times, or to have an unexpected encounter and act appropriately. It comes from the instructions preparatory to the exodus from Egypt (Exod. 12:11) as had already been used by Philo (*Abel* 63) to describe the service of God. It appears in this sense in Ephesians 6:14, while 1 Peter 1:13 and above all Didache 16:1 (where both images are found) are more concerned with the eschatological coming of Christ. This fits with 9:51; 13:22, etc.

[36] The marriage feast is not an eschatological image—the lord departs from it—but only the reason for returning home in the dead of night. [37–38] In the present form, the astonishing promise framed by the double macarisms (cf. vs. 43) constitutes the real focus. As is often true in Jesus' parables, what is stated is not inconceivable but far surpasses—like Jesus' own actions in 22:27 and John 13:4–5!—normal experience; here it also is incongruous with the midnight hour. Thus by means of a kind of alienation (see the excursus following Mark 4:1–9) it points attention to the salvation that is being accorded to the listener. Later 22:27 will show the basis of this promise that surpasses all expectations.

[41] The totally Lukan question, distinguishing sayings addressed to the disciples from those addressed to everyone (see the discussion of 6:20*a*), [42] leads to substitution of a steward for the servant (see the introduction to Matt. 24:45–51). Luke is thus still thinking in terms of special instruction for the disciples (vs. 22). He therefore sets vs. 42 in the future: [44] after Easter Jesus will entrust his dis-

ciples with leadership of his community (see the discussion of 22:26). They are promised something great but also have a greater responsibility. **[47–48]** This is made clear in two double sayings unique to Luke. The first describes the principle of graduated responsibility in antithetical terms (cf. the lack of knowledge in 23:34 and Wisd. 6:6–8), the second in parallel: here only the one to whom much is entrusted, i.e., the Apostle, is under discussion. The image of the steward who provides his fellow servants with their necessities dominates these sayings as well (vs. 42). They are part of Luke's special material but can hardly originate with him, as is shown by the change to the third person plural as periphrasis for God (see the introduction and discussion of 6:38).

All three parables focus on the coming of Jesus. It has certainly receded into the background. Only the wicked servant thinks that the master is delayed; only Luke explicitly adds "in coming." But his coming is, however, seen more as an event that already dominates the present; therefore Luke speaks of it here and in 17:20–37 (cf. also 19:11–26), rather than leaving the theme to a final chapter of instruction by Jesus (Mark 13; Luke 21).

There are shifts in emphasis. In vss. 39–40, the coming of Jesus is viewed as a threatening catastrophe for which one must be prepared at all times. Vss. 35–38 are formulated as a promise in which the glory of what is to come bursts the form of the parable. Here, too, the emphasis is on being always ready. Vss. 42–46, by contrast, show that the interim of waiting demands responsible action on behalf of others. Jesus answers Peter's question indirectly by speaking of the steward and those in his charge. The point is not rights and authority but greater responsibility and also a greater temptation to lord it over others (vs. 45). The promise (vss. 35–38) and warning (vss. 39–40) that are addressed to all hold true even more for the Apostles and hence for the leaders of the community (vss. 47–48).

### Trial by Fire and Baptism (12:49–53)
Cf. Matthew 10:34–36; 5:25–26

49"I came to cast fire upon the earth, and how I wish that it were already kindled. 50I have a baptism to be baptized with, and how I am constrained until it is accomplished. ⁵¹Do you think that I have come to give peace on earth? No, I tell you, but rather division; ⁵²for henceforth in one house there will be five divided, three against two and two against three they will be divided, ⁵³father against son and 'son against father,' mother against daughter and 'daughter against mother,' mother-in-law against daughter-in-law and daughter-in-law against mother-in-law."

(Vs. 53—Mic. 7:6.)

Jesus twice describes his mission, then adds his wish with an interrogative particle (vss. 49–50). A question directed to those listening expresses a misunderstanding (vs. 51a); its rejection (vs. 51b) is motivated by a clause using the future tense (vs. 52a), which is expanded in traditional biblical language repeating the verb "divide" (vss. 52b–53). Vss. 49–50 are special Lukan material; vss. 51–53 are a revision of Matthew 10:34–36 (q.v.), linguistically pre-Lukan. The two sections may have been combined before Luke (Q; "cast" in vs. 49 and Matt. 10:34).

[50] "Baptism" and "baptize" stand for Jesus' death; the image probably comes from Jesus himself (see the discussion of Mark 10:38). The word is also used in Greek for the "burden" or even "death" of the soul (Plutarch *Education of Children* 9 B; Hercher, *Erotici* 2; Charitonos *Aphr.* 3. 2. 6; Libanius *Orationes* 64, 115). The real meaning of Jesus' deliberate journey to Jerusalem, which began in 9:51, can now be seen. He is going to his death. [51] Just as Jesus promises his disciples in Mark 10:38 that they will share in this baptism, so he promises them here not peace but division. [52] Biblical sayings that once referred to the eschaton "from now on" become reality: the closest family ties are dissolved.

[50] Jesus' baptism appears to let loose "waves of death and torrents of perdition" (2 Sam. 22:5), where one "sinks in deep mire, comes into deep waters and is overwhelmed by floods" (Ps. 69:3). Jesus' "constraint" or "affliction" shows that these images must not be spiritualized. [49] In vs. 49, Jesus calls this, in typically cryptic language, the fire that he wishes were already kindled. The parallelism between vss. 49 and 50–51, which describes both the fire and the division as to the purpose of Jesus' coming, shows that fire,

baptism, and division refer to the same event. Fire is an image of judgment (see the discussion of Mark 1:7–8; also Luke 3:9; 9:54; Rev. 8:5; 20:9). The word used in vs. 50 means "being afflicted," "totally constrained" (by fear or a plan or an act of will); vs. 49 gives clearer expression to Jesus' desire. The combination of these statements is possible because according to Zechariah 13:9; Malachi 3:2–3, God's fire of judgment is also a purifying fire (cf. Luke 3:16–17). It passes through the people in God's word (Jer. 5:14; 23:29; cf. 22:29; Ecclus. 48:1). A noncanonical saying of Jesus clearly expresses this quality of judgment and salvation: "Whoever is near me is near the fire; whoever is distant from me is distant from the kingdom" (Gospel of Thomas 82); "fire" and "kingdom" stand in parallel and ultimately mean the same. What was promised in Luke 2:34 (q.v.) is being realized. Only through the fire of judgment does one find the kingdom. God's fire brings affliction and fear of death, but division and assault lead to entrance into the kingdom, where table fellowship (vs. 37) and identity (vs. 44) are found.

And so there is a double truth. Jesus does not bring the peace and quiet that we would expect, but in the ultimate and deepest sense he is "our peace" (Eph. 2:14). Nothing is said of vicarious suffering on the part of Jesus (see the excursus following 22:30, a). But Jesus does go his way to the baptism of death in order that others following him may be granted something of his burning heart, to make them firebrands of a difficult and sometimes violent but amazingly helpful love for humankind.

### Blindness to God's Signs (12:54–59)
Cf. Matthew 6:2–3

54He also said to the crowd, "When you see a cloud rising in the west, you say at once, 'A shower is coming'; and so it happens. 55And when you see the south wind blowing, you say, 'It will be hot,' and it happens. 56Hypocrites, you know how to interpret the appearance of earth and sky, so why do you not know how to interpret the present time?

57"Why do you not judge for yourselves what is right? 58For when you go with your accuser before the magistrate, make an effort to settle with him on the way, lest he drag you to the judge, and the judge hand you over to the officer, and the officer put you in prison. ⁵⁹I tell you, you will never get out until you have paid the last penny."

The saying in the second person singular in vss. 58–59 has been linked secondarily with vss. 54–56, in the plural, by means of the Lukan vs. 57 ("for yourselves," also inserted by Luke in 21:30). Vss. 54–56 lead with two parallel "if . . . then" clauses from everyday observation to the critical question addressed to the listeners. Vss. 58–59 move from the definition of a situation introduced by the comparative particle to the necessary action (imperative) and the consequences to be avoided (negative purpose clause). Only with the emphatic warning in vs. 59, however, do we see that vss. 58–59 are actually dealing, [54] like vss. 54–55, with a far more serious situation.

[57] Luke introduces the crowd as Jesus' audience and emphasizes how obvious his demand really should be. [54–56] The first saying belongs to Luke's special material (see the discussion of Matt. 16:2–3); it is meant to underline the urgency of the admonition, found also in Matthew 5:25–26 (q.v.), [58–59] which Luke has formulated in terminology borrowed from the legal language of Rome. The context is clearly eschatological although Luke himself may have in mind a decision for or against the community (vss. 51–53). Both images, then, share the same meaning: knowledge of what is to come (vss. 54–56) must issue in appropriate action while there is still time (vss. 57–59). [54–55] The west wind from the sea brings rain, [56] the desert wind from the south brings heat. Anyone can interpret (literally "distinguish") that. But the listeners cannot distinguish the present as the special "time" of God's incursion from the simple continuity of unfulfilled "time" (the Greek uses two different words) (on "hypocrites," see the discussion of 12:1). Therefore they lack the consequent critical ability to "distinguish" the will of God (Rom. 12:2; Phil. 1:10; 1 Thess. 5:21) from their own will, or the requirements of God from their own way of life (1 Cor. 11:31; 2 Cor. 13:5). [57] The two are intimately connected, as vs. 57 shows: the ability to "distinguish" the time set apart by God leads to the ability to determine and do what is "right." [58] Considered in itself, vs. 58

only depicts the urgency of such action, but Luke's expression "be reconciled with him" is probably meant to recall that reconciliation with God, which delivers one from judgment, is the one thing necessary.

# C. REPENTANCE AND THE COMING KINGDOM (13:1–21)

This must be taken as a separate unit; the restatement of Jerusalem as Jesus' destination in vs. 22 marks the beginning of the central section, vss. 22–35. Vss. 1–9 are an urgent call to repentance, addressed to the people already addressed by 12:54–59. In deed (vss. 10–17) and word (vss. 18–21) the coming kingdom of God is proclaimed (vss. 18, 20). The result is division, (vs. 17).

### Time to Repent (13:1–9)

[1]There came to him at that time some who told him of the Galileans whose blood Pilate had mingled with their sacrifices. [2]And he answered and said to them, "Do you think that these Galileans were worse sinners than all the [other] Galileans, because they suffered thus? [3]No, I tell you; but unless you repent you will all likewise perish. [4]Or those eighteen upon whom the tower in Siloam fell and killed them, do you think that they were worse offenders than all who dwell in Jerusalem? [5]No, I tell you; but unless you repent you will all likewise perish."

[6]And he told this parable: "A certain person had a fig tree planted in his vineyard, and he came seeking fruit on it and found none. [7]And he said to the vinedresser, 'Behold, these three years I have come seeking fruit on this fig tree, and I find none; cut it down. Why should it use up the ground?' [8]But he answered him and said, 'Lord, let it alone this year also, till I dig about it and put on manure, [9]to see if it will not bear fruit in the future; but if not, you may cut it down.'"

Vss. 1–5 comprise two sayings of Jesus that are parallel even to their wording: the first is introduced in typically Lukan manner (see the discussion of 11:1) by the question of "some," the second by

Jesus himself (vs. 4a). In each case the question is followed by Jesus' counterquestion and his warning, with only minor stylistic changes. The inhabitants of Jerusalem are introduced alongside the Galileans. By vss. 1–5 the parable in vss. 6–9 is interpreted beforehand. This is also the case in Luke 10:29, 37; 11:9; 12:21(41); 16:9–13; 18:14b; especially typical of Luke is a summary statement at the beginning: 12:15, 35; 15:1–2; 18:1–9; 19:11. The statement of the situation (vs. 6) is followed by the reasoning of the owner (vs. 7). The vinedresser's objection leaves the decision open.

[1] Behind vs. 1 stands the universal question of God's justice; therefore neither the inquirer nor the setting is further defined. The "they" whom Jesus answers also includes more than those who ask the question (see the discussion of vs. 23). Josephus (*Ant.* 18. 85–87) tells of some Samaritans who were massacred at Pilate's command on their way to the sanctuary but that was after Jesus' death and on Mount Gerizim. He also (ibid., 60–62) tells of a Jewish demonstration in Jerusalem around the time of Jesus that Pilate brutally suppressed. [2] Jesus' response rules out the dogma that particular sinfulness leads to particular disaster, and thus the notion that we are indeed "all sinners" but not as bad as some. [3] Introduced with special emphasis, it rejects the question of the onlookers and thus also refuses to explain how God acts. It is wrong for human beings to call God into question or justify his ways by imputing particular sinfulness to someone who is struck by disaster; it is rather God who calls the questioner into question. Of course this is scandalous: who would dare to abolish such differences without taking into consideration how religious or irreligious the victim was?

[4] The collapse of the tower is also unattested, but the fact that nothing like that happened during the building of the sanctuary (Bill.) does not prove that it could not have happened, for example, during the construction of the city wall or the aqueduct leading to the Pool of Siloam (Josephus *De bello jud.* 5. 145, 275; *Ant.* 18. 60). [5] It is to the God who poses unfathomable riddles that one must turn in repentance.

[6–9] This is also the urgent message of the parable. Luke 13:3, 5 undoubtedly mean "perishing" like the Galileans or inhabitants of

Jerusalem, i.e., historical catastrophe, the fall of Jerusalem. Vine-yard and fig tree also symbolize Israel (Isa. 5:1–7; Hos. 9:10; Mic. 7:1; Jer. 8:13). But no one who has heard vss. 1–5 can believe any longer that God apportions temporal and eternal punishments pre-cisely as deserved, so that every disaster is the consequence of a particular offense. Jesus' parable cannot be used to emphasize a spe-cial guilt on the part of the Jews of Jerusalem. But Luke does have Jesus address his own age rather than proclaim eternal verities; he knows the truth incarnate in Jesus that it is not simply judgment that comes over his hearers (as suggested by the story of the barren fig tree in Mark 11:12–14, which Luke omits) but that the time of Jesus, with all its terrible events caused by human guilt or not, is an invi-tation to salvation.

This is reflected in the conversation between the owner and the gardener, for which there is not parallel in similar parables (Ahikar 8. 35; Bill. 4. 474). The use of the present tense in vs. 8 (see the introduction to 16:23) shows that it is pre-Lukan, probably a genuine saying of Jesus. Something of the mystery of Jesus can be seen in the image of God against God in order that grace may be offered to all. Jesus is present again and again wherever anyone will allow him to come to life (see the discussion of 4:21). Therefore this section follows the call to both disciples (12:35–53) and crowd (12:54–59) to be ready for God's coming. The questions in vss. 2 and 4 are addressed to all readers; they are told that God cannot be explained, but can be experienced.

## The Sabbath as a Sign of God's New Creation (13:10–17)

[10]Now he was teaching in one of the synagogues on the sabbath. [11]And behold, there was a woman who had had a spirit of infirmity for eighteen years, and she was bent over and could not fully straighten herself. [12]When Jesus saw her, he called her and said to her, "Woman, be freed from your infirmity." [13]And he laid his hands upon her, and immediately she was made straight, and praised God. [14]But the ruler of the synagogue, indignant because Jesus had healed on the sabbath, an-swered and said to the crowd, "There are six days on which work ought to be done. Come on those days and be healed, and not on the sabbath day." [15]But the Lord answered him and said, "Hypocrites, does not each

of you on the sabbath untie his ox or his ass from the manger and lead it away to water? [16]And this woman, who is a daughter of Abraham, whom Satan bound, behold, for eighteen years, should she not be loosed from this bond on the sabbath day?" [17]And when he said this, "all his adversaries were put to shame," and the whole crowd rejoiced at all the glorious things that were done by him.

(Vs. 17—Isa. 45:16.)

The miracle story ends with vs. 13, where Luke has presumably added the statement about praising God (see the discussion of 17:15). The appearance of the helper (vs. 10) and those who need help (vs. 11), including a typical description of the severity of the case, is followed by healing word and gesture, success, and praise to God (vss. 12–13). But the crux comes with the objection in vs. 14, answered by two counterquestions (vss. 15–16), which divide the listeners into shamed opponents and a rejoicing crowd. This is the focus of the text. Vss. 10–13 (Jesus approaches a woman!) and 17 are linguistically Lukan; vss. 14–16 are equally un-Lukan. The plural "sabbaths" is often used for a single sabbath, probably originally and also here. Luke, however, always uses the singular except in the phrase "sabbath day" (4:6; traditional?); he also corrects Mark and Q (6:1, 7, 9; 14:3, 5). Mark 2:24, "Why are they doing on the sabbaths what is not lawful," which uses the plural although it refers only to the day on which Jesus' disciples are actually plucking the grain, is corrected in Luke 6:2 to read, "Why are they doing what is not lawful on the sabbaths" because Luke uses the plural for more than one sabbath. Our story probably used the plural originally, as in vs. 10. Luke changed this to a singular, including the phrase "sabbath day" in vss. 14–16, but left the plural in vs. 10 because he was thinking of continued teaching "on the sabbaths." The question "who among you . . ." (cf. vs. 15), which is typical of Jesus, is associated with the problem of the sabbath in 14:5 and Matthew 12:11 (q.v.). Since sabbath healings do not appear as a problem either in the primitive Christian community or in Judaism, they probably go back to Jesus himself; if so, this probably holds true also of an argument like vs. 15, which would be meaningless apart from its setting and also uses the expression "loose" symbolically.

[10] Luke pictures Jesus as teaching during (or after?) synagogue worship: 4:16, 31, 33 (Mark 1:21, 23); 6:6 (where "teach" is an addition); cf. Acts 13:5, 14; 14:1; 17:1–2; etc. [11] Since women were not admitted to synagogue worship, the encounter is not possible until afterward. Does Luke picture Jesus calling the woman out of the crowd (vs. 12)? Illnesses, like possession, were ascribed to spirits, expressing the sense of a superior power that holds the upper hand.

[12] Jesus' initiative (cf. 6:8 = Mark 3:3; 14:3–4) is even more striking when a woman is addressed (see the discussion of 8:3). We are never told of a Jewish woman who asks Jesus for help (cf. only Matt. 20:20; John 11:20–22), but Jesus does address himself to them. [13] Luke also stresses the features of physical contact (cf. Ps. 145:14: 146:8; and the discussion of Luke 4:39–40) and praise of God (cf. the discussion of 17:15), who has acted through Jesus. The crucial point is the indignation (cf. 15:2) of the ruler of the synagogue (see the discussion of Mark 5:22), who stays with the letter of the law, which is still in force, and cannot see that now God is doing something new. [15] Jesus calls this "hypocrisy" (see the discussion of 12:1).

The watering of cattle on the sabbath was later permitted only with strict limitations (Bill.): the halter must be removed with a single hand, and the well must be inside the fence surrounding the property. A similar regulation appears in CD 11:5–7 (cf. the discussion of Matt. 12:11). The argument is not persuasive, since healing could also take place on the following day (vs. 14b). [16] Only the striking reference to Satan and above all to the covenant with Abraham (cf. 19:9), [17] together with the echo of the age of salvation when the enemies of Israel will be put to shame but the people will be saved (Isa. 45:16), show that we are dealing here with something more than rational liberalism.

Luke, who often omits double traditions, includes sabbath healings in 6:6–11 (= Mark 3:1–6) and 14:1–6 as well as here although the question of the sabbath was no longer a concern in his community. He felt that there was something deeper behind this practice on the part of Jesus. The very fact that a woman is involved points in a way to the new age when there will be "neither male nor female," but all will be "one" in Christ (Gal. 3:28). More important is the appeal to the covenant with Abraham. The statement is not uncommon (Bill. 2. 200: "If every woman that others gossip about at their spinning wheels were dismissed, there would be no daughter left to Abraham who could remain with her husband"). Here, however, it contrasts with the sovereignty of Satan, which is broken by Jesus' healing, as he restores the covenant between God and Israel. The new attitude of Jesus toward the sabbath, the most obvious point of difference between the Christian community and Judaism, does not separate from Israel but rather brings God's way with Israel to its goal. The point therefore is not liberal versus restrictive interpretation of the sabbath regulations, which could be a matter of debate, but a fundamentally false doctrine (hypocrisy) versus openness to God's new eschatological act. The sabbath is the day God finished all his work (Gen. 2:1–3), and therefore its every observance suggests the final completion of God's saving work for all the world (Heb. 4:9–11; see the discussion of Matt. 12:1–8). The sabbath joy of Israel was buried under a cancerous growth of rules and prohibitions; Jesus uncovers it once more (see the discussion of Mark 2:27). Recourse to Scripture need not have a conservative effect.

Perhaps this is why 14:1–6 is told in the context of a sabbath meal replete with conversations that look forward to the time of joy to come—indirectly in vss. 7–14, openly in 15–24. Did Jesus refuse to wait until the following day because he wanted to point to the long-awaited liberating sabbath of God, dawning in his ministry? Is this why Luke, or an editor before him, associated this story with the call to repentance addressed to Israel in 13:1–9 and the sayings about the kingdom of God being opened to the nations in vss. 18–21? And is 14:3 an echo of the fact that Jesus posed the fundamental question of the sabbath? If so, then Jesus has indeed released us from our self-alienation and restored us to a meaningful life (Mark 2:27).

## The Littleness and Greatness of the Kingdom of God (13:18–21)
Cf. Mark 4:30–32; Matthew 13:31–33

¹⁸Now he said, "What is the kingdom of God like and to what shall I compare it? ¹⁹It is like a grain of mustard seed that someone took and

sowed in the garden, and it grew and became a tree and 'the birds of
the air made nests in its branches.' "
    20And again he said, "To what shall I compare the kingdom of God?
21It is like leaven which a woman took and hid in three measures of
meal, till it was all leavened."

(Vs. 19—Ezek. 17:23; 31:6.)

On the two parables, see the discussion of Matthew 13:31–33. The
double introduction (triple in vss. 18–19a) is also reminiscent of
Mark 4:30. It is typical of Q and appears to have been abbreviated
by Matthew (likewise Luke 6:47b, 48a; 7:31). Vs. 19 speaks of a
garden instead of a field. For Luke, the parables are related to the
healing on the sabbath. Like 14:7–14, they say that in the healing of
this one woman the eschaton is seen to dawn; its coming cannot be
halted.


# D. JERUSALEM: CITY OF DECISION
# (13:22–35)


About this central section the period of journeying is organized
(see the discussion of 9:51—19:27). Jerusalem is therefore mentioned at its beginning and end. Vss. 22–30 have strong eschatological overtones, like 12:35–59; now, however, they are clearly applied
to Jesus' contemporaries (13:26), and extend beyond Israel in vss.
29–30. It is therefore better to include these verses with the crucial
statement of Jesus' mission in vss. 31–35 than to draw a line between vss. 30 and 31.


### The Nearness to Jesus of the Distant (13:22–30)
Cf. Matthew 7:13–14, 22–23; 8:11–12

    22And he went on his way through cities and villages, teaching and
journeying toward Jerusalem. 23But someone said to him, "Lord, will
those who are saved be few?" And he said to them, 24"Strive to enter
by the narrow door; for many, I tell you, will seek to enter and will not

be able. ²⁵When once the householder has risen up and the door is shut and you begin to stand outside and to knock at the door, saying, 'Lord, open to us,' he will answer you, 'I do not know where you come from.' ²⁶Then you will begin to say, 'We ate and drank in your presence, and you taught in our streets.' ²⁷And he will speak to you and say, 'I do not know where you come from; depart from me, all you workers of iniquity.' ²⁸There will be weeping and gnashing of teeth when you see Abraham and Issac and Jacob and all the prophets in the kingdom of God, and you yourselves thrust out. ²⁹And they will come 'from east and west and north and south' and recline at table in the kingdom of God. ³⁰And behold, there are last who will be first, and first who will be last."

(Vs. 27—Ps. 6:9. Vs. 29—Ps. 107:3.)

As usual (see the discussion of 11:1), "someone" asks a question (vs. 23a). Jesus frames his admonition in vivid imagery (vs. 24a; see the the discussion of 12:35) and gives the reason (vs. 24b). The parable follows in vss. 25–27. It begins with a temporal clause in the subjunctive, setting the scene; with the householder's words of judgment the main clause is introduced (with incorrect grammar) (vs. 25). After the protest (vs. 26), the householder repeats his words (again with a superfluous "begin") and increases their severity by adding a dismissal in the imperative (vs. 27). The traditional description of the judgment (vs. 28a; see the discussion of Matt. 8:12) is once more followed by a temporal clause in the subjunctive (vs. 28b), which issues in a main clause (vs. 29) whose promise of salvation constitutes the positive counterpart to the words of judgment (end of vs. 25). Vss. 25–27 are already in future tense, formulated as direct address in the second person plural. Vs. 27 and above all vss. 28–29 destroy the scene.

The closed door derives from a true parable (Matt. 25:10–12, q.v.), the words of judgment for a direct declaration of judgment (Matt. 7:23, q.v.), and the promise of the influx of the nations from Matthew 8:11–12 (q.v.), a saying of Jesus still in the third person. The concluding verse is a familiar proverb cited in another context in Matthew 20:16 (and in reverse order also in Mark 10:31 = Matt. 19:30). Vss. 25–27 at least are un-Lukan in language; the objection made by those who are turned away resembles that in Matthew 7:22, where it also stands in proximity to the image of the narrow door, though used there as an example of merely saying "Lord, Lord," already condemned in Luke 6:46 (Matt. 7:21). The statement "I do not know of you" (so literally in Matt. 25:12 = Luke 13:25) has attracted the statement "I do not know" (Luke 13:27 = Matt. 7:23: "I never knew you"), and the catchword "outside" appears in both vs. 25 and vs. 28. At the same time, the vocative "Lord" has recalled the saying in Matthew 7:22 (Luke 13:26) with its warning against saying "Lord, Lord." Here it no longer refers to charismatic prophets but to contemporaries of Jesus in Palestine. This restriction is not Lukan (see the conclusion to 13:1–9); neither is the present participle "thrust out" (vs. 28) or the reference to the faith of the Gentiles (see the discussion of vs. 29). Perhaps the various sayings had already been brought together in catechetic tradition, so that Luke merely revised them stylistically and assimilated them to each other. His style appears in vss. 22–24.

[22] The destination of Jerusalem once again dominates all that follows. Again Jesus' teaching is emphasized (see the discussion of vs. 10). [23] Asked by "someone" about "the saved" (Isa. 37:32 LXX), Jesus answers "them," i.e., he addresses everyone.

[24] This is the problem discussed by rabbis and apocalypticists. On the one hand, we read: "All Israel shares in the world to come" (Bill. 1. 883); on the other: "The Most High created this world for the sake of many, but the world to come for few" (2 Esd. 8:1, also followed by a parable). But the direct address of Jesus leaves this plane of theological discussion. The "striving" (literally "contest") of the martyrs is already mentioned in 2 Maccabees 13:14, and Christians have often borrowed the metaphor. The "many/few" antithesis is already linked with the image of the narrow door in Matthew 7:13–14. There, however, the door is hard to find because the way to it is narrow. The rabbis speak also of the narrow "gate" through which one must venture onto the broad sea (Bill. 1. 461). In Luke 13:24 it is unclear why the many "will not be able" (a Lukan expression) to pass through. The antithesis is also not a broad gate (in

Greek the same word as door) with easy access but a closed door, whose narrowness or wideness is irrelevant. Luke is using traditional language in which the metaphors have lost their concrete vividness.

[25] The householder, too, is now only a symbol for Jesus and is therefore addressed as "Lord" and "you" with reference to his actions in the environment of the listeners. In contrast to Matthew 25:10, where the bridegroom is seated at the banquet, he rises here to shut the door. His features are more those of a judge. [26] The reference to the historical situation of Jesus' ministry shows that before Luke the passage dealt with the limited time given Israel; Luke has generalized the application by adding vss. 23–24 and made it a call to decision addressed to all. [27] "All you workers of iniquity" is a Lukan expression, as is "all the prophets."

[28] When Luke or one of his predecessors appended vss. 28–29 to the judgment saying, their order was reversed. Now the image at the beginning expresses the protests of the rejected; then follows the image of the influx from all sides. The opposite order appears in Matthew 8:11–12 (q.v.). [29] Vs. 29 speaks only of those who are distant and therefore not among the Palestinian contemporaries of Jesus (Matt. 8:12: "sons of the kingdom" = Israel!) (cf. the conclusion to 11:37–54), not the Gentiles explicitly although they are certainly included (see the discussion of 8:39).

[30] Vs. 30 does not say "many who are first" or even "the first" (Matt. 19:30; 20:16) but "there are first who. . . ." In other words, vs. 30 corrects vss. 28–29: there are Gentiles and also Jews who have faith. As in Matthew 20:16 (contra 19:30), the promise comes at the beginning. Like the general admonition at the beginning, Luke probably added the proverbial maxim at the end.

This collection of ethical admonitions, drawing on already schematic metaphors, warns against self-sufficiency. Mere confession of the Lord is of no more profit than appeal to Abraham, even for those who were his actual table companions. The daughter of Abraham must first be set free (vs. 16), those who are distant are coming to him (vs. 29). Both take place in the authoritative ministry of Jesus, which fails to reach only those who think they already have everything and need no help.

## Jerusalem, City of Decision (13:31–35)
Cf. Matthew 23:37–39

[31]At that very hour some Pharisees came and said to him, "Depart and journey elsewhere, for Herod wants to kill you." [32]And he said to them, "Go and tell that fox, 'Behold, I cast out demons and perform cures today and tomorrow, and the third day I am consummated. [33]But I must journey today and tomorrow and the day following, because it cannot be that a prophet should perish away from Jerusalem.' [34]Jerusalem, Jerusalem, killing the prophets and stoning those who are sent to you! How often would I have gathered your children together as a hen gathers her brood under her wings, and you would not! [35]Behold, 'your house will be forsaken.' But I tell you, you will not see me again until it comes about that you say, 'Blessed be he whom comes in the name of the Lord.'"

(Vs. 35—Jer. 22:5; Ps. 118:26.)

Jesus' words are occasioned by a warning from outside (vs. 31; see the discussion of 11:1). The words describe his work in three clauses (vs. 32) and confront him with God's imperative (literally: "it must be that . . ."), motivated by a "because" clause. An apostrophe to Jerusalem follows, which contains a retrospective description of Jesus' ministry and a future threat. It agrees almost verbatim with Matthew 23:37–39. It was originally linked with 11:49–51 (q.v., introduction) but is also appropriate to 13:26–30 on the assumption that the words were spoken in Jerusalem. The metaphor in vs. 34, however, where the hen is feminine like wisdom or the "presence" of God (for which the same image is used; see the discussion of Matt. 23:37), clearly belongs to a wisdom passage like 11:49–51.

Stylistically Lukan are vs. 31 and the expression "the day following" (Acts 20:15; 21:26), which contradicts the three days already mentioned in vs. 32. Un-Lukan are probably the expression "it cannot be" and Jesus' reference to himself as a "prophet." Did Luke then introduce the three days (or just the third) in vs. 33 because for him the way of the cross also forms part of Jesus' "journeying" (eighty-eight occurrences in Luke and Acts)? Did he eliminate, as he often does, a place name to which "elsewhere" once referred (vs. 31)? If so, the traditional text would merely have said that God alone determines the end of Jesus' three-day ministry, and that he must then go to Jerusalem to die.

[31] Historically, the warning could have come through Herod's initiative since he would be glad to be rid of Jesus. According to Mark 3:6, also, the Pharisees and Herodians were one in their opposition to Jesus. But none of this is suggested by Luke, who interprets the warning more as an act of friendship. Herod and Jerusalem (vs. 34) wish for Jesus' death, while the Pharisees and Romans (see the discussion of vs. 35), although in a twilight zone, are at least not simply opponents of Jesus. Vss. 34–35 probably did originate as the conclusion of a discourse against the Pharisees (Matt. 23:27). According to Luke, however, many of them are open to Jesus. They issue him invitations (7:36; 11:37; 14:1). In comparison with Mark, their reaction is either toned down (6:11) or omitted (11:15–16; 16:18 [cf. Mark 10:2]; 20:19–20). Only in 5:17, 21 does he add them to the scribes. He takes Q in a sense less hostile to the Pharisees than Matthew does. In L or Lukan redaction, their teaching comes in for particular criticism (7:30, 39; 11:37–44, 53–54; 12:1; 14:3; 15:2; 17:20; 18:10–14; 19:39), but there are also Christian Pharisees (Acts 15:5; cf. 5:34), and Paul is pictured as a true Pharisee (see the conclusion to Luke 16:14–18). Here Luke has preserved an accurate tradition. Although Pharisees sat on the court, except in Matthew 27:62 (and John 18:3) they never appear in the actual Passion narrative. They are not the driving force there but rather the upper-class Sadducees, who were particularly concerned to reach a political accommodation with Rome. The Pharisees, who were certainly at odds with Jesus in conflicts over the sabbath and discussions about cultic regulations, were forced into the role of Jesus' real enemies because they later determined dogmatically what Jewish practice was and thus came into conflict with the community of Jesus, especially after the destruction of Jerusalem. Historically seen, both groups were forced to maintain strictly separate identities. Judaism had no desire to be absorbed into a universal religious syncretism, and the community of Jesus was unwilling simply to remain a Jewish sect.

[32] A "fox" symbolizes someone who is insignificant or cunning (Bill.). As in 7:21, exorcisms and "cures" (the verb and noun are almost exclusively Lukan, and so this is a Lukan addition) are cen-

tral, as expressions of Jesus' God-given authority. They will cease in Jerusalem (except in 22:51). The three days are the period allotted by God; this is Jesus' great freedom, that all he does and its appointed end belong to God. That is the sense of "consummate." The root is the same as in "fulfill" and may suggest for Luke even here that the life of Jesus, in fulfillment of God's will, is moving toward his exaltation and the consummation of God's plan of salvation.

[33] Jesus journeys under a divine imperative (see the discussion of 9:51). His going is not subject to his own pleasure or fear of Herod. It is seldom reported that Jerusalem killed prophets (Jer. 26:20–23; cf. 2:30; 2 Chron. 24:21; cf. 1 Kings 18:4, 13; 19:10, 14). But there are legends to that effect (see the discussion of Matt. 23:29–30), and Jewish confessions of sin looked upon this as typical behavior on the part of Israel (see the conclusion to Luke 11:37—12:1). Jesus places himself in this company of prophets, albeit as the last in the series (see the discussion of 3:19–20 and the excursus following 22:30, a). Jesus astonishingly accepts this element of Jewish confessions and thus his own fate as a prophet. But this very acceptance does not simply condemn a disobedient and ignorant people but offers a salvation in which last can be first (vs. 30). The statement about the death of the prophets is extremely important to Luke: Jerusalem (which he mentions ninety times, in comparison to forty-nine occurrences in the rest of the New Testament) is exalted above all cities of the world by human sin and God's action. [34] Luke connects this with vss. 34–35 (see the discussion of 11:49–51): Jesus will die not only in but at the hands of Jerusalem.

[35] This changes the meaning of the text decisively. The macarism in vs. 35 now comes in a different place than in Matthew 23:39. Here it is incorporated in Jesus' answer to Pharisees in the territory ruled by Herod. It will be heard again in 19:38. The statement that they will not see him again thus refers only to the time preceding the entrance into Jerusalem, which already looks forward to its fall (19:39–44). The time is therefore not the final time of crisis indicated by the phrase "from now on" in Matthew 23:39.

It is in this light that Luke interprets the "text" about the forsaken house, which is no longer really appropriate. He also has the Pharisees reappear in 19:39, albeit as those who reject the call of the "great crowd of disciples" (only Luke 19:37). That will be the time of decision. Until then, Jesus and those who come to warn him go their separate ways; until then they still have time to repent; afterward the end of Jerusalem will come. For Luke, this is its conquest by the Romans (cf. vss. 1–9).

A saying that was originally eschatological (cf. Matt. 23:39) is seen by Luke as being fulfilled in the fate of Jesus in Jerusalem, which points in turn to the fall of Jerusalem in A.D. 70. This does not mean that eschatology is unimportant to Luke (see the excursus following 21:38) but that what is essential to him is the time for decision given to people in their historical situation. Therefore the fall of Jerusalem is also a warning to his readers. Vss. 22–30 have this double emphasis: concern for the human lifetime as the time of spiritual "striving" (vs. 24), and an understanding of Israel as a warning against all kinds of self-sufficiency, which will prove unavailing in the last judgment. Vs. 31 connects these verses closely with the saying that follows.

The Pharisees are not devils. They are human beings who have nothing against Jesus but are happiest when he does not get too close to them (vs. 31) with his radicalism which refuses to adapt. Luke contrasts them with Jesus' uncompromising subordination to God, whereby he also finds solidarity with people, especially those who suffer.

This must not be misinterpreted as a mere enthusiasm. It is already under the sign of that "third day" and, because Jesus knows this, he can live with full intensity (vs. 32) and maintain God's solidarity with us to the bitter end. This is exemplified by the prophets, and Jesus is so termed in vs. 33. Prophetic speech is also represented in the participial and question form of vss. 34–35, as well as the sequence: address—invective—threat—appeal to God's faithfulness—prophecy. But the messenger formula "thus says the Lord" does not appear in Jesus' words, nor is there a corresponding element in his signs. He speaks and acts on his own authority, and thus is both a call to repentance and a proclamation of salvation because he shows the human situation—and also the situation of God, who maintains his love for humankind all the way to the cross. For God there is no room in the world (2:7), and yet the divine is on the way toward the world (13:33)!

The terrifying element is that it is the city of the devout that has the exclusive right to kill the prophets because it, more than the Pharisees of vs. 31, thinks it knows all there is to know about God. But when the living God forsakes the house, the walls of magnificent temples and churches may remain standing (cf. 21:5), but all the religious activity and all the theological expertise cannot conceal the fact that they are empty, "deserted by all good spirits," and that it is only a question of time until the fall to ruin (vs. 35). They will be visited only by tourists with an interest in art history, whose guides repeat the terrifying echo, "This is the temple of Yahweh" (Jer. 7:4).

In Jesus, however, God's living presence (see the discussion of Matt. 23:37) comes over Jerusalem—again, not over a special community he is to found. Therefore the warning of judgment to come is also God's urgent invitation. It is addressed to the inflexible devout, to the doubting Pharisees who stand apart, and to the half-Jew Herod, but also to the disciples of Jesus (half and whole). For them all there will be times when they no longer see Jesus, but it is important to be ready until he once more proves himself the living Christ.

# E. THE JOY OF REPENTANCE
## (14:1—15:32)

Together with 13:1–21, this section frames the central section 13:22–35, which focuses entirely on Jerusalem. As in 13:10–21, the coming kingdom of God (13:18, 20/14:14, 15) is proclaimed in deed (14:1–6, a sabbath healing like 13:10–16) and word (14:7–14, parables like 13:18–21). As in 13:10–21, the result is division (13:17/ 14:6). In 13:1–9, there is an initial call to Israel to repent; the same call follows here in 14:15—15:32. It is enormously expanded, which shows how important it is that those who were really not expected can repent and return (14:15–24; 15:1–32). Luke 15:1 is a new introduction, but the tax collectors and sinners represent those who are

named in 14:21, 23, while the Pharisees and scribes represent those
named in 14:24.

## Table Conversation as Call to the Kingdom of God (14:1–24)

### (1) Sabbath Healing (14:1–6)

¹And it happened, when he went to the house of a ruler of the Pharisees to dine on the sabbath, they were watching him. ²And behold,
there was a person before him who had dropsy. ³And Jesus answered
and said to the lawyers and Pharisees, "Is it lawful to heal on the sabbath, or not?" ⁴But they were silent. Then he took him and healed him
and let him go. ⁵And he said to them, "Which of you having a son or
an ox that has fallen into a well would not immediately pull him out on
the sabbath day?" ⁶And they could not reply to this.

Vss. 1–24 are placed in the setting of a meal to which Jesus is
invited; cf. 7:36; 10:38; 11:37; also 5:29. This literary form was
used by Plato and Plutarch, as well as in Hellenistic Judaism (Arist.
187–300); vss. 7–14, which sound like Jewish wisdom aphorisms,
are appropriate here. The Lukan expressions in vss. 1, 7, 12, and 15
show that Luke is responsible for this choice of form. Since, however, it is only Jesus who speaks (except in vs. 15), Luke probably
took as his model the Last Supper as the setting for Jesus' teaching
(22:24–30; John 13–16; cf. the discussion of vs. 24 and Acts 20:7;
2:42). The tone of eschatological rejoicing (vss. 11, 14, 16) also fits
this setting. Since vss. 2–6, 8–14 (without 12a), 16–24 contain non-
Lukan material, they probably belonged together before Luke; therefore he also incorporated the healing (vss. 1–6) into the setting of
the meal.

[1–6] Like a miracle story, vss. 1–2 begin by introducing the helper
and the sufferer. But opponents are also mentioned at the outset. It
is unusual for Jesus to ask the fundamental question that silences his
opponents (vss. 3–4a) before the healing takes place (vs. 4). Only
then come the argument and the aporia of the opponents (vss. 5–6).
The story has thus been transformed by a dominant interest in the
fundamental question; this reveals the central concern (cf. the con-

clusion to 13:10–17). Stylistically, vss. 1, 2*a* (reflecting 6:6–7?), 4, 6 are clearly Lukan; the question in vs. 3 and the argument in vs. 5 are related to Matthew 12:10–11 (q.v.). Together with a brief introduction (the word for "before" in vs. 2*b* is un-Lukan) and a statement of the healing, they may have been a saying of Jesus associated with vss. 7–24, so that it might have been Luke who turned them into an actual story (in fact a doublet).

[1] The Pharisee probably sees in Jesus a teacher sympathetic to his own ideas. Traveling rabbis were often invited to homes, especially to the noon meal (11:37; literally "bread-eating," see the discussion of vs. 15) following sabbath worship (Bill. 1. 589–90, 611–15; 2. 202–203). On other days there were only morning and evening meals.

[3] The question is not theoretical; Jesus always asks in very specific situations what the will of God is here and now. The striking phrase "a son or [even just] an ox" (see the discussion of Matt. 12:9–14) has been emended by many copyists.

[4] For Jesus, the poor and the liberation that comes to them are an integral part of any celebration and feast.

[6] It is possible to be open to Jesus (cf. the discussion of 13:31), delight in discussing his teachings, and still miss the encounter with him because, faced with a practical problem, one does not want to surrender principles and therefore remains silent. Jesus' reason for challenging his host is to open him to the incursion of God's new act. God's sabbath joy seeks to free him from his moralism, which bars the way to his suffering neighbor.

## (2) The Life Shaped by the Coming Kingdom (14:7–14)

7Now he told a parable to those who were invited, when he marked how they chose the places of honor, saying to them, 8"When you are invited by anyone to a marriage feast, do not recline in a place of honor, lest someone more eminent than you be invited by him, 9and he who invited you both will come and say to you, 'Give place to this person,' and then you will begin with shame to take the lowest place. 10But when you are invited, go and recline in the lowest place, so that when he who invited you comes, he may say to you, 'Friend, go up higher.' Then you will be honored in the presence of all those invited. [11]For everyone who exalts himself will be humbled, and whoever humbles himself will be exalted."

[12]He said also to the man who had invited him, "When you give a noon or evening banquet, do not invite your friends or your brothers or your relatives or rich neighbors, lest they also invite you in return and you be repaid. [13]But when you give a feast, invite the poor, the maimed, the lame, the blind, [14]and you will be blessed, because they cannot repay you. But you will be repaid at the resurrection of the just."

The two sayings exhibit parallel structure: "When you . . . , then [negative command] . . . lest; but when you . . . then [positive command using a different verb]. . . ." In both cases, two verbs in the future tense give the result in both earthly and eternal life. This fact and the introductory characterization of the passage as a parable show that it is more than a lesson in etiquette. Vs. 11 appears also in 18:14 and Matthew 23:12 (cf. James 4:6; 1 Pet. 5:5; 1 Clem. 30:2; Ignatius *Eph.* 5:3); it was obviously a familiar and frequently quoted saying. On vs. 13, see the discussion of vs. 21; on vss. 7–10, see the conclusion to Matthew 20:20–28.

[8–10] Even in Jesus' day table precedence was a ticklish problem; later, age replaced honor or wealth as the criterion, so that no one would be offended. And so vss. 8–10 appear to be wise counsel for someone who is hungry for special honor: "Stay two or three places below your own (even modesty must not be exaggerated!) and wait until someone says, 'Come up . . .'" (Bill.; similar advice in Prov. 26:6–7). [11] But vs. 11 and the striking macarism in vss. 14–15 (see the discussion of 12:37–38) show that Jesus intends to illuminate quite other depths.

[12–14] Vss. 12–14 likewise appear to be purely social rules (on "the lame and the blind," cf. the discussion of Matt. 21:14). Again, however, the use of the term "repay" in the concluding clauses (12, 14*a*) shows that Jesus has something more comprehensive in mind. [14] The resurrection of the just (only) is also mentioned in 20:36 (q.v.); Josephus *Antiquities* 18. 14 (cf. 2 Macc. 7:9). In contrast to Daniel 12:1–3 it brings only salvation (also 20:35), not judgment (see the conclusion to Mark 12:18–27 and the excursus following Mark 5:21–43). But it would be wrong to look for doctrinal instruction in the phrase, or from the opposite image in 16:23 (q.v.).

It would be a total misunderstanding to take Jesus' words as a demand for a Christian "humility" that says "I am nothing," still focusing all its attention on itself. This attitude does not free the self for others but secretly expects contradiction and thus greater honor. A person who attaches no value to him- or herself cannot truly value others. Neither is the point a somewhat utopian rejection of social distinctions for the brief hours of a celebration but an escape from the usual comfortable circle. It is nearer to the mark to say that Jesus would like to free his listeners from the need always to advance their own cause and come out on top or to count the profit. Not to have to impress others with our talk or with our silence, with our accomplishments or our social status (only to be outdone), not to have to think, "Someday they could also do something for me," but to be unconditionally generous—that would indeed set us free to lead truly human lives. Then we could really celebrate with others and live in the joy of a new age. Then we could take our places without worrying whether we were second or tenth, where we were lame or where we were blind.

But only the concluding words render these admonitions transparent. They say that it is God alone who gives us identity, honor, and position. The fact that Jesus speaks them is not irrelevant; he is himself a guest, dependent on invitations from others (vs. 1) and at one with all who are in the same position (Matt. 25:35). Thus he frees us from the need always to be first, to compare ourselves with others and define our own value on that basis (vs. 8), and makes us people in whose company others can find happiness, as the tax collectors did with Jesus.

At the same time, he is also the host, who invites the outsiders and the unimportant (15:2; cf. 14:21) and thus gives freedom for a meaningful life on behalf of others (vs. 13), in which the one who needs help often gives the helper more than the helper gives. The common grace ". . . and be our guest" takes its profound meaning (cf. also Gen. 18:2–5 and Heb. 13:2) from the meal at which Jesus both presides and serves (22:15, 27), thus freeing his disciples from domination by social, moral, or religious hierarchies that close off access to those who stand higher or lower on the scale (cf. Phil. 2:5–11). But this must be practiced with common sense in a human and very concrete way depicted in vss. 8–10, 12–14a.

## (3) The Kingdom of God as a Banquet (14:15–24)
Cf. Matthew 22:1–10

[15]When one of those who reclined at table with him heard this, he said to him, "Blessed is he who shall eat bread in the kingdom of God." [16]But he said to him, "A person once gave a great banquet and invited many. [17]And he sent his servant at the time for the banquet to say to those who had been invited, 'Come, for it is now ready.' [18]And they all alike began to make excuses. The first said to him, 'I have bought a field, and I must go out and see it; I pray you, have me excused.' [19]And another said, 'I have bought five yoke of oxen, and I go to examine them; I pray you, have me excused.' [20]And another said, 'I have married a wife, and therefore I cannot come.' [21]And when the servant came to him, he reported this to his lord. Then the householder in anger said to his servant, 'Go quickly to the streets and lanes of the city and bring in the poor and maimed and blind and lame.' [22]And the servant said, 'Lord, what you have commanded has been done and still there is room.' [23]And the lord said to the servant, 'Go out to the highways and hedges and compel people to come in, that my house may be filled. [24]For I tell you, none of those men who were invited shall taste my banquet.'"

The parable that follows is introduced in typical Lukan fashion by an interruption on the part of one of the guests (see the discussion of 11:1). This emphasizes that the preceding and following sections refer to the kingdom of God (also in Matt. 22:2). But it also says that a faithful longing for God's eschaton is not enough if it forgets that the invitation must be accepted here and now, that the crucial question is not when the kingdom will come but who will share in it (see the discussion of 19:11–27).

[15] "Eating bread" (used, as in 14:1, for the entire meal) may allude to the table fellowship established by the breaking of bread and the prayer of thanksgiving (Luke 24:30; Acts 2:46; etc.). [16–

**20]** On the whole, vss. 16–24 are simpler than in Matthew 22:1–10 (q.v.). Besides property ownership and work, sexuality now also comes into consideration although it is not necessary to waste much time discussing why the invited guest prefers the company of his wife to that of the banquet (cf. Deut. 20:5–7 and the discussion of Luke 17:26–33). **[20]** Vs. 20 is lacking in Mathew 22:5; it is also phrased differently from the other excuses. If it were not part of the original parable, those invited might have expressed their willingness to come later, just not at the moment. Then the passage would refer to those who attach great importance to God's final salvation that is to come but do not see that it is now coming to them in Jesus. But this is certainly not true of the present text, which describes fundamental rejection and centers on the invitation, not on the conflict with opponents.

**[21]** Luke himself probably added the list of the wretched in vs. 21*b*, which is identical with vs. 13, and possibly the "many" in vs. 16. Through the inclusion of this list he may in fact be responsible for the distinction between an invitation within the city (Israel) and a second outside the gates (Gentiles; see the discussion of Matt. 22:8–10). In this case, some un-Lukan terms ("quickly," "bring in," "and he said," "room," vss. 23*b*, 24*a*) appeared in what was originally a single invitation, and the parable was intended to conquer the possible hesitation in every listener between acceptance and rejection (vs. 24). Luke would then have altered it to refer concretely (see the discussion of 13:9) to the rejection of Jesus and the subsequent mission to Jews and Gentiles (see the discussion of 13:28–30).

It is unlikely, if only because of the new beginning in vs. 15, that it was Luke's purpose merely to exhort the rich or those who had not yet suffered persecution, after the fashion of vs. 13. Furthermore, for Luke the poor and those with bodily infirmities symbolize all who need God's help, just as the tax collectors and sinners of 15:1–2 symbolize all who are open to this help, whether within Israel or not. Therefore for him their healing by Jesus and the community (Acts 2:43; 3:6–7; etc.) is a sign of the mighty incursion of God, who seeks to heal the far deeper need and alienation of each person from God and therefore from himself (4:21–27; 7:21–23; see the discussion of 10:17). Vs. 21a, in which the "person" and "house-holder" (vss. 16, 21b) is called "lord," also contains Lukan language.

[23] It is unlikely that the guests are to be "compelled" (an un-Lukan expression) because in the Near East an invitation must first be declined (Gen. 19:2–3) or because of a necessity in salvation history (see the discussion of 13:33), which was later even used to justify forced conversions by fire and sword. [17] Only the urgency of the invitation is underlined, as it also is by the reference to the "time for the banquet" when "all is ready" [24] and the term "taste," which is also used for the community meal (Acts 20:11). It is un-likely that this refers to tidbits that were sometimes sent to those who could not be present.

The parable, then, is a totally open invitation. It is the real focus of the entire section. This is underlined by the invitation to the whole city and countryside, which is conceivable but goes far beyond all expectations. Those who are warned in the last verse have done nothing evil; they have merely failed to notice how minor their pressing bus-iness was in comparison to the inconceivable greatness of the invi-tation. They are like the elder son in 15:25–32 and the contemporaries of Noah and Lot in 17:27–28. Morality, immorality, everyday af-fairs—all can be a curse for someone whose goodness or wicked-ness or normality is more important than the Lord. God seeks to break through all that to call the wicked as well as the good (Matt. 22:10), the poor and the sick as well as those who lead a normal life (Luke 14:21, 23) because nothing brings God more joy than to have his creatures share his feast and fill his house.

By referring directly to acceptance of the gospel by Jews and Gen-tiles, Luke underlines the fact that what matters is not theory but practical decisions. The interpretation of vs. 23 as referring to the Gentiles is possibly further supported by the fact that here all appear to be invited, not just the poor (vs. 21). The danger of looking for the reprobate only among the Jews of Jesus' own day who rejected him (see the discussion of vss. 34–35) is checked by the sitting together of Jews and Gentiles at the banquet and also by vss. 12–13 which require people to continue in their social actions the good God has done for them, and by the radical demands of vss. 25–33. In addition, one must remember the original form, in which both possibilities are open to every listener.

### Considered Discipleship (14:25–35)

[25]Now a great crowd assembled, and he turned and said to them, [26]"If anyone comes to me and does not hate his own father and mother and wife and children and brothers and sisters, yes, and even his own life, he cannot be my disciple. [27]Whoever does not bear his own cross and come after me cannot be my disciple. [28]For which of you, desiring to build a tower, does not first sit down and count the cost, whether he has enough to complete it? [29]Otherwise, when he has laid a foundation and is not able to finish, all who see it begin to mock him, [30]saying, 'This man began to build and was not able to finish.' [31]Or what king, going to encounter another king in war, will not sit down first and take counsel whether it is possible for him with ten thousand to meet him who comes against him with twenty thousand? [32]And if not, while the other is yet a great way off, he sends an embassy and asks terms of peace. [33]So therefore whoever of you does not renounce all that belongs to him cannot be my disciple.

[34]"Now the salt is good, but if the salt has lost its taste, how shall it be seasoned? [35]It is fit neither for the land nor for the dunghill, and so they throw it away. The one who has ears, let him hear."

Vs. 25 defines the situation. Two parallel clauses follow ("If anyone comes to me and does not . . ." and "Whoever does not . . ." vss. 26–27), summarized in vs. 33 ("Whoever does not . . ."; from Luke himself?). All three end in the same way. In between come two parables formulated as questions; the first is a single statement introduced by "Who among you . . ." (see the discussion of Matt. 12:11); the second, following the question, expresses the alternative (which is hardly conceivable with respect to Jesus). Vss. 26–27 appear in similar form in Matthew 10:37–38 (q.v.; also Mark 8:34), vss. 34–35 in Matthew 5:13 (q.v.), in each case with different wording. Separate sayings have been combined here to emphasize the urgency of deciding for Jesus, which is further stressed by the addition of "comes to me" in vs. 26, going beyond vss. 27 and 33. The sayings have influenced each other in the course of tradition. In vs. 26, "yes, and even his own life" has been added, because vs. 27 appears in Mark 8:34–35 alongside the saying about losing one's own life, which appears in John 12:25 in the form "hating one's own life." Since the parables describe the time before a decision is made, Luke (following vss. 21 and 23!) has them addressed to the crowd that has not yet decided to follow Jesus. Vs. 34 has been influenced by Mark 9:50 but also (like vs. 35) by Matthew 5:13 (Q).

[25] The phrase "a great crowd" is Lukan (Greek plural as in 5:15; singular: 7:11; 8:4; 9:37); it recalls vss. 21 and 23. [26] The division among family members corresponds to Mark 10:29, except that wives are also mentioned, as in Luke 18:29. "Hate" is understood not as an emotion but as radical objective subordination, perhaps even as "forsake," as in the case of the Hebrew verb.

[28–32] The private citizen who builds a tower in his vineyard (Isa. 5:2) can simply forget the project to avoid the scorn of his neighbors, but a great king would be forced to submit to his enemy (2 Sam. 8:10; Test. Jud. 7:7). The two cases are therefore not equivalent; they may have been combined on the basis of Proverbs 24:3–6, which describes wisdom as building her house wisely and waging her war well. This could have been predicated of God or Jesus in a sermon (excursus following Matt. 25:39). In this case it would be a call to follow him who has already built a house and achieved the victory. But none of this appears in the present text. Neither can it mean that whoever follows Jesus must, in contrast to farmer or king, renounce all means of achieving success; for vs. 33 concludes by saying "So therefore. . . ." The parables therefore state that those who, like the crowd, run after Jesus must consider carefully whether they are prepared for total discipleship.

[33] Together with vss. 28–32, which describe the situation before decision for Jesus, vs. 33 must be addressed to all the people, even though it has in mind the most radical form of discipleship. As in vss. 26–27, all are called to be prepared for it although it will not be the reality for all (cf. the discussion of 6:20a). Of course Luke 9:23 has already spoken of following Jesus continually in contrast to the single decision to do so (Mark 8:34), and this is the theme of the

refrain that dominates the entire section: ". . . cannot be [not: 'become'!] my disciple." And so Jesus' warning is also addressed to those readers who already belong to the community.

[34] This is underlined in vss. 34–35: salt symbolizes discipleship (Matt. 5:13). Although the described use of salt cannot be explained convincingly, vs. 35 therefore states even more forcefully than its parallels that a disciple who is not really a disciple is more useless than someone who has never set out to follow Jesus. As in Matthew 22:11–14 (q.v.), this protects against misinterpreting the parable of the banquet as referring only to Jesus' unbelieving contemporaries (see the conclusion to vss. 15–24).

Love claims the beloved totally. Therefore the God of the Old Testament is a jealous God, making equally radical demands of those who would be his priests (Deut. 33:9; also 4QTest 15–17). Whoever would be exposed to this love must consider what he is getting into. In vs. 33, Luke is thinking especially of possessions. The necessary equipment for discipleship consists in having nothing. That is every bit as essential as the means for building a tower or waging war. Of course Luke is also aware that sometimes families must be forsaken (vs. 26), other times brought into the community (Acts 16:33; 1 Cor. 7:12; Col. 3:18–21); sometimes the cross must be borne (vs. 27), other times food and drink and clothing must be accepted (12:22–32; 14:1); sometimes everything must be given up (vs. 33), other times property must be used for oneself and others (5:29; 7:37; 10:38; 22:10–12). Of course not all are called in the same way to the same form of discipleship. But it is equally sure that there is no such thing as a totally middle-class discipleship where there is only preservation of one's heritage and radical renunciation can never flower.

## Two Seekers (15:1–10)
Cf. Matthew 18:12–14

[1]Now the tax collectors and sinners were all drawing near to hear him, [2]and the Pharisees and the scribes murmured, saying, "This man receives sinners and eats with them."

[3]But he told them this parable, saying, [4]"Which of you, having a

hundred sheep and having lost one of them, does not leave the ninety-nine in the wilderness and go after the one which is lost, until he finds it? [5]And when he has found it, he lays it on his shoulders, rejoicing, [6]and when he comes home he calls together his friends and his neighbors, saying, 'Rejoice with me, for I have found my sheep which was lost.' [7]Even so, I tell you, there will be joy in heaven over one sinner who repents more than over ninety-nine righteous persons who need no repentance.

[8]"Or what woman who has ten drachmas, if she loses one coin, does not light a lamp and sweep the house and seek diligently until she finds it? [9]And when she has found it, she calls together her friends and neighbors, saying, 'Rejoice with me, for I have found the drachma which I lost.' [10]Even so, I tell you, there is joy before the angels of God over one sinner who repents."

Vss. 4–10 contain two parallel parables aimed at those who "murmur" (vss. 1–2, Lukan; cf. 5:30 and the discussion of 13:1–5). They are followed in vss. 11–32 by a further parable that is open-ended. Similar triplets are found in 9:57–62; 11:42–52; 14:18–20; 20:10–12 (but cf. the discussion of 19:13). In 16:1 Jesus addresses the disciples once more.

The first two parables are identical in structure. In 14:28/31 we find "Which of *you* . . ." (see the discussion of Matt. 12:11 analogously only at the beginning of the first parable). The alternation between participle and conditional subordinate clause ("having lost"/ 'if she loses," vss. 4a/8a) is common (see the discussion of 12:8–9). In minor details, Luke has adapted the second parable more closely to his style. Only in the first does it make sense to speak of leaving the ninety-nine and repeat the motif in vs. 7. Losing and finding are each mentioned three times in the parables (losing only twice in vss. 8–10). Both are obviously necessary to the story. In each case, friends and neighbors are called in to share in the rejoicing. This joy is all that is mentioned in the interpretation, so it is the point of the narrative.

The first parable appears also in Matthew 18:12–13 (q.v.). The statement, "Even so, I tell you, there will be joy . . . over one sinner . . . more than over ninety-nine . . ." is stylistically un-Lukan (cf. the discussion of 19:40). It therefore belonged to the tradition although possibly it came within the parable, as in Matthew 18:13

("over the one [sheep]"). "Heaven" in the singular is Lukan, as are "righteous" and the entire relative clause (both lacking in vs. 10!); the repentance of the sinner is important to him. This really has nothing to do with the parable since the sheep (unlike the son in vs. 20) has not "returned." This tension shows that the parables are pre-Lukan (Jesuan; see the discussion of Matt. 18:10–14). "Righteous persons who need no repentance" makes sense only in contrast to the one who allows himself to be found: Luke and the third parable are well aware that it is precisely these who are called to repentance. It is against the "righteous" that God's festival must be defended (vss. 2, 32!). The triplet corresponds in a way to Jeremiah 31:10–14, 15–16, 17–20, but this is probably accidental.

[1] Luke speaks of "all" the tax collectors and sinners in order to emphasize their fundamental willingness to hear Jesus. [2] The Pharisees similarly represent fundamental rejection of Jesus. They accuse him of "eating and drinking," as in 5:30 (both expressions only in Luke), perhaps because according to Deuteronomy 21:20–21 (cf. Bill. 4. 608 and Prov. 23:20–21) a son who has become a "glutton and drunkard" (Luke 7:34) should be stoned. This same passage is cited in the Qumran Temple Scroll (64:5), where lines 8–12 discuss crucifixion.
[3] All that follows is treated as a single parable (see the discussion of 6:37–42) and understood as a unit. [4] Once again, Jesus frames vs. 4 as a question demanding the listener's opinion. The conduct of the shepherd contradicts 1 Samuel 17:28. Has the leaving of the rest (not found in vs. 8) been added in order to bring out the astonishing element in Jesus' actions (vss. 2, 7)? In Judaism, God's intervention on behalf of Joseph in Egypt is likened to a person who, having twelves beasts of burden, goes after one that has run into a Gentile warehouse (Bill. 1. 785). Carrying the sheep on the shoulders might recall Greek statues of Orpheus, but the image is found as early as the eighth century B.C. in northern Syria and is an obvious way to emphasize special solicitude. The joy spoken of in vss. 6–7, 9–10 is already introduced here (by Luke?). [6] It takes on dimensions far beyond the expected. [7] The interpretation runs counter to rabbinic perception, which gives higher status to those

who have remained righteous (Bill.). Nothing is said here to deny their righteousness or to censure them. The Greek uses a word that merely means "than" or "or," but it must be translated "more than" as in 17:2; Mark 9:43 (where the "more" appears in the parallel clause in vs. 42), and frequently in the LXX. It is also understood in this sense in Matthew 18:13. In Luke 18:14, the translation could well be "but not," but the formulation is different in the original text. Whether there are in fact righteous persons who can give up their claim to a special place in heaven is another question (cf. Retrospect 1). But the parable is to be understood only as a message of God's great joy (2:10).

[8] Vs. 8 depicts the great effort involved in searching within a windowless Palestinian house and resembles a Jewish commentary (Bill.): "He who studies the law is like a person who, having lost a coin or necklace in his house, lights many lamps until he recovers it." This, however, refers to someone illuminated by study of the law. A drachma (roughly equivalent to one denarius) is the daily wage of an unskilled laborer; it may be part of a woman's dowry, sewed into her head covering (see the discussion of 8:3). Here the rejoicing is even more exaggerated; in the interpretation, it is described by means of the present tense rather than the future, as in vs. 7.

Both parables are concerned with joy. The search is emphasized, and the joy described surpasses all expectations. The sheep went to no trouble and certainly not the coin, but they are the object of rejoicing. The door is being left open to the sinner far more than a crack—here, as the interpretation says, all heaven rejoices over one's return.

Luke has set the parables in Jesus' own situation. Those who are lost are not nebulous figures but people who employ highly dubious business methods (tax collectors; see the discussion of 3:13) and avoid any religiosity that could bother their middle-class lives (sinners). Nor are the opponents bogies but devout people who impose great sacrifices on themselves in order really to serve their God: Pharisees (see the discussion of 3:7) and scribes (trained theologians).

But there is another point that is crucial: Luke is saying that Jesus himself is the interpretation of his parables. Luke does not talk about God's fatherly love in general, he does not instruct the reader in God's nature but tells of God's acts that are taking place now in the ministry of Jesus and are therefore already (see the discussion of vs. 10) the cause of rejoicing in heaven.

Cyril (died A.D. 444) is not wrong to interpret the shepherd as standing for Jesus, the ninety-nine sheep as the angels, and the one sheep as humankind (*Homilies*, 21), but Jesus expresses what is taking place in his ministry through the parable as interpreted by the situation, here the Pharisees and tax collectors.

## The Powerless Almighty Father (15:11–32)

[11]And he said, "A certain person had two sons, [12]and the younger of them said to his father, 'Father, give me the share of the property that falls to me.' And he divided his living between them. [13]And not many days later the younger son gathered all he had and took his journey into a far country. And there he squandered his property stupidly. [14]But when he had spent everything, a great famine arose in that country, and he began to be in want. [15]And he went and joined himself to one of the citizens of that country, and he sent him into his fields to feed swine. [16]And he desired to fill his belly with the carob pods that the swine ate, but no one gave him any. [17]Then he came to himself and said, 'How many of my father's hired servants have bread enough and to spare, but I perish here with hunger! [18]I will arise and go to my father and say: "Father, I have sinned against heaven and before you. [19]I am no longer worthy to be called your son. Make me one of your hired servants."' [20]And he arose and went to his father. But while he was yet at a distance, his father saw him and had compassion and ran and embraced him and kissed him. [21]But the son said to him, 'Father, I have sinned against heaven and before you; I am no longer worthy to be called your son.' [22]But the father said to his servants, 'Bring quickly the best robe and put it on him and put a ring on his hand and shoes on his feet [23]and bring the fatted calf and kill it, and let us eat and make merry, [24]for this my son was dead and is alive again, was lost and is found.' And they began to make merry.

[25]"But his elder son was in the field, and as he came and drew near to the house, he heard music and dancing [26]and he called to one of the servants and asked what this meant. [27]And he said to him, 'Your brother

has come, and your Father has killed the fatted calf because he has received him safe and sound.' [28]But he was enraged and refused to go in. His father came out and entreated him. [29]But he answered and said to his father, 'Behold, these many years I have served you like a servant and I never disobeyed your command, and yet you never gave me even a kid that I might make merry with my friends. [30]But now that this son of yours comes who has devoured your living with harlots, you have killed for him the fatted calf!' [31]And he said to him, 'Child, you are always with me, and all that is mine is yours. [32]It was fitting to make merry and be glad, for this your brother was dead and has come to life again; he was lost and is found.' "

The initial situation is briefly stated (vs. 11, with the father as subject); there follow the fundamental inward separation of the younger son from his father (vs. 12), its outward manifestation (vss. 13–15, aorist) and consequence (vs. 16, imperfect), and the son's inward (vss. 17–19) and outward (vss. 20a, 21) conversion (aorist, with the son as subject throughout). The flow is interrupted by the father's intervention (vs. 20b, with the father as subject), which puts an end to the separation first in principle and then outwardly (vss. 22–24) and makes possible something more than bare physical survival (as in vss. 17–20a). In vss. 25–28a the outward separation of the elder son (vs. 25a, imperfect) becomes a fundamental inward separation (vss. 25b–28a, 29–30, aorist). But the father intervenes once more (vs. 28b) and refuses to allow such separation to continue (vs. 31). Vs. 32 states the obligation to rejoice; the acceptance or rejection of this obligation determines whether the initial situation (vs. 11) is restored.

The parable begins and ends with the father. In both sections he interrupts what his son is saying, and his interruption is decisive. His joy is the criterion by which all else is measured (vs. 32). The dialogue, in which the events of the narrative are queried as to their meaning and thus made the raw material of theological reflection, describes the relationship of the father to his sons but also that of the younger son to his employer and above all to himself and that of the elder to the whole business. No more words are needed for the younger son, only the act of rejoicing, but more needs to be said to the elder

son, who has yet to be won over. He must still be given the freedom
to say yes or no.

It is actually the father who gives both sons the possibility of sepa-
rating from him. He acts in totally unexpected ways, like the shepherd and the woman in the preceding section, especially when one
considers the contemporary educational ideal, by which one must
constantly see to it that a beloved son should feel the rod (Ecclus.
30:1–13). The behavior of the sons, on the contrary, fits the expected
pattern. It is easy to identify with them but not with the father.
Therefore the whole parable turns totally on him. It begins with him,
it ends with him; he alone unites both portions.

[12] The son's request goes beyond normal expectations. It is impossible to grant by any standard of Jewish or Hellenistic law appli-
cable, say, to emigration. Normally the father continues to have
usufruct of the third that belongs to the second son by Deuteronomy
21:17. Even what the son sells goes to the buyer only after the death
of the father. Thus the parable makes it clear that the son merely
wants something from the father, not the father himself. [13] The
father is left behind; the son is his de facto survivor. "Gather" may
also mean "convert into cash." No immorality is mentioned; he merely
squanders his money "stupidly" (cf. the stupidity of the rich man in
12:20). [14] Neither is his situation entirely his own fault. [15–16]
Along with hunger ("When the Israelites need to eat carob, they will
repent," Bill., d), he suffers loss of religious identity. Swine have
been unclean since Leviticus 11:7; only Gentiles eat their flesh (Isa.
65:4; 66:17), and "whoever tends swine is cursed" (Bill. 1. 493).
[17] The son has become a nonperson.

Repentance is the recollection of how good things are at his father's house; it causes the son to "come to himself." [18] It leads to
the realization that he has taken the wrong road. Israel speaks in
similar terms (Jer. 31:18–19; Hos. 2:9). A distinction is made between God and the father (as between God and Israel in the words
of Pharaoh in Exod. 2:16); the father is not simply the allegorical
equivalent of God.

[19] The son knows that he has no claim on his father, whose
household lacks nothing; at best he can be in his service, without

any covetous designs on his wealth. **[20]** His father is already present in his memory, but also in the fact that his father continues to look for him (cf. Jer. 31:20). For his father to run to him is contrary to all custom; in the Near East, a mature man loses all his dignity when he runs. It is possible in the case of Esau, who is younger (Gen. 33:3), but it reveals strong emotion. Many painters have rightly seen here the heart of the parable.

**[21]** The son is forgiven before he can confess; his confession is really a kind of postscript and cannot even be finished, because it is already irrelevant. **[22]** Forgiveness is performed, not pronounced. Ring, robe, (Gen. 41:42; Ezek. 16:10), and shoes (in contrast to slaves, who go barefoot) indicate even more: a position of honor. There may be echoes of the Jewish rite of restitution of someone who had been expelled from the community. **[23]** The special roast—meat is rarely eaten in Palestine in any event—makes the whole event a holiday.

**[24]** The father's reason is not a reproof of his son but a public affirmation. It speaks not only of finding what was lost (vss. 6, 9) but of the resurrection of the dead. Psalm 41:13 also uses this image because separation from God always represents the realm of death. Nothing is said of penitence, probation, progress, or trial, only of immediate rejoicing (vss. 6–7, 9–10).

Other younger brothers who enjoy God's favor include Abel, Isaac, Jacob, Joseph, Benjamin, David, Gideon, and Judas Maccabeus (cf. Gal. 4:21–31).

**[25]** Typically, the elder brother is at work. A point is made of his being far from lost. He lives—outwardly—with his father but not inwardly. The noise of the festivities—this is the first we hear of music and dancing—is the antithesis to his pique. **[27–28]** All that matters to the servant is that the younger son is safe at home. He sees what is in the foreground; what is said in vs. 24 does not concern him. The elder son's rage (aorist) reveals his self-centeredness; it is met by the continued efforts (imperfect tense) of the father.

**[29–30]** The omission of the vocative "Father" and the refusal to use the term "brother" ("this son of yours") completes the elder son's separation from his father. He will have no more to do with his father's incomprehensible actions than with his brother's reprehensible actions. He can only regret that the world and even his own father have no sense of morality. It is he who speaks of harlots, of whom the narrative says nothing, because he wants to preserve his own righteous conduct, perhaps even resisting similar desires. Separation from his father takes the form of separation from his brother, and his primary reproach is that his father has shown compassion.

[31] In response, the father affirms his son; he has no need to protect his own worth by putting someone else down. [32] The father does not defend himself or his younger son. He only calls for rejoicing because that alone sets one free from calculation and comparison, and he refuses to dismiss his elder son from his love.

The parable is the story of a father (see above), and thus brings God into living reality. Considered abstractly, this father is an almighty father. He could refuse the younger son his inheritance ("You can't wait until I'm in the ground?") or merely assign him the interest or raise his allowance ("Then we'll see how you do"). He could bring him back from the far country or send a friend or even the police after him ("Didn't I tell you what would happen?"). He could let the son feel his power ("Now you can work a few years as a servant!"). He could have two servants get the elder son into the house in five minutes ("I don't owe you any explanations"). But this almighty father has no power at all. He has decided once and for all in favor of love and knows that if he acted in this fashion, he would have lost his sons forever.

Therefore he can only let his younger son depart, worry about him, and look for him daily. Therefore it is also impossible to take a snapshot of the feast, with the father sitting at the head of the table dispensing food and drink and happiness to his returning son and the whole company, and paste it in an album, as though we had captured the image of the all-merciful and almighty father. Without doubt this is *also* a true picture of what God is, but because God is a living God, the picture must change. Within five minutes, in Jesus' parable, the father is standing outside in the dark, where he could catch pneumonia, facing his elder son with no means but words to express what is in his burning heart.

In Jesus' narrative the kingdom of God becomes real. But a few weeks or months later he will hang on the cross, equally powerless, mocked by all: "Are you not the Christ? Save yourself and us!"

(23:39). All his power resides in his loving heart, which invites others to God: "Today you will be with me in paradise" (23:43).

God becomes real only among persons. This is so true that we can actually follow the psychoanalytic history of the two sons. The Oedipal situation is clear: the younger does away with his father by leaving him and claiming the inheritance that is his only after his father's death, but his father continues to pursue him. He squanders his substance (and his sexuality?), thus divorcing himself from all that belongs to his father, seeking a father figure in his new master, who turns out to be harsh. Now he "comes to himself," recognizes his "shadow side," the loss of meaning in his life, but he is still trapped by his past. Is the solution to become a servant, an "object" belonging to his father, so that his sonship is destroyed?

The elder son also does away with his father by identifying with him—but in fact with his father as he would like him to be. Thus he also divorces himself from him. Is it possible to meet the father only by adapting totally to him and remaining infantile? But this would be the God created by a person's own subconscious.

The God of Jesus' parable overcomes this God, who is a human creation. The striking actions of the father in the parable repeatedly shatter the expected picture. He has no need to possess anything or control anyone. The law is present in the parable: the younger son transgresses it, the elder son obeys it. But both types of conduct are overthrown by the father's incredible actions, which do not correspond to the law, and his overwhelming joy at the return of his son, who is accepted back into his father's love almost sacramentally, without any preaching.

Thus the parable brings great joy in the very act of telling because the listener can really do nothing but agree with the father's final statement. And yet the parable remains open, ultimately toward Jesus' own fate in Jerusalem, in which is made clear how hard it is for human beings to live this natural joy. What the tax collector in 18:13 recognizes, what Paul says when he states that no one can boast of his own righteousness (Phil. 3:9) or wisdom (1 Cor. 2:6–7) before God—this is what takes place when someone can hear this parable, can perhaps even in one's last extremity catch an echo of God's approaching steps. Then one discovers that one has no claim to the miracle that takes place in the parable: the fact that a human being can call God "Abba, father." In Galatians 4:6; Romans 8:15; 1 John 3:1; Revelation 21:7, too, this is understood as an eschatological miracle.

Jesus does not appear in the parable, but only because it is he who tells it and lives it to the point of death does the joy of restoration it recounts become reality. In the parable "there is no room left for any mediator between God and the sinner" (Jülicher); it is all the more incomprehensible, however, without a mediator. It was not simply Jesus the teacher who discovered God to be the father of mankind; without his ministry the parable would not be true. Jesus does not define God in the parable; wherever the parable truly comes to life, God uses it to show the significance of Jesus, to "define" him. The truth of the parable cannot be assumed as long as its first narrator, Jesus, is not alive in the particular situation of the listener or reader. A musical performance cannot be transmitted didactically without becoming an audible event; neither can the content of this parable, which—contrary to Luke's usual practice (see the introduction to 13:1–5)—cannot be captured in a summary statement. In his introduction, Luke has emphasized the error of the "righteous" (cf. the introduction and conclusion to vss. 3–10), and perhaps also that of the sinner (vss. 7, 10, 18b, 19a, 21?). This might tempt us to shift the focus from what God does to what persons do. But Luke is rightly concerned that the word address "friend and foe alike" (A. Pötzsch: "A word went forth . . ."), that readers read the parable in such a way that it may shape their lives. This is stated in Matthew 21:28–32, a parable that exhibits related features, as well as in Luke 16, where vs. 14 mentions the Pharisees again. Luke is also well aware that God's amazing action precedes all repentance (19:5–10; 24:46–47; etc.).

# F. DISCIPLESHIP AND POSSESSIONS (16:1—17:10)

Like 12:35–59 (cf. the discussion of 9:51—19:27), the parable in 16:1–8, which is also addressed to the disciples, speaks of readiness for what is to come and ends with a more general admonition. Like 12:2–34, 16:9–13 deals with use of possessions and the faithfulness that is expected above all of disciples. Each passage is much shorter than the parallel in chapter 12. There follows in 16:14–18, as in 11:37—12:1, a controversy with the Pharisees, again much abbreviated. But the story of Lazarus must be included on account of vs. 14. Luke 17:1–10 is a bridge passage, clearly directed at the disciples, who are mentioned only briefly in 12:1.

## Liberation for God's Future (16:1–13)
Cf. Matthew 6:24

[1]He also said to the disciples, "There was a rich person who had a steward, and charges were brought to him that he was wasting his goods. [2]And he called to him and said to him, 'What is this that I hear about you? Turn in the account of your stewardship; you can no longer be steward.' [3]But the steward said to himself, 'What shall I do? For my lord is taking the stewardship away from me. I am not strong enough to dig, and I am ashamed to beg. [4]I have decided what to do, so that, when I am put out of the stewardship, they will receive me into their houses.' [5]So, summoning his lord's debtors one by one, he said to the first, 'How much do you owe my lord?' [6]And he said, 'A hundred measures of oil.' But he said to him, 'Take your bill and sit down and quickly write fifty.' [7]Then he said to another, 'But you, how much do you owe?' And he said, 'A hundred measures of wheat.' He said to him, 'Take your bill and write eighty.' [8]And the lord commended the unrighteous servant because he had acted prudently, for the sons of this world are wiser toward their own generation than the sons of light. [9]And I tell you, make friends for yourself by means of unrighteous mammon, so that when it fails they may receive you into the eternal habitations.

[10]"Whoever is faithful in a very little is faithful also in much, and whoever is unrighteous in a very little is unrighteous also in much. [11]But if now you are not faithful in the unrighteous mammon, who will entrust to you that which is true? [12]And if you are not faithful in that which is another's, who will give you that which is your own? [13]No servant can serve two lords; for either he will hate the one and love the other, or he will be devoted to the one and despise the other. You cannot serve God and mammon."

The Lukan introduction addresses the parable to the disciples. If it ends with vs. 8*a*, "the lord" is Jesus, as in 18:6, and vs. 8*b* is an interpretation, somewhat awkwardly appended by the conjunction. Or "the lord" may be the lord of the parable (as in vss. 3, 5; cf. 14:23), because Jesus speaks in vs. 9 with an emphatically antithetical "I." But why should he praise the "unrighteous" (vs. 8!) steward? Possibly because he had merely deducted the interest (which would be fifty percent according to vs. 6) forbidden by Deuteronomy 23:19? Or is this merely an ironic expression of resignation in the presence of other property owners? In any case, vs. 9 is an isolated saying that has been assimilated to vs. 4. To it are appended two further sayings (vss. 10–12, 13) intended to describe how the teaching of the parable can be put into practice. Vs. 10 might derive from 19:17 (Q). Vs. 13 agrees verbatim with Matthew 6:24 (q.v.) except for the Greek word for "servant," which describes the disciple as a steward. All the rest is Lukan special material, of which "someone" in vs. 1 is typical (see the discussion of 11:1).

[1–2] The steward is charged with doing what the younger son did (15:13). The abbreviated narrative assumes that the charges are true. [3] The crucial point is depicted in typically Lukan fashion as a monologue on the part of the accused. His horror of begging (Ecclus. 40:28) and his lack of strength for construction work (Aristophanes *Birds* 14, 32) are described in common idioms. Perhaps there is also an echo of the low status assigned laborers in Ecclesiasticus 38:27 (albeit in comparison with scribes, 38:34–39:5). [5] The debtors might be tenants or merchants—in any event, the steward acts with the routine of a smart businessman not troubled by ethical scruples. [6–7] The sums involved are large, and the values are roughly equal.

[8] "Steward of unrighteousness" (the literal translation of the Greek) cannot mean "steward of unrighteous mammon"; it is merely the common Semitic idiom to indicate that he is unrighteous. This makes the praise accorded to him even more striking. The point is therefore neither the demonic effects of wealth nor the right use of property but the sagacity of the steward. He is smart because he knows what is coming and adapts to it. Thus the parable understands the present as the possibility of adapting to the future: in fact, it calls urgently

for such adaptation (cf. 12:42–46). Vs. 8*b* is a comment about the proper approach to interpretation: considered in isolation, the steward is far from exemplary; he is a "son of this world." But if even he acts so sagaciously, how much more must the "children of light." This is true, but in this generalized and resigned form it no longer opens the horizon of the future; instead it looks back and bemoans the lack of understanding on the part of Jesus' listeners. The antithesis between sons of light and sons of darkness is typical (cf. En. 108:11; 1QS 1:9–10; 3:13, 20–21; but also John 12:36; 1 Thess. 5:5; Eph. 5:8). But far from emphasizing this antithesis, the parable holds up the man of this world as a model for the sons of light.

[9] What follows is a new extension dealing with the right use of wealth, which was actually not discussed in the parable, or at least not the use of one's own wealth. Is it "unrighteous" (cf. also En. 63:10) because it tempts us to unrighteousness or because it fails us (Zeph. 1:18: in the day of judgment)? "Mammon" (not an Old Testament term) originally meant "that in which one trusts," and so could comprehend everything that one makes one's god. But even if this is true and we are not dealing with a Canaanite loanword having a different meaning, who would still be aware of it? The image of being "received" reflects vs. 4*b*. The action takes place at the last judgment; this is true whether "they" are the poor who have been given alms, the angels, or God (see the discussion of 6:38). The "habitations" (literally "booths" or "tents") recall the exodus from Egypt (cf. the discussion of Mark 9:5). The sagacious action of the steward is not only an image for the conduct of the believer, which is not described in further detail, it is now understood as an example to be imitated. Of course this does not refer to the property of others—a possibility that shows the danger of allegorizing the individual features. The point is that the disciples are called upon not only to think but to act sagaciously, which naturally includes more than sensible use of money. The emphatic "I" points expressly to Jesus, whose teaching and conduct should determine that of the sons of light. This is a necessary addition as soon as Jesus is no longer the narrator.

[10–12] Different again is the application in which the conduct of the steward is turned into a horrible example for Jesus' disciples. Alongside a radical criticism of mammon (vs. 13) stands a practical exhortation to use it rightly. The contradiction is lessened by vss. 11–12, which develop the fundamental principle of vs. 10 and emphasize that true riches are something else again, if the reference really is to spiritual riches of which the disciples are stewards and not, say, to the greater financial responsibility of the community leaders. The former interpretation is supported by 19:17 and above all by the wording of vss. 11–12, for what is "true" in contrast to "mammon" can only be spiritual. Similarly "what is yours" (as the oldest manuscripts read, not "what is ours") stands in contrast to "what is another's," i.e., what is truly given in faith in contrast to all other possessions. Epictetus makes a similar statement: "Nothing belongs to a person, everything is alien" (4. 5. 15).

The parable stresses decision in the light of Jesus' presence; he makes it possible to live for an assured future. Vs. 8 interprets this to mean that Jesus' demands determine our fate at the judgment. Vss. 10–12 show that this is not to be understood as flight from the world but as faithfulness within the world, which makes us capable of faithfulness in spiritual things, while the concluding verse reemphasizes the radical nature of the decision concerning to whom one chooses to belong. The later additions in vss. 9–13 are unrelated to the central meaning of the parable, but they help us to live it. To find the meaning of life not in the accumulation of goods but in "friends," including those who suffer and lead marginal lives, to be faithful in everything, from minor details to ultimate spiritual truths, from the proper management of household funds to the life of prayer—these are concrete existential possibilities. The surrounding verses remind us of the radical principle: whoever is ruled by possessions has lost even the sagacity of the children of this world and cannot be counted among the children of light.

## The Function of the Law (16:14–18)
Cf. Matthew 11:12–13; 5:18, 32; 19:9

[14]The Pharisees, who are lovers of money, heard all this, and turned up their noses at him. [15]And he said to them, "You are those who justify

themselves before others. But God knows your hearts because what is exalted among persons is an abomination in the sight of God.

[16]"The law and the prophets were until John. Since then the kingdom of God is preached as good news, and everyone is invited urgently. [17]But it is easier for heaven and earth to pass away than for one dot of the law to become void.

[18]"Everyone who divorces his wife and marries another commits adultery, and whoever marries a woman divorced by her husband commits adultery."

Vss. 16–18 appear also in Matthew 11:12–13; 5:18; 19:9 (q.v.) with the same rare words ("is invited urgently" [see the discussion of vs. 16], "dot") but formulated entirely differently. Probably Luke found them thus in his prototype and added vss. 14–15 as an introduction (see the discussion of 11:1 and 23:35). Vs. 16a is closer to the original form than Matthew 11:13, where "law" is out of place; but Matthew 11:12 is probably earlier than Luke 16:16b. "Justify oneself" (10:29; 18:19) and the word for "before" are Lukan. The "because" clause (without a verb; un-Lukan) is a traditional maxim.

[14] The Pharisees (see the discussion of 13:31) are subjected to the judgment of vs. 13 (vs. 14). [17] The emphasis on the law (vs. 17) is appropriate in this context. [15–16] The two verses frame vss. 15–16: outward correctness does not justify anyone since God weighs the heart. Now the law is left behind and the kingdom of God is preached: [18] its commandments, as the postscript in vs. 18 shows, are far more radically demanding. But the train of thought is not really clear.

[14] Jesus is laughed at by his opponents because he looks like an illusionist who wants to change the world and does not see reality, though according to vss. 9–12, this charge cannot be brought against the Lukan form of Jesus' words. [15] His reply therefore shows that he is not concerned simply for an unrealistic ideal but that people open their hearts entirely to God, so as not to become an "abomination," seeking to rise by condemning others (cf. the conclusion to 14:7–14; also 1:51–52; 18:9–14; Isa. 2:11–19; 5:14–16).

[16] Vs. 16 is difficult. The identical word is translated "suffers violence" in Matthew 11:12. The verb (with the addition of a prefix,

as often in Luke without change of meaning) means "invite urgently" in 24:29 and Acts 16:15. This is the best parallel to "preach" and probably represents what Luke is trying to say. The form can also mean "enter violently," the usual translation, but does "everyone" do this?

A more important question is whether "until John" includes him or not. His day is a transitional period, like that between Easter and Pentecost (also between Luke 9:31 and 9:51?). For this reason the resurrection and ascension are mentioned both at the beginning of Acts and at the end of the Gospel, and Pentecost is already alluded to in Luke 24:49. It is true that Luke never states directly that John preached the kingdom of God though he "preaches good news" (3:18), thus linking law and prophets with the coming kingdom of God. Nevertheless, according to 3:1–2 the new age begins with him. Luke brings forward the quotation in 3:4–6 and then leads into John's preaching with "therefore," characterizing him as the fulfiller of the prophecy. Therefore he is also more than a prophet, the herald of him who is to come (7:26; see the conclusion to 3:15–20). According to 7:29–30 and Acts 1:21–22, all of his baptismal ministry (Acts 10:37; 13:24–25), not just his baptism of Jesus (he is not even mentioned in 3:21!), belongs to the age of salvation. In Luke 1—2 his life is totally interwoven with that of Jesus. Although his day is not itself already the presence of God's kingdom, as in the case of Jesus, for Luke it is nevertheless fundamentally a part of the new age. Even in the age of Jesus one may be invited "into the kingdom of God" [17] without eliminating the possibility that the law, as newly interpreted by Jesus' preaching of the kingdom, will continue in force as the norm of morality (cf. vs. 29). [18] In Jesus' interpretation the law comes to its true fulfillment. As in the preaching of the prophets, much is no longer required, e.g., fulfillment of the cultic regulations; but for Luke there is no sharp separation between the two ages. Vs. 18 is added in its Q form, but in its mention of two ways for a person to sin it is more typically Jewish than Matthew 5:31–32 (q.v.).

The fact that Marcion (see the discussion of 4:31) had to reinterpret vs. 17 as referring to Jesus' words shows how some of Paul's radical statements could lead to rejection of the Old Testament when statements like Romans 3:31 and 7:12 were forgotten. Luke presents instead a new understanding of the law, given through Jesus (see the excursus following 21:24, b). What he says concerning love of riches (vss. 14–15) and the continued validity of the law (vss. 16–18) is taken up once more in vss. 19–31.

## Wealth as Separation from God (16:19–31)

[19]"There was a rich man who was clothed in purple and fine linen and feasted sumptuously every day. [20]And a poor man named Lazarus, full of sores, was laid at his gate, [21]who desired to be fed with what fell from the rich man's table, and even the dogs came and licked his sores. [22]It happened that the poor man died and was carried by the angels to Abraham's bosom. The rich man also died and was buried. [23]And in the underworld he lifted up his eyes, being in torment, and sees Abraham far off and Lazarus in his bosom. [24]And he called out and said, 'Father Abraham, have mercy on me and send Lazarus to dip the end of his finger in water and cool my tongue; for I am in anguish in this flame.' [25]But Abraham said, 'Child, remember that you in your lifetime received your good things, and Lazarus in like manner evil things, but now he is comforted here, and you are in anguish. [26]And besides all this, between us and you a great chasm has been fixed, in order that those who would pass from here to you may not be able, and none may cross from there to us.' [27]And he said, 'Then I beg you, father, to send him to my father's house, [28]for I have five brothers, so that he may testify to them, lest they also come into this place of torment.' [29]But Abraham says, 'They have Moses and the prophets, let them hear them.' [30]And he said, 'No, father Abraham, but if someone would go to them from the dead, they would repent.' [31]He said to him, 'If they do not hear Moses and the prophets, then they will also not be convinced if someone should rise from the dead.'"

[19–24] Vss. 19–21 describe the situation of the two persons; vs. 23 tells what happens after their death (vs. 22). In vs. 20 the poor man looks covetously at the rich man; the opposite is true in vs. 23 because now the rich man is no longer "up" but "down" and must "lift up" his eyes. In each case only the one who is suffering is aware of the other. No words are exchanged between them; [25–26] and all that passes between the rich man and Abraham is confirmation that the separation is absolute (vss. 25–26).

[27–31] In vss. 21 and 24, food and drink were at issue; in vss. 27–31, it is the word as sufficient guide to life. In formal parallel with vs. 24, Abraham is called upon in vs. 27 to send Lazarus for the purpose defined in vs. 28. [23] As the present tense in vss. 23 and 29 shows (Luke removes ninety-two of the ninety-three uses of the present tense in Mark!), Luke was drawing on an extant story (on Lazarus, cf. vss. 29–31).

The story is based on an Egyptian tale of a god who becomes the child of earthly parents, to whom he shows Hades and paradise, where, after the magnificent funeral of a rich man, the rich furnishings of his tomb are given to a poor man: "Whoever does good [evil] upon earth, to him will be done good [evil] in the realm of the dead." Influenced by this story, Judaism told of the honorable burial of a rich tax collector, which rewarded him for his one good deed, while a devout man received a wretched burial, which atoned for his one sin (once having put on the phylacteries on his forehead before those on his arm [see the discussion of Matt. 23:5]!); thus in the next world both can be fully rewarded (Bill.; many similar stories). The same idea is behind Enoch 103:5–6: "Woe [to those who say]: Blessed are the sinful, they have seen good fortune in their lives all their days and die illustrious, and no judgment has come during their lifetime." For them a special place of punishment is reserved in the next world (22:10, which also speaks of their burial).

[19] The rich man is not depicted as a profiteer. He lives according to contemporary standards (see the discussion of 12:16–19), considers wealth and poverty the gift of God, who knows why. [20–21] The terrible thing is the innocence (cf. 17:27–28) with which he lives his life of ease, avoiding contact with what surrounds him. Like the priest and the Levite in 10:31–32, he does not even see the sufferer. Therefore absolutely nothing happens in this first sense.

The mention of a name, highly unusual in an exemplary narrative or parable, is appropriate here. The poor man is not just someone; his name is short for Eliezer, "helped by God." This accent was lost when copyists introduced a name (Neves) for the rich man as well. Since this name first turns up in Egypt, it may have been a part of the Egyptian tale. Lazarus appears to be a cripple ("was laid"). Dogs were considered unclean; the point is therefore not that they showed more compassion than the rich man but that the poor man was in desperate condition.

[22] Only in the case of the rich man is anything said about burial; only his burial is noteworthy. [23] In the Bible, the "underworld" is never hell but the place of the dead awaiting judgment. "Going" or "being gathered" to one's fathers (Gen. 15:15; 47:30; Deut. 31:16; Judg. 2:10) and being with Abraham (Matt. 8:11) directly after death, on the other hand, describes a final state of peace. The image probably suggests the place of honor next to Abraham at a banquet (cf. John 13:23). The story is not a guidebook to the next world; it is impossible to say whether it is thinking of various places of waiting before the resurrection (En. 18—27) or expects the final state, described in 2 Esdras 7:36 as "hell" or "paradise," to follow directly after death (see the discussion of 23:43). [25] The story also uses the word "life" atypically for "lifetime on earth" (also En. 103:5; see the introduction above) because its purpose is not to provide theological instruction about the next life but to emphasize vs. 29.

For this reason, too, the description of the poor man's good fortune is not meant as a consolation in terms of an afterlife in which circumstances will be reversed (cf. Ezek. 17:24 and also Isa. 55:13; 60:17). On the contrary, the purpose is to condemn the wrong done him on earth; [24] the torment of the rich man is pictured as making him long for what had been the focus of his life.

Mere appeal to Abraham is unavailing (cf. 3:7–8); the rich man has dug an unbridgeable chasm by his way of life. [27–28] Like 12:30 (cf. 13:30; 16:8), vss. 27–28 presuppose that the necessity of repentance is obvious and that sin is a form of stupidity that does not look beyond the moment. [29–31] It can only be countered by God's word. Even if someone should "rise from the dead" (Christian terminology), it would be to no avail. This is proved by the Lazarus of John 11:43–53. Does Luke or his prototype have in mind that Jesus' resurrection did not always lead to repentance and conversion (Acts 3:15–17; 13:27–30; 17:30–31), or did a need for community members after the personal experience of Easter produce this statement?

In contrast to all the parallels, nothing is said about the goodness of the poor man. At most it is suggested that he has no one to help him but God. Neither is the rich man a villain, but his innocence does not excuse him. It is a form of stupidity that ignores a fellow human being lying in plain sight on one's doorstep and thereby ignores God. There is also no suggestion of an ideal world without poverty after death (Deut. 15:4; Plato's *Republic*) as a consolation for suffering in this life. The bliss enjoyed by the poor man is seen only by the eyes of the rich (vs. 23). The problem of God's distributive justice is not addressed (cf. the discussion of 13:1–9). The whole story focuses on the rich man, or more precisely on his surviving brothers and on those who read Luke's text. It is they whom the word of God must liberate from their perverse and stupid self-assurance. It is they whom it must teach to look in the other direction, whom it must open to table fellowship with all the poor and disadvantaged, as given by Jesus' interpretation of "law and prophets" (24:27–31). Luke emphasizes something that is extremely characteristic of both the Old Testament and Jesus: God's partiality toward the poor. But one must open oneself to the word in order to understand this partiality. Then when someone rises from the dead it can be a sign (Acts 10:40–41); otherwise even resurrection leads only to hardness of heart.

## The Life of a Disciple (17:1–10)
Cf. Mark 9:42; Matthew 18:6–7, 15, 21–22; 17:19–20

¹And he said to his disciples, "Stumbling blocks are sure to come; but woe to him by whom they come. ²It would be better for him if a millstone were hung round his neck and he were cast into the sea, than that he should cause one of these little ones to stumble. ³Take heed to yourselves. If your brother sins, rebuke him, and if he repents, forgive him. ⁴And if he sins against you seven times in the day and turns to you seven times and says, 'I repent,' you must forgive him."

⁵And the Apostles said to the Lord, "Give us faith." ⁶But the Lord said, "If you have faith like a grain of mustard seed, you could say to this sycamine tree, 'Be rooted up, and be planted in the sea,' and it would obey you.

⁷"And which of you has a servant plowing or keeping sheep will say

to him when he comes in from the field, 'Come at once and recline at table'? [8]Will he not rather say, 'Prepare supper for me, gird yourself and serve me, till I have eaten and drunk, then afterward you shall eat and drink'? [9]Surely he will not thank the servant because he did what was commanded? [10]So you also, when you have done all that was commanded you, say, 'We are worthless servants; we have only done what was our duty.' "

[1] When the disciples are addressed, it is emphasized that the danger previously discussed confronts them in a special way. They request help from Jesus and receive it (vss. 5–10; see the discussion of 16:1–13). [2] Vss. 1–2, originally an eschatological warning, formed a unit even before Luke (see the discussion of Mark 9:42; Matt. 18:7), probably in the wording of Q taken over and altered by L. [3–4] The same is true of vss. 3–4 (see the discussion of Matt. 18:21–35). In their Lukan context they warn against endangering any of the weak; examples are given in 16:19–21 for the material life of the community, in 17:3–4 for its spiritual life. Like Matthew 18:15 (q.v.), Luke 17:3 probably refers to a person within the community. Unlike the Matthean parallel, however, the disciple is affected personally by that person's sin since vs. 4 ("against you") is closely associated. Furthermore, like the Testament of Gad 6:3–4 (6–7), Luke assumes that the person "turns" and "repents" (terms often used for returning to God). Luke is greatly concerned that Jesus' summons be lived in everyday life.

[5–6] There follows a saying that also appears in Matthew 17:20 (q.v., and the discussion of Mark 11:23) in response to a question asked by the disciples (see the discussion of 11:1). This question is triggered by the demands in vss. 1–4. L is familiar with faith bestowed through Jesus as as aid against the temptations of Satan (22:31–32); the association of vss. 5–6 with vss. 1–2 may therefore go back to L rather than to the catchword "sea" (vss. 2/6). This is also suggested by the double reference to "the Lord" (see section 2c of the Introduction).

Following the parable in 16:1–8, the Pharisees were made dependent on the continued validity of the law as interpreted by Jesus' preaching of the kingdom; the disciples are similarly dependent on faith, which they can only pray for as a gift (see the discussion of 22:31). Of course there cannot be "more" or "less" if they "have" (not "had," contrary to fact!) true faith; no matter how small, faith is efficacious (Mark 4:31). This is true even if the image of the mustard seed suggests growth. The somewhat alienating picture of the tree has no Jewish parallels and is unexpected in the Christian community; does it possibly bear the stamp of Jesus himself?

[7–10] Vss. 7–10 belong to Luke's special material. Perhaps the interpretation (vs. 10), which somewhat misses the point (see below), and the details in vs. 8bc were not present in the earliest (Jesuan) version. The formula "Which of you . . ." (see the discussion of Matt. 12:11) with a relative clause or participle and an apodosis is typical of Q (12:25, 42–43, abbreviated in Luke: 11:1–2; 14:5) and L (11:5–7; 14:28, 31; 15:4, 8; 17:7–9). "Plowing" and "keeping sheep" serve no function in the parable except to illustrate exhausting labor; there is no allegorical reference to missionaries and community leaders. [8–9] Nothing is said to justify the master's attitude (cf. 12:37); it is merely stated. [10] The conclusion is what is important: if a servant on a farm doesn't pat himself on the back for doing what is required, how much less should a disciple of Jesus! Today the master's attitude is not so obviously acceptable from the standpoint of labor relations, but for a disciple of Jesus, going on strike is never a weapon to be used in defining one's duty to God.

What vs. 10 requires is not a degrading confession of sin but love that knows that its duty is never done. A disciple of Jesus is not "worthless" because he is nothing and can do nothing but because he can never begin to fulfill everything that is left to do. This holds true also for community leaders, whom Luke may be thinking of. It goes well beyond Jewish teaching: "When you have much fulfilled the law, do not be proud of what you have done; for this purpose you were created. . . . Do not be like servants who serve their master because they receive a reward" (Bill. 2. 235; 4. 19k). This sets us free from all conceit which leads in turn to judgment and comparison and feelings of inferiority, giving insight into the fact that a life made meaningful by service is a gift. Requested by his disciples to give with the fullness of his authority (vs. 5), Jesus sets them free to be natural and to live a self-evident life on behalf of those who need their service. Nothing heroic is required. All comparison, all measurement is wrong, whether one measures one's faith and judges it to be especially great (or shamefully little) or seeks to determine that one has finally done enough and that anything more is an extraordinary achievement. "We belong to God with all that we are and have; that is why it is so stupid to want to settle accounts with God" (Calvin). This is also the principle of vss. 1–4: only when forgiveness is offered without limit and without measure can the "scandal" (Greek) be avoided that endangers "these little ones."

# G. JERUSALEM AND GOD'S FINAL JUDGMENT (17:11—19:27)

One might ask whether the eschatological discourse (17:20–37) is not intended to be framed by sections dealing with prayer (17:11—19; 18:1—8) and conceit (17:7–10; 18:9–14). But 17:11 clearly marks a new beginning, and vss. 11–19 do not really deal with prayers of thanksgiving. It is therefore better to look on 17:11–19 as an introduction taking up the theme of vss. 5–10 and interpreting faith (vss. 5–6, 19; 18:8) as conscious grateful acceptance of the life that has been given. In this case a certain reverse parallelism to 9:51—11:36 (q.v.) can be noted. As in 11:14–36, misunderstanding of Jesus' healing work is rejected in 17:11–19, overenthusiasm in vss. 20–25, and false expectations in vss. 26–37. The section on prayer (18:1–14) clearly corresponds to 11:1–13 (which also contains two parables, albeit in conjunction with other material). The question about eternal life in 10:25 is repeated verbatim in 18:18. In 18:15–30 infants and disciples, in 10:38–42 Mary and Martha contrast with the questioner who, one could add, is not ready to follow Jesus. Finally, 18:31—19:10 tells of the discipleship of a blind man and the obedience of Zacchaeus, while 9:57—10:24 contains sayings concerning discipleship, the sending of the seventy, and their return. Jesus' rejoicing in 10:21–24 corresponds in a way to the fundamental saying about the Son of Man (19:10). In 19:11, Jerusalem, the stated goal of 9:51, is near; and the parable concerning the responsibility of the disciples before God's judgment in 19:12–27 recalls the judgment of God threatened by the disciples but rejected by Jesus in 9:52–56. The correspondences are not always clear and are sometimes probably accidental. It is more probable that the sequence is determined by the desire to end the eschatological discourse (17:20–37) with two parables (18:1–14) containing ethical admonitions (18:8, 14b), as is likewise true of the eschatological discourse in 21:6–28, followed by vss. 29–33 and 34–36, and in 12:35–59, where admonitions (13:1–5) and parable (13:6–9) appear in reverse order.

In 18:15, Luke returns to his Markan material without any new beginning. Only in 19:28, with the geographical approach to Jerusalem, does he mark the beginning of a new period. He omits the conflict over Jewish divorce regulations as being no longer topical; the crucial point has already been made in 16:18 (Q). The new place Jesus gives to infants (18:15–17) follows easily after vss. 9–14. The conflict with the sons of Zebedee (Mark 10:35–45) is not included because of 22:24–27 (q.v.), not because Luke is trying to protect the disciples (cf. 9:54–55 and the discussion of 18:28). It is more likely that the disciples cannot understand Jesus' Passion (vs. 34), and therefore also his martyrdom and heavenly glory (Mark 10:37–39). The healing of the blind man (vss. 35–43) and the story of Zacchaeus (19:1–10) must be included at this point because they are set in Jericho before Jesus goes up to Jerusalem and because they depict discipleship. The parable in 19:11–27 precludes any misunderstanding of the triumphal entry that follows (cf. the discussion of 13:1–9).

## Healing and Salvation (17:11–19)

[11]And it happened, while he was journeying to Jerusalem he passed through the midst of Samaria and Galilee. [12]And as he entered a village, he was met by ten lepers, who stood at a distance. [13]And they lifted up their voices and said, "Jesus, Master, have mercy on us!" [14]And when he saw them, he said to them, "Go and show yourselves to the priests." And it happened, while they were going they were cleansed. [15]Then one of them, when he saw that he had been healed, turned back, prais-

ing God with a loud voice. ¹⁶And he fell on his face at his feet to thank him. And he was a Samaritan. ¹⁷Then Jesus answered and said, "Were not ten cleansed? But where are the nine? ¹⁸Was no one found who returned to give glory to God except this foreigner?" ¹⁹And he said to him, "Rise and go, your faith has healed you."

Vss. 11 and 19 are Lukan in style. They show how he understands the story theologically. It runs a clear course: The helper and those who need help appear (vs. 12). The request for help (vs. 13) is followed by a promise and its realization (vs. 14). Then the reaction of a single individual is recounted (vss. 15–16), leading up to the point, the question asked by Jesus (vss. 17–18). At the beginning and end of the second section, a contrast is made between the ten and the one; in between, the conduct of the nine is described in two questions. The tradition of lepers being healed (Mark 1:40–45; cf. 2 Kings 5:1–19) may have been drawn on here to make this point. Apart from this there are scarcely any parallels. The story may have been associated already with the eschatological discourse because the healing of leprosy was looked on as a kind of resurrection, probably because it appeared equally difficult (Bill. 4. 751).

[11] For Luke the new reference to Jesus' journey to Jerusalem functions as a signal: only faith, as depicted here, is prepared for the coming of the Son of Man, who must first suffer in Jerusalem (17:25; cf. 19:11). The geographical statement is totally obscure. "The midst of Samaria and Galilee" would indicate a journey from Jerusalem to the extreme north. Therefore copyists have emended the text to read "between," which at best would make sense if it meant "along the border." But Luke's only purpose is to account for the presence of a Samaritan (see the discussion of 9:52; 10:33) among the Jews.

[12] The lepers observe the sanitary regulations of Leviticus 13:45–46 and keep at a distance, [13] which they bridge at once by crying out (see the discussion of 5:5). [14] The healing of lepers must be confirmed by priests (5:14). The associated sacrifice could be offered only in Jerusalem (vs. 11!). But vs. 14 is probably meant only to pave the way for the return of the one (without the nine). The fact that the healing does not take place until they have left is not to be

taken as a test of faith; neither does Jesus' adherence to the law serve as a counterpoint to what the Samaritan does (see the introduction to 5:12—6:11).

[15] This praise, which is directed to God rather than deifying the healer, is important to Luke; he adds it in 5:25 (vs. 26 = Mark 2:12); 18:43 ("praise" and "glory," as in 2:20); 19:37; 23:47 (?) and incorporates it when found in L (1:64; 2:20; 7:16; 13:13; cf. 5:8; 9:43; Acts 3:8; 4:21; 11:18; 13:48; 21:20, and the discussion of Luke 10:17). It does not appear in the story of the sabbath healing (6:10) which is borrowed from Mark and in the related story (14:4) which also has common features with Matthew 12:10–11. From the praise of God the healed man proceeds to the thanks given Jesus, intensified by the act of prostration. In the later church, the Lord's Supper is called "thanksgiving" (eucharist), and the cry "Have mercy," as well as the terms "rise" and "arise" (cf. Eph. 5:14) become liturgical. But there is no trace of this yet in Acts.

[17–18] The interpretation begins in vs. 17; possibly the additional mention of giving glory to God (see the discussion of vs. 15) and the fact that the healed leper is a Samaritan are Lukan. [19] This is probable in the case of the concluding sentence.

"Healing" and "salvation" are the same word in Greek. Acts 27:20, 31, 34; 28:4 use it in a purely secular sense. The statement that elsewhere ascribes bodily healing to faith (8:48; 18:42 = Mark 5:34; 10:52) is here addressed only to the one; in 7:50 (q.v., conclusion) it is even addressed to a woman with no bodily infirmities. The breaking of social barriers (7:37–43) and the healing of disease (17:14) are themselves part of the process of salvation; and the very fact that there is only a single word for them shows how impossible it would be for the true word of salvation to dispense with them. But even the amazing faith of the nine, who are confident in the miracle upon the mere word of Jesus, and the remarkable revolutionary courage with which the woman ignores the social barriers in her way, are not salvation until they arrive at a knowledge of God's merciful action, a knowledge that takes form in great love (7:44–47) and thankfulness (17:15–16, 18). Otherwise the persons concerned remain isolated from God, indeed even more than before, because they deify themselves in their revolutionary actions or search for healing.

It has already been stated (e.g., 11:37—12:1; 14:1–6) that staying with the status quo of what the law demands and ignoring the plight of the sick equally lead away from salvation. The Samaritan is an outsider (vs. 19), like the woman in 7:50. For him especially healing and salvation go together because he does not stop with healing. His faith has brought him to real salvation, namely to the one who bestowed it on him. Just as the created world becomes an idol when we do not see the Creator through it, so bodily healing can lead away from salvation when we only want "something" (health or political liberation or social security or whatever) and not God in this "something." Naaman, after he was healed, took two baskets of earth back with him so that among the many gods involved in his worldly service he would not forget what God had done for him (2 Kings 5:17–19). He needed a piece of sacred ground to stand on. For the same reason Jesus gives his community the eucharist as a remembrance. The same meaning attaches to wayside crosses, shrines, and the somewhat old-fashioned thank-offering box—or even better a modern congregational ordinance (in the mountains of New Guinea) that requires all members to make an annual accounting to the elders, telling what God has given them and what they have done with it.

A Christian community where the sick are not healed is a spiritually poor community. A community in which the healing does not take place quietly but is placed in the center for its propaganda effect is a spiritually endangered community. Whether healing takes place through extraordinary means such as prayer or through "ordinary" means, such as the faithful ministrations of a doctor, is not the most important question. What matters is whether or not the bodily healing leads to a new life with God. Here the sign of healing through prayer can be helpful, and its total absence is an unnatural condition for the community.

## Present and Future of the Kingdom (17:20–37)
Cf. Matthew 24:23–28, 37–41, 17–18; 10:39; Mark 13:19–23, 14–16

20When he was asked by the Pharisees when the kingdom of God would come, he answered them and said, "The kingdom of God is not coming in such a way that it can be observed [with observation]; 21they will not say, 'Behold here, behold there!' For behold, the kingdom of God is in the midst of you."

²²And he said to the disciples, "The days will come when you will desire to see one of the days of the Son of Man, and you will not see it. ²³And they will say to you, 'Behold here, behold there!' Do not go, do not follow them. ²⁴For as the lightning when it flashes shines from one horizon to the other, so will the Son of Man be in his day. ²⁵But first he must suffer many things and be rejected by this generation. ²⁶And as it was in the days of Noah, so will it be in the days of the Son of Man. ²⁷They ate, drank, married, and were given in marriage until the day when Noah entered the ark, and the flood came and destroyed them all. ²⁸Likewise as it was in the days of Lot, they ate, drank, bought, sold, planted, built. ²⁹But on the day when Lot went out from Sodom, 'he rained fire and brimstone from heaven' and destroyed them all. ³⁰So will it be on the day when the Son of Man is revealed. ³¹On that day, let him who is on the roof with his goods in the house not come down to take them away, and likewise let him who is in the field not turn back. ³²Remember Lot's wife. ³³Whoever seeks to gain his life will lose it, but whoever loses his life will preserve it. ³⁴I tell you, in that night there will be two in one bed; one will be taken and the other left. ³⁵There will be two women grinding in the same place; one will be taken and the other left." [³⁶Two men will be in the field; one will be taken and the other left.] ³⁷And they answered and said to him, "Where, Lord?" But he said to them, "Where the body is, there the vultures will be gathered."

(Vss. 27, 32—cf. Gen. 7:12; 19:24–26.)

From 17:23 on Luke follows Q. In Matthew 24, vss. 37–39 originally followed vss. 26–27 (q.v.) directly, as in Luke. Luke has added vs. 25 for theological reasons. In vss. 28–29, looking ahead to the mention of Lot's wife in vs. 32, Lot has been added alongside Noah as a second example. The sentence structure still reveals the secondary interpolation clearly. Even the warning against going back into the house in vs. 31 (Mark 13:5) was probably in Q but was omitted by Matthew because he had already included it in vss. 17–18, following Mark. This is suggested by stylistic details and the linking phrase "in the field" (Matt. 24:18, 40). The warning against "turning back" (vs. 31) has been understood in a spiritual sense by Luke, as in 9:62 and 14:26, 33. This led him to add the reference to Lot's wife and the admonition about not seeking to save one's life (vss. 32–33). The saying about the carcass probably came at the end in Q, as it does in Luke (vs. 37); Matthew may have brought it forward to 24:28 because Matthew 24:26 speaks of the desert.

Luke has added vss. 20–22 to introduce this discourse. The juxtaposition of "They will not say . . ." and "They will say . . ." (vss. 21, 23), although possible in terms of meaning, is stylistically harsh, indicating that introduction and discourse are not homogeneous. Has Luke taken a familiar saying about the impossibility of calculating the time when the kingdom will come (vss. 20b, 21a) and set it off from a purely apocalyptic future expectation by a question from outside (see the discussion of 11:1) and above all by the saying about the presence of the kingdom of God? If so, did he even compose vs. 21a after the model of vs. 23? But without the crucial statement about the presence of the kingdom, there would be no point to the passage. It is much more likely, therefore, that vs. 21b, with its unusual expression "in the midst of you," which probably (like 11:20) goes back to Jesus, was already part of the tradition, and that Luke used vss. 20a and 22 to introduce it and link it with the discourse that follows.

As in the missionary discourse, then, Luke has incorporated Q in 17:23–37 and Mark in 21:5–33, whereas Matthew combined the two versions. Q contained vss. 23–24, 26–27, 30–31, 34–35, 37; Luke interprets them by the addition of vss. 25, 28–29, 32–33. The warning against false expectations is followed by the announcement of the coming of the Son of Man, which is corrected immediately by the reference to the Passion (vs. 25). Vss. 26–30 shift to the human response to the certain judgment to come; this is underlined by the interpretation in vss. 31 and 32–33. Vss. 34–37 close with a stress on division. Like Mark 13, L (Q) appears to have concluded Jesus' ministry before the Passion with an eschatological discourse followed by two related parables (18:1–14), which had already been placed before the entry into Jerusalem.

[20] The question of when the kingdom of God will come is always posed in connection with Jerusalem (vs. 11; cf. 19:11; 21:7;

Acts 1:6). Luke rejects the expectation of a kingdom limited to Israel (Acts 1:6). This may be why it is the Pharisees who ask the question. Does this verse refer to the "observation" of the law (Gal. 4:10) that would hasten the coming of the kingdom? According to the rabbis, redemption would come if Israel would observe two sabbaths perfectly (Bill. 1. 1600, b). Or is the reference to the night of Passover (cf. the discussion of vs. 34), in which the kingdom was expected? In some Greek translations, Exodus 12:42 calls it the "night of observation." But Acts is directed, not against either of these interpretations, but against disciples who ask about "times and seasons." At least for Luke, therefore, the verse probably has in mind a search for signs that would enable the time of the coming to be calculated (Bill. 4. 1015: "Whoever calculates the end has no portion in the world to come").

[21] For similar reasons the place cannot be determined. Acts 1:6–8 censures erroneous geographical expectations (not just Israel!) as well as their temporal equivalent. If the kingdom is present, there can be no possibility of limiting it to a "here" or "there" (cf. vs. 24). This can already be seen in the present.

Another possible translation is "within you," i.e., in human hearts. This is attested by a papyrus (Hennecke 1. 63): "The kingdom of God is within you and [whoever] knows [himself] will find it." A similar statement appears in the Gospel of Thomas: "The kingdom of God is internal within you and [not?] external. If you know yourselves, then you will be known . . ." (3, cf. 113). This is also the interpretation of most of the early Christian writers. One can then emphasize the hiddenness of the treasure and the leaven (Hippolytus), the participation of the believer in God (Origen), the Christ who dwells mystically within us in the word (Athanasius), or the moral (Erasmus) or ecclesiastical (Calvin) sovereignty of God in human hearts.

Calvin sees the problem and states that Jesus' answer is in fact addressed to the disciples (not mentioned in the text until vs. 22). This interpretation, along the lines of Mark 7:15 (cf. Matt. 18:3–4) is not impossible although for Jesus inward attitude and outward way of life usually go together. It would also be possible for Luke in the sense of 16:15 (cf. Eph. 3:17), but there (as elsewhere) he uses a different word for "in," and in his account the statement is addressed to Pharisees. This would be possible only if the meaning is "within your power," i.e., it is up to you whether the kingdom is present (first proposed by Goguel, then by Lichtenhan with respect to the futurity of the last judgment). This is Tertullian's understanding: it depends on our will. If so, we have a shift from passive expectation to active involvement. But the evidence supporting this translation is not convincing, and so "in the midst of you" is still the most probable translation (Deut. 5:14; also Xenophon *Cyrus* 5. 13). Cyril also reads the verse thus but with the further meaning "within you" for the disciples.

But how are we to understand this translation? As referring to the future, when the kingdom will suddenly be present (Loisy)? Then the verse would not only have to read "they will say," like vss. 23–24, but also "it *will* be" or "it is coming," like vs. 20. Again, this might have been the original meaning; but Luke at least (as even Loisy admits) maintains in opposition to vss. 22–37 that, although the visible coming of the Son of Man lies in the future, this is not true of the kingdom of God (cf. the excursus following 21:3, b). As God's great gift, it already invades human life in Jesus' words and deeds; it is intended to produce the concrete results illustrated in vss. 15–19. In Jesus it is already in the midst of them; they need only open themselves to it. This is probably also Luke's understanding of 1:33 (cf. Rom. 14:17).

[22] What follows is instruction addressed to the disciples. The plural "days of the Son of Man" probably derives from vs. 26, where it means the period preceding the judgment, like the days of Noah before the deluge; "the day" in vss. 24, 30–31 is the day of the coming of the Son of Man (as in 21:34; 10:12). Luke is fond of using "days" to designate a period of time (9:51; Lukan also in 4:2; 5:35; 6:12; 9:36).

But what does this actually mean? In 21:6 (q.v.) as well as 5:35, "the days will come" refers to the time after Jesus' death. This would agree with 17:26, 28, which has in mind a period of danger and temptation. But what then would be the "days of the Son of Man" that people desire to see? Surely not this same period, as in vs. 26. Are they the days of the earthly Jesus, which are likened in 10:12 to those of Sodom (like the time between Easter and the end of the world in Luke 17:28) and in 11:29–32 to those of Jonah, who will come forward as a witness against the generation that rejects Jesus when the Son of Man appears? Is 17:22 saying that after Jesus' death people will yearn for the time of decision they ignored during Jesus' earthly ministry but that it will be too late? But the statement is addressed to the disciples, and throughout the entire passage the "Son of Man" is one who will come in judgment. This means that vs. 22 must refer to one of the days of the coming kingdom, as in 22:30, when the disciples will be in the company of the Son of Man. The idea would be clearer if we could translate the Semitic idiom "one of," which also appears in Acts 20:7, as "the first." But this would be possible only if the article were present and is attested only in the common phrase "the first day of the week." However easily it would fit with 21:28, Luke cannot have been thinking of the first day of redemption, the day of Jesus' coming.

In any case, the introduction describes the coming time as a time of temptation (Acts 14:22), in which the disciples, who have already made the decision with which the Pharisees are confronted in vs. 21, long for Jesus' coming. Those who would see the glory must learn faith.

[23] Luke has assimilated the warning to vs. 21a (as he often does: 23:35/37/39; also 8:21/11:28; 10:25/18:18; 12:11/21:14; 22:2/4; cf. section 2a of the Introduction). The false teachers are doing something that cannot in fact be done (vs. 21). [24] Even more than in Matthew 24:27 (q.v.) the shining of the lightning from horizon to horizon is emphasized (cf. Apoc. Bar. 53:8–9: lightning "illuminated the whole earth and healed its lands"). [25] As in vs. 31, *the* day is the day of the coming of Jesus. As in 19:11, the idea of glory without the Passion is rejected; Luke uses an early formula (9:22; see the introduction to Mark 8:27–33) that speaks only of Jesus' suffering at the hands of "this generation" (see the discussion of Matt. 11:16; a similar statement appears in 9:44; cf. Acts 14:22).

[26–30] Sodom is not mentioned in Matthew 24:37–39. It is added here not with its notorious sins but with its typical everyday activities of trade, farming, and building. "The days of the Son of Man" refers here to the time at the end of which will be his final coming (vs. 30). But since this day is unknown, the whole period after Easter can be this final age. Noah's "entrance" into the ark is described in biblical language, as is the judgment that follows Lot's "going out." The two are also combined in 2 Peter 2:5-6, as well as Wisdom 10:4-7; Philo *De Vita Mosis* 2. 53-56; Bill. 1. 574; 3 Maccabees 2:4-5; and the Testament Naphtali 3:4-5. Vs. 26 speaks of the days of the Son of Man in conjunction with the days of Noah; vs. 30, like Matthew 24:39, speaks of "the day" on which the Son of Man is "revealed." The verb also means the eschatological "revelation" of Christ in 1 Corinthians 1:7 and 2 Thessalonians 1:7; elsewhere it is used in a different sense (Rom. 1:18; 2 Thess. 2:3-8).

[31] In this context, vs. 31 (see the discussion of Mark 13:15-16) probably means only that at the coming of Jesus no one will be able to collect one's possessions. [32] Lot's wife is introduced as a warning example. In Genesis 19:17, the admonition not to look back probably means that no one can be a mere observer at God's judgment: one either escapes by looking only to the goal given by God or perishes. But the mention of "life" has reminded Luke of the Q saying in vs. 33 (see the discussion of Mark 8:35 and Matt. 10:39). He also inserts a saying from Q in the second eschatological discourse (21:18). He therefore interprets her looking back as dependence on earthly possessions and urges the inward freedom that must be practiced during one's earthly life. It is certainly not a warning against conservatism (see the discussion of 21:19).

[33] To "gain" one's life (used in Ezek. 13:19 in contrast to "put to death") has overtones of "through one's own efforts" in Greek; the parallel "preserve" (Exod. 1:17; Acts 7:19) suggests "arouse" and "bear witness." Luke stresses the element of human involvement, conceiving acceptance of him who comes as an admonition for the present; he does not limit the saying to martyrs.

[34-35] Unlike Matthew 24:40-41, vss. 34-35 expect the judgment to come at night, during a banquet (cf. Gospel of Thomas 61*b*) or while the men are asleep and the women (cf. the discussion of 8:3) are grinding grain before sunrise. Or is the image that of a husband and wife asleep while the maidservants are already at work? Probably the "night" is only related to the idea of "watching" (Mark 13:35), which is not stressed here although it is linked with this

double saying in Matthew 24:42, albeit in association with the "day" of Jesus' coming (Matt. 24:36, while the "hour" of the night appears in vss. 43–44).

[36–37] Vs. 36 (Matt. 24:40) does not appear in any of the ancient manuscripts. Vs. 37, with an un-Lukan introduction in the present tense (see the introduction to 16:23), concludes the discourse and rejects once more any geographical limitation (see the discussion of vs. 21). The "body" is an image of God's judgment (see the discussion of Matt. 24:28), as in Job 39:30: "Where the slain are, there is he" (the vulture).

The whole discourse emphasizes that we cannot picture what is to come in spatial or temporal terms. It therefore uses a variety of images intended to set people in motion and shape their present lives, described in vs. 22 as temptation. Therefore the eschatological discourse does not come at the end of Jesus' ministry, just before the Passion, like Mark 13 (Luke 21), but within the account of Jesus' journey. The first two verses rule out the security of being an outside observer. We cannot make objective, scientific "observations" and then come to a personal decision, as though we could choose to relate to the kingdom of God. In fact the kingdom of God chooses to relate to us by coming into our midst. Therefore we cannot assign the kingdom to its proper place in the present or in the near or distant future. The kingdom rather assigns us to our proper place because in Jesus' work it shapes the entire present. Anyone who looks for signs of its future coming expects a period of time, however short, to consider whether or not to accept it. In the kingdom of God, however, the future is not understood as being separate from the present; it already includes the present. As something that will reach its consummation in the future, it is already present—like the leaven raising the dough, the living seed in the ground, the master for whom the servants labor.

To understand it as merely making us God's children is to spiritualize it wrongly and to forget how it seeks to comprehend the world, indeed the universe, and transform their basic structures. To understand it only as hope for a miraculous future end of the world is to apocalypticize it wrongly and to forget how it seeks to determine our lives today and shape their every detail. Therefore it is as wrong to retreat into interiority as it is to identify the kingdom with any utopia, secular or sacred, or the success of any program, reactionary or conservative.

The kingdom of God is neither here nor there (vs. 23). The real danger is that we will continue to live our inoffensive everyday lives of middle-class propriety, closing our eyes to God's future (vss. 26–30). Above all we must give up any dreams that the glory of paradise will be realized immediately. Like Jesus himself (vs. 25), his disciples must be free for what is coming, no longer bound to what is passing away (vss. 31–32). This may appear as senseless as Noah's building of the ark or Lot's flight (vss. 27, 29), and a disciple can never prove what Jesus tells him: that a life one seeks anxiously to preserve or create is appearance, a life bestowed by faith, reality (vs. 33).

As Lot's wife demonstrates, even those who are chosen for deliverance are in danger. Therefore knowledge of the separation to come (vss. 34–37) should produce a life of prayer that puts its total trust in God (18:1–14). The admonition is urgent; the parables that follow show that its purpose is to give courage for a life of prayer set free from that which all the world thinks important. This may involve suffering, and its meaning cannot simply be demonstrated to everyone. It is a life, however, that no longer ignores God but centers on the divine. It is impossible and wrong to picture Jesus' coming in human terms, but it is possible to live a life determined by that ultimate encounter with him that will bring final peace, far beyond anything given by historical tradition or even the Holy Spirit in the face of temptation. In this encounter we shall see that God has the face of Jesus, and that every encounter with Jesus in our lives on earth is a preparation for that day when very God, in the form of Jesus Christ, brings us into final life with God.

## Perseverance in Prayer (18:1–8)

[1]And he told them a parable, to the effect that they ought always to pray and not lose heart, [2]and said, "In a city there was a judge who neither feared God nor heeded any person. [3]But there was a widow in

that city who kept coming to him and saying, 'Vindicate me against my adversary.' [4]And for a long time he refused. But then he said to himself, 'Though I neither fear God nor heed any person, [5]yet because this widow bothers me, I will vindicate her, lest she finally come and treat me roughly.'" [6]And the Lord said, "Hear what the unrighteous judge says. [7]But will not God vindicate his elect who cry to him day and night, and will he delay long over them? [8]I tell you, he will vindicate them speedily. Nevertheless, will the Son of Man when he comes find faith on earth?"

The parable includes vss. 2–5. The helper is described in terms of his manner of life, the woman in need of help in terms of her actions (vss. 2–3). It is the helper's manner of life that stands in the way (vs. 4, repeating). It is overcome by the actions of the petitioner (vss. 4–5). The interpretive introduction in vs. 1 (cf. the discussion of 13:1–5), with its stereotyped reference to "praying always," is Lukan (see the discussion of 5:36). The wording of vs. 5 recalls 11:7–8. Vs. 8b is an isolated saying or the original conclusion after 17:37; its style is un-Lukan. Did Luke add it here as a concluding appeal to the reader (cf. 15:25–32), as in 17:19, where he also speaks of "faith" after the thanksgiving (prayer) of the leper? Vs. 6 recalls 16:8a; here "the Lord" is clearly Jesus. Apart from vs. 7 (and 8a), the parable would be meaningless unless Jesus had spoken it in a situation that made its meaning unambiguous. This means that the very first narrator must have added at least vs. 7. Vs. 8a repeats vs. 7 with stronger emphasis on the speediness of the help, which conflicts with the image of the judge.

The end of vs. 7 is difficult. Should we assume an Aramaic prototype and translate it ". . . even if he delays long"? This does not represent the Greek; 2 Corinthians 13:4 does not provide a parallel for such a construction. Furthermore, we would expect an aorist subjunctive or future. We could translate it ". . . and he is patient with them." But this conflicts with the parable and above all with "speedily" in vs. 8a, whether the reference is to the disciples whose prayers God hears or to those for whom God's patience still provides a chance to repent (2 Pet. 3:9–12). We would at least expect the conjunction "but." Therefore it is also unlikely that an original form of vss. 2–5, 7–8 emphasized on the one hand the certain coming of the Son of Man, and on the other his great patience, thus accounting for the eschatological discourse in 17:20–37. And so we must translate it "delays" and take the concluding clause as a question although the verb is more often used for patient waiting.

[1] As in 11:8, Luke puts more emphasis on continuous or continual prayer, even to the point of "nagging," than the certainty of the (imminent) coming of the end, as that which is to shape life in the present (see the conclusion to 17:20–37). "Oh that one could pray throughout the entire day!" is the desire of a rabbi (Bill.).

[2] Josephus (*Ant.* 10. 83) describes Jehoiakim as being "neither devoted to God nor kind to others." [3] In property disputes, a man of recognized probity could decide the question alone (Bill. 1. 289). [5] The expected conduct of the widow is described coarsely (literally: "by continued [present tense] blows under the eye"), whether we translate as above or "incessantly" (despite apparent futility). The meaning "cause me to lose face" is highly unlikely.

[6–7] What even the unrighteous judge (literally: "judge of unrighteousness"; cf. 16:8) does at last, God will do much sooner (cf. the discussion of 11:8). "Impudence conquers the evil one, even more the All-Merciful of the world" (Bill. 1. 456). The vindication God gives for the benefit of the weak and defenseless is God's purpose but again continual prayer is inculcated. The expression "delay long over them" may echo Ecclus. 35(32):13–22(18!), which describes a judge who helps a widow without bias.

[8] Vs. 8 looks for "speedy" help. Luke may have in mind its "sudden" coming, but compare the discussion of 21:32. An appeal to 1 Timothy 5:22 is insufficient to justify the translation "without hesitation" (instead of "speedily"). The final question is not whether God will act but whether we are prepared for that action. It is unusual for a question to follow a parable, except (as in 7:42*b*) when addressed directly to the listener to indicate the point of the whole parable. Vs. 8*b* is therefore an addition intended to introduce another important point of view.

The earliest form of the parable culminated in "how much more." It inculcated the certainty that God hears the prayers of the oppressed "widow," i.e., the community, which prays for the coming of the kingdom. The parable would be entirely altered if the appellant were a wealthy property owner with all kinds of connections, who could bring a variety of pressures to bear in order to receive vindication. The parable thus also tells the community that its prayers reflect its relationship to God. It cannot, and need not, coerce. It can take comfort in the knowledge that it is entirely dependent on God and learn to pray even in times when prayer seems totally meaningless. God in freedom will give the community the kingdom, when and wherever the time comes. This confidence springs from the fact that it is Jesus who tells the parable (or that the community traces it back to him), for in Christ the kingdom is already coming to those who can really hear the parable.

Later it became important that the kingdom come *soon* (vss. 7*b*, 8*b*). The admonitory question in vs. 8*b* was also added. Finally, Luke takes a sober look at the community of his own day and recognizes that prayer plays far too small a part in its life; he, therefore, puts more emphasis on the summons to pray (vs. 1). In the context of 17:22–37, he probably is thinking of prayer for the coming of the Son of Man.

## Right Self-Assessment Before God (18:9–14)

⁹But to some who trusted in themselves that they were righteous and depised others, he told this parable: ¹⁰"Two men went up into the temple to pray, one a Pharisee and the other a tax collector. ¹¹The Pharisee stood and prayed thus with himself, 'God, I thank thee that I am not like other people—extortioners, unjust, adulterers—or even like this tax collector. ¹²I fast twice a week; I give tithes of all that I purchase.' ¹³But the tax collector, staying far off, did not even venture to lift up his eyes to heaven, but beat his breast, saying, 'God, be merciful to me a sinner!' ¹⁴I tell you, this man went down to his house justified rather than the other; for every one who exalts himself will be humbled, but he who humbles himself will be exalted."

The introduction, Lukan in style, interprets the exemplary narrative (cf. the discussion of 13:1–5). This narrative with its asyndetic clauses is undoubtedly pre-Lukan, and was already linked with vss. 2–8 (cf. "vindicate," vs. 7 and "justify," vs. 14 have the same root in Greek). It probably goes back to Jesus.

Vs. 10 introduces the two characters. Their "going up" in vs. 10 parallels their "going down" in vs. 14. Both have their minds set on the "temple" and "God"—"vertically upward." Both are characterized by their prayer (vss. 11–13). The first man's prayer is very long, and its subject is "I" throughout; the prayer of the second man is short and its subject is God.

The first man, in line with the ideal of righteousness described in such texts as Psalm 26, takes his attention from God and turns it "horizontally," to comparison with others. The second man, following the model of such texts as Psalm 51, places God above whatever he himself is in comparison with others. The entrance of the first man is described briefly, that of the second man in detail. Jesus' words appraise the story (vs. 14a). God's judgment alone ("vertically downward") defines the relationship of one to the other, even on the "horizontal" plane. A common aphorism generalizes what has been said (vs. 14b). The rabbis know a human righteousness that could reconcile the whole world (Bill. 1. 211–12; B. Sukk. 45b). On the other hand, Qumran texts (1QS 11:2–5; 1QH 11:3, 10–18, 30–31; 13:16–17) speak of the God who justifies sinners, albeit so that they can then fulfill the law.

[11] The manner of the Pharisee's approach is emphasized; perhaps "praying with himself" is meant to suggest that he remains caught up in his monologue. His gratitude is genuine; similar expressions are found in Jewish prayers and even in texts like Psalm 26. "Whoever concerns himself with paradise in the synagogue rather than with hell in theater and circus should give thanks to God," say the rabbis (Bill.). But what he lists are not temptations for him. He lives within a social stratum or group in which "one does not do that"—the tax collector does not.

[12] Fasting is obligatory only on the Day of Atonement. But Didache 8:1 shows that at that time the "hypocrites" (i.e., the Jews)

observed Monday and Thursday as fast days (in contrast to the "good Christians," who observed Wednesday and Friday), a real sacrifice since it included drink as well as food. To put a tenth of one's purchases into the poor box goes beyond what the law requires; it is a precaution in case the seller has not already done so. The Pharisee does not leave open any back doors by which he might evade the service of God. His willingness and devotion are admirable. There really is nothing that he can pray for.

[13] Not so the tax collector (see the discussion of 3:13). His prayer, however, appears hopeless, for only those can be reconciled with God who have been reconciled with all they have injured (Bill. 2. 375), and that is impossible. But the tax collector vindicates God, even against himself. Therefore he does not have to worry about himself and his status in comparison with others. His humility is not a conscious "Christian virtue," which focuses on his own ego but with a negative self-image. It does not appear just in his thoughts or his words but with total naturalness in his entire attitude. Therefore nothing is said about his "putting himself" before God (cf. vs. 11). He is simply "staying" there, "far off" (presumably from the center of the forecourt or the entrance), not even "venturing" (Semitic idiom; literally: "wishing") to lift up his eyes (cf. En. 13:5: "They could no longer speak or raise their eyes to heaven out of shame for their sins").

[14] That it is God's verdict that determines salvation or condemnation is something Paul learned from Jesus. The literal rendering is "beyond/past the other"; perhaps we should translate it "and not the other." [9] Luke interprets this as a rejection of all self-justification (see the discussion of 16:15; on the formulation cf. Ezek. 33:13), [14] and emphasizes his perspective by adding the saying in vs. 14b (see the discussion of vs. 16 and the conclusion to 14:7–14), which with its future tense looks forward to the coming judgment of God and thus links the passage with 17:20–37.

What the Pharisee (see the discussion of 13:31) says is true, praiseworthy, and pleasing to God. The tax collector is equally correct in calling himself a sinner. Despite the way the scene is often pictured, the Pharisee is probably thin and ascetic, the tax collector stout and comfortable. "This" (not every) tax collector is righteous before God; "this" (not every) Pharisee is far from it. What is wrong is not the piety of the Pharisee; even the comparison is accurate as far as it goes (cf. Gal. 1:14; 2:15; Phil. 3:6). Such comparisons are important in the case of examinations, competitions, etc.; there must be superiors and inferiors if an organization is to function. Even in the lives of the faithful this can be a stimulus. Therefore those who hear this story will not just identify with the tax collector but discover also something of the Pharisee within themselves.

What is pernicious is what takes place between the Pharisee's "going up" and his "going down," the turning point at which he tries in his prayer to commit God to condemning the tax collector. The rabbis, too, condemn the righteous who are not merciful toward God's creatures (Bill. 3. 223). He is no longer willing to let God be God but remains trapped in a world where persons seek recognition without God.

In vs. 14, however, in Jesus' authoritative words, God steps forth from hiddenness and reveals the real truth. Before God vanish all the differences that may be necessary for earthly life. If a group is to be photographed, the ones in back must stand on higher steps; from the perspective of an airplane, not to mention the sun, these differences vanish. But the statement in vs. 14 goes even deeper. It reveals a God who bears no resemblance to the God pictured by either man. God is not a court that automatically rewards piety and punishes impiety. In that case God would be unnecessary. God would become a machine whose functions we could control, which we could therefore use as a means of final reward.

In fact, God loves those who come with empty and dirty hands no less than those who have labored mightily for God—and does not wait until they are reconciled with all they have injured (see the discussion of 19:8). There is no reward in feelings of inferiority, only in the discovery of this inconceivably merciful God (Calvin). Whether a whirlpool turns right or left while it sucks a swimmer down does not matter. The person must be rescued from the center of the whirlpool and given another center, the one who saves. The parable sets us free from the notion of achievement, which revolves about what we have accomplished, and from that of incompetence, which revolves about lack of self-esteem, from the enthusiasm of success and the resignation of failure. It frees us to risk our lives without depending on ourselves any longer.

Whoever will let God be the only court of judgment can see their own lights and shadows—that they labor more than all the rest (1 Cor. 15:10) and that Satan harasses them so that they can never boast (2 Cor. 12:7). The image of a heart of "flesh" (i.e., living) in contrast to a heart of stone (Ezek. 11:19) is therefore better than that of a "broken" heart (Ps. 51:19) because even a stone that has been ground into sand still has edges on every grain. Such a living heart can only be the gift of God. It is given in the miracle of such a story from the mouth of Jesus. Thus the parable becomes God's self-revelation against all human idols. In vss. 9 and 14b, Luke has interpreted it as an exhortation to rely completely on this God, and not to pass by the divine in our lives.

## Childlikeness and Freedom from Possessions (18:15–30)
Cf. Mark 10:13–22; Matthew 19:13–22.

[15]Now they were bringing even infants to him that he might touch them. And when the disciples saw it, they threatened them. [16]But Jesus called the infants to him, saying, "Let the children come to me and do not hinder them; for to such belongs the kingdom of God. [17]Truly [Amen], I say to you, whoever does not receive the kingdom of God like a child shall not enter it."

[18]And a ruler asked him and said, "Good teacher, what shall I do to inherit eternal life?" [19]And Jesus said to him, "Why do you call me good? No one is good but the One God. [20]You know the commandments: 'Do not commit adultery, do not kill, do not steal, do not bear false witness, honor your father and mother.' " [21]But he said, "All these I have observed from my youth." [22]And when Jesus heard it, he said to him, "One thing you still lack; sell all that you have and distribute it to the poor, and you will have a treasure in heaven, and come, follow me." [23]But when he heard this, he became sad, for he was very rich. [24]Jesus, looking at him, said, "How hard it is for those who have riches to enter the kingdom of God! [25]For it is easier for a camel to go through the eye of a needle than for a rich person to enter the kingdom of God." [26]Those who heard it said, "And then who can be saved?" [27]But he said, "What

is impossible with human beings is possible with God." [28]And Peter said, "Behold, we left our possessions and followed you." [29]And he said to them, "Truly [Amen], I say to you, there is no one who has left house or wife or brothers or parents or children for the sake of the kingdom of God [30]who will not receive manifold more in this time and in the world to come eternal life."

(Vs. 20—cf. Exod. 20:12–16; Deut. 5:16–20.)

[15] Luke follows Mark almost verbatim. In vs. 15 he speaks of "infants," bringing into sharper relief their total dependency, their inability to care for themselves. They are among those that cannot justify themselves, who are not yet conceited (just as those who truly believe are no longer conceited). [17] Since vs. 17 has become associated with baptism in the course of tradition (see the introduction to Matt. 18:3), the change might even be related to the practice of infant baptism (see the excursus following Mark 10:16). [16] Does the statement that nothing should stand in the way of baptism (Acts 8:36; 10:47; 11:17) indicate that there was a baptismal liturgy that included something like Luke 18:16–17, and possibly even vs. 14*b*, seeing that Matthew 18:3 is also linked with a similar saying (18:4)? It is probably accidental, though, that Jesus "calls" in both Matthew 18:2 and Luke 18:16. If this is the case, Luke inserted vs. 14*b* to make the transition. But this is pure speculation.

The idyllic picture of Jesus, the friend of children, laying his hands on them in blessing (Mark 10:16), is absent in Luke, perhaps because vs. 17 does not apply to these infants or because the imposition of hands at baptism, commissioning, and healing has already become institutionalized (Acts 6:6; 8:17; 9:17; 13:3; 19:6; 28:8; cf. 14:23); this would argue against any connection with infant baptism. [15] The disciples' lack of understanding is similar to that in vs. 34. The section teaches a faith that is childlike (not childish): it depends entirely on God for salvation, not on one's own accomplishments. It is like the faith exhibited by the tax collector in vss. 9–14.

[18] Vs. 18 follows directly (contra Mark). Again someone steps forward who, like the Pharisee in vss. 9–14, must surrender his sources of security although they are of a different nature. [20] Only Luke says that he was a ruler. He lists the commandments in a different

order. [21] In Luke (except 8:14 = Mark 4:19; but cf. 16:13 = Matt. 6:24) Jesus never speaks of dangerous riches but of rich persons who are in danger, or of being rich. More than in Mark, too, the setting in Jesus' journey to Jerusalem is emphasized. Jesus leads the way (see the discussion of vs. 31) in practicing a childlike life that renounces self-assurance and is focused entirely on God. Thus Jesus also makes this life possible for others. The disciples provide an example. [28] In 5:11(q.v.), 28 and 18:22 (going beyond Mark!) he adds that the disciples leave "all," but he drops the term in Mark 10:28 and merely has Peter say that they left their possessions. Peter does not brag.

It is therefore all right for the disciples to ask about the meaning of such discipleship: does faith make life poorer or richer? [30] By omitting Mark 10:31, Luke makes "eternal life," which the ruler asks about in vs. 18, Jesus' final word: they will find it in discipleship. This promise they may have; they cannot mistake it for a guarantee giving them some kind of claim. They have all been called to discipleship by Jesus; we are told of none who sought it on their own accord and had the strength to follow through. Discipleship, even in this special sense of radical renunciation of everything, is a gift.

[29] Vs. 29 speaks of the kingdom of God, not of the gospel or the name of Jesus like Mark 10:29 or Matthew 19:29. Since Luke even adds "for my name's sake" in Luke 21:12 for the period after Easter, he may omit it here in order to set the words more clearly in the time of the earthly Jesus and his disciples (cf. the beginning of the excursus following 4:30). That also explains other Lukan emendations.

[24-25] The ruler does not go away; vss. 24-25 are therefore addressed to him personally, not to the disciples as in Mark 10:23. Therefore the present tense is used: *he*, who is "very rich" (vs. 23), should *now* "enter the kingdom of God" (not the future tense, as in Mark 10:23). Therefore Luke also omits the general statement that it is difficult to do so (Mark 10:24). [26] And in vs. 26 it is not the disciples but some listeners that ask who can be saved. All of this shows that Luke is focusing on this particular instance.

Jesus promises the rich man salvation through the commandments. The very fact that God makes demands of us, thus giving our life meaning, is salvation. The rich man must understand this. It is not Jesus' intent to offer a new way of salvation. But the rich man keeps talking (vs. 21) and thus blocks his own retreat. He has not yet found peace. Jesus does not respond with doctrinal instruction which he could swallow and thus do what was required even if it went against his own common sense. Jesus challenges him to rely totally on God, but for him this means to rely on nothing. What was stated in 6:20a is confirmed: for every believer there is a specific way of life that relies entirely on God; beyond this, there is discipleship in a narrower sense, in which someone, through radical renunciation, may act as a sign helping others to this way of life. Such discipleship can succeed only when Jesus himself issues the call and makes it possible by leading the way. The Taizé Community makes careful provision for health and old age insurance, then each year gives away all the rest of its possessions; this, alongside many other actions less well known, is such a sign. It lends courage.

## Blindness to God (18:31–43)
Cf. Mark 10:32–34, 46–52; Matthew 20:17–19, 29–34

[31]And he took the Twelve and said to them, "Behold, we are going up to Jerusalem, and everything that is written by the prophets will be accomplished in the Son of Man; [32]for he will be delivered to the Gentiles and mocked and shamefully treated and spit upon, [33]and after they have scourged him, they will kill him. And on the third day he will rise." [34]But they understood none of these things, and this saying remained hidden from them, and they did not grasp what was said.

[35]And it happened, as he drew near to Jericho, a blind man was sitting by the roadside begging. [36]When he heard the crowd going by, he inquired what this meant. [37]And they told him that Jesus the Nazarene was passing by. [38]And he cried, "Jesus, Son of David, have mercy on me!" [39]And those who were in front threatened him, telling him to be silent. But he cried out all the more, "Son of David, have mercy on me!" [40]And Jesus stopped and commanded him to be brought to him. And when he came near, he asked him, [41]"What do you want me to do for you?" And he said, "Lord, let me receive my sight." [42]And Jesus said to him, "Receive your sight; your faith has helped you." [43]And immediately he received his sight and followed him, glorifying God. And all the people who saw it gave praise to God.

[31] This prediction of the Passion (see the excursus following 22:30, a) also follows Mark but is linked more closely with what precedes. As in 12:50 and 22:37, emphasis is on the culmination of God's plan; 13:32 also makes a similar, though not identical, statement. [32] This is why all the verbs in vs. 32 are passive (see the discussion of 21:8–9). God is behind every human action. Luke 22:71 also leaves out the death sentence pronounced by the priests and scribes (Mark 10:33), not to spare the Jews (see the discussion of 23:25 and cf. Acts 3:13–14; 13:28), but because the human subjects are unimportant: what befalls the Son of Man is only what fulfills the writings of the prophets (vs. 31, Lukan). Here Luke comes close to the viewpoint of John 19:28, 30. Therefore he also incorporates Mark's mention of spitting and scourging (Isa. 50:6; see the discussion of Mark 14:65), which he omits or does not stress in his Passion narrative. He emphasizes the "shameful treatment" at the hands of the Gentiles (Romans), whose guilt he elsewhere downplays, using a word that in Psalm 94:2–7; 123:4; Zephaniah 3:11–12; Ecclesiasticus 10:12–18, etc., stands for haughty people who persecute the "lowly" righteous.

[34] Luke adds a statement, repeated three times, of the disciples' inability to understand the Passion (see the discussion of 9:31), not the messiahship, of Jesus; this incomprehension will only be overcome by the risen Lord (24:26–27, 46; cf. vss. 6–7). It is almost inconceivable that anyone could fail to understand the plain words of vss. 32–33; this very fact reveals Luke's theological interest: here lies the real difficulty standing in the way of faith (first 9:20–21 [q.v], 45; then Acts 2:23; 3:18; 17:3; 26:22–23).

[35] We would expect the story of Zacchaeus, which takes place in Jericho (19:1) at this point instead of Mark 10:35–45 (see the discussion of 18:15—19:27 and the introduction to 19:10) because according to Mark 10:46 the healing of the blind man took place as Jesus was leaving the city. Luke makes this change because he does not incorporate Mark's strong emphasis on the blind man's following Jesus as a disciple (see the introduction to Mark 10:32–34) but does find in Zacchaeus an outstanding example of both discipleship and the attitude demanded by the parable of the money held in trust (19:11–27), whereas the healed blind man provides a contrast to vs. 34. Contrary to his usual custom (see the discussion of 5:12–16),

Luke includes the location because it illustrates Jesus' proximity to Jerusalem but omits the name of the blind man. **[36, 39]** He also adds a mention of the crowd preceding Jesus (vss. 36 [Lukan] and 39; cf. 19:37), **[43]** as well as of the praise of God on their lips and those of the healed man (vs. 43; see the discussion of 17:15). **[42]** In vs. 42 he adds "receive your sight," so that in vss. 41–43 the words of the prophetic text in 4:18 are repeated three times. Acts 9:17–18 also links physical opening of the eyes with that which also opens the heart to faith (Luke 18:34!; cf. 24:45; Acts 26:18; Eph. 1:18). Nowhere else except in 20:41–44 = Mark 12:35–37 (where it is rejected) does Luke use the title "Son of David," which suggests a revolutionary nationalistic Messiah, although David appears frequently in Luke 1—2. Here he incorporates it from the tradition because it cannot be misunderstood in a political sense from the lips of someone seeking healing. It is unlikely that Luke understood the title as referring to a miracle worker because David's son Solomon was so considered (Bill. 4. 533–34; cf. Matt. 12:23, 27).

## The Repentance of Those Far Off (19:1–10)

¹And he entered and passed through Jericho. ²And behold, a man, called Zacchaeus by name, and he was a chief tax collector, and he was rich. ³And he sought to see Jesus, who he was, and could not on account of the crowd because he was small of stature. ⁴And he ran on ahead [of all], and climbed up into a sycamore tree to see him, for he was to pass that way. ⁵And when he came to that place, Jesus looked up and said to him, "Zacchaeus, make haste and come down, for today I must stay at your house." ⁶And he made haste and came down and received him joyfully. ⁷And seeing this they all murmured and said, "He has gone in to be the guest of a sinful man." ⁸But Zacchaeus came and said to the Lord, "Behold, Lord, the half of my goods I give to the poor, and if I have extorted anything from anyone, I restore it fourfold." ⁹But Jesus said, referring to him, "Today salvation has come to this house since he is also a son of Abraham; ¹⁰for the Son of Man came to seek and save the lost."

The appearance of the helper in vs. 1 is followed (in contrast to 18:35) by a detailed description of the other party and his actions (vss. 2–4). Jesus' initiative (vs. 5) leads to their meeting (vs. 6). The objection voiced by "all" (vs. 7) is answered by Jesus (vss. 9–

10). In between comes the promise of Jesus' host (vs. 8), so that vss. 9–10 are now directed to him. According to normal usage, the quotation is introduced by ". . . said to him" (originally: "to them"?), but since Jesus speaks of him in the third person (vs. 9*b*), a forced translation like that above is necessary. It is not grammatically impossible; 20:19 (literally "told to them") probably includes the sense "referring to them." Vs. 8 can therefore hardly have been part of the story in its original form. But was it added by Luke? Vs. 10 probably derives from him. The expression "For the Son of Man came to . . ." recalls Mark 10:45, which Luke omitted here, and is probably modeled upon it. Jesus himself would hardly have spoken of "saving" in the present (7:50 and 17:9 also appear to be Lukan). The only other mention of "the lost" in the New Testament is Luke 15:6, 24, 32, apart from the Old Testament expression "lost sheep" (Matt. 10:6 = Ps. 119[118]:176; cf. Jer. 50[27]:6). "To seek and to save" parallels God's eschatological act through his servant David in Ezekiel 34:4, 16 (cf. Isa. 11:12). If Luke thus emphasizes the coming of Jesus as the ground for salvation, then someone before him probably added vs. 8, which bases the salvation spoken of in vs. 9 on the conversion of Zacchaeus and appears to be familiar with Jewish law. Repentance and conversion are important to Luke, and he borrows formulas that describe salvation as the offer of repentance (Acts 5:31; see the conclusion to 11:37—12:1). He is also concerned with the practical realization of knowledge in everyday life (cf. the discussion of 17:32; 18:1), and he emphasizes the gratitude that glorifies God for mercy (see the discussion of 17:15). It is unlikely, however, that alongside vs. 10 he also composed vs. 8 and changed the meaning of vs. 9. In the Greek text the position of "my" is un-Lukan; the rare word for "extort" appears in 3:14 in L. With its many repetitions of "and," the story is pre-Lukan even in form although he has revised it stylistically. It says nothing about "following" Jesus either explicitly or implicitly.

[1–2] The location and the man's name probably belong to the original form of the story. "Zacchaeus" may mean "pure" or "righteous" (but cf. Ezra 2:9; Neh. 7:14; 2 Macc. 10:19). His profession points up the problem of accommodating the structures necessary in the secular world to the call that comes from God. If he offers the highest bid, the chief tax collector receives a tax monopoly from the Romans; he collects the money through his employees, the tax collectors (see the discussion of 3:13 and Mark 2:14).

[3] Whether he is moved by anything more than curiosity is not stated. The problem is somewhat minor; what is needed to overcome it is not the "sword of faith" but a little common craftiness. [4] Of course he runs the risk of making himself ridiculous; at least he is seriously curious, and that is something. Curiosity sometimes conceals an unconscious yearning to see God. Herod, too, was curious (9:9), but he stayed in his palace and waited; when Jesus really did come, it was too late (23:11).

[5] As in Mark 1:16, 19 (q.v.), the turning point comes when Jesus looks and calls. God's mercy precedes self-awareness and repentance. The urgency is underlined by "make haste" (also in vs. 6; 2:16) and "today" (also in vs. 9; 2:11; see the discussion of 4:21). "Stay" implies some length of time. [6] Here, too, there is no mention of doctrinal instruction, followed by confession of sin and faith; grace comes in the call to act and the resulting joy. It comes as an event; it is not accepted intellectually as a proposition.

[7] The objection demonstrates that "all" (cf. 5:30; 15:2) have understood what has happened here. [8] Zacchaeus "comes forward" (as in 18:11), taking the initiative. A fifth of one's wealth and future income was considered the most that could be given away (Bill. 4. 547, to prevent the abuse of charity). In cases of fraud, restitution plus twenty percent of the total taken was required (Bill.) Only stolen cattle were repaid four or fivefold (Exod. 22:1; 2 Sam. 12:6).

[9] Jesus pronounces salvation not only for Zacchaeus but for his entire house (cf. Acts 10:2; 11:14; 16:15–31; 18:8; and the excursus following Mark 10:16). As in 13:16, the reason is not Zacchaeus' act of penance but his solidarity with Abraham, that is, God's free grace. [10] What was made clear in the event is not expressed in words: God's covenant faithfulness is fulfilled in the work of the Son of Man.

Just as 18:35–43 was the counterpart to 18:(31)–34, so 19:1–10 (with vs. 8!) is the counterpart to 18:18–30. Here, however, the story begins (like all genuine stories of discipleship) with Jesus; what is concentrated in a single clause in the case of the other tax collector

(5:27) is here developed in detail. Just as Luke has Jesus heal Simon's mother-in-law before he looks at him and calls him (4:38–39; 5:2–4), so the news of Jesus has already made Zacchaeus curious. Just as Jesus asks a small service of Simon, and thus prepares him for discipleship, so does Jesus ask Zacchaeus here (vs. 5). Jesus is already at work; he is already a guest in Zacchaeus' house before Zacchaeus responds with his promise. Reconciliation has taken place before he has made any restitution (see the discussion of 18:13). Prostitutes and tax collectors find the way into the kingdom of God (Matt. 21:32). Whether he is devout in the sense of the confession of faith, whether he is longing for God or only looking for a little variety, some small sensation, is unimportant. What is important is that Jesus breaks into his normal everyday life. This is underlined by the opposition it arouses. But everything depends on whether Zacchaeus can do the very thing the devout are least able to do, whether he can sense what has taken place and respond to it. The answer is already given in vs. 8; we do not have to wait until vs. 10. The effect of Jesus on the life of Zacchaeus puts the murmurers to shame. It also places the idea of restitution within the framework of what God has done for him in the person of Jesus (vss. 5 and 9–10). Therefore it is no longer necessary for Zacchaeus to repress anything—he can speak of his extortions and for the first time be open to himself. He believes not only with heart and voice but also with legs and hands—but not with the result that he flees the world. On the contrary, he practices his discipleship in the "world" and its institutions (cf. Mark 5:19). No more than in the discipleship stories is the difficulty of his undertaking described, what it means as a high official, known throughout the city, to go from door to door and admit cases of fraud, and later to pay the sum he has contracted for without resort to fraud or extortion (see the discussion of vs. 2). His conduct is not important as a special achievement but as praise of God, in which Jesus' saving act in him takes shape.

### Life That Looks for God's Coming (19:11–17)
Cf. Matthew 25:14–30

[11]As they heard these things, he added a parable, because he was near to Jerusalem and they supposed that the kingdom of God was to

appear immediately. [12]He said therefore, "A nobleman went into a far country to receive a kingdom and then return. [13]Having called ten of his servants, he gave them ten minas and said to them, 'Trade with these while I travel [or: come].' [14]But his citizens hated him and sent an embassy after him, saying, 'We do not want this man to reign over us.' [15]And it happened, when he returned, having received the kingdom, he commanded these servants to whom he had given the silver to be called to him, that he might find out what they had gained by trading. [16]The first came before him, saying, 'Lord, your mina has made ten minas more.' [17]And he said to him, 'Well done, good servant! Because you have been faithful in a very little, you shall have authority over ten cities.' [18]And the second came, saying, 'Your mina, Lord, has made five minas.' [19]And he said also to him, 'And you are to be [placed] over five cities.' [20]And the other came, saying, 'Lord, here is your mina, which I kept laid away in a napkin; [21]for I was afraid of you because you are a severe man; you take up what you did not lay down and reap what you did not sow.' [22]He says to him, 'Out of your own mouth will I condemn you, you wicked servant! You knew that I was a severe man, taking up what I did not lay down and reaping what I did not sow? [23]And why did you not put my money into the bank, and I would have come and collected it with interest?' [24]And he said to those who stood by, 'Take the mina from him and give it to him who has the ten minas.' [25]And they said to him, 'Lord, he has ten minas [already]!' [26]'I tell you, to everyone who has will more be given; but from him who has not, even what he has will be taken away. [27]But as for these enemies of mine, who do not want me to reign over them, bring them here and slay them before me.'"

The parable also appears in Matthew 25:14–30 (q.v.); its introduction is entirely Luke's (cf. the discussion of 17:20). The train of thought is interrupted in vss. 14 and 27 by a different idea (in plainly un-Lukan style). This is shown by the awkward reintroduction of the servants in vs. 15 and the return to that story in vs. 27 after vs. 26 has already generalized about the situation. Vss. 14 and 27 are not about "servants" but "citizens." The "kingdom" in vss. 12b and 15a also belongs to this strand. Did Luke introduce these verses in order to explain allegorically why God's kingdom does not come immediately (vs. 11)? But Luke's concern is not with its delay but with its presence and above all with what the community does in the interim. Neither does he say (like Matt. 25:19) that the master returned "after a long time," while he has the vineyard owner in 20:9b go off "for a long while." There, however, the subject is God and the period from the prophets to Jesus and the beginning of the Gentile mission. Furthermore, "far country" is an un-Lukan expression although it might come from 15:13. Vss. 14 and 27 undoubtedly are concerned only with the enemies who attack the lord after he has left and are punished for their act; Luke is probably thinking of 19:42–44; 20:2; etc. But the historical event reflected in these verses was an actual competition for a kingdom (Josephus *Ant.* 17. 299–303, 339; see the discussion of Matt. 25:28). Its mention in the prototype of vss 12 and 15a led Luke to the introduction of vs. 11. None of the parables in his special material has an introduction that mentions the kingdom of God (cf. Matt. 25:1!); Luke 14:15 (cf. Matt. 22:2) also adds such an introduction redactionally. Finally, the appointment of the servants as governors of cities (vss. 17, 19) is probably also due to this expansion. Luke therefore found the parable already highly elaborated. Vs. 22a also contains an un-Lukan present tense (see the introduction to 16:23).

[11] The proximity to Jerusalem is emphasized. It is misunderstood. Jesus helps people by the roadside and in the trees of Jericho but not in such a way that God's kingdom is made clearly visible to all, as the "hearers" (cf. the discussion of 21:5) expect. On the contrary, it will come in him whom Jerusalem kills like the prophets before him (13:31–35). It is unlikely that a polemic is intended against enthusiasts who saw Jesus' final coming in his Easter appearances and identified the community of Jesus with the kingdom of God. A group of troubled people is more likely. Since Acts 1:6–8 also attacks hopes for a visible realization of the kingdom within Israel, Luke may be thinking of Jewish objections based on the invisibility of the kingdom announced by Jesus.

[12] The image from contemporary politics may suggest to Luke that Jesus does not take the kingdom himself but receives it (22:29). In any case, he emphasizes Jesus' "return," using a verb that occurs thirty-three times in Luke-Acts and only five times in the rest of the New Testament (vs. 15 also contains Lukan terminology). For Luke the return is still important (Acts 1:11!) but not "when."

[13] Although only three servants appear in vss. 15–24, ten are mentioned here. The three are examples. A mina consists of a hundred drachmas, a hundred days' wages for laborers—not an earth-shaking amount. Faithfulness is required in insignificant forms of service, apparently affecting nothing. Vs. 17 (cf. 16:10) is therefore accurate. "While" (instead of "until") "I am coming" (the usual meaning of the verb translated "travel") is striking. Does it suggest the present time, already marked by the coming of the Lord?

[14] The shift to vs. 14 may echo the experience of a hostile world in which the community must serve. The citizens' "unwillingness" recalls 13:34.

[15, 17] Luke emphasizes the "actions" and "faithfulness" of the servants while in the parable the mina itself is the subject; it has made ten more. [16] In contrast to Matthew 25:21, Luke keeps the image that emphasizes both the disproportionate size of the reward (cf. 12:32) and its nature as service. The point is not that "the reward for fulfillment of the commandments is [more] fulfillment of the commandments" (Bill. 1. 249) but that the final glory is participation in God's work (22:30; 1 Cor. 6:2), not just empty idleness. [18–19] The second servant illustrates vividly that there is no fixed goal to be achieved by all. There are gradations, but they have more to do with the talents given each individual than with reward. In any case he is not reproached for being less successful but praised for his faithfulness even in lesser success.

[20] The action of the third servant is described in more foolish terms than in Matthew 25:18, 25 (q.v.). [21] He speaks in cliches (vs. 21b; also Josephus Ap. 2. 216; Philo Hypothet. 7. 6; Aelian Not. 3. 46). In contrast to Matthew 25:30, he is not punished (cf. 1 Cor. 3:15; someone who fails is saved "as through fire"). He remains just a servant as he was before vs. 13.

[25] Vs. 25 has been interpolated clumsily (cf. the discussion of Matt. 25:28). [26] A reply from the nobleman is expected. Instead, Jesus himself answers, concluding the parable. Luke omits the awkwardly appended "from him" (Matt. 25:29; Luke 8:18/Mark 4:25/Matt. 13:12). [27] It is impossible to say whether Luke is thinking in vs. 27 of the destruction of Jerusalem, as vss. 28–44, which follow directly, would suggest, or of the last judgment. Luke in-

cludes vs. 27 because for him the crucial question is not "When will the kingdom of God come?" but "Who will share in it and who will not?" (see the introduction to 14:15–24).

Also important to Luke is the setting at the end of Jesus' journey to Jerusalem. Jesus did not capitalize on the revolutionary messianic mood of the people. Thus Luke's readers are called away from fantasies of a visibly triumphant Jesus community to discipleship that follows the way of the cross (17:25; 19:11). Even before Luke the parable focused on conduct in the interim, with its disproportionate reward of all the profit (vss. 24–25) and appointment to office (vss. 17, 19), and its minatory reference to the fate of Israel. It is Luke himself who emphasizes the return of the Lord. Even before his return, Jesus is present in the community but as a rule indirectly in spirit, name, and power (see the excursus following 21:38, b). Full redemption comes only with his return (21:28). It is also the return of the judge (Acts 10:42; 17:31), who already determines the conduct of the community in the interim. Luke introduces this notion here once more. But the judgment will involve distinctions: what is required of all (cf. the discussion of vss. 18–19 and 18:18–30). There are both valley Christians and mountainclimbers. What matters is the faithfulness that is revealed in action (vss. 15, 17). The disciples have left their possessions; in the community they find their new home, above all at the consummation (18:28, 30). The blind man cries out to Jesus and then follows him (18:38, 43). Zacchaeus leaves his villa and goes to those of whom he has taken advantage (19:3, 8). The act in itself is not salvation—the enemies are very active (vss. 14, 27)—but is the act of a disciple who knows that, like a child, one is totally dependent on God and opens oneself to God (18:31–34). This is precisely what Jesus himself will do in the Passion narrative, pioneering the way for his disciples.

# IV

## PASSION AND RESURRECTION
### (19:28—24:53)

As in Mark, we may divide the narrative into the days in Jerusalem (19:28—21:38), the Passion proper (22:1—23:56), and the Easter stories (24:1–53). On questions of fact, compare the introduction to Mark 11:1–16:8; on Luke's sources, see the excursus following 23:25.

## A. DAYS IN JERUSALEM
### (19:28—21:38)

Luke follows Mark but inserts the saying about Jerusalem (19:39–44) and omits the cursing of the fig tree (see the discussion of 13:6–9) and the question about the greatest commandment (see the discussion of 10:25–28). He seems to assume an extended ministry in Jerusalem (19:47; 21:37–38; 22:39; see the discussion of 22:1).

### Jesus Takes Possession of the Temple (19:28–48)
Cf. Mark 11:1–17; Matthew 21:1–13; John 2:13–17

²⁸And when he had said this, he journeyed on ahead, going up to Jerusalem. ²⁹And it happened, when he drew near to Bethphage and Bethany, at the mount that it called Olivet, he sent two of the disciples, ³⁰saying, "Go into the village up ahead; in it on entering you will find a colt tied, on which no one has ever yet sat; untie it and bring it. ³¹And if anyone asks you, 'Why are you untying it?' you shall say this: 'The Lord has need of it.'" ³²Those who were sent went away and found it as he had told them. ³³And as they were untying the colt, its owners said to them, "Why are you untying the colt?" ³⁴And they said, "The Lord has need of it." ³⁵And they brought it to Jesus, and throwing their garments on the colt they set Jesus upon it. ³⁶And as he journeyed

along, they spread their garments on the road. [37]When he drew near to the descent of the Mount of Olives, the whole crowd of the disciples began to rejoice and praise God with a loud voice for all the mighty works that they had seen, [38]saying, "Blessed be he who comes, the king, in the name of the Lord! In heaven peace and glory in the highest!" [39]And some of the Pharisees in the crowd said to him, "Teacher, rebuke your disciples." [40]And he answered and said, "I tell you, if these are silent, the very stones will cry out."

[41]And when he drew nearer and saw the city, he wept over it, [42]saying, "Would that even on this day you had recognized the things [that make for] peace! But now they have been hidden from your eyes. [43]For the days shall come upon you, and your enemies will cast up a bank about you and surround you and hem you in on every side [44]and dash you to the ground, you and your children within you, and will not leave one stone upon another, because you did not recognize the time of [God's] visitation."

[45]And he entered the temple and began to drive out those who sold, [46]saying to them, "It is written, 'And my house shall be a house of prayer'; but you have made it 'a den of robbers.'"

[47]And he was teaching daily in the temple, but the chief priests and the scribes sought to destroy him, and the principle leaders of the people. [48]And they could not find anything they could do, for all the people hung on him and listened to him.

(Vs. 38—Ps. 118:25–26. Vs. 44—Ps. 137:9. Vs. 46—Isa. 56:7; Jer. 7:11; Zech. 14:21; Isa. 60:7.)

[28] Luke links the narrative closely with vss. 11–27: the entry must not be misunderstood as a final triumph. Therefore he also underlines Jesus' "journeying" to Jerusalem as the disciples' leader ("ahead"). The word "journey" appears here for the ninth time since 9:51, and again in vs. 36—so important is it to Luke. [31, 34] He abbreviates, but by repeating "the Lord has need of it" he emphasizes Jesus' lordship and initiative. [35] The word Luke uses for "setting" Jesus upon the colt is used in 1 Kings 1:33 (but not in vs. 38) for Solomon as he rides to his coronation (cf. also the discussion of Mark 11:8).

[37] The mention of the descent of the Mount of Olives (with an un-Lukan construction) is new. What is the source of this geograph-

ical information, which is better than vs. 29 = Mark 11:1 (q.v.)? Does this mark the beginning of a new source, which may not have included the colt? Great emphasis is put on the "crowd" of disciples (see the discussion of 6:17–18), their joy, and their praise of God for Jesus' mighty works (see the discussion of 17:15). **[38]** "Hosanna" is omitted in the acclamation, as in 13:35 (q.v.; cf. 8:54; 23:23); instead, the ending is assimilated to 2:10, 13–14, where the "crowd" of angels "praise God" and proclaim "great joy." The focus is not on the kingdom promised to David, as in Mark 11:10. Peace and glory are accorded to Jesus himself but "in heaven" and "in the highest"; there is as yet no peace on earth. But Jesus is on the way to receive his kingdom (19:12). In addition, the order of the second line is (as in 2:14, q.v.) reversed with respect to the first one: "in heaven peace and glory in the highest" (see 24:26). "Heaven," however, takes the place of "earth" (2:14). Thus Jesus' entrance with his band of disciples points to the final fulfillment of the Christmas promise. Therefore Jesus may already be called king, a title used only by Luke and (less awkwardly) John 12:13.

**[45]** Jesus enters the temple, i.e., the "religious" section of Jerusalem, not the city (Mark 11:11, 15). **[39–44]** Vss. 39–44 are unique to Luke. Introduced by an objection from outsiders, Jesus interprets a prophetic saying metaphorically to predict what is going to take place; therefore vs. 40 uses "will," not "would," in spite of the subjunctive in the premise (literally "were silent"). Vss. 43–44*a* go into detail, anticipating 21:6, 20; 23:28–30. The framework is provided by vss. 42 and 44*b*, an indictment in prophetic style. This mysterious fate is also guilt, but it cannot be measured in moral terms. Both are true: "They have been hid" (vs. 42*b*) and "You did not recognize" (vs. 44). The latter statement has already appeared, using the same form of the Greek verb, in vs. 42*a*.

**[41]** The repetition of the location emphasizes the fact that Jesus' words apply to the whole city. Jesus' weeping is the symbolic action of a prophet. It reveals inward involvement, as is found in Greek authors, but also 2 Kings 8:11; Jeremiah 9:1; 14:17; 15:5; and in similar form Isaiah 48:18. **[39–40]** As in 13:31–35, the warning by the Pharisees leads to the saying about Jerusalem, which has an un-Lukan introduction (see the Introduction, 2, c). Both passages appear only in Luke, who may be thinking (as in 13:31–35) of a well-intentioned warning that fails to understand Jesus (cf. Matt. 21:16). The "crying out" of the stones may be understood as an indictment, as in Habbakuk 2:11 (cf. Bill.). Vs. 44 (= 21:6) describes the outcome. Rejoicing (vss. 37–40) and tears (vs. 41) stand close together.

[41–44] Vss. 41–44 are also unique to Luke. [42] Jerusalem, meaning "vision of peace" (Philo *Dreams* 2. 250; cf. Heb. 7:2; Ps. 122:6; 147:12–14) has hidden from it the things that make for peace, probably because God has already turned his back on the city that has rejected Yahweh. [43] The eschatological "coming of days" is also an expression used by the prophets (seventeen times in the LXX, also Apoc. Bar. 70:2; similarly 1 Sam. 2:31; 2 Kings 20:7). But Luke always uses a different verb from the one used here (5:35 = Mark 2:20; 17:22; 21:6; yet another in 23:29). Is Luke's stylistic artistry responsible for the five repetitions of "and," the un-Lukan forms in vs. 40 and the beginning of vs. 43, and the change in formulation when compared to 21:6, 20; 23:29*a*? More likely these are signs of a special tradition. The "children" of Jerusalem are also mentioned in 13:34 (cf. Nah. 3:10; real children in Luke 23:28; cf. Hos. 10:14). "Encirclement" of the city, a "bank," and siege towers are prophesied in Isaiah 29:3 (cf. Jer. 6:6–21), the dashing of children to the ground in Psalm 137(136):9. "No stone upon another" may anticipate 21:6 (Mark 13:2), but the different form (third person plural) suggests a pre-Lukan tradition; the word "hem in" could reveal his redaction.

The joy of a great crowd of disciples praising God is much more vivid than in Mark. The Christmas promise is being fulfilled. But Jesus is still journeying (vs. 28); the rejoicing will cease and the stones will cry out (vs. 40). Jesus must go on to his destination, where peace and glory already reign (vs. 38), for Jerusalem has ignored the offer of peace. Jesus plays the role of a prophet. His inward involvement and the prediction of the final judgment on Jerusalem (not the world) do not yet set him significantly apart from others—but this does, that the all-important "visitation" of God (see the discussion of 1:68) takes place in Jesus' unprepossessing entry.

Of course this cannot simply be observed (like the future entry of the Roman victor!). It can only be believed and experienced through Jesus' word.

As in chapters 1—2 (cf. the excursus following 2:52, b), the pivotal point is Jesus' coming including, however, his whole life, now especially his coming to his death. This is already announced: Jerusalem, so important to Luke that he is responsible for 94 of the 143 times it is mentioned in the New Testament, has played its role in God's history. It is the city in which God dwells (Ps. 84:1), to which all the tribes go up to worship God (Psalm 122), built on the mountain of God as the goal for all nations (Isa. 2:1–5), surrounded by the power of God (Psalm 125). Luke speaks of it in terms that suggest the eschaton (vs. 43a); but it is a historical judgment that brings its era to an end, its destruction by the Romans in A.D. 70.

At the same time, however, Jerusalem is the site of Jesus' departure and ascension. The story is told in Luke 24 and Acts 1, so that the time of Jesus and the time of the community are closely linked. Above all, the preaching of the gospel begins in Jerusalem. "Out of Zion shall go forth instruction, and the word of the Lord from Jerusalem" (Isa. 2:3). Jerusalem becomes almost a "geographical symbol" of the continuity of God's actions. Therefore the temple is here already the place where Jesus and the Apostles exercise their ministry (2:41–50; 19:17; 24:53; Acts 2:46; 3:1, 12–26; 5:20–21, 42; cf. 21:27–30; 22:17). Its "occupation" by Jesus and his band (vss. 45–48) is a sign that the new age has dawned. In it Israel reaches fulfillment by opening itself to the nations, so that in the history of God, which now encompasses the entire world, its capital no longer remains the capital (see the excursus after 21:24 and 21:38, a). And so this warning still calls to repentance those who do not justify themselves but are expectant, open to God's new act. This holds true also for the reader, who must take the warning personally, without any sense of superiority over others, e.g., Jerusalem.

[45–48] The cleansing of the temple is reduced to the barest minimum; it leaves room for Jesus' daily teaching (cf. 22:53 = Mark 14:49), which seems to extend over a considerable period (cf. 20:1). [45] According to Luke, Jesus does not enter the city but goes directly into the temple (cf. 2:46), where he only speaks, neither over-turning tables (Mark) nor using a whip (John). [46] There is no mention of "all nations" (Mark 11:17), perhaps because it is the risen Lord who leads to them (see the discussion of 8:39), or because Jerusalem was a pagan Roman sanctuary in Luke's day, or [47] because Luke seeks to emphasize the true meaning of the temple as the site of Jesus' teaching, against which the intrigues of the officials (see the discussion of 20:1) cannot prevail. The statement opens Jesus' ministry in Jerusalem, as 4:14–15 opens his ministry in Galilee. Nor is Jerusalem the final goal; from there Jesus' teaching will go throughout the world. [48] Already "all people" hear it. In this sense the cleansing of the temple is also a sign of God's eschatological act. In itself, criticism of the cult is unimportant; what matters is Jesus' teaching, which gives the temple its meaning, a meaning that it will also annul. In like fashion, Acts 7:40–48 contrasts the cult with the "living oracles" of Moses (vss. 37–38), which point to Jesus. For "people" (Mark 11:18), Luke uses the biblical term for the people of God seventeen times between 19:43 and 23:35 (see the discussion of 2:10). It is distinct from its officials (20:1, 9, 19; 21:38; 22:2). In 23:4 the crowd (23:13 the people) is present, but is distinguished from the leaders (23:2, 5) although the crucifixion is demanded by all (23:18–23; also Acts 13:27–28). Did Luke borrow this idea from Mark 15:11–14? Were originally only the leaders mentioned (see the discussion of 23:5)? In any event, according to Acts 2:41; 4:4; 5:14; 6:7; 21:20 thousands from among this people will be numbered among Jesus' followers, who will then preach his message to the nations.

## Jesus' Teaching in the Temple (20:1—21:4)

### (1) The Authority of His Teaching (20:1–8)
Cf. Mark 11:27–33; Matthew 21:23–27

¹And it happened on one of the days when he was teaching in the temple and preaching the good news, the chief priests and the scribes with the elders stepped forward against him, ²and they spoke and said to him, "Tell us by what authority you do these things, or who it is that gave you this authority." ³But he answered and said to them, "I also will

ask you a question, and you will tell me: ⁴the baptism of John, was it from heaven or from human sources?" ⁵And they discussed it with one another, saying, "If we say, 'From heaven,' he will say, 'Why did you not believe him?' ⁶But if we say, 'From human sources,' all the people will stone us to death; for they are convinced that John was a prophet." ⁷And they answered that they did not know whence it was. ⁸And Jesus said to them, "Neither will I tell you by what authority I do these things."

[1] Luke follows Mark throughout but makes a clear distinction between the people (of God; cf. the discussion of 19:48) and the officials, who even fear assault at the hands of the crowd. [2] According to Luke, it is Jesus' teaching and proclamation of the gospel that provokes the question of authority, not his cleansing of the temple. Therefore he omits "to do them" (Mark 11:28). The spirits are distinguished by the positive statement of God's presence, addressed to all the people. [1] As in Mark 11:27, the elders are counted among the officials, but Luke subordinates them to the others, just as he tacks them on at the end in 19:47 (contra Mark 11:18).

[4] Jesus' question is even more explosive because according to Luke 3:21–22 the Holy Spirit descended in "bodily form" and before all "the people" (of God). [8] This brings the discussion in which arguments in defense of one's own position are important but one can also admit ignorance to a stage that admits only a "yes" or "no." [1] Thus even for Jesus' opponents it is an offer of the good news (vs. 1). This is all the more true because in Luke, unlike Mark, there is no great emphasis on the cleansing of the temple and the break with the Jewish cult but rather on its continuity in the teaching of Jesus in the temple of Israel.

## (2) The Parable of the Rejected Messenger (20:9–19)
Cf. Mark 12:1–12; Matthew 21:33–46

⁹And he began to tell the people this parable: "A man planted a vineyard and let it out to tenants and went into another country for a long while. ¹⁰And when the time came, he sent a servant to the tenants, that they should give him of the fruit of the vineyard. But the tenants, having beaten him, sent him away empty-handed. ¹¹And he decided to send another servant. But they, having beaten him and treated him shame-

fully, sent him also away empty-handed. ¹²And he decided to send a third. But they, having wounded him, cast him out also. ¹³Then the lord of the vineyard said, 'What shall I do? I will send my beloved son; it may be they will respect him.' ¹⁴But when the tenants saw him, they considered and said to themselves, 'This is the heir; let us kill him, that the inheritance may be ours.' ¹⁵And having cast him out of the vineyard, they killed him. Now what will the lord of the vineyard do to them? ¹⁶He will come and destroy those tenants and give the vineyard to others." When they heard this, they said, "God forbid!" ¹⁷But he looked at them and said, "What then is this that is written: 'The very stone which the builders rejected has become the cornerstone.'? ¹⁸"Every one who falls on that stone will be broken; but when it falls on anyone, it will crush him."

¹⁹And the scribes and chief priests sought at that very hour to lay hands on him, and yet they feared the people; for they perceived that he had told this parable about them.

(Vs. 17—Ps. 118:22.)

[9] Once more the listeners are the people of God (cf. the discussion of 8:10). The lengthy absence of the lord is emphasized, i.e., the period of responsibility (in Israel!). [10–12] Luke describes only three servants, as in 19:13–23 although he there presupposes ten. The three thus represent the "many others" (Mark 12:5, making the reference to the prophets even clearer). [15] The crimes mount, culminating in the murder of the son; in Mark and Matthew, some of the servants are also killed (see the excursus following 22:30). [13] In addition, the decision to send him is described as the result of careful deliberation, which is aware of the risk of an unfortunate outcome ("it may be"). [15] The son is cast out before he is killed (contra Mark 12:8, as in Matt. 21:39, q.v.), possibly because Israel had already rejected Jesus before Good Friday.

[16] Since Luke distinguishes the people from the officials and mentions only the latter in vs. 19, and (contra Mark 12:9) speaks of "those" tenants, he probably has in mind those responsible for leadership in Israel. The "others" to whom the vineyard is given are then the Apostles (contra Matt. 21:43). [17] Vs. 17 speaks of those who reject the "stone" and of God, who uses this rejection for salvation. [18] But vs. 18 emphasizes only judgment (contra Mark 12:11; cf.

Dan. 2:34–35, 44–45; Isa. 8:14–15; see the discussion of Matt. 21:44), as in the Jewish proverb: "If the stone falls on the pot, alas for the pot; if the pot falls on the stone, alas for the pot" (Bill. 1. 877). Those who threaten Jesus are in fact the threatened. Gospel of Thomas 65 contains a related form that urges the reader to seek the kingdom of God as vigorously as the tenants, but it is unlikely that this was known to Luke.

Like the pre-Markan parable, Luke sees the fate of Jesus in the line of the prophets (see the conclusion to 11:37—12:1), but only Jesus is finally rejected and slain. Does he omit the death of the Baptist and of Paul for the same reason (but cf. Acts 7:54–60)? It is as the rejected stone that Jesus becomes the foundation stone of that which God desires to build and also the destruction of those who reject him. Thus Good Friday and Easter are emphasized as end and new beginning (see the excursus following 4:30, b).

### (3) A Trick Question: Religion and Politics (20:20–26)
Cf. Mark 12:13–17; Matthew 22:15–22

[20]And they watched him and sent spies who pretended to be righteous that they might catch him in what he said, so as to deliver him up to the authority and jurisdiction of the governor. [21]And they asked him and said, "Teacher, we know that you speak and teach rightly, and show no partiality, but truly teach the way of God. [22]Is it lawful for us to give tribute to the emperor or not?" [23]But he perceived their craftiness and said to them, "Show me a denarius. Whose likeness and inscription has it?" [24]They said, "The emperor's." [25]He said to them, "Then render to the emperor the things that are the emperor's, and to God the things that are God's." [26]And they were not able to catch him by what he said in the presence of the people, but marveling at his answer they were silent.

[20] Unlike Mark 12:13, Luke does not mention the Pharisees (see 13:31) but pillories self-righteousness (see the discussion of 18:9) and mentions the intent to have Jesus put to death (cf. the discussion of 23:25). The attempt to catch Jesus in a suspicious utterance against the Mosaic or Roman law has already been brought out in 11:53–

54; 19:47. This very fact reveals his innocence. **[21]** Jesus' teaching is mentioned twice. The "way of God" (Mark 12:14) appears in Acts 18:26 (cf. 18:25; 9:2; 16:17; 19:9, 23; 22:4; 24:14, 22) as a term for the totality of the Christian faith, which is understood as a journey (cf. Luke 1:79). It includes not only thought but also will and action. **[26]** The failure of the trap is emphasized. Once again Luke stresses the opposite attitude of the people (of God) and perhaps also Jesus' positive attitude toward the state (vs. 20 speaks of the "governor").

It is impossible to make a fundamental distinction between the realms of church and state. We must continually decide before God whether to resist the state like the Zealots, cooperate with it like the Sadducees, or, like the Pharisees, reject both possibilities and perform some other service required by God. The answer, which demands that we always continue to ask God's will, is not prejudged.

### (4) The Theology of the Resurrection (20:27–40)
Cf. Mark 12:18–27; Matthew 22:23–33

[27]There came to him some of the Sadducees, those who say there is no resurrection. They asked him [28]and said, "Teacher, Moses wrote for us: 'If someone's brother dies' having a wife and 'no children,' 'his brother must take the wife and raise up children for his brother.' [29]Now there were seven brothers, and the first took a wife and died without children. [30]And the second [31]and the third took her, and likewise all seven left no children and died. [32]Afterward the woman also died. [33]The woman now, whose wife will she be in the resurrection? For the seven had her as wife."

[34]And Jesus said to them, "The children of this world marry and are given in marriage, [35]but those who are accounted worthy to attain to that world and to the resurrection from the dead neither marry nor are given in marriage; [36]for they cannot die any more because they are equal to angels and are children of God, being children of the resurrection. [37]But that the dead are raised, even Moses showed in the passage about the bush, where he calls the Lord the God of Abraham and the God of Isaac and the God of Jacob. [38]But he is not God of the dead but of the living, for all live to him." [39]And some of the scribes answered

and said, "Teacher, you have spoken well." ⁴⁰For they no longer dared to ask him any question.

(Vs. 28—Deut. 25:5–6. Vs. 37—Exod. 3:6.)

[27] Acts 23:8 also states that the Sadducees (see the excursus following Mark 1:21–28) deny the resurrection (in stronger terms than Mark 12:18). [34–35] Strangely, the references to Scripture (cf. vs. 37) and the power of God (Mark 12:24) are omitted. Instead, "that world" is contrasted to this world and its "children." What is under discussion is not survival of the soul (see the discussion of 8:55) but "resurrection from the dead" (similarly Mark 12:25). It is not vouchsafed to all but is clearly understood as a gift of God (see the discussion of 14:14). Do 16:23 and the emphasis on the judge in Acts 10:42; 17:31; 24:25 (cf. Luke 11:31–32; 12:47–48, 58) allow the conclusion that Luke introduced such a doctrine of resurrection on his own?

[36] Just as 16:8, using a Semitic idiom, speaks of the "children of this aeon," so vs. 36 speaks here of the "children of God" or "children of the resurrection," or, using the terminology of vs. 35, "children of that aeon" (= that world); cf. similarly "child of peace" in 10:6. According to Wisdom 5:5, 15–16, also, the righteous appear among the "children of God" because the kingdom of glory is intended for them. Some manuscripts omit the expression, possibly to emphasize that Jesus alone is God's son. They are equal to the angels in their future immortality, not just in not being married (Mark 12:25). Some manuscripts read "do not beget and are not begotten" in vs. 34, which is appropriate but not likely to be original.

[37] While Mark 12:26–27 cites the passage in the "book" of Moses as evidence, here Moses himself appears as witness to *Jesus'* proclamation of the resurrection, [38] which culminates in the statement that "all live to him." Does this mean only, like 4 Maccabees 16:25, that after their death (as martyrs) they "live to God like Abraham, Isaac, and Jacob, and all the patriarchs" (cf. 7:19)? But the present tense recalls Romans 14:8: those whose lives are open to God already belong to God. They already experience the incursion of God and thus of a life that is not subject to physical death.

**[39]** The praise of the "scribes" recalls Mark 12:32 and agrees in content with Acts 23:8–9. **[40]** On this point Jesus is at one with them. Since the following conversation is omitted (see the introduction to 10:25–28), its conclusion (Mark 12:34) comes here.

In contrast to Greek notions of an inherently immortal soul, Luke emphasizes the resurrection from the dead, which is a gift. It is given to those who "live to God," who have experienced that God, whose will is life and not death, who has promised them personally to be their God. The continuity between earthly life and future resurrection therefore resides in God, whose life already invades the existence of the believer. This life does not end with physical death but will one day find fulfillment in the resurrection. Luke does not reflect on the time between death and that last day—presumably with reason because time in our sense can hardly exist apart from human life.

### (5) Jesus' Counterquestions (20:41—21:4)
Cf. Mark 12:35–44; Matthew 22:41–46; 23:1, 6

⁴¹But he said to them, "How can they say that the Messiah is David's son? ⁴²For David himself says in the Book of Psalms,

'The Lord said to my Lord:

Sit at my right hand,

⁴³ until I lay thy enemies at thy feet.'

⁴⁴David thus calls him Lord, and so how is he his son?"

⁴⁵And while all the people were listening, he said to his disciples, ⁴⁶"Beware of the scribes, who like to go about in long robes, and love salutations in the market places and the best seats in the synagogues and the places of honor at feasts, ⁴⁷who devour widows' houses and for a pretense make long prayers. They will receive all the more severe judgment."

¹And he looked up and saw the rich putting their gifts into the treasury. ²And he saw a poor widow put in two lepta ³and said, "Truly, I tell you, this poor widow has put in more than all of them; ⁴for they all contributed out of their abundance, but she out of her poverty put in all the living that she had."

(Vss. 42–43—Ps. 110:1.)

[41] The scribes mentioned in vs. 39 do not need to be maintained again (as in Mark 12:35) although the expression "they say" actually implies that they are no longer present. [44] Jesus' words are less a criticism than a question, asking how the Messiah, as David's son, can also be Lord. The answer will not appear until Acts 2:34-36. [42] The quotation is emended to agree with the LXX. Instead of the Holy Spirit (Mark 12:36), Luke refers to the Book of Psalms, probably to prevent any misunderstanding to the effect that the Spirit speaks only in Scripture and not also in the present (cf. however, Acts 1:16; 4:25; 28:25).

[45] In contrast to Mark 12:37-38 (and Matt. 23:1), the warning is addressed to "the disciples." This dative and the expression "beware of" are un-Lukan but not Markan. Is this an echo of the conclusion of the woes discourse in Q (see the discussion of 12:1)? Vs. 46 has already appeared in 11:43 (q.v., introduction) in its Q form; there, but not here, it uses the same word for "love" as Matthew 23:6 (Q). Anyone can put on a long robe, but it is the particular dress of scholars (Bill. 2. 31, 33). Rabbis later also sat facing the people (Bill. 1. 915-16). Luke views this more as a general warning against ambition and greed than as a special warning addressed to community leaders; it is hardly likely that robes and seats of honor were the trend in Luke's day, any more than prayers for show and administration of widows' property, as is later attested (Ignatius *Polyc.* 4:1; Apost. Const. 2. 25. 2; cf. Didascalia 2. 4. 1; 5. 2) and protected against abuses (Apost. Const. 4. 6. 4; Hermas *Sim.* 9. 26. 2).

[21:1] The next story, which follows Mark with minor abbreviations, is more closely linked with what precedes. Jesus is sitting as a teacher and therefore "looks up." Luke no longer says that the rich give "much"; much or little does not matter, only whether the gift comes from abundance or poverty.

## Presence and Future of God's Kingdom (21:5-38)
Cf. Mark 13:1-32; Matthew 24:1-25, 29-36; 10:17-22

⁵And as some spoke of the temple, how it was adorned with noble stones and offerings, he said, ⁶"These things which you see—the days

will come when there shall not be left one stone upon another that will not be thrown down." ⁷But they asked him and said, "Teacher, when will this be? And what is the sign that this is about to take place?" ⁸And he said, "Take heed that you are not led astray; for many will come in my name, saying, 'I am he,' and, 'The time is at hand.' Do not go after them. ⁹And when you hear of wars and rebellions, do not be terrified, for this must first take place; but the end [will] not [be] at once."

¹⁰Then he said to them, "'Nation will rise against nation, and kingdom against kindgom,' ¹¹and there will be great earthquakes, and in various places famines and pestilences, and terrors and great signs from heaven will be seen. ¹²But before all this they will lay hands on you and persecute you, delivering you up to the synagogues and prisons, and bringing you before kings and governors for my name's sake. ¹³This will result in a testimony for you. ¹⁴Receive it therefore into your hearts not to worry beforehand how to answer;¹⁵for I will give you eloquence [a mouth] and wisdom, which none of your adversaries will be able to withstand or contradict. ¹⁶But you will be delivered up even by parents and brothers and kin and friends, and some of you they will put to death, ¹⁷and you will be hated by all for my name's sake. ¹⁸But not a hair of your head will perish. ¹⁹By your endurance you will gain your souls.

²⁰"But when you see Jerusalem surrounded by armies, then know that its desolation has come near. ²¹Then let those who are in Judea flee to the mountains, and let those who are inside it depart, and let not those who are in the country enter it, ²²for these are 'days of vengeance,' so that all that is written may be fulfilled. ²³Woe to those who are with child and to those who give suck in those days! For great distress shall be in this land [upon earth] and wrath upon this people [of God], ²⁴and they will fall by the mouth of the sword and be led captive among all nations. And Jerusalem will 'be trodden down by the Gentiles,' until the times of the Gentiles are fulfilled.

²⁵"And there will be signs in sun and moon and stars, and upon the earth distress of nations in perplexity at the 'roaring of the sea and the waves,' ²⁶people fainting with fear and with foreboding of what is coming on the world; for 'the powers of the heavens will be shaken.' ²⁷And then they shall see the Son of Man coming in a cloud with power and great glory. ²⁸But when these things begin to take place, look up and raise your heads because your redemption is drawing near."

²⁹And he told them a parable: "Look at the fig tree, and all the trees; ³⁰as soon as they come out in leaf, if you see it, then you know for

yourselves that the summer is already near. ³¹So also, when you see these things taking place, know that the kingdom of God is near. ³²Truly [Amen], I say to you, this generation will not pass away till all has taken place. ³³Heaven and earth will pass away, but my words will not pass away.

³⁴"But take heed to yourselves lest your 'hearts' be 'weighed down' by hangover and drunkenness and worries about subsistence, and that day suddenly ³⁵come 'upon you like a snare.' For it will come upon 'all who dwell upon [the face of] the whole earth.' ³⁶But watch, praying at all times that you may have strength to escape all these things that will take place, and to stand before the Son of Man."

³⁷And every day he was teaching in the temple, but at night he went out and lodged on the mount called Olivet, ³⁸and early in the morning all the people came to him in the temple to hear him.

(Vs. 9—Dan. 2:28. Vs. 10—Isa. 19:2. Vss. 22–23—Deut. 32:37; Hos. 9:7. Vs. 24—Zech. 12:3 LXX; sa. 63:18; Dan. 8:13. Vs. 25—Ps. 65:8–9. Vs. 26—Isa. 34:4. Vs. 27—Dan. 7:13. Vs. 34—Exod. 7:14. Vs. 35—Isa. 24:17.)


The discourse reproduces Mark 13:1–37 but is clearly delivered in the temple (vss. 5, 7). The events in vss. 10 and 11 do not take place until after those in vss. 12–24 (vs. 12). and vss. 20–24 make major changes in Mark 13:14–20. Vs. 11 has been assimilated to vss. 25–26. Do the three sections vss. 5–11, 12–19, 20–28 each seek to describe the time from the fall of Jerusalem to the end? Luke says nothing about Jesus' ignorance of the day of the consummation (Mark 13:32), and the concluding admonitions differ because Luke has already included material like Mark 13:33–37 in 12:38–40 and 19:12–13. The reintroduction of Jesus in vss. 10 and 29 shows that Luke can hardly have been thinking of an uninterrupted discourse.

[34–36] Vss. 34–36 contain un-Lukan expressions, including some that are biblical and early Christian. Exodus 7:14 speaks of a "heart weighed down"; 1 Thessalonians 5:3–7 tells of the "day" with its terror that will "suddenly come upon" those who are "drunken." Ephesians 6:18 exhorts to "watch" and "pray at all times" and 1 Timothy 6:9 warns of the "snare." Lukan expressions include "take heed to yourselves" (17:3; Acts 5:35) and "the face of the whole earth" (Acts 17:26; see the discussion of vs. 34 below). Mark 13:33–37 is suggested at most by the call to "watch." Nowhere else does Luke speak in this tone; in Acts he never uses such biblical language to warn about the sudden coming of the day. This section therefore probably represents a special tradition.

Can the discourse proper be read as a Lukan reinterpretation of Mark 13:1–37? **[25–28]** Vss. 25–28 could be a reinterpretation of Mark 13:24–27. The sun, moon, and stars of vs. 25 appear there, but the Lukan text is much abbreviated. Then follow echoes of Psalm 65(64):8–9 (LXX): ". . . who causes the sea to roar, the surge of its waves; the nations are in an uproar, and they are afraid at thy signs." Similar terrors are described, for example, in Revelation 6:12–17 (to which vss. 10–11 are also related; see below). Vss. 26b–27 are Markan once more, but the ingathering of the elect is omitted for no apparent reason (Mark 13:27). Vs. 28 is new and goes well with vss. 25–26 but not with vs. 27 since it speaks of the "beginning" of these events. Do we have here a tradition that included vss. 25, 26a, and 28 but not the coming of the Son of Man (vs. 27)? Then vs. 28 had to be placed after vs. 27 because vs. 27 is still speaking of people in general, rather than being addressed directly to the disciples like vss. 28 and 29–33.

**[20–24]** Vss. 20–24 also appear initially to be an interpretation of Mark 13:14–23, of which the beginning ("When you see . . ."), the catchword "desolation," and Luke 21:21a, 23a have been incorporated. In this case, Luke emended vss. 20–22 to refer to the siege of Jerusalem and the departure of the Christian community from the city. He omitted Mark 13:15, 21–23 because he had already used this material in 17:31, 23. He historicized the mysterious apocalyptic reference to the "abomination of desolation" and the details of eschatological terror in Mark 13:14, 19–20 and also introduced the statement about the "times of the Gentiles" (vss. 23–24). All this is possible. But in vs. 21b "depart" and "enter" surely refer to the city of Jerusalem, as in vs. 20. This makes sense only in the context of a tradition that did not yet contain vs. 21a. Would Luke not have written "from Jerusalem" if he had been writing on his own, rather than use the Markan vs. 21a, which breaks the continuity, to expand on the already fixed tradition of vss. 20, 21b? Above all, Luke never refers in Acts to the destruction of Jerusalem, so that the statements that refer to it here, with their biblical allusions, more likely derive from a second source.

**[8–19]** In vss. 8–9, 12–19 there are also striking changes. Vss. 14–15 contain a variant of the words of comfort for those brought before the court because Luke 12:11–12 has already given the Q version. Here belongs the other word of comfort, to the effect that no hair shall perish (vs. 18), which appears also in a somewhat different form in 12:7 in the context of the first saying; it is quite unexpected, however, after 21:16–17, which has martyrdom in view. Does this mean that both sayings were already present in a prototype? In vs. 11, only Luke speaks of pestilence. This brings the list of apocalyptic signs in Mark 13:7–13, 24–27 (q.v.) into agreement with Revelation 6. Is this an accident, or did Luke preserve an original version? Above all, vss. 10–11 disturb Luke in their present place, as "before all this" in vs. 12a shows. Luke's hesitation about simply letting vss. 10–11 follow vs. 9 can also be seen in the new introduction in vs. 10, which is elsewhere used only to introduce a parable (5:36; 6:39; 21:29; cf. 12:42). If Luke had only changed the entire discourse so fundamentally on the basis of the Markan prototype, why would he not have inserted vss. 10–11 before vs. 25, where he thinks they belong? Since it is unlikely that all the changes were made by Luke, especially the Old Testament expressions (biblical in content as well as form), the contradiction between vss. 16–17 and 18, and the interruption caused by vs. 21a (q.v.), it is more likely that he was familiar with another variant besides Mark 13, which had developed from a still earlier form along a trajectory similar to that of Mark 13 and which stood closer to Luke 17:23–37 (Matt. 24:17–18, 23–28, 37–41). This would also confirm what was said concerning 17:31 (q.v., introduction; also the discussion of 21:21) (cf. the excursus following 23:25).

**[5]** In contrast to Mark 13:1, Jesus does not leave the temple. "Some" (see the discussion of vs. 12 and 11:1) point out the ashlar, fastened as for eternity (Josephus *Ant.* 15. 399), and the votive offerings on display, e.g., the golden vine donated by Herod (*ibid.*, 395), not just the walls and buildings visible from without (Mark

13:1). Unlike 12:42; 17:22 (q.v., and cf. the discussion of 8:10), this discourse and the appended parables are addressed to all (like 19:11–27), not just to the disciples, like Mark 13 and Matthew 24–25.

[6] An anacoluthon and a biblical formula (see the discussion of 19:43) accent the prediction of the temple's destruction. According to Luke, it is part of the act of God that leads to the eschaton. That it has taken place proves that the rest of Jesus' predictions will come to pass. In a similar way, in chapters 1–2 Zechariah and Elizabeth enter into God's history before Jesus, and Simeon already sees the eschatological salvation of God (2:30). Just as God's preparatory acts can be seen in historical proximity to Jesus, so too can his culminating acts (see the excursus following vs. 38, a). In addition, 24:7 points to the fulfillment of Jesus' prophecy already at Easter.

[7] It is not the disciples who ask Jesus, as in Mark 13:3–4 (q.v.) and Matthew 24:3 but those named in vs. 5; the disciples never call Jesus "teacher." "This" refers only to the destruction of the temple, not the final consummation (Mark and Matthew), which Luke does not mention until vs. 10. [8–9] Vss. 8–9 have been revised stylistically. The three verbs with "not" all have the same ending in Greek (also in 18:32) and begin with the same letter. The statement that "the time" (determined by God) is at hand (see the discussion of 12:56) Luke brands here as heresy (cf. also 17:23; 12:45). He does not expect the end as soon as Revelation 1:3; 22:10, where this very statement is proclaimed. Luke has also added "rebellions," probably because they were more common then than "wars." All of this "must first take place" (see the excursus following 22:30, b), and is therefore not grounds for terror.

[10] Vss. 10–11 are set apart by a new introduction, a conclusion that points ahead to vs. 25 ("signs" from heaven) and "before all this" in vs. 12. The direct address form of vss. 8–9, 12–20, further heightened by vs. 16 (q.v.), is also dropped here. The statement that this marks "the beginning of the sufferings" (Mark 13:8) is omitted; for Luke it is the final time before the end. [11] The mention of "pestilence" could be an old tradition (see the introduction above). The destruction of Jerusalem is a sign that the age is coming to an end, but only the cosmic signs show that the end is imminent. The

fact that they have not yet appeared is protection against false security and false certainty about God's plan.

[12] Persecution does not belong to this complex of events; it comes "before" all this (cf. the conclusion to Matt. 10:17–25). Perhaps vs. 12 replaces the Jewish courts (sanhedrins, Mark 13:9) with "guard stations" or "prisons" because the former are no longer of any importance. Luke 8:13 omits Mark's reference to persecutions, and as to martyrdoms, Acts has only the story of Stephen and the brief note about James (7:58; 12:2). Acts tells how Paul overcomes all his afflictions (e.g., 14:19–20) but says nothing of his death. As an Apostle, he is the target of hostility, and Acts 14:22 also promises "tribulations" for the community. Luke 9:23–24 deals with the daily life of faith not with martyrdom (more likely in Mark 8:34–35), so that Luke 21:12–19 applies more to the early period of the community, when according to Acts 5:36–37 false messiahs (Luke 21:8) also appeared. Here, then, the emphasis is more on vss. 15, 18–19. The "name" of Jesus (also vs. 17 = Mark 13:13) is the mode of his presence after Easter (see the discussion of 18:29 and the excursus following 4:30, a).

[13] Vss. 5, 7, and 10 notwithstanding, these words are addressed to the disciples or the Christian community. For them, this is an opportunity for witness (somewhat different from Mark 13:9; cf. the discussion of 8:39). Or does the statement mean that their persecution will bear witness (against the persecutors) at God's judgment? [14] The introduction, like 1:66, agrees almost verbatim with Malachi 2:2 LXX, while the similar statement in Luke 9:44 associates this passage with Exodus 17:14. Does this indicate use of a source? Not only are they not to be anxious (12:11 Q), they are not even to prepare their defense (also 12:11). [15] The place of the Spirit (12:12; Mark 13:11) is taken by the Lord. Of course he also speaks in the Spirit, because God, who has been revealed in Jesus Christ, comes to us in the Spirit (cf. Acts 18:9 alongside 16:6–7, 10), but would Luke have made this change apart from a prototype? Only in a vision or state of ecstasy (usually at night) does the "Lord" appear, probably from heaven (Acts 9:10; 18:9; 22:17–19; cf. 23:11). When this is not the case, the speaker is an angel sent by the Lord (Acts 12:9;

cf. 10:3; 11:5, 8 [addressed as "Lord"]; 27:23) or the Spirit. The fact that no one can resist the Lord (cf. Acts 6:10!) does not preclude the possibility that, against this better knowledge, enemies will put "some of them" to death. **[16]** Luke changes vs. 16 to the second person, linking it more closely with vs. 15. The biblical reference to the persecution of parents by their children (Luke 12:53; also Bk. Jub. 23:16–21) is dropped. **[18]** Vs. 18 follows immediately (cf. 12:7). The statement is proverbial (1 Sam. 14:45; 2 Sam. 14:11; 1 Kings 1:52; Acts 27:34), but what does it mean to Luke, who records both instances of miraculous preservation and martyrdom (vs. 16; Acts 7:57–60; 12:2)? **[19]** Vs. 19 could also be translated, "By your patience you will save your lives," in the sense that those who do not let themselves get carried away will be safe from persecution. But the statement undoubtedly refers to endurance in the faith and the true life of the resurrection ("your souls," cf. the discussion of 8:55). Therefore Luke also formulates it more actively than Mark 13:13, speaking of "gaining." In *this* sense they will lose nothing (vs. 18).

Luke stresses that although persecution is possible for both Jesus (17:25) and the disciples (cf. the excursus following 22:30, b.3), the help of the living Lord will be stronger. This his readers should inscribe upon their hearts.

**[20]** "The abomination of desolation" (Mark 13:14, literally) is now the siege that brings desolation, and the place "where it ought not to be" is Jerusalem. In the background are texts like Jeremiah 4:7; 7:34; 22:5; 25(32):18; 44(51):6, 22, not Daniel as in Mark 13:14. **[21]** The warning not to go back into the house because the Son of Man is coming at once (Mark 13:15) has appeared already in the eschatological discourse proper (17:31). Here instead the inhabitants of the countryside are warned not to enter Jerusalem; Acts 8:1 uses the same word to contrast city and countryside. Of course vs. 21*a* comes in between (literally identical with Mark 13:14*b*), so that the warning is actually against entering Judea, which is nonsense, since the mountains are part of Judea (see the introduction above). The new interpretation is connected with Luke 11:49–51; 19:41–44; 23:28–31. What the generation of A.D. 70 (already passed away in Luke's day) is called on to "know" (vs. 20) refers to a historical catastrophe. **[22]** This, too, was predicted in Scripture—the final prediction, so that "all" that is written may be fulfilled. The cosmic apocalyptic events (cf. the discussion of vss. 25–26), on the contrary, are prophesied only by Jesus (vs. 33).

Luke remains grateful when thinking of Jerusalem as the mother of the community, but she no longer has a role to play in salvation history. The community has "departed." But the fact that her destruction was prophesied helps faith to see God even in such terror and calls on it to recognize deity in time, so that what comes will not be condemnation.

**[23]** Vs. 23*a* again follows Mark 13:17 verbatim but is made to refer to the siege of Jerusalem in A.D. 69/70 rather than the unparalleled terrors of the flight described in Mark 13:15–16, 18–20, which Luke omits. Vs. 23*b* no longer speaks of eschatological distress but only of the distress that shall be upon "this people," so that the earlier Greek word should probably be translated "land" rather than "earth." Therefore what follows is the description of a historical event, in the various details of which prophecy (see above) is fulfilled. **[24]** Revelation 11:2 also speaks of being trodden down by the nations (or: Gentiles) and its allotted time (cf. Zech. 8:13, 22; Tob. 14:5–6). The "time of the Gentiles" can therefore hardly be that of the Gentile mission but rather the period of Roman sovereignty, which is of course also that of the Gentile Christian community (on Jerusalem see the conclusion to 19:41–44).

The entire passage borrows eschatological expectations from Mark 13:14–20 or its prototype and the Old Testament but relates them to the fall of Jerusalem, already past history in Luke's day. A post-Easter event has thus found an important place in the Gospel. Only in Revelation and the Old Testament does historical experience take on this revelatory character. A distinction is made, of course, between these events and the end of the world (already in vss. 10–11); everyone knows the world did not end in A.D. 70. But Luke wants to stress the material connection, perhaps even to associate it directly with the final coming of Jesus, just as the earliest Christians associated it with the resurrection. In any case, Luke omits "in those days after that tribulation" (Mark 13:24) and appends vs. 25 directly without any break to the time of the nations, because with the fall of

Jerusalem everything predicted by Scripture has been fulfilled. The gospel has already come to Rome before it (Acts 28:26–28), so that it can point directly to the final consummation. It warns against living a life that ignores God but introduces the age that leads inexorably to the coming of the Son of Man. Although a fixed time cannot be set, it is close at hand (17:24–37; cf. 12:45; 21:32). In this sense the fall of Jerusalem is eschatological (see the excursus following vs. 38, a).

**The Significance of Israel** (cf. the excursus following 2:38). (a) Luke begins his Gospel in the Jerusalem temple and ends it there (1:8–10; 2:22–38, 41–50; 19:47; 21:37; 24:53). Jewish spirituality shapes Jesus and his community. Paul is depicted as a Pharisee, so that the only matter of dispute is whether there is a resurrection and whether or not it has already taken place in Jesus (Acts 4:2; 23:6; 24:15, 21; 26:8). Jewish belief in a Creator and the enlightened Hellenistic view of God provide a basis to which is added only an additional Christian message of resurrection and judgment (Acts 17:24–31). But there is also a break. Jerusalem's role has ended (see the conclusion to 19:28–44). Luke 21:20–24 replaces Mark 13:14–20 (q.v., conclusion, and the conclusion to Luke 13:1–9). Luke 19:41–43 and 23:28–31 present this as the fulfillment of Jesus' prophecy, 21:22 as the fulfillment of Scripture. The temple has become the site of Jesus' teaching (see the discussion of 2:47; 19:47); this is why it is so important that the preaching that extends beyond the Jews should begin in Jerusalem (Acts 8:14–17). But the community no longer gathers in the temple.

With Paul the proclamation of the kingdom of God and the teachings of the Lord Jesus Christ move from Jerusalem into the Gentile world as far as Rome (Acts 28:31), albeit only after Israel has decided. In Jerusalem first three thousand, then five thousand, then even more, and finally tens of thousands (see the discussion of Luke 12:1) accept the gospel (Acts 2:41; 4:4; 5:14; 6:1, 7; 12:24; 21:20). Among the Jews of the diaspora and the God-fearers, this acceptance is even more natural (Acts. 9:42; 13:43; 14:1; 17:11–12; cf. the conclusion to Luke 11:37–54).

In the first speech addressed to Gentiles, the gospel sent to *Israel* is preached (Acts 10:36, 42; cf. 13:23–24). In Abraham's offspring all nations are blessed (Acts 3:25), and Israel remains a people in the full sense (see the discussion of Luke 2:10). Does Acts 26:18 say that the Gentiles receive their portion in Israel, those "sanctified" by God, as in Romans 11:17–18? But the "saints" of Acts 9:13, 32, 41; 26:10 are Christians, albeit in Jerusalem and its environs. The closest parallel, Acts 20:32, should certainly not be taken in this sense, and Acts 26:17 probably also is speaking of Jews and Gentiles who find their portion among the "sanctified," i.e., in the community of God. Only exceptionally (Acts 15:14; 18:10) does Luke call the community of Jesus "people" (of God), and never "the true Israel." Though the nations join the Israelites who have accepted the gospel and though the continuity remains important, the name "Israel" is never applied to the community although the Jews as a body have rejected God's offer (Acts 28:26–28).

(b) Something similar appears in the problem of the law. The parents of the Baptist and of Jesus are exemplary in its fulfillment (Luke 1:6; 2:22–24, 27, 41), and it is important to do what it commands (3:10–14; 8:15, 21; 10:37). According to Acts 7:53, it is the Jews who do not observe the law, while Paul as a devout Pharisee follows it and can keep it even after his call to be an Apostle (Acts 16:3; 18:18; 26:5; cf. 16:4, 13). Now, of course, he uses the "law and prophets" to preach the kingdom of God (Acts 28:23; cf. Luke 16:31). But the righteousness demanded by the law is present in every nation (Acts 10:35), for the ritual law does not matter although a minimum must be kept (Acts 15:10, 19–21; 21:24–25)—a position no Pharisee would ever have accepted. Therefore true faith is present even in pre-Christian Israel, not just as for Paul (Gal. 3:6–18) in Abraham, who lived before the time of the law. Luke thinks in terms of a transition from the law to the gospel, which annuls the law's imperfections (Acts 13:38–39; 15:10, 19–20). He omits Mark 7:15 and the antitheses in Matthew 5:21–48. On the other hand, the law is radicalized (cf. the discussion of Luke 16:17). Is the point, then, to eliminate unnecessary or exaggerated ritual requirements in order to concentrate on the central ethical commandments?

All this is, of course, far removed from the clarity with which Paul contrasts the law with the gospel. And yet, like Paul, Luke knows the danger of self-justification (10:29; 16:15; 18:9; 20:20), in which a person thinks God is no longer needed. This is an abuse of the works, good in themselves, required by the law. It makes love impossible because it leads to measurement and comparison so that one can stay "on top" (cf. the conclusion to 15:29–30). But Luke no longer encounters it in the form of precise fulfillment of the Mosaic law. It would be more in place to fault him for associating self-justification only with fulfillment of the law in 10:29; 16:15; 18:9. But he knows that true faith exists only when one waits before God empty-handed (see the excursus following 2:52, c). Therefore figures like the rich in 12:16–21 and 16:19–31 (cf. the discussion of 18:8!), the elder son (15:25–32), the Pharisee in 7:36–50, or the onlookers in 13:1–5 who want to disassociate themselves from the sinners, but also Luke's references to the present meaning of Jesus' warnings (see, for example, the conclusion to 14:15–24; 14:33; 17:1–4)—all these "translate" false self-justification into the new situation. Because legalistic Jewish spirituality is hardly a danger any longer, so that the Mosaic law is no longer a way of salvation, Luke, with the prophets, can understand it as a sign of the gospel and (like Paul in Rom. 3:31; 7:12) a good expression of God's will. It is Luke who shows how wealth or ambition lead to false self-assertion before God. On the other hand, one who has learned to live from what God gives can use it as a guidepost, showing the direction in which the way should go. Luke finds the error more in the practical conduct of life than in intellectual assent to a way of salvation based on the law rather than on grace. Therefore the division passes through the midst of both Jews and Gentiles and reappears continually in the Christian community.

[25–26] The cosmic wonders of Mark 13:24 are summarized briefly as "signs" (cf. vs. 11); so that the quotation from Isaiah 13:10; 34:4 vanishes and only the biblical expression "powers of the heavens" remains (the host of the stars, Dan. 8:10; also 2 Kings 17:16). Instead the terror of the nations is described, an earthly event, with echoes of Psalm 65:8–9 (cf. also Matt. 24:30).

[27] In contrast to Daniel 7:13; Mark 13:26; 14:62; and Revelation 1:7, only one cloud is mentioned, as at the transfiguration. Accord-

ing to Acts 1:11, the disciples will see Jesus coming as he departed from them because his coming is the consummation of his exaltation (cf. the discussion of Mark 14:62). The cloud (singular) is also a sign of God's presence and glory in Exodus 19:16; 24:16; Numbers 11:25; etc. (cf. 9:26). The sending of the angels by the Son of Man (Mark 13:27) is omitted (cf. the discussion of 9:26); they are associated with God (12:8-9; 15:10), not the Son of Man (Matt. 13:41; 16:27; 24:31; 25:31). The function of judge, in itself important to Luke (Acts 10:42; 17:31) is here deemphasized in the case of the Son of Man. Probably Jesus considered himself not the judge but the key witness at the last judgment (cf. 12:8; not even mentioned in 12:9), as is already expected of the righteous sufferer in Wisdom 5:1-5 (see the end of the excursus following Mark 8:27-33). As such he appears on behalf of his own (Acts 7:56). [28] Therefore the section closes with a call to rejoice, again in the form of direct address. It promises "redemption" (cf. En. 51:2: "the day of their redemption is near") from the present troubles, which are taken very seriously. This redemption is the "kingdom of God" (vs. 31), which comes after the judgment.

Luke pictures a double reaction, not mentioned in Mark 13:24-27, at the coming of Jesus. It is not the community who must be afraid (vss. 9, 14-15) but rather those whom its members are tempted now to fear. The consummation also affects the world, but the darkening of the sun and moon, the fall of the stars, are of no interest. At most they arouse curiosity instead of calling to a life that leads to final hope rather than fear and terror.

[29] Luke provides the parable from Mark 13:28-32 with an introduction (see the introduction to 6:37-42) and speaks of "all the trees," turning the parable into a universal law of nature, [30] which should be obvious to anyone (cf. 12:57) and eliminating the original reference to Joel 2:22. [31] The "kingdom of God" is a Lukan addition, which has already been used in vss. 16, 19, and 28 to underline the reference to the disciples. But how are we to understand its "nearness"? Its presence in Jesus (as in 9:27, q.v.) cannot be meant because it is preceded by cosmic signs and the coming of the Son of Man. [32] And who is "this generation"? According to 17:25; 11:29-32, and 50-51, it should be the generation of Jesus' day, meaning

that Luke expected the kingdom of God before the death of the last witnesses, who are addressed in the second person in vss. 28–32, i.e., within the next twenty or thirty years. Perhaps Luke really means this (cf. 18:8). If so, "all" (vs. 32) would have to include the coming of Jesus in vs. 27. This is unlikely; otherwise Acts could scarcely have been written almost without allusion to this end of the world and without any use of apocalyptic language. Does "this generation" then refer to the Jews? The fact that they cannot be absorbed among the other nations would then be a sign of God's history (Romans 9—11). But would Luke have limited himself to such an obscure statement of so important a point? Would he not at least have had to mention it in Acts 28:26–28? The Christians are never called "this generation." Is therefore the entire human race meant, as in 16:8? The kingdom will come as certainly as the human race will not die out. But this idea would be expressed in rather banal language. Most likely Luke means that since Easter all belong to the generation of the eschaton, which also appears to comprise several generations (1QpHab 2:7; 7:2) because "the time of the end is extended" (7:7). Luke therefore stresses that no one knows the date of Jesus' coming (Acts 1:7), except, of course, Jesus—Mark 13:32 is omitted!

[34] The conclusion is without parallel. It is more admonitory than vss. 28 and 31, but hope for final redemption, exhortation to pray without ceasing, and the question of human reaction also occur together in 18:1–8. As in that passage, Luke accepts his tradition (see the introduction) and affirms it. Drunkenness is the condition in which "the senses grow heavy with wine" (Homer *Od*. 19. 122; 3. 139; cf. Philo *Drunkenness* 104 [desires and passions], 131), so that one can no longer see reality and lives in illusions, including what we realistically call "worry about subsistence" (8:14; 12:22; cf. 12:13–34, 45; 17:26–30). One forgets "that day" (10:12; 17:31) and falls into it like an animal into a snare (also 1 Tim. 6:9). [35] The extension to all the inhabitants of the earth comes from Isaiah 24:17 and underlines the appeal to the individual. [36] Continual prayer (cf. 18:1; Eph. 6:18) gives strength to flee from all these terrors to the Son of Man; not to the judge (as in 2 Cor. 5:10), but to him before whom one may "stand upright" as a believer (the same word as in Rom. 14:4). Like 12:8, this may be a genuine saying of Jesus.

**[37–38]** Vss. 37–38 go with 19:47–48 and 20:1 and conclude the period of teaching in Jerusalem (see the discussion of 22:1). As at the beginning, the people appear to be on Jesus' side (cf. the conclusion of Moses' teaching in the presence of the people: Deut. 31:1; 32:44–45). John 8:1–2 is related in vocabulary but could be based on Luke 21:37 since John 7:53—8:11 appears in a manuscript between Luke 21:37 and 21:38. But John 18:2, like Luke 22:39, presupposes that Jesus often stayed upon the mount "called" (although already mentioned in 19:37; cf. 22:39) Olivet. This sets the scene for Jesus' arrest. Like Mark 13, the eschatological discourse concludes the public ministry of Jesus.

The end does not come simply at some future time; it determines life in the present. Therefore Jerusalem plays an important role, while the natural catastrophes of the eschaton fade into the background. Its fall marks the beginning of the eschaton of God, the "time of the Gentiles," which Luke links closely with the last coming of Jesus. Therefore the objective description in vss. 16, 18–19, 28 is recast in the form of direct address, while exhortations like Mark 13:33–37 have already been developed extensively in 12:35–59 and 17:22–37. "Drunkenness" and "hangover," triumph and distress, can so fill the heart that there is no room for what is truly important: the knowledge, through faith, that the end is the beginning of ultimate joy. This knowledge must give rise to a salutary discontent that establishes new values.

**Final Coming and Eschatological History.** (a) The events of the eschaton with the final coming of the Son of Man are important to Luke. Luke 19:12 is emended to underline the return of the Lord. Far more than in Mark, references to this event pervade the entire Gospel. Luke provides not one but three eschatological discourses (12:35–59; 17:20–37; 21:5–36), while omitting some Markan texts (e.g., 4:30–32; 6:1–6; 9:42–50; 10:2–12) when he has already included similar material (e.g., from Q). The first discourse inculcates watchfulness. The second emphasizes the suddenness of Jesus' coming. The third depicts the interim and the eschaton, their differences and similarities, while Acts 1:6–8 speaks explicitly of the Spirit.

Luke makes a clear distinction between events that have already happened, like the conquest of Jerusalem and the persecution of the community, and the eschaton proper, which will affect the cosmos (21:10a, 12a, 20–24). In the case of the former, he omits typically apocalyptic expressions (the "abomination" in Mark 13:14) or shifts them to the final period (17:31). What has already taken place is not secular history but a part of God's eschatological action, for which biblical language is also used (see the discussion of 12:52; 21:22). In 21:10–11, the cosmic events follow upon what has already taken place. Above all, the time of the Gentiles, no longer limited to the apocalyptic three-and-a-half years (Rev. 11:2), passes directly into that of the coming of the Son of Man. Luke 21:25 omits "in those days" (after that tribulation), which marks the eschaton proper (see the discussion of vs. 23). According to Acts 2:17–21, "the last days" have begun and the time of the Spirit passes without interruption into the time of cosmic miracles, the darkening of the sun, and the last judgment.

That the fall of Jerusalem was not the end of the world, everyone knows. For Luke's readers, this concerned an obscure corner of the Roman Empire. But Luke underlines its material connection with the events of the eschaton proper. The death of Paul was also not the end. His farewell address does speak of the "wolves" to come (Acts 20:29–30), which were expected in the eschaton (see the discussion of Matt. 7:15), but this, like Luke 10:3, describes the time of persecution before the final period. Luke is certainly not thinking of centuries; the end can come at any time. It is awaited by the eschatological community, shaped by the Spirit. Indeed, according to 21:32 (q.v.), it seems to be coming soon. The mission to Israel is over (Acts 28:28), and the preaching to the Gentiles has probably also reached its goal with the death of the Apostle. Of course the preaching is to continue (Acts 28:31), but Acts 20:28 is thinking not of mission but of pasturing the flock (now termed "watching," vs. 31!; see the conclusion to 10:17–20). The problem of preserving the teaching for future generations (2 Tim. 2:2) has hardly yet arisen.

On the other hand, Luke writes a Gospel (like Mark!) in which exhortation (like Mark 13:34–37, q.v.) has already shifted its focus to responsible conduct in the interim. Acts does emphasize the resurrection of the dead (24:21, etc.) and the judgment together with its required righteousness (24:25), but we hear nothing of cosmic eschatological events and the coming of Jesus, which is only hinted at in 3:20–21 in a traditional expression. A related observation is that the Passion and resurrection of Jesus, the fall of Jerusalem, and the preaching to the nations are all included in the prophecies of the law and prophets (Luke 21:22; 24:26–27, 46–47; Acts 17:3; 26:22–23, 27; probably also 3:21–26; cf. 2 Cor. 5:19) but not the events of the eschaton. Biblical expressions do appear in the description of the final period even outside the Markan parallels (17:29; 21:25, 35), but they are not characterized as such and may have been borrowed by Luke. Above all they point to the judgment awaiting humankind. The passages dealing with the eschaton thus take on the function of reminding readers of the judgment and the glory that await them (21:28, 36; Acts 10:42; 17:31).

(b) The "kingdom of God" is also ambiguous. In the consummation hoped for by the people (19:11) and the disciples (Acts 1:6) it has not yet dawned; it comes only after the Lord's return (19:12, 15). Jesus (in his exaltation?) has already entered into the "legacy" of the Father and in turn appoints the kingdom as a "legacy" to his disciples, who will share in it with him in the future (22:29–30). Similarly, the community will enter into the kingdom of God only "through many tribulations" (Acts 14:22). But instruction concerning the kingdom (Acts 1:3) and its preaching on the part of Jesus (Luke 4:43) and the disciples (Luke 8:1; Acts 28:31) are certainly not to be conceived merely as a discussion of the events of the eschaton. The disciples, announcing the coming of *Jesus* (Luke 10:1, redactional), declare to the city that rejects them that the *kingdom* has come near them (10:11). The Lukan emendation in 18:24 (q.v.) stresses entering into the kingdom in the present.

But for Luke, both probably describe a decision for the future kingdom. The parables in his special material have no introductions alluding to the kingdom of God, but he adds such an introduction in 14:15 and 19:11 to two parables that emphasize the present decision to live in the expectation of the kingdom. In the Matthean parallels (22:2; 25:1) it appears within the parable but in a clearly eschatological context. This is also the sense in which he probably understands the statements he borrows about the presence of the kingdom (11:20; 17:21; cf. also the discussion of 10:19), and so he can also borrow 13:18–21 from Q.

When the question of "when" arises (17:20; 19:11; 21:7; Acts 1:6–7), he points to the coming future. As in the case of Jesus himself (excursus following Mark 1:14–15), it is less appropriate to ask whether the kingdom is present or future than in what way it is present or future. Luke, however, does not give the paradoxical answer of Matthew 11:12 (q.v.) but stresses the immediate requirement of openness to what will come. It is future in the sense of final redemption from all tribulation (Luke 21:28–31; Acts 14:22), of unbroken communion with the Lord (Luke 22:30), and thus of an end to hiddenness (19:11; cf. 13:19*b*, 28–29). Time and place are reserved to God's decision (see the discussion of 17:20 and 21). It is present in the ministry and person of Jesus (cf. the conclusion to 17:11–19 and the Retrospect), to which one must be open. "With him" the disciples will enter into the kingdom and are therefore in a certain sense already there (22:28–30; 23:43; Acts 7:56). For them it is already prepared although it is not identical with the community (12:32). They can already "see" it (see the discussion of 9:27).

Acts 1:6–8 not only rejects foreknowledge of place and time but replaces such foreknowledge with the worldwide ministry of the disciples and their proclamation of Jesus as the Christ (5:42; cf. 10:36) in the power of the Holy Spirit, without actually using the expression "kingdom of God." For neither their ministry, before (cf. 10:20 alongside 18) or after Easter, nor the life of the community is identical with it. But Paul proclaims the kingdom of God (Acts 28:31) by proclaiming the Lord Jesus Christ (not: Jesus of Nazareth, Luke 24:19). Thus God's effectual sovereignty, already visible in the earthly life of Jesus, is granted the exalted Lord as "his [Jesus'] kingdom" (Luke 19:12, 15; 22:29) because he rules in God's name.

(c) In this case it is wrong to say that Luke understands the earthly ministry of Jesus as the midpoint of time, followed by another period comparable to the period before Jesus, until God's intervention ends all history. Of course the death, resurrection, and ascension of Jesus define a period between two ages, which Luke 24:50–53 and Acts 1:1–14 both distinguish and picture as merging. But Luke stresses the intimate connection between the two (cf. the excursus following 4:30, b), in which both ages together, as fulfillment of the prophets (see above, a, end), are distinct from the age of prophecy. The saving events of Jesus' life, death, and resurrection have precedence over faith; but the fact that in Acts Luke tells the history of faith, once again the result of God's action, shows that he is aware that they are not saving events unless they are preached and understood by faith (see the discussion of 4:21 and the excursus following 4:30, c). If for Luke the presence of the kingdom consists above all in the possibility of being open to it and receiving it, this holds true even more for the post-Easter proclamation of the Lord, to whom the kingdom has been given. But only the final communion with Jesus (22:29–30) will bring the fullness of the kingdom, no longer "paradoxical" (5:26), promised the disciples.

(d) The earliest community was able to understand the period after Easter together with that of the earthly Jesus as the eschaton in the strict sense because they expected the end so imminently (Mark 9:1; 13:30; 1 Thess. 4:17; 1 Cor. 15:51) that the preaching to Israel and later to the nations represented the outside limit. They may even have understood the experience of the Spirit as the beginning of Jesus' coming to judgment. Paul was still able to think along similar lines (1 Thess. 4:17; 2 Cor. 6:2). Twenty years after Paul's death, when Luke was writing, this was no longer possible. Following Paul, one could say with John that in Jesus the eschaton was already present because what took place in him transcends all ages, bringing salvation to those who have faith and uniting them with Christ. In this case the coming of Christ and the last judgment mean only that the curtain is drawn aside and what had always been hidden is visible to all.

The danger here is Gnosticism, for which all that matters is knowledge of a salvation already achieved, so that life in the world becomes incidental (cf. the excursus following 4:30, a). Then all interest is lost in God as Creator of the world, and with it concern for nature, society, and the state. For this reason Paul put it that, although we have died with Jesus, we must rise with him in our way of life that we may one day share in the final resurrection (Rom. 6:8–11). To counter the misunderstandings at Corinth, he made a sharp distinction between the resurrection of the dead as an eschatological event and the situation now (1 Cor. 15:21–28), a distinction he maintained until Philippians 3:20–21 (*pace* 1:23). Even John set clear statements about the future resurrection of the dead alongside those about the present resurrection (as he incorporated 3:5 alongside 3:3; see the introduction to Matt. 18:3–4), or at least was later corrected along these lines (5:28–29; 6:39; cf. 1 John 2:28).

God's final act, bringing humankind and the world, not just a few souls, to the goal envisioned by God in creation, is essential to faith. Therefore one can do as Revelation does, albeit only in prophetic imagery, placing this final act in the center and stressing all that is discussed in the conclusion to Mark 13:1–27. The danger then is flight into a fantasy world that once more refuses to take seriously the world and the time remaining before the expected end. If we want to avoid both dangers, we must follow Luke in holding fast to expectation of a consummating final act of God but placing the major emphasis on human conduct in the interim as determined by this final act (see the discussion of 12:35; 18:1; 21:34–36). This is so true for Luke that in Acts (cf. also Luke 16:23; 23:43) it is no longer clear whether he expects resurrection and judgment only as the conclusion of each individual human life, perhaps even directly after death, or as the final goal of the world.

(e) Luke escapes the other danger of confusing the kingdom of God with human activity, whether religious or secular. He associates the kingdom of God strictly with Jesus (see above, c), hopes for salvation from God's eschatological act, sees the life of the Holy Spirit, whom even those that have already received must continually be granted and accept (Acts 4:8, 31; 13:9; etc.), and faith as the gift of God (Luke 17:5; Acts 3:16: "the faith which is [given] through him"; 16:14). The incursion of God into human life, which has already taken place in Jesus, and the focus on God's consummation thus shape those belonging to the age of the community in the event of the Spirit. Luke does not even speak of Christ's dwelling in us or of our life in him, as do Paul and John, but of the exalted Lord enthroned in heaven, who deals with us from heaven through the Spirit. For this period, too, Luke knows nothing of a salvation history in the sense of progress toward an end that could be described by the historian (see the excursus following 4:30, a), but he means something more than that the Christ-event produces some effects and after-effects in history or that it repeatedly and in fundamentally the same way serves as a sign of God's will and grace (see *ibid.*, c). In the history of the community, God creates the faith that sees the kingdom to come at the end of this history and opens itself to it. Therefore the last days (Acts 2:17) begin with Jesus and the gift of the Spirit (see the discussion of Luke 21:6).

# B. JESUS' PASSION
## (22:1—23:56)

Although Luke basically follows the outline of Mark, in the story of the Passion he departs significantly from him; see the excursus following 23:25.

## Passover Preparations in the Shadow of the Cross (22:1-13)
Cf. Mark 14:1-2, 10-16; Matthew 26:1-5, 14-19

[1]Now the Feast of the Unleavened Bread drew near, which is called Passover. [2]And the chief priests and scribes were seeking how to put him to death, for they feared the people.

[3]Then Satan entered into Judas, called Iscariot, who was one of the number of the Twelve. [4]And he went away and conferred with the chief priests and captains how he might betray him to them. [5]And they were glad and promised to give him money. [6]And he agreed and sought an opportunity to betray him to them in the absence of the crowd.

[7]Then the day of Unleavened Bread came, on which the Passover had to be slaughtered. [8]And he sent Peter and John, saying, "Go and prepare the Passover for us, that we may eat it." [9]But they said to him, "Where would you have us prepare it?" [10]He said to them, "Behold, when you have entered the city, a person will meet you carrying a jar of water. Follow him into the house which he enters, [11]and say to the householder, 'The Teacher says to you, Where is the guest room, where I may eat the Passover with my disciples?' [12]And he will show you a large upper room, furnished with carpets. There make ready." [13]And when they went away, they found it as he had told them, and they prepared the Passover.

[1] Omission of the anointing episode (see the introduction to 7:36–50) has brought the decision to put Jesus to death into conjunction with Judas' offer (Mark 14:1–2/10–11). The anointing planned for later (23:56) is overtaken by the resurrection. The period of two days (Mark 14:1) is omitted; Luke knows nothing of any distribution of events over a week (Palm Sunday to Easter; see the discussion of 19:28—21:38). The imprecise identification of the two feasts (see the discussion of Mark 14:1) is widespread (cf. Josephus *Ant.* 3. 249; 14. 21; 18. 29; *De bello jud.* 2. 10; 17. 213; 20. 5), but "the day" (not "the first day" as in Mark 14:12) in vs. 7 is almost impossible (but cf. Josephus *De beilo jud.* 5. 99). Furthermore, the Day of Passover begins after sundown, not in the morning, as the Greeks reckon days (cf. vs. 34). Of course the lamb is slaughtered earlier and the leaven removed from the house.

[2] Once again the people are distinguished more clearly from the officials than in Mark (see the discussion of 19:48). [3] Judas' treachery is ascribed to Satan (see the discussion of 8:12), as in John 13:2, 27 ("Satan [the only occurrence in John!] entered into him"). The Martyrdom of Isaiah 3:11 says similarly of Beliar ( = Satan) that he took up residence in the heart of Manasses. [4] The only question is "how" (cf. vs. 2). Luke singles out the temple police (see the introduction to vss. 47–53), emphasizes Judas' assent, and gives the reason for involving Judas: it is to be carried out "in the absence of the crowd." [7] Does the "had to be" allude to the necessity of Jesus' death (24:26; Acts 8:32)? But Luke does not understand Jesus as the Passover lamb, and vs. 15 argues to the contrary. [8] Jesus, not the disciples, takes the initiative and sends "Peter and John" (see the discussion of 8:45). [6] The "opportunity" (vs. 6) is not yet at hand since Judas does not know where the room is.


## Passover (22:14–38)
Cf. Mark 14:17–31; 10:42–45; Matthew 26:20–35; 20:25, 28; 19:28; John 13:1–38

¹⁴And when the hour came, he reclined and the Apostles with him. ¹⁵And he said to them, "Desirously I have desired to eat this Passover with you before my suffering. ¹⁶For I tell you I shall not eat it until it is fulfilled in the kingdom of God. ¹⁷And he took a cup, pronounced the

thanksgiving, and said, "Take this and divide it among yourselves; [18]for I tell you that from now on I shall not eat of the fruit of the vine until the kingdom of God comes." [19]And he took bread, pronounced the thanksgiving, broke it, and gave it to them, saying, "This is my body which is given for you. Do this in remembrance of me." [20]And likewise the cup after supper, saying, "This cup is the new covenant [or: the new testament] in my blood which is poured out for you. [21]"But behold, the hand of him who betrays me is with me on the table. [22]For the Son of Man goes as it has been determined, but woe to that person by whom he is betrayed." [23]And they began to question one another, which of them it could be that would do this.

[24]A dispute also arose among them, which of them was to be regarded as the greatest. [25]And he said to them, "The kings of the nations exercise lordship over them, and their powerful ones are called benefactors. [26]But not so with you; rather let the greatest among you become as the youngest and the leader as one who serves. [27]For which is the greater: one who reclines at table or one who serves? Is it not the one who reclines at table? But I am among you as the one who serves.

[28]"You are those who have continued with me in my trials. [29]And I appoint to you, as the Father has appointed to me royal sovereignty [or: a kingdom], [30]that you may eat and drink at my table in my kingdom, and sit on thrones judging the twelve tribes of Israel.

[31]"Simon, Simon, behold, Satan demanded to have you, that he might sift you like wheat. [32]But I have prayed for you that your faith may not fail. And you, when you have turned again, strengthen your brothers and sisters." [33]And he said to him, "Lord, I am ready to go with you to prison and to death." [34]He said to him, "I tell you, Peter, the cock will not crow this day until you have denied three times that you know me."

[35]And he said to them, "When I sent you out without purse or bag or sandals, did you lack anything?" And they said, "Nothing." [36]He said to them, "But now, let him who has a purse take it, and likewise a bag, and let him who does not have one, sell his mantle and buy a sword. [37]For I tell you that what has been written must be fulfilled in me, namely, 'And he was reckoned among the transgressors.' For what concerns me comes to an end." [38]But they said, "Lord, behold, here are two swords." And he said, "It is enough."

(Vs. 37—Isa. 53:21.)


The beginning of the meal (vs. 14) parallels the departure (vs. 39), which introduces the arrest. The phrase "and Jesus said to them"

introduces sayings concerning the meal (including the announcement of Jesus' betrayal, vss. 15–24) and the future of the disciples
(vss. 25–34), as well as the admonition to buy swords (vss. 35–38).
"For I tell you" emphasizes Jesus' prediction of his own fate (vss.
16, 18, 37). Only vss. 31–38 are dialogue (but cf. vss. 23–24).

[15–20] The sayings during the meal are remarkably interwoven.
The saying concerning the Passover and that concerning the cup both
comprise a solemn introduction followed by a prospect of the kingdom of God (vss. 16, 18). The introduction to the saying concerning
the cup in turn parallels that in the saying concerning the bread (vss.
17, 19), while the sayings concerning the betrayal follow vs. 20
without any transition. On the words of institution, cf. the excursus
following Mark 14:22–25. Vss. 19a and 20 (end) correspond to Mark
14:22, 24 (except for "thanksgiving" [prayer] instead of "blessing").
Vss. 19b (beginning with "for you") and 20 (up to "blood") follow
the version in 1 Corinthians 11:24–25 but not precisely. These were
probably the words of the liturgy familiar to Luke in his community.
In one ancient manuscript vss. 19b–20 are omitted, but they are
found in all the others, including those closely related to that one,
and in the earliest papyrus. Since vs. 19a without vss. 19b–20 would
be an extremely abrupt conclusion, and since other manuscripts or
ancient versions place vss. 17–18 after vs. 19 (and 20), or substitute
them for vss. 19b–20 or omit them entirely, the short text is best
explained as yet another attempt to get rid of the two cups (the one
in vs. 17 before the bread, the one in vs. 20 after) since only one
was used in the Lord's Supper. If so, it is admittedly surprising that
vss. 17–18 were not omitted and that vs. 19b (assimilation to Mark?)
was.

In vs. 20, the phrase "poured out for you" has been borrowed
mechanically from Mark 14:24: it is in the nominative while "blood"
is in the dative. Strictly speaking, it should modify "cup," but a cup
is not poured out. Two traditional formulas are in conflict here; the
grammatical discrepancy cannot be reproduced in English. Compare
also the excursus following Mark 14:22–25. Vss. 14–18 are probably familiar to Luke from a special tradition; they contain un-Lukan
expressions although his editorial hand is visible. Since he did not
have any first-hand knowledge of a Passover meal, it is hard to imag-

ine him introducing a cup before the bread and shifting the designation of the traitor so that Judas still receives bread and wine. But in
an account that records the words before and over the first cup, this
designation has to appear here on account of vs. 21b (on "but" see
section 2, c of the Introduction). Furthermore, the unusual references in vss. 16 and 18 to the Passover lamb and the (first) cup are
probably earlier than the reference to the cup of the Lord's Supper
in Mark 14:25.

[24–30] Vss. 29–30 are related. The disciples are given a portion
in that which Jesus expects for himself (vss. 16, 18)—the kingdom
and its festal eating and drinking. In between come vss. 25–27, which
point to Jesus' serving, now illustrated in the context of the meal but
also determinative of his entire life and death, as the basis for the
service of the disciples. The saying itself is a variant of Mark 10:42–
45, not yet developed to the point of explicitly mentioning the atonement (see the introduction to Mark 10:35–45).

The transitional vs. 24 is Lukan (cf. 9:46) and possibly vs. 28.
The form for "greatest" (literally "greater") is found only here and
in 7:28 (Q); 12:18 (L); and 9:46 (Mark), but it appears in Matthew
23:11 in contrast to "servant" (cf. the introduction to Mark 9:33–
37); we are probably dealing with a special tradition. The use of
"exercise lordship" (a weaker term than that used in Mark 10:42),
the prefix in "recline at table," and similar features, as well as the
double question in vs. 27, are un-Lukan. Vs. 30b is a variant of the
special saying recorded in Matthew 19:28b (q.v.). The change in
form of the verb from vs. 30a might indicate that vs. 30b was originally handed down separately. The elimination of Judas is not reflected in the saying. The word "appoint" or "bequeath" comes from
the same root as "covenant" (in Acts 3:25 the two words are used
together; cf. 2 Sam. 5:3 LXX). Vs. 20, which speaks explicitly of the
covenant, is thus all the more likely to have been part of the original
text of Luke.

Was there then a tradition comprising vss. 14–18, (25–26), 27,
29–30, and perhaps including a description of the Passover meal? It
would have emphasized the renewal of the covenant and the final
consummation to come. It has even been suggested that originally
there was a Christian Passover celebration, during which night the

Son of Man was expected to come (cf. the night of redemption in
Judaism: Bill 1. 85). There is evidence of this for later Christian
groups; for the pre-Lukan period it is pure conjecture (cf. the discussion of 17:34–35).

[31–34] Vss. 31–34 contain a totally different saying (un-Lukan in
style) addressed to "Simon" (cf. the introduction to 5:1–11). The
name "Peter" in vs. 34 is Lukan. Only in the prediction of the betrayal itself does this passage echo Mark 14:30. Contrary to Mark
14:26, it is spoken in the upper room (see the discussion of vs. 31).
Here, too, we are dealing with a special tradition. This is also suggested by its echoes of the Johannine tradition (see the discussion of
vs. 3), which, like vs. 14, speaks of Jesus' "hour" (13:1; but cf.
Mark 14:35) and knows of Peter's "later" discipleship and pastoral
role, as well as the form of address "Simon" (son of John) (John
13:36; 21:15–17). John 13:38b is formally closer to Luke 22:34 than
Mark is.
[21–23] Vss. 21–22 (John 13:21) follow Mark 14:18 (cf. Ps. 41:10
in John 13:18). But in John 13—16, too, the saying addressed to
Simon Peter comes between the Last Supper, which included Jesus'
exemplary service to his disciples, and the farewell discourses, which
look forward to a future consummation (see the excursus following
Mark 14:22–25).
[35–38] Vss. 35–38, again appended directly, are without parallel. Vs. 36b contradicts vs. 51; for this reason and because it is so
hard to interpret, it was certainly in Luke's prototype. The quotation
in vs. 37, which is close to the Hebrew text and is introduced with
an un-Lukan article, was also not added by Luke, if only because he
would have placed it after vs. 53. Furthermore, vs. 35 cites the saying addressed to the seventy(-two) (10:4 Q?), rather than that addressed to the Twelve. Did vss. 36 and 37 circulate together and
become framed by vss. 35 and 38 (before Luke, on stylistic grounds)
to form a short story?

[14] The difficulty of having Jesus arrive with the "Twelve" although two have gone on ahead (Mark 14:17) is avoided. Instead
Luke describes the beginning of a festive meal at which all are re-

clining. The "hour" (cf. John 13:1) is the hour of the Passover meal (see the discussion of 2:41) but also the hour appointed by God for Jesus' departure.

[15–16] "This Passover" (lamb) refers to the lamb lying before them, so that Jesus' statement probably means that he is eating of it for the last time, not that he is now refusing to eat. The Greek form could be used in an oath but also appears in quotations and traditional sayings of Jesus in a purely future sense: 1:15; (12:29); 13:35; 18:7; (21:33). In any case, the eschatological fulfillment is stressed. At the same time, Luke emphasizes human company as prefiguring this fulfillment. It is important to him that what is actually unimaginable can be experienced, if not precisely defined. In the new Passover, the table fellowship of the Lord's Supper, something of the consummation to come (cf. 14:15–24) is lived proleptically.

[17] Although lamb and wine belong to the Passover meal, not the Lord's Supper, the taking of the cup and the thanksgiving over it recall the latter. The benediction over the first cup (cf. the excursus following Mark 14:12–16) is pronounced at Passover and other solemn banquets by one person, usually the father of the household, on behalf of all: "Blessed art thou . . . who didst create the fruit of the vine" (Isa. 32:12; Bill. 4. 62. 621). He takes the first drink. The command to share the cup emphasizes the fellowship.

[18] Strictly speaking, vs. 18 would imply that Jesus does not drink of the cup in vs. 20; this may account for the shift of this saying in Mark 14:25. The promise of the kingdom follows in vss. (19–20), 29–30. If vss. 14–18, 25–30 in fact represent an early special tradition, there would be special emphasis on the lamb and the wine, in keeping with the joyous expectation of the eschatological banquet. The coming of the kingdom is entirely up to God; Jesus shares in it and promises a share in it to his own but does not bring it about. Whether anything was said about bread in this tradition we do not know. In any case, we have no evidence here for the "breaking of bread" (Acts 2:42, 46; 20:7, 11) as a special form of the Lord's Supper, without wine and the idea of atonement, but replete with eschatological hope.

[19] "Take this" (Mark 14:22) has already appeared in vs. 17 and is not repeated. "Remembrance" means far more than recollection.

The historical event is brought so into the present that it takes effect today. [20] The cup is identified with the new covenant or testament, not the wine with Jesus' blood. The Passover is replaced by the new fellowship with God that even now becomes reality in Jesus and (according to vss. 29–30) will one day be established visibly. The blood that is poured out corresponds to the body that is given. Thus salvation is based on Jesus' sacrifice on the cross, not simply on the cultic meal.

[21] Vs. 21 is simpler than Mark 14:20; it does not (yet?) contain the image of dipping in the same bowl, the person of the traitor is represented by his "hand," and the echo of Psalm 41:10 is omitted. [22] Vs. 22 speaks of what has been determined (by God) instead of Scripture (cf. Acts 2:23). [23] The confusion of the disciples reflects Mark 14:19 (but "one another" suggests John 13:22). It reveals the human situation, even of those obedient to Jesus: anyone could be Judas. Perhaps something of the mystery of evil can be seen: there is also an election to evil (never simply excusing anyone) that ultimately serves God (see the discussion of Mark 14:10). The shift has made vss. 21–23 the beginning of Jesus' farewell discourses (cf. Deut. 1:1–5; 32:45—33:1; Tob. 4:3–20; 14:3–11; Test. XII; John 14—16; Acts 20:18–38).

[24] The statement of the situation (see the discussion of 11:1) resembles 9:46, but vss. 25–27 (like 9:46/48) are hard to imagine without such an introduction. It is therefore not likely that Luke is thinking of a quarrel over seats in the assembly (James 2:2–4). [26] In contrast to Mark 10:43, vs. 26 speaks of someone who truly is great, a leader, but he is great in service. This is especially true of the Apostles. The terms "leaders" (Acts 15:22; Heb. 13:7, 17, 24) and "young men" (Acts 5:6, [10]; 1 Pet. 5:5; cf. 1 Tim. 5:1–2; Tit. 2:6) might suggest special positions in the community, but at most as a later interpretation (as in 12:42) since the term "servant" (Mark 10:43), which also means "deacon," is absent here. But in contrast to Acts 2:42–43 and 13:1–3, there is already perceptible here the danger of an episcopate or presbyterate misunderstood as power. Nothing is said of humility in the abstract; Jesus exhibits the attitude required of the disciples in active service. He does not talk of a virtue but points to something that he does. This corresponds in

substance to John 13:1–17. In Luke 22 (vss. 11, 15), Jesus is in fact the lord of the household; perhaps Luke has in mind a prophetic symbolic act (like Jesus' washing the disciples' feet in John 13) that shows what his whole life has been and above all will be the next morning and astonishingly fulfills 12:37.

[28] Vs. 28 stresses the perseverance, Matthew 19:28 the "following" of the disciples. The retrospect (see the discussion of 4:13) [29] is matched by a prospect. Both are part of the farewell. The "new covenant" (vs. 20) is made in the covenantal promise of full table fellowship; in Greek "bequeath" is based on the same root as "covenant." This is the only passage in the Gospels where "kingdom" (of God) or "sovereignty" appears without the article. This usage is found elsewhere only in the formula about inheriting the kingdom of God in 1 Corinthians 6:9–10; 15:50; and Galatians 5:21; therefore the translation above is suggested (cf. Rev. 1:9). Does the expression belong to both the main clause and the subordinate clause, or does it refer only to the sovereignty given Jesus? It makes little material difference since the disciples share in it in any case (cf. Rom. 5:17; 1 Cor. 4:8; 6:2–3; 1 Pet. 2:9; Rev. 3:21; 5:10; and especially 2 Tim. 2:12a).

[30] This is described in vs. 30. It is impossible to visualize both images simultaneously since thrones symbolize judgment and sovereignty (Dan. 7:9; Rev. 20:4; cf. 1 Cor. 6:2), but Revelation 3:20–21 also links table fellowship and thrones, and Enoch 62:14 looks forward to the banquet with the Son of Man, who first judges all the nations. On Easter God gives Jesus sovereign lordship (Acts 2:36). Now his disciples are subordinate to it; one day they will share it (see the discussion of 1:33 and 23:42). Nothing is said about the dominion of the church over Israel; *now* it is a (suffering) witness before Israel (21:12–13; Acts 1:8). The farewell meal is also a testament that shapes the future (as in Test. N. 1).

The words of the liturgy twice say "for you" (vss. 19–20). The context develops this idea. Just as Jesus' table fellowship with the tax collectors brings them into fellowship with God (5:30; 15:2; 19:7), so God makes a new covenant with God's own in the eating and drinking Jesus shares with his band of disciples (cf. the conclusion to 24:13–35). Fellowship is not just declared, it is created. Of course it would remain idle if God were not one day to redeem this sign in a fellowship that is not fragmentary and symbolic but comprehends all that makes up life. Hence the enormous, expectant joy of the primitive Christian celebration of the Lord's Supper (see the discussion of 2:41); it would be nothing but a pious illusion if it did not so shape the lives of the participants that they became lives of service. Hence the extraordinary influence of the primitive Christian celebration of the Lord's Supper on everyday life (Acts 2:46, 45). The Lord's Supper is a foretaste of the future consummation and an aftertaste of the life Jesus lived for us.

**Understanding Jesus' Death on the Cross.** (a) Luke records the "for you" of the liturgy, but just as "the blood outpoured" of 22:20 is not linked grammatically to the rest of the sentence, neither is the phrase "with his own blood" in Acts 20:28, referring to God instead of Jesus, a formula that recalls Psalm 74(73):2 and Revelation 5:9. Luke uses the verb "save" (or "heal," "help") more than thirty times (including 19:10) but never in connection with Jesus' death. But Jesus' Passion is emphasized more strongly in Luke than in the other Gospels (see the discussion of 9:31 and 20:15). Indeed, Luke borrows the Christian neologism of the "Passion" or "suffering" of Christ (Mark 8:31; 9:12), which means his death, as it does in the interpretive passages 2 Corinthians 4:10 and Philippians 3:10. In contrast to Luke's usage, it came to be used in the Christian community primarily in an ethical sense (2 Cor. 1:5–7; Phil. 3:10; Col. 1:24; Heb. 2:9–10, 18; 5:8; 9:26; 13:12; 1 Pet. 2:21, 23; 3:18; 4:1, 13; 5:1, 9).

(b) (1) Luke's interpretation is unique: according to him, it is the *function of Christ* that he "must suffer." This idea is neither Jewish nor universally Christian. In this function Jesus is seen as the righteous sufferer, or more precisely the suffering prophet, whose path is marked by God's "must" (13:31–33). Hebrew has no term for this necessity although it appears in the Greek idea of fate (Herodotus 8. 53: according to God's prophecy, all Attica "had" to be subject to the Persians), but Jewish apocalyptic took up this "must." Just as the dream sent by God "must" be fulfilled in the eschaton (Dan. 2:28 LXX), so must the prophecy of Jesus (Mark 13:7; Rev. 1:1). Mark 8:31 already sees in Jesus' fate the eschatological act of God; Luke sees in it fulfillment of Scripture (22:37; 24:25-27). But since this does not predict the cosmic eschatological catastrophes, in 21:9 ( = Mark 13:7) Luke separates what "must" take place from these catastrophes and associates it particularly with Jesus' death, resurrection, and exaltation, together with the suffering these imply for the community that bears witness to Jesus (also 17:25; 24:7; Acts 1:16; 9:16; 14:22; 17:3; 19:21; 25:10).

(2) The place of Mark 10:45 is taken by Luke 19:10 and 22:27. Both statements describe Jesus' entire life, not just his death. If one inquires into the *salvific significance* of Jesus' service, which leads to death, 19:10 finds it in "seeking and saving the lost." This is why it is so important for Luke that the crucified Jesus is found among the transgressors (22:37), that he turns to them in love and gives them repentance (19:8; 22:51; 23:32, 34 [q.v.], 40-42), as he has done throughout his entire ministry. According to Mark 15:34, the crucified Jesus emphasizes only the terrible loneliness of this death. According to John 19:26-28, 30, he shows his sovereignty in caring for his mother and the beloved disciple, consciously fulfills the Scriptures, and dies with a shout of victory. In Luke all three words from the cross show Jesus' love for humankind and his Father in heaven.

(3) If one inquires into the effect of the Passion *within the community*, 22:27 emphasizes that his service in suffering gives the community the possibility of service, making possible a kind of "aftertaste" (cf. the conclusion to 4:1-13) of the power of God. The prayers of Jesus on the cross are repeated on the lips of Stephen (Acts 7:59-60), whose blood is "poured out" (Acts 22:20) like that of the prophets (Luke 11:49-50, where the "Apostles" are added by Luke) and Jesus himself (Luke 22:20). Paul's journey to Jerusalem recalls that of Jesus (Acts 19:21; 20:22; 21:4, 11-15), even in its structure (divine prediction of suffering [Luke 9:31], farewell discourse, council, Roman governor, Herodian king: Acts 9:16; 20:18-25; 22:30; 23:33; 25:23). Like the Son of Man, Paul, too, is "delivered into the hands of the Gentiles" (Acts 21:11; Luke 18:32; 24:7; Bk. Jub. 1:19). Of Acts, 23.5 percent tells of Paul during his imprisonment; according to 9:16 (cf. "for"), the basis of his election is suffering for the name of Christ. Like Jesus the community must enter the kingdom of God

through tribulation (Luke 24:26; Acts 14:22). Jesus' Passion is described in such a way that it comprehends his entire life of service, in which a new possibility of human life and death is created. If faith is more than just acceptance of some formula or schema, there must be certain analogies between the experience of Jesus and that of his disciples (cf. Phil. 2:5–8; 3:10–11). Perhaps this is why echoes of the Lord's Prayer appear so often in Luke's Passion narrative (22:18, 40, 42; 23:34), as well as motifs deriving from Jewish martyrdoms: temptation by Satan, struggle, hope for aid from heaven and its arrival, political charges, announcement of judgment for the persecutors, and declaration of innocence (Mart. Isa. 3:6, 11; 2 Macc. 7:6, 12, 14, 19, 24, 30, 31–35; 3 Macc. 4:11; 5:7–9; 6:18; 4 Macc. 6:4, 6; 8:6–9; 9:10, 30–32; 17:10–11). Here Jesus is "the faithful witness," who makes his disciples faithful witnesses (Rev. 1:5; 2:13). Thus Luke 22:15–30 (38) becomes a testamentary farewell discourse.

(c) Luke, then, sees three things. (1) Jesus' ministry, which consummates the fate of the Old Testament prophets, is a road to suffering, deliberately taken. He emphasizes the greatness of the temptation, the "power of darkness," and Jesus' submission to God's will. (2) This effects salvation in Jesus' love for humankind, thus (3) making possible the post-Easter way of service and suffering taken by the community. But just as in Revelation 5:9 (see a above) only Jesus is the lamb that has purchased a people for God, so for Luke, too, Jesus' Passion remains the absolute foundation for all later experience: the Gospel precedes Acts (cf. the excursus following 21:38). Here he is revealed as the Christ. Only he has the authority to promise the kingdom (20:29–30) and paradise (23:43, q.v., conclusion), in other words, salvation.

[31] In contrast to Mark 14:26–31 (q.v., introduction), Jesus' words to Simon follow directly. As in John 13:37–38, they are therefore spoken in the upper room. [33] As in John, Peter addresses Jesus as "Lord" and expresses his readiness to die (vs. 33, not in Mark 14:29). [34] As in John, vs. 34 reads "not . . . until. . . ." Together with vss. 21–23, this passage states that no one can be certain before the event and that whoever feels strong will be abandoned to his weak-

ness. **[32]** Only through repentance does true faith come, experienced as a gift.

**[35–38]** Again we have a retrospect and prospect but now looking to a time when swords are needed. **[36a]** Vs. 36a annuls the requirement of 10:4 (= vs. 35), which applied only to the unique situation of preparing for the coming of the earthly Jesus himself, and advises taking the necessities. This was Paul's principle. As soon as the gospel moved from rural Palestine, where lodging could be found with fellow believers, into the Hellenistic cities, and missionaries wanted to push forward into new territories (Rom. 15:20), such a procedure was inescapable. Whoever took Jesus' command literally (see the excursus following Matt. 7:23, 7) would have to stay within the orbit of existing Christian communities. Paul may well have been charged with carrying money (which he had earned himself!) (Acts 18:3) rather than following Luke 10:4 and relying entirely on hospitality (1 Cor. 9:6–15). But he lived the fine carelessness of Jesus' messengers in other ways (Acts. 20:33–35; Phil. 4:12–16). For Luke, then, Jesus' instructions are not engraved in stone (cf. the discussion of Matt. 10:5–6) but are to be adapted in practice to changing situations (see the discussion of 6:20b).

**[36b]** Nevertheless, the admonition that whoever does not have a sword (or a purse) should buy a sword is striking. Is it a proverbial expression for a time of distress when a sword is more important than the blanket that keeps one warm at night? Is the period of the nascent church similar to that of Nehemiah 4:18? Is it suggested that the mere possession of a sword will keep one from being attacked? In any case, Luke 22:49 explicitly raises the question of the use of the sword, which is answered negatively in 22:51. **[38]** Jesus' response in vs. 38 cannot therefore be taken as approval. Probably it is a brusque rejection ("Enough of that!"; cf. 1 Kings 19:4; Deut. 3:26 [Moses' farewell discourse]), not irony ("More than enough!"). It is simply not possible that the two swords are meant to suggest the two armed men between whom Jesus is crucified or that **[37]** the "transgressors" of vs. 37 are the disciples and that the two swords are "enough" evidence. Equally impossible is the hypothesis that Jesus planned an armed revolution; two swords are certainly not enough for that, and the disciples are not touched when Jesus is arrested (vs. 54). Neither is it likely that the statement justifies self-defense in certain cases. The point is probably just that times have changed: the course taken by Jesus (vs. 37; cf. the excursus following vs. 30, b.1) calls forth the sword (Matt. 10:34; cf. Luke 12:50/51). Now the disciples have to take their necessities with them. They can no longer simply proclaim peace without purse, bag, or sandals (10:4–5). The traditional saying of Jesus in vs. 36b had to be incorporated somehow. Luke understands it symbolically: just as for Jesus everything must come to its consummation in the Passion (cf. 18:31, Lukan), so, too, for the disciples hard times are at hand; Acts 9:31 is followed by 12:1, etc. But despite vs. 51, this passage was used to derive the theory that one sword belongs to the church, the other to the state. This shows how fatal it can be not just to preserve obscure sayings of Jesus but to try to understand them at any price.

## Jesus' Struggle with God's Will (22:39–46)
Cf. Mark 14:32–42; Matthew 26:36–46

³⁹And he went out and went, as was his custom, to the Mount of Olives. And the disciples followed him. ⁴⁰And when he came to the place, he said to them, "Pray that you may not enter into temptation." ⁴¹And he tore himself away from them, about a stone's throw apart, and knelt and prayed ⁴²and said, "Father, if thou art willing, let this cup pass me by; nevertheless, not my will but thine be done." ⁴³But there appeared to him an angel from heaven, strengthening him. ⁴⁴And being in agony he prayed more earnestly, and his sweat became like drops of blood falling down upon the ground. ⁴⁵And he rose from prayer, came to the disciples, and found them sleeping for sorrow. ⁴⁶And he said to them, "Why do you sleep? Rise and pray that you may not enter into temptation."

The text agrees with Mark only in some of Jesus' words, but there are no un-Lukan expressions. Is Luke following an oral tradition that also included Jesus' prayer (Matt. 26:42; Luke 22:42!) or L? After the introduction, the section begins and ends with a saying of Jesus (vss. 40b, 46). Jesus' return corresponds to his withdrawal (vss. 41, 45). All four verses mention his praying. Vss. 42–44 constitute the core. Vss. 43–44 do not appear in some ancient manuscripts but are stylistically so Lukan that they could hardly have been written later. Also typically Lukan are the continued prayer, the response through an angel, and the parallel to 9:28-32 (prayer on the mountain—heavenly messengers—reference to suffering—sleep of the disciples). Without these verses the passage would have no real point; later copyists probably found them too human.

[39] Only at this point does Jesus leave the upper room and go to the Mount of Olives (Mark 14:26; cf. the discussion of Luke 21:37–38). The name Gethsemane (also unknown to John) is omitted, as is the name Golgotha. As yet there are no sacred sites. Possibly the "following" of the disciples is stressed because the story is intended to shape the life of the community. [40] They are not told to stay awake, nor are they chastized for sleeping (vs. 46); they are instead told (in Lukan style) to pray, as in vs. 46. [41] Jesus does not take three of the disciples with him, as in Mark 14:33, but "tears himself away" (Acts 21:1). As in Acts 7:60; 9:40; 20:36 (farewell); 21:5 (also 1 Kings 8:54), the prayer that follows is said kneeling (not standing, as in 18:11, 13).

[42] The middle of the prayer agrees with Mark 14:36 ("this cup," identical in Greek with vs. 20), but the beginning and end have been altered in form (probably before Luke). In the Old Testament, the cup stands for God's judgment, which, since Mark 10:38 (q.v.) does not appear in Luke, takes place in the overall rejection of Jesus, not simply in his death. "Thy will be done" (Matt. 11:10; 26:42, somewhat different in form) does not appear in the Lukan version of the Lord's Prayer. Even the hour of darkness, the hour of Satan (vss. 53, 3), can be willed by God. [43] "Strengthening" by an angel is mentioned in Daniel 10:13, 15–18; Jewish legend says the same of Daniel when he was thrown into the fiery furnace (Bill. 4. 454, on vs. 3; cf. Isa. 42:6 [the suffering servant]). [44] It does not do away with "agony" but gives strength to deal with it. The root is the same as in "strive" (see the discussion of 13:24) and thus suggests "unceasing" prayer (also in Acts 12:5). "Like drops of blood" leaves open the question whether blood was mixed with Jesus' sweat; in any case, Jesus is not depicted as a Stoic (cf. sweat as a sign of wrath, rejection, and remorse in Joseph and Aseneth 4:9; 9:1). [45]

The sleep of the disciples is excused; it is just not the time for it. [46] The conclusion does not look back (Mark 14:37*b*), only forward. The saying about the weakness of the flesh and Jesus' two additional prayers (Mark 14:38–42) are omitted.

As in Hebrews 2:17 and 5:7–10, Jesus is pictured as one who was "made like his brethren in every respect." Only thus is it possible to incorporate his Passion into the life of faith rather than merely accepting it intellectually. What was stated in the excursus following vs. 30 is confirmed: it is important to Luke that faith should share in the way of Jesus and be shaped by it, but the angel comes only to Jesus, and only he is not asleep at the crucial hour.

## The Hour of Darkness (22:47–53)
Cf. Mark 14:43–52; Matthew 26:47–56; John 18:2–12

47While he was still speaking, behold, there was a crowd, and the one called Judas, one of the Twelve, was going before them, and he drew near to Jesus to kiss him. 48But Jesus said to him, "Judas, would you betray the Son of Man with a kiss?" 49And when those who were about him saw what would follow, they said, "Lord, shall we strike with the sword?" 50And one of them struck the slave of the high priest with the sword and cut off his right ear. 51And Jesus answered and said, "Let it suffice [or: pass]," and he touched the ear and healed him. 52But Jesus said to the chief priests and captains of the temple and elders, who had come out against him, "How have you come out as against a robber, with swords and clubs; 53when I was with you day by day in the temple, why did you not lay hands on me? But this is your hour and the power of darkness."

There are several points of agreement with John against Mark: Jesus initiates the action (vss. 48, 51, 53*b*). Judas appears as leader of the multitude. Some captains (one in John 18:12) are present. It is unclear whether Judas actually kisses Jesus (vs. 48 is new). The slave's "right" ear is cut off even before Jesus is arrested. And the disciples do not flee. Some expressions have been borrowed from Mark. There are no clearly un-Lukan passages, but some details attract attention.

**[47]** Vs. 47, like Matthew 26:14 at the beginning of the Passion, speaks of "the one called Judas," as though he were being mentioned for the first time (cf. Acts 3:2; 6:9; and the discussion of Luke 21:37–38). **[49]** Since only the disciples (and Jesus' enemies) are present, the expression "those who were about him" is strange; in Mark 4:10 and Acts 13:13 it refers to an otherwise undesignated group (cf. Matt. 26:51). **[52]** Finally, chief priests, captains, and elders are not mentioned until vs. 52 (cf. Mark 14:43). The captains probably belong to the temple police although Acts 4:1; 5:24, 26 speak of only a single captain. Do we have here the beginning of an early Passion narrative? The fact that Mark 14:7 also mentions "those standing by" and that the word "disciple" does not appear again after Mark 14:32 (except for 16:7)/Luke 22:45, although Luke says nothing of their flight, may indicate that they fled at the moment of Jesus' arrest and that their absence continued to influence the Lukan tradition (cf. the discussion of 23:49).

**[48]** "Betray the Son of Man" is a fixed idiom (9:44; 18:32; 22:22; 24:7; also Mark 14:41). **[49]** The sword is clearly intended for self-defense; Jesus has not yet been arrested (see the discussion of vss. 35–38). **[50]** But since Mark 14:47–48 states that the sword was actually used, **[51]** Luke is forced to postpone Jesus' negative response. It contains only three words (Matt. 26:52–54 uses forty-two!)—"Leave [off? it be?] until here"—but a more eloquent action. **[53]** Darkness is Satan's realm (vs. 3; Acts 26:18). Jesus confirms this and allows himself to be arrested.

The question of force is posed explicitly. It is answered by Jesus' readiness to suffer and even to heal his enemy. Both belong to Jesus' way. He does not contest Pilate's authority or his military power, but for himself he rejects use of the sword. It is his will to give life, not to take it. This does not solve the problem, but it establishes a guide-post (cf. the excursus following Matt. 7:29, a.3 and c.2, 4).

## Peter's Denial and Jesus' Confession (22:54–71)
Cf. Mark 14:53–72; Matthew 26:57–75; John 18:13–24

⁵⁴When they had taken him prisoner, they led him away and brought him into the high priest's house. But Peter followed at a distance. ⁵⁵And

when they had kindled a fire in the middle of the courtyard and sat down together, Peter sat in their midst. [56]When a maid saw him sitting by the fire and looked him in the eye, she said, "This man also was with him." [57]But he denied it, saying, "I do not know him, woman." [58]And a little later someone else saw him and said, "You also are one of them." But Peter denied it, saying, "Man, I am not." [59]And after about an hour had passed, still another insisted, "In truth, this one also was with him, for he is also a Galilean." [60]But Peter said, "Man, I do not know what you are saying." And immediately, while he was still speaking, the cock crowed. [61]And the Lord turned and looked at Peter, and Peter remembered the word of the Lord, how he had said to him, "Before the cock crows, you will deny me today three times." [62]And he went out and wept bitterly.

[63]And the men who were holding him mocked him and beat him [64]and blindfolded him and asked, "Prophesy! Who is it that struck you?" [65]And they spoke many other blasphemies against him.

[66]And when day came, the assembly of the elders of the people gathered together, both chief priests and scribes, and they led him before their tribunal [67]and said, "If you are the Messiah, tell us." But he said to them, "If I tell you, you will not believe, [68]and if I ask, you will not answer. [69]But from now on the Son of Man shall be seated at the right hand of the power of God." [70]And they all said, "Are you the Son of God, then?" But he said to them, "You say it; I am [or: let me be]." [71]And they said, "What further testimony do we need? For we have heard it ourselves out of his own mouth."

Luke knows of Peter's denial during the night but only of one trial the next morning (vs. 66; cf. the introduction to Mark 14:53–55). Both reports differ almost as much from Mark as from John. The tradition that Luke is most likely drawing on here must have many primitive elements. It has many expressions in common with Mark, especially a portion of Jesus' saying in vs. 69, but a large number of stylistic and factual details agree with John, and vs. 67 recalls the dialogue in John 10:24–25. Above all, Luke and John depict the course of the trial similarly (see the excursus on the trial following Mark 14:53–72). What is even stranger, vs. 62 and the question in vs. 64 agree verbatim with Matthew 26:75, 68 (q.v.). Purely oral tradition cannot explain these observations. Un-Lukan expressions are not frequent but the content of the narrative has been changed substantially. Do we have here the same source as in vss. 31-34?

[56] Luke speaks of a woman, who would have carried little weight as a witness then, and two men; according to Deuteronomy 19:15, at least two witnesses are required. [58] Peter addresses only the second questioner directly, the opposite of Mark 14:67, 69. [56] Temptation thus approaches him more closely. Earlier it was just a maid's chatter, not enough to keep him from staying close by to find out what was happening to Jesus. Therefore Peter does not draw back, as in Mark 14:68. [59] The third man speaks an hour later. Perhaps Luke is saying that apparent calm can be deceptive. Here, too, Peter is not asked a direct question, and he answers obliquely, "I do not know what you are saying," without stating directly that he knows nothing of Jesus, as in Mark 14:71.

[61] Only Luke reports that Jesus turns to Peter. Jesus is clearly being kept prisoner in the same courtyard where Peter is. Or else he is inside the "house" (vs. 54), where Peter can see him through an open window. Is it (as in John 18:13) the house of Annas, the high priest (see the discussion of 3:2)? In any event, Jesus is not brought before the tribunal until vs. 66, possibly in the palace of Caiaphas (John 18:24). [62] Even as a prisoner he effects a decisive change in Peter, a change given even more weight than in Matthew 26:75 by Luke's account of Peter's witness after Easter in Jerusalem, Samaria, and among the Gentiles. Acts also speaks of "the word of the Lord"; in it the Lord is present and restores us when we have gone astray.

[63] Although Peter has just been the subject, "him" refers to Jesus; he is the protagonist throughout. In contrast to Mark 14:65, it is not the members of the council but the guards on watch in the courtyard who "mock" him (as in Mark 15:20), [64] cover his face, strike him, and call on him to prophesy. The echoes of Isaiah 50:6 have vanished. [65] Instead Luke interprets their treatment as blasphemy. The mockery is less malicious than in Mark, but even someone who is not wicked "blasphemes" by living as though God did not exist and seeking to convince oneself of this fact through one's own provocations.

**[66]** The next morning Jesus is brought before the court. The "assembly of the elders" could be a generic term for a group made up of chief priests and scribes, but in 20:1; Acts 22:5; and probably also 5:21, all three groups are distinguished. Nothing is said about witnesses, the saying concerning the temple, and Jesus' silence, nor does the high priest appear. **[67]** Instead the question of Jesus' messiahship is asked at once, probably not out of a desire to assimilate the account to later martyrdoms. The question indicates from the outset that "Son of God" (vs. 70) is to be understood in the Old Testament sense, not as a Greek demigod; in 4:41, also, the two titles are used together (cf. 1:32–35). Jesus' answer is similar to that in John 10:25–26 (cf. vs. 36, and formally also Jer. 38:15). **[68]** In truth it is he who asks the question and they who must answer (cf. 20:7). **[69]** As in John 18:36–37, Jesus accepts the question and gives an affirmative answer but in a different sense than the questioners intended. "From now on" (cf. Matt. 26:64!) emphasizes that Luke is thinking of Jesus' exaltation, not the last coming; therefore he omits the statement about "coming with the clouds" and "seeing" in the future. **[70]** As in Daniel 7:13, "Son of Man" (cf. the excursus following Mark 8:27–33) designates the one who is exalted to God and can therefore be equated with "Son of God" (vs. 70). Do we have here, despite the Lukan language, an ancient tradition that originally followed directly after vss. 67–68? Or does the text interpret Jesus' prophetic answer, with its mysterious reference to the Son of Man in vs. 69, in the sense of Acts 13:33 and Romans 1:4, so that in the resurrection Jesus is exalted to Son of God?

In the Judaism of the first century C.E., "Son of Man" and "Son of God" never appear to be identified. This does happen in 2 Esdras 3:3, 32, but the Latin text probably represents an original title "Servant [not: Son] of God." In Enoch 48:10 [49:3]; 52:4, the Son of Man and the Messiah are equated, but we do not know when this section of Enoch was written. Or did Luke add vs. 70, replacing the reference to Jesus' last coming, which he proclaims in 21:27, with a reference to Jesus' divine sonship? "You say it" suggests that fundamentally they know the answer, or that their formulation of the question is unsatisfactory because Jesus has yet to enter into the sovereignty of the office. (1:32–33).

[71] Although elsewhere Luke shifts the burden of guilt from the Romans to the Jews, he does not take over the Jewish death sentence in Mark 14:64; neither does it appear in Luke 18:32. He is obviously following a different account. From the formal legal point of view, the council acts correctly, without mistreating the accused, but its rejection of Jesus is less honest and much more profound than that of the servants in the courtyard.

Even more than in Mark and Matthew, Jesus is here the protagonist. He is the focus of the conversation in the courtyard. His look helps Peter back on the right road, and the hearing centers solely on the question of who he is. What is in view is not the end of the world but the time of the community, which is given to know its heavenly Lord, who is ready to receive it (Acts 7:56).

## "Before King and Governor" (23:1–25)
Cf. Mark 15:1–15; Matthew 27:1–2, 11–26; John 18:28—19:16

¹And the whole company of them arose and brought him to Pilate. ²And they began to accuse him, saying, "We found this one perverting our nation and preventing them from giving tribute to Caesar, and saying that he is the Messiah King." ³But Pilate asked him and said, "Are you the King of the Jews?" And he answered him and said, "You say it." ⁴And Pilate said to the chief priests and the crowd, "I find no guilt in this person." ⁵But they became more urgent, saying, "He stirs up the people with his teaching throughout all Judea, from Galilee to this place."
⁶When Pilate heard this, he asked whether this person was a Galilean, ⁷and when he learned that he was from Herod's jurisdiction, he sent him over to Herod, who was himself in Jerusalem in these days. ⁸When Herod saw Jesus, he was very glad, for he had long desired to see him because he had heard about him and he was hoping to see some sign done by him. ⁹So he questioned him with many words, but he answered him nothing. ¹⁰The chief priests and scribes stood by, vehemently accusing him. ¹¹And Herod with his bodyguard treated him with contempt and mocked him, arrayed him in gorgeous apparel, and sent him back to Pilate. ¹²And Herod and Pilate became friends with each other that very day, for before this they had been at enmity with each other.

¹³Then Pilate called together the chief priests and the leaders and the people ¹⁴and said to them, "You brought me this person as one who was perverting the people, and behold, I have examined him before you and I have found no guilt in this person of any of your charges against him, ¹⁵and neither did Herod, for he sent him back to us. Behold, nothing deserving death has been done by him. ¹⁶I will therefore chastize him and release him."

¹⁸ But they all cried out together, "Away with this one and release to us Barabbas," ¹⁹who had been thrown into prison for an insurrection started in the city and for murder. ²⁰But Pilate spoke to them once more, with the desire to release Jesus. ²¹But they shouted out, "Crucify, crucify him!" ²²A third time he said to them, "What evil has this one done? I have found in him no guilt deserving death. I will therefore chastize him and release him." ²³But they urged him with loud cries and demanded his crucifixion, and their voices prevailed. ²⁴And Pilate determined that their demand should be fulfilled. ²⁵The one who had been thrown into prison for insurrection and murder, for whom they had asked, he released, but Jesus he delivered up to their will.

The trial is organized around three declarations of innocence made by Pilate: vss. 4, 16, and 22. In between come the scene with Herod, reported only by Luke, and the discussion about Barabbas; at the beginning comes a brief hearing, and at the end a verdict. There is almost no verbal agreement with Mark expect for the question, "Are you the King of the Jews?" and Jesus' answer (vs. 3), both of which also appear in John 18:33, 37 (see the discussion of vs. 4).

[1] The "crowd," described with increasing precision in vss. 10 and 13 (q.v.), can only refer to the council in this context (Acts 23:7). The binding of Jesus (Mark 15:1) is omitted; he continues to act freely. [2] As is logical, the charge is cited before the hearing (contra Mark 15:2, 3) and is formulated for the ears of the Roman official: disturbing the peace, financial risk, lese majesty against the emperor; therefore "Christ" is coupled with "King." The council is apparently defending only Roman interests (cf. John 11:48–50). [3] "You [emphatic in Greek] say it" can hardly be understood as a question, like John 18:34, but only as an affirmative answer, like 18:37 (also Bill. 1. 990, the only example!). Of course it also implies that

Jesus would have put it differently (see the discussion of Matt. 26:63–64). **[4]** Pilate's declaration of innocence is all the more surprising. Does Luke understand Jesus' answer to mean, "*You* say it" (but it is not true)? But in this case the clause in parentheses would have to be present. More likely he thinks Pilate is not taking the matter seriously. In John 18:38 almost the identical formula follows the same answer on the part of Jesus; there, however, Jesus states that he is King in a spiritual sense. Now vs. 14 assumes that Pilate has conducted an actual hearing in the presence of the people, who suddenly turn up without having been introduced. Is Luke following a source that had more to tell? Why else would he incorporate only vs. 3 (unchanged!) from Mark 15:2?

**[5]** Unlike vs. 2, vs. 5 uses the term that designates the people of God (see the discussion of 19:48) for "people," and once more presupposes opposition between the leaders and the people. In vs. 10 and 24:20 only the former are involved (see the discussion of 19:48). The people do not mock but mourn (23:35, 48). In Acts 1—5 too, the people are on the side of the disciples, in opposition to the leaders. Did Luke add the "crowd" or the "people" (a Lukan expression) in 23:4, 13 (q.v.), 35 (cf. vss. 18, 23), while the tradition clearly distinguished the people from the leaders who were Jesus' enemies? In Acts, too, it is at first only the officials, and then gradually the people, who oppose the Apostles and the gospel. Vs. 5*b* parallels Acts 10:37. "Judea" probably means the whole country (see the discussion of 4:44); Galilee is appended as a bridge to vs. 6. The charge of sedition (vs. 2) is leveled, which the reader knows is false (19:42; 20:25; 9:21–22). The hearing is limited to the question of Jesus' kingship, which appears in all the Gospels, and ends with a statement of Jesus' innocence.

**[6]** Vss. 6–16 contain Lukan expressions and hardly anything un-Lukan. Are they based entirely on oral tradition? It is fair to accuse the Galileans of insurrection; that is where the rebellion against Rome began in the sixties (cf. also 22:59; John 7:52). **[7]** But Pilate has a different reaction: as a Galilean, Jesus comes under Herod's jurisdiction. And so he "sends" Jesus to him (a technical term used also in vs. 15). This is smart politically, if not courageous. He is honoring Herod and may be getting rid of a difficult case. Pilate's derisive "this one" takes on theological substance in the "Behold, the person" of John 19:5.

[9] Jesus' demeanor is politically unwise but courageous and above all right; his silence is also politically relevant. [8] Herod is open if God sends an unambiguous sign, but signs are given only to those who surrender themselves to God (see the conclusion to Mark 8:11–13). This has been shown already in 4:1–13, 23 (cf. the conclusion to 19:1–10).

[9–11] The accusation of the chief priests, Jesus' silence, and mockery with royal garments (Josephus *Ant.* 8. 185–86) are placed by Mark 15:3–4, 17–20 (q.v.) in the hearing before Pilate. They underline Jesus' inoffensiveness, which does not bother Herod at all. Vs. 11 does not mean that Herod himself put on the white robe (which is textually possible; he does "mock" Jesus). Therefore one early translation even omitted vss. 10–12 (on account of vs. 15!).

[12] Pilate has achieved one aim but not the other: the hostility between himself and Herod (cf. Philo *Emb.* 24. 38) is ended, but he still must take responsibility. Nowhere else is anything said of friendship between Pilate and Herod. Certainly something more is meant than a symbolic reference to reconciliation between Gentiles and Jews (Eph. 2:11–32). Perhaps this friendship has been derived from Psalm 2:2, which states that "kings" and "leaders" have taken counsel against the Christ. Acts 4:26–27 cites this passage in connection with Herod and Pilate, an association that must predate Luke: according to him they both want to save Jesus, and for him Herod is not a "king" (see the discussion of 9:7). When he speaks of "leaders" (sixteen times), they are always Jewish officials, except when he applies the term to demons. [13] Like vs. 13, 24:20 distinguishes chief priests and leaders. The calling together of the officials and the people is striking. According to vs. 10, Jesus' accusers have stayed with him; did the people stay in the vicinity of Pilate's residence? Is this based on the same tradition as John 18:38, 39*b*; 19:1? There Pilate also appears before the people (or the Jews), declares Jesus innocent, suggests his release, and has him scourged. Or was the original reading "leaders of the people" (as in 19:47)? Did Luke make the change or introduce the people (of God) on his own because (according to Mark 15:11–34) they request Barabbas? [14–15]

In any case, the significance of the declaration of innocence is underlined; Herod, too, now joins in it as a second witness (Deut. 19:15). **[16]** Instead of "scourging" (Mark 15:15), Luke speaks of "chastizing"; he never records its being carried out.

**[18]** The cry for Barabbas is unmotivated; nothing is said of any custom of a Passover amnesty. It sounds more like a suggested exchange. Is Luke's tradition still aware that this was an isolated case (see the introduction to Mark 15:2–15)? **[17]** Some manuscripts have reinserted a mention of the custom in vs. 17 because otherwise Pilate's acquiescence is almost incomprehensible. The expression "away with him" and the repeated "Crucify, crucify" parallel John 19:6, 15. Linguistically the verses are Lukan; emphasis is on the "general" cry for Barabbas (see the discussion of vs. 5). As in John 18:40, it is only afterward explained who he is, in sharp contrast to Jesus' innocence (vss. 14–15, etc.).

**[19]** Only Luke reports that the insurrection took place in Jerusalem. Jesus is accused of being a revolutionary; at once all the people take up the cause of the real revolutionary. Instead of argument, we have a contest to see who can shout the loudest (cf. vs. 23!). God's curse is upon crucifixion (Deut. 21:23, emphasized in the Qumran Temple Scroll). A group of proper citizens, impressed by Jesus as individuals, are blinded as a mass. Does this show that they really are more comfortable with Barabbas than with Jesus, who is in many ways mysterious and never predictable?

**[22]** As in John 18:38; 19:4, 6, Pilate states three times, "I find no guilt in him" (vss. 4, 14) and repeats the suggestion of vs. 16. As in John 19:2–3, Jesus is mocked (by Herod's soldiers in Luke 23:11) *before* being handed over to be crucified. **[24]** A real verdict is never pronounced (but cf. 24:20). **[25]** The guilt of the released Barabbas is repeated in the words of vs. 19. Jesus is handed over to "them." Since the soldiers do not "come up" until vs. 36, the uninitiated reader would have to assume that the Jews crucified Jesus (similarly 24:20; but cf. 20:20; Acts 13:28; and, for the shift of subject, e.g., Luke 23:32, 33). In any event, Luke does not explicitly ascribe Jesus' crucifixion to the Romans and puts the actual blame on the people (Acts 2:23, 36; 4:10; 13:28), but compare the conclusion to 11:37—12:1.

The leaders are dominated by fear of unrest; the people go along and join the chorus because all are afraid to expose themselves before others; the governor has good intentions toward Jesus and wants to save him by cunning, but with all the power at his disposal he falls victim to his own diplomacy and cannot escape. Only one person is free: he who appears almost reduced to an object, referred to contemptuously as "this one." Only once does he appear, silent, as subject (vs. 9), and once he speaks two words, with which he disclaims responsibility for the crucial statement (vs. 3).

**Luke's Special Source (L).** Is Luke's special source (L) in the Passion narrative? The question cannot be answered with certainty. Luke omits the following: anointing, the details of Gethsemane, the flight of the disciples and its prediction, the night hearing, Jesus' silence before the council and Pilate, the introduction of Barabbas, the mockery of the Roman soldiers (vs. 36 instead) and the people, Pilate's wonder, the first offer of drink, and the question about Elijah (Mark 14:3-9, 26-28, 33-34, 38b-42, 55--61a, 64b; 15:3-5, 6-10, 16-20a, 23, 25, 29-30, 34-35, 44-45). He changes the order of the following: designation of the traitor, journey to the Mount of Olives, Jesus' arrest, the mockery of Jesus, crucifixion of the two criminals, offer of drink, inscription, preparation for anointing (Luke 22:21-23, 39, 54, 63-65; 23:33, 36, 38, 56). Everywhere else, when he changes the order of Mark he also has a different wording, reflecting a special tradition: (3:19-20); 4:16-30; 5:1-11; (6:17-19); 8:19-21; 10:25-28; 11:14-23, 37-41; 12:10; 13:18-21; 14:34-35; 17:1-2, 23-24, 31. Special traditions that belong together and appear to be connected with earlier traditions include the Last Supper, with the saying addressed to Simon and the saying concerning the sword; Gethsemane; (Peter's denial); morning hearing before Pilate and Herod (cf. 9:9b; 13:31); the saying over Jerusalem (cf. 19:41-44); crucifixion (see the discussion of vss. 26-49); the women before and after the visit to the tomb (cf. 8:2-3); and Easter appearances (cf. 24:6): 22:15-17, 24-38, 39-53 (54-65) 66-71; 23:2, 4-16, 22-23, 27-32, 33b, 34a, 35-37, 39-43, 46b (47) 48, 55-56; 24:10b-12, 13-53. Here we also find quotations from Scripture, not just general references to its fulfillment: 22:37; 23:30, 35, 46 (49?) (q.v.).

Now 1 and 2 Chronicles, Pseudo-Philo, the Book of Jubilees, and Josephus show how freely Judaism of this period retold the biblical narrative and enriched it with new elements, but it is certain that Luke did not invent all this himself. A half century later Papias stated: "What comes from books I did not consider as valuable as what proceeds from the living . . . voice" (Eusebius *Hist. eccl.* 3. 39. 4). Did Luke think along similar lines? If we picture him as knowing the Markan Passion narrative almost by heart, it is conceivable that he enriched it with new material and set it down in a different order. But the scene in the upper room exhibiting an accumulation of un-Lukan expressions and above all tensions involving the two cups and the saying about the sword makes the theory of a written source virtually necessary (cf. also the discussion of 23:5, 27, 29). This is suggested also by the parallels with John: see the introduction to 22:31–34, also the discussion of 21:37–38; 22:3, 14, 23, 27, 31, 32, 47–53, 54–71; 23:4 (and introduction), 13, 18–25 introduction; 24:12, 40, 41; and section 2.b of the Introduction. It is even possible that John 18:22–23 provides the basis for Acts 23:2–5, as Mark 14:53–58 does for Acts 6:13–14.

Furthermore, the crucifixion is described differently, frequently with un-Lukan expressions; certainly it was not Luke himself (23:35; cf. the discussion of vs. 49) who chose to use different words from Psalm 22(21):8 than those used in Mark 15:29 since Luke, although able to write in the style of the LXX, often ignores references to specific verses (19:38?; 20:9; 21:16, 25–28, 39; 22:21, 63; see the discussion of 23:35). The conversation with the two criminals appears to be inserted into a fixed schema (see the introduction to 23:33–48). On the other hand, the scenes in Gethsemane, before Pilate, and before Herod contain Lukan expressions, and almost no non-Lukan ones. Luke 24:1–12 diverges markedly from Mark and presupposes familiarity with Jewish tombs sealed by rolling stones (vs. 2). The Emmaus story clearly exhibits several stages of development and cannot be harmonized with the appearance to the group of disciples that follows. The saying addressed to Simon (22:31–32) and the scene before Pilate (cf. the participation of the people, the sudden appearance of Barabbas, the lack of an official inquiry) are also not homogeneous. Is it conceivable that Gethsemane, the hearing before Pilate (and Herod?), the crucifixion, and the Easter story continued to be recounted with relative freedom in the worship of the community, so that Luke, in reproducing his sources (Mark and L) in these sections, was especially apt to introduce his own style? Does the clear preponderance of Lukan expressions in these sections indicate the particularly strong influence of oral tradition alongside the inclusion of written sources? A person, for example, who has often heard and recounted the Christmas story tends increasingly to tell it in his or her own language, even when following the outline of Matthew 1—2 and Luke 1—2. He or she is open to the influence of Old Testament Advent prophecies heard in church, Christmas carols learned by heart, traditional legends surrounding the celebration, etc. The whole problem is discussed in section 2 of the Introduction.

## The End as a Sign of the New Beginning (23:26–56)

The account of Jesus' crucifixion more or less follows Mark but with a different choice of words and in a different sequence (see the excursus above). New materials include the Jerusalem saying (see the discussion of vss. 28–29), which is related to 19:41–44; the double mention of the criminals crucified with Jesus (vss. 32 [with the remarkable phrase "two other criminals"] and 33b ["there" is not typical of Luke]); the conversation with them (vss. 39–43); Jesus' last words (vss. 34a, 46); the explanation of the darkness (vs. 45), and the reaction of the people (vs. 49). Agreements with Mark appear only in vss. 26, 34b (35b [q.v.], 38?), 44 (45b, 46a, 46c, 47?), and sometimes appear to be interpolations (vss. 34b, 38). The sixth and ninth hours are mentioned in vs. 44 but not the third (Mark 15:2, 5). Each of the four sections (vss. 26–32; 33–38; 39–43; 44–49) includes a saying of Jesus (see the discussion of vs. 34).

### (1) The Way of the Cross (23:26–32)
Cf. Mark 15:20–21; Matthew 27:31–32; John 19:16–17

26 And as they led him away, they seized one Simon of Cyrene, who was coming in from the field, and laid on him the cross, to carry it behind Jesus. 27And there followed him a great multitude of the people

and of women who bewailed and lamented him. [28]But Jesus turning to them said, "Daughters of Jerusalem, do not weep for me, but weep for yourselves and for your children; [29]for behold, the days are coming when they will say, 'Blessed are the barren, and the wombs that never bore, and the breasts that never gave suck!' [30]For then they will begin to say to the mountains, 'Fall on us,' and to the hills, 'Cover us,' [31]for if they do this when the wood is green, what will happen when it is dry?"
[32]And there were two other criminals led away with him to be executed.

(Vs. 30—Hos. 10:8.)

[26] Only Luke adds that Simon was to "carry the cross behind Jesus." He has also emphasized "bearing the cross daily" in 9:43 and 14:27, albeit with other words for "carry" and "behind." Nevertheless he probably sees in Simon an image of discipleship. Perhaps he even means to say that an involuntary "cross" can be a blessing since Simon is "seized" for this service. Luke does not say "compel," like Mark 15:12, probably because he also does not mention the Roman soldiers who have that authority. [27] He also mentions another kind of "following," voluntary and more deliberate, but for the moment unable to do more than weep. "Who" refers only to the women. Did Luke add the "great multitude of the people" (also 6:17; cf. 1:10; Acts 14:1; 15:12; 17:4; 21:36; and *passim*) to a source fragment dealing only with the women, which contains un-Lukan expressions in vss. 28–31? In Zechariah 12:10–14 (see the discussion of Matt. 24:30), the women are mentioned separately when Jerusalem mourns (the same Greek word) for an only son.

[28] Jesus, however, seeks not pity but repentance. He expresses his own anguish over Jerusalem, as at his entry (19:41–44), so now at his departure (for a similar expression, see Seneca *Agam.* 659–60). In both cases the fate of the children is singled out for special mention. [29] Only here, as in the LXX, do we find the present tense "are coming" (see the discussion of 19:43), which jars with "will say"; the macarism appears to be entirely traditional. It is a striking image but has nothing to do with Galatians 4:27, where the community of Jesus is identified with Sarah, who was barren. A similar threat appears in 21:23 (= Mark 13:17). Luke has made both refer clearly to the fall of Jerusalem (see the excursus following 21:38, a).

**[30]** In Revelation 6:16, the same quotation describes the cosmic catastrophes of the eschaton. **[31]** If fire can destroy living, green wood, it will certainly destroy the dry. The fate of Jesus, like that of the prophets, is sure to befall his enemies (cf. Prov. 11:31; Bill. cites a similar saying concerning a righteous person who is crucified; cf. 1 Pet. 4:17–18).

Prophecies of terror appear in Hellenism (vs. 28) and Jewish apocalyptic literatures (vss. 29–30). That the martyrdom of a prophet or righteous person calls others to repentance is known to Judaism (cf. the conclusion to 11:37—12:1). But the figure of Jesus and his mourning over Jerusalem (vs. 28; 19:41–44) dominate the whole section. Therefore we are also told of one who carries the cross behind Jesus, thus mysteriously sharing in God's blessing, and above all of the Galilean women, clearly set apart from the inhabitants of Jerusalem, who follow after him and serve even after death (vss. 39, 55–56).

### (2) Jesus' Crucifixion and Death (23:33–49)
Cf. Mark 15:22–41; Matthew 27:33–56; John 19:17–30

<sup></sup>33And when they came to the place which is called Skull, they crucified him there and the criminals, one on the right and one on the left. 34But Jesus said, "Father, forgive them; for they do not know what they do." "And to divide his garments they cast lots." 35And the people stood by, watching. But the leaders also sneered and said, "He helped others; let him help himself if he is the Christ of God, the Chosen One." 36The soldiers also mocked him, coming up and offering him vinegar 37and saying, "If you are the King of the Jews, help yourself!" 38There was also an inscription over him: "This is the King of the Jews."

39One of the crucified criminals blasphemed against him: "Are you not the Christ? Help yourself and us!" 40But the other answered and rebuked him and stated, "Do you not fear God since you are under the same judgment? 41And we indeed are receiving justly the reward of our deeds. But this man has done nothing wrong." 42And he said to Jesus, "Remember me when you come in your kingdom." 43And he said to him, "Amen, I say to you, today you will be with me in paradise."

44And it was already about the sixth hour, and there was darkness over the whole land until the ninth hour ⁴⁵since the sun lost its light. And the curtain of the temple was torn in two. ⁴⁶And Jesus cried with a loud voice, "Father, 'into thy hands I commit my spirit,' " and having said that, he breathed his last. ⁴⁷But when the centurion saw what had taken place, he praised God and said, "Certainly this person was righteous." ⁴⁸And all the crowd that had assembled to see the sight, when they saw what had taken place, beat their breasts and returned. ⁴⁹But all "his acquaintances" and the women who had followed him from Galilee "stood at a distance" and saw these things.

(Vs. 34—Ps. 22:19. Vs. 46—Ps. 31:6. Vs. 49—Ps. 38:12; 88:9–10.)

The account comprises four tripartite sections: crucifixion, Jesus' intercession, and division of Jesus' garments; "Help yourself," said by the officials, the soldiers, and the criminals; three signs: darkness, the curtain, and Jesus' cry; effects on the centurion, the people, and acquaintances. The conversion of one of the criminals (vss. 40–43) has been interpolated into this schema. **[33]** The name "Golgotha" is omitted (see the discussion of 22:39), as well as the mixture of wine and myrrh (Mark 15:22–23); John 19:29 also speaks only of vinegar (Luke 23:36). But the crucifixion of the two criminals, already mentioned in vs. 32, comes in its proper place (as in John 19:18), with no reference to the fulfillment of 22:27.

**[34]** The first of the words from the cross (see the excursus following 22:30, c) is not found in the earliest papyrus and several good manuscripts. Possibly it was omitted because it appears to exonerate the Jews. Jewish Christians may have been thinking of Leviticus 4:2, according to which unwitting sins are atoned for by the death of the sacrificial animal, in this case by the death of Jesus. A similar group of manuscripts drops the exoneration of the Jews on account of ignorance in Acts 13:27, while keeping it (17:23, 30) or even adding it (16:39) in the case of Gentiles and places more of a burden of guilt on the Jews as distinct from the Christians in 3:17. A totally different type of ignorance is meant in the addition in Luke 6:5 (q.v.). Vs. 34 is appropriate to Luke (Acts 3:17; 13:27; cf. also Luke 12:48a), and Stephen echoes both this and Jesus' final word, albeit with different wording (Acts 7:59–60). Furthermore, it brings the total to three words from the cross (see the introduction to vss. 26–32) and takes the place of the usual confession of guilt on the part of the condemned person or the curse upon his enemies (2 Macc. 7:19; 4 Macc. 9:15). Jesus' death is therefore more than a call to repentance (vs. 31). In his intercession even on behalf of his tormentors, he opens the possibility of God's forgiveness of even the most terrible sin and at the same time pioneers a way for his disciples to let God's love shine forth through them (see the excursus following 22:30, b.2, 3). Allusions to Psalm 22(21):19 (vs. 34b; see the discussion of Mark 15:24), 8 (vs. 35); 69:22 (vs. 36) are less pointed than in Mark (see the excursus following vs. 25).

[35] Vs. 35 has been changed substantially vis-à-vis Mark. Now it is not all the people standing by but only the leaders (see the discussion of vss. 5, 13) who "sneer" or "turn up their noses" (see the introduction to Mark 15:27–32). This very rare word appears also in Luke 16:14. Does it derive here from Psalm 22:7, and was it added by Luke in 16:14? Is Luke using "but . . . also" to assert, contrary to his tradition, that the people likewise mocked Jesus? The term "people" (of God) probably derives from him. The reference to Jesus' saying about the temple is also omitted (see the discussion of 22:67). The political title "King" is put in the mouth of the soldiers (vs. 37) and replaced here by a good Jewish title ("Christ of God"; see the discussion of 9:20; "the Chosen One," 9:35; cf. the Messiah in En. 39:6; 40:5; 45:3–4). We are not told that the leaders were prepared to believe if they witnessed a miracle. The challenge to Jesus to help himself corresponds to Mark 15:31, but it is formulated as a third person imperative, which agrees more with Mark 15:30 and 32. The challenge is repeated verbatim in vss. 37, 39. [36] The drink of vinegar is pure mockery; the mistaken suggestion that Jesus is calling on Elijah is omitted. [37–38] The inscription is not mentioned until this point, where its absurdity is underlined by the soldiers.

[39] In contrast to Mark 15:32, Luke describes different reactions on the part of each of the criminals, illustrating the possibilities of faith as the acceptance of salvation, unfaith as its rejection (cf. 7:36–50 instead of Mark 14:3–9; also 15:24–32; 18:9–14). For Luke, the demand to see miracles and focus on purely outward deliverance is blasphemy. [40–41] The fear of God (cf. 1:50; 18:2, 4; Acts 10:35)

consists in self-knowledge and acceptance of God's judgment but also in bearing witness to Jesus' innocence, which issues in a plea that goes beyond what is outwardly visible. **[42]** "Remember us, Lord . . ." (Ps. 106[105]:4) also appears in Jewish funerary inscriptions (*Israel Exploration Journal*, 5:4, pp. 234 ff.). Diodorus Siculus (34:2, 5–8) tells of a slave who claimed the kingship on account of his miracles and visions; he was invited as a joke and admonished, "When you become king, remember this good deed." The kingdom of *Jesus* is also mentioned in 1:33; 22:30 (q.v.). **[43]** "Today" is especially emphasized if we follow several ancient manuscripts in reading vs. 42 as above (rather than "*into* your kingdom"), or another group that reads, "on the day of your coming." Jesus counters a hope that centers on a distant future with a statement of salvation that is already present. Probably this is meant to stress that whoever lives "with Christ" already shares in the present kingdom and thus enters the Christian fellowship of paradise upon death; no detailed thoughts about a life after death are intended (see the excursus following 21:38, b; the discussion of 16:23 and of 8:55; and cf. Phil. 1:23). The absolute otherness of the life consummated in God is no longer expressed by the temporal distance of the last day but by the spatial distance between earth and paradise. It is unlikely that Luke is thinking of a paradisiacal intermediate state before the resurrection of Jesus on Easter and of the criminal on the last day. Just as he stresses the "today" of salvation in 4:21 (q.v.) and 19:9, so he does here, albeit in combination with "you will be," since the paradise, the fulfillment, lies on the other side of earthly pain and struggle. In addition 22:69 says "from now on" although Easter and the ascension are yet to come. A proposed reading "Today I say to you . . ." is most unlikely.

**[44]** The sixth hour (with a Lukan "about") is mentioned because darkness at noon (Amos 8:9) is extraordinary. **[45]** Luke "explains" the darkness as an eclipse, which is scientifically impossible during the Passover full moon. Just as night turned to day at Jesus' birth, so now day is turned to night (cf. 22:53!). The tearing of the temple curtain is moved here from its place after Jesus' death in Mark 15:38; the "seeing" of the centurion (vs. 47) cannot refer to it. The miracle in the heavens is matched by the miracle in the temple.

[46] As in Mark 15:34, 37, Jesus dies "crying with a loud cry" (the literal text, emphasizing the significance of the moment). But the inarticulate cry in Mark 15:37 is omitted, and Jesus' words are not a cry of despair but of faithful trust. Jesus has indeed been delivered into human hands (9:44; 20:19; 22:53), but he commits himself to the hands of his Father. In Psalm 31(30):6, which is cited here, "my spirit" stands for "me," simply designating the totality of the living person. Mark 15:37 reads literally "breathed out [his] spirit"; this led to Matthew 27:50 ("yielded up [his] spirit," q.v.) and Luke 23:46. The use of "Father" to address God (as in 10:21; 11:2; 22:42; 23:34) is unique to Jesus (see the excursus following Mark 14:36). There is no notion of a disembodied "spirit" continuing to exist after death (see the discussion of 8:55).

[47] According to vs. 47, everything that has taken place, the miracle of the darkness and the conduct of Jesus, causes the centurion to praise God (see the discussion of 17:15) and utter his judgment of Jesus. Instead of "Son of God," he calls him "righteous." Does Luke make the change because "Son of God" from the mouth of a Gentile would awaken false ideas, or do we have here an ancient tradition that sees in Jesus the righteous innocent sufferer (cf. Acts 3:14; 7:52; 22:14; the excursus following Mark 11:1—16:8; introduction to Mark 15:22-24; conclusion to Mark 15:27-32)? [48] We can even see the effect of Jesus' death on the crowd. They have only assembled to "see the sight," which is probably not the same as the "seeing" of the crucial event that had taken place (vs. 47). The Greek text uses two different verbs, which are also used in John 16:19 to distinguish outward seeing from spiritual seeing. But they are in fact moved, and have some sense of guilt (cf. 18:13!). They "return"— but only in the sense of going back home to the city. The real return to God that comes through repentance will not be possible until Acts 2:37-38. [49] Besides the crowd, Luke mentions Jesus' "acquaintances," and the women (see the discussion of 8:2-3) but not the disciples (see the introduction to 22:47-53). As Galileans, the women are distinguished clearly from the "daughters of Jerusalem" (vs. 28). Whether Psalm 38(37):12; 88(87):9 influenced this verse is uncertain; "at a distance" also appears in Mark 15:40.

Even more clearly than Mark, Luke does not proclaim and interpret Jesus' death but narrates it (cf. Retrospect, 3). But he does so in such a way as to reveal a wealth of interrelationships and meanings. In dying, Jesus also shows his love toward humankind. Do awareness of guilt, affirmation of Jesus, and prayer to him give reason for a promise of salvation? But the scene begins with Jesus in the very place where criminals are tortured to death (22:37!). In him we can see God's solidarity with humankind that makes such insight possible. The dying and rising with him spoken of in Romans 6 are presented in narrative form. Within the identity of experience, however, the superiority of Jesus is clearly maintained; outwardly as powerless as the criminals, he can accord sovereign authority. In this sense he is crucified "for" this criminal. One may well ask whether a narrative can show this. Without the reserve of Mark and the didactic explanation given by Paul, it would remain too vague. On the other hand, without the contribution of Luke, faith would remain largely abstract. The uniqueness of Jesus is not found in titles. He is the green wood alongside the dry (vs. 31), the innocent alongside the criminals (vs. 41), but above all the one who can rightfully say, "Father" (vss. 34, 46), and promise paradise (vs. 43). The eclipse and the curtain of the temple indicate who it is that dies here. Salvation comes in such a way that God's love for humankind is seen in Jesus' love for executioners and victims (vss. 34, 43), that the people are moved, a Gentile praises God, and an outsider performs a due act of love (vss. 50-53). Finally, the nascent community can be sensed in him who must follow after Jesus against his will but especially in the words of Jesus that others will later echo (vss. 34, 46).

## (3) The Burial of Jesus (23:50–56)
Cf. Mark 15:42–47; Matthew 27:57–61; John 19:38–42

[50]And behold, a man named Joseph, who was a member of the council, a good and righteous man—[51]he had not consented to their decision and deed—from Arimathea, a city of the Jews, one who was looking for the kingdom of God—[52]he went to Pilate and asked for the body of Jesus. [53]And he took it down and wrapped it in a linen shroud, and laid him in a rock-hewn tomb, where no one had ever yet been laid. [54]And it was the day of preparation, and the sabbath was dawning. [55]But the

women who had come with him from Galilee followed and saw the tomb and how his body was laid. [56]Then they returned, and prepared spices and ointments.

Through the sabbath they rested according to the commandment.


[50] Joseph of Arimathea is mentioned in all of the Gospels. This proves that none of the disciples were present to perform the most important duty of piety. [51] A "righteous" man looking for "the consolation of Israel," the "kingdom of God," appears at both the beginning of Jesus' life (2:25) and at the end. Beside the Roman (vs. 47) stands the Jew (cf. Acts 5:34). [52–53] Vss. 52–53 resemble Matthew 27:58–59 very closely, especially at the beginning, in the word for "wrap," and in the abbreviation of the Markan text. Like John 19:41–42, Luke emphasizes that the tomb is new and also mentions here for the first time that it was Friday. [54] The "dawning" (literally "shining forth"—of the evening star or the sabbath lamp?) of this sabbath may be symbolic for Luke: the promise of God's consummation already shines over Jesus' tomb, as it afterward shines over those of Jesus' community. [55] Luke emphasizes that the women saw the tomb: on the morning of Easter, in other words, they did not go to some other tomb (24:1). They have followed Jesus as his disciples since Galilee (vs. 49); their discipleship is now demonstrated in one final act of service (cf. 8:3). In contrast to Mark 16:1 (according to almost all the manuscripts), they buy what they need on Friday evening. [56] Obedience to the commandments is emphasized here as it was in 1:6; 2:22–24, 27. It is the last sabbath before the "Day of the Lord" dawns (cf. Rev. 1:10).


# C. NEW BEGINNING—
# GIFT OF THE RISEN LORD
# (24:1–53)


Only vss. 1–12 agree to some degree with Mark 16:1–8. All the rest of the material is unique to Luke.

## God's Message to the Women (24:1–12)
Cf. Mark 16:1–8; Matthew 28:1–8; John 20:1–13

[1]But on the first day of the week, at early dawn, they went to the tomb, taking the spices which they had prepared. [2]And they found the stone rolled away from the tomb. [3]But when they went in, they did not find the body of the Lord Jesus. [4]And it happened while they were at a loss over this, behold, two men stood by them in dazzling apparel. [5]And as they were frightened and bowed their faces to the ground, they said to them, "Why are you seeking the living among the dead? [6]He is not here but has been raised. Remember how he told you, while he was still in Galilee [7]and was speaking of the Son of Man, that he must be delivered into the hands of sinful persons and be crucified and on the third day rise." [8]And they remembered his words [9]and returned from the tomb and told all this to the Eleven and to all the rest. [10]And it was Magdalene Mary and Joanna and Mary of James and the other women with them. They told it to the Apostles. [11]And these words seemed to them like a fairy tale and they did not believe them. [12]But Peter rose and ran to the tomb; stooping and looking in he sees the linen cloths and ran off and wondered to himself at what had happened.

[1] The only points of agreement with Mark are the statement of the day of the week (vs. 1), five words in the message of the angel, and the expression "to/from the tomb" (but cf. the discussion of vs. 6). Much of the material could be pre-Markan. [12] Vs. 12 is omitted in a portion of one group of manuscripts; in wording it resembles John 20:3–6, 10. That can hardly be its source, however; why would the other disciple (John) not be mentioned, especially since vs. 24 speaks of more than one witness? In contrast to John 20:12, the angel appears even before the arrival of Peter (also in vs. 23). Stylistically, the beginning and end are typically Lukan but not the present tense "sees" (see the introduction to 16:23) and the phrase "to [or: by] himself," which can modify "wondered" (as in the translation above) or "ran off." In the latter case, an Aramaic idiom would support the translation "ran home." This is how John 20:10 takes it. This suggests that the verse originally read, "wondered to himself" (cf. 18:11) and was known to John in this form. Possibly the verse was omitted in order not to compete with the first appearance to Peter (vs. 34).

[2] As in John 20:1, the stone is mentioned here for the first time, rather than in the context of Jesus' burial or the discussion of the women. It is a fixed element of the Easter story. [3-4] As in John 20:12, the "two" (also 9:30; Acts 1:10) angels do not appear until after the astonishment of the women at discovering the tomb empty. It is hard to imagine that all the women (vs. 10!) entered the tomb. The earliest account probably thought only in terms of the three mentioned by name. [5] There is a Jewish saying against necromancy: "Is it customary to look for the dead among the living, and the living among the dead?" (Bill.). Because Jesus is alive in the same sense that God is alive, he is not to be sought among the dead (cf. the discussion of Mark 12:27), either as a troublemaker who has finally been taken care of or as a teacher remembered with reverence and honor. The gaze is directed away from the tomb. [6] "He is not here" (placed first, as in Matt. 28:6, q.v.) makes a good continuation. The (pre-Lukan?) alteration of Mark 16:7 results in the odd mention of Galilee and the inappropriate "you" (in Mark 16:7 correctly identified with the disciples). Galilee is past; nothing more takes place there (see the discussion of 4:44); after Easter it is mentioned only once (Acts 9:31). [7] The formula in vs. 7a recalls 9:44; the word "sinful" or "sinner" recalls Mark 14:41; Luke never uses it in Acts and never introduces it on his own in Markan material. "Crucify" does not appear in any summary of the Passion. "Rise" appears in the formulas Luke 24:46; Acts 10:41; 17:3 but could be traditional there since Luke changes or omits the term in Mark 8:31; 9:31. The proleptic position of "Son of Man" in the original text is even more remarkable, but Acts 13:32 (cf. Luke 9:31; Gal. 4:11) is comparable. It is therefore likely, although not certain, that Luke used an existing formula.

[9] In contrast to Mark 16:8, the women do as they are told but without encountering Christ, as they do in Matthew 28:9-10. [10] Only now (Acts 1:13-14) are we told the women's identities. The names differ from those in Mark 16:1 (q.v., introduction): "Magdalene" before "Mary" is unique (cf. the discussion of 8:2); on Joanna, see the discussion of 8:3; "Mary of James" should mean she is his wife (but cf. Mark 15:40, 47; 16:1). Even stranger is the repetition of vs. 9b, with special mention of the Apostles, who play an impor-

tant role for Luke (vss. 9, 33 and Acts 2:14: "the Eleven"). Did Luke insert vss. 10–11 into the traditional story on the basis of an oral tradition preserving the names?

[11] The disciples' disbelief is first reported in Luke 24:11, 41 (cf. the discussion of Mark 16:9–10). Disbelief, of course is not the same thing as rejection of the message of the resurrection (Acts 17:18, 32). [12] Even Peter's personal inspection of the tomb leads only to wonderment, which of course includes openness to future experience. "Not from people nor through a person" (Gal. 1:1) is the assurance of the resurrection given to the Apostle (vs. 34).

## Word and Sacrament—Gift of the Risen Lord (24:13–35)

[13]And behold, two of them were journeying on that very day to a village about sixty stadia from Jerusalem, named Emmaus. [14]And they were talking with each other about all these things that had happened. [15]And it happened, while they were talking and discussing together, that Jesus himself drew near and went with them. [16]But their eyes were kept from recognizing him. [17]And he said to them, "What kind of words are these that you are exchanging with each other as you walk?" And they stood still, looking sad. [18]Then one of them, named Cleopas, answered and said to him, "Are you the only visitor to Jerusalem who does not know the things that have happened there in these days?" [19]And he said to them, "What things?" And they said to him, "Concerning Jesus of Nazareth, who was a prophet mighty in deed and word before God and all the people, [20]and how our chief priests and leaders delivered him up to be condemned to death, and crucified him. [21]But we had hoped that he was the one to redeem Israel. Yes, and besides all this it is now the third day since this happened. [22]Moreover some women of us amazed us, who were at the tomb early in the morning [23]and, being unable to find his body, came back saying that they had seen a vision of angels, who said that he was alive. [24]And some of those with us went to the tomb and found it just as the women had said, but him they did not see." [25]And he said to them, "O foolish and slow of heart to believe all that the prophets have spoken! [26]Was it not necessary that the Christ should suffer these things and enter into his glory?" [27]And beginning with Moses and all the prophets, he interpreted to them in all the Scriptures what was said concerning himself.

[28]And they drew near to the village to which they were journeying,

and he made as if to go further. [29]And they urged him, saying, "Stay with us, for it is toward evening and the day is now far spent." And he went in to stay with them. [30]And it happened, when he reclined at table with them, he took the bread, said the blessing, and broke it and gave it to them. [31]And their eyes were opened and they recognized him. And he vanished from them. [32]And they said to each other, "Did not our heart burn within us while he talked to us on the road, while he opened to us the Scriptures?" [33]And they rose that same hour and returned to Jerusalem, and found the Eleven gathered together and those who were with them, [34]saying, "Indeed the Lord has risen, and has appeared to Simon." [35]And they told what had happened on the road, and how he was known to them in the breaking of the bread.

The departure of the two disciples (vss. 13–14), the coming of Jesus (vs. 15), and their failure to recognize him (vs. 16) are paralleled in reverse order by their recognition (vs. 31a), Jesus' disappearance (vs. 31b), and their return (vss. 33–35). In between comes the meal (vss. 28–30). It is preceded by a conversation that begins with Jesus' question (vs. 17) and ends with his interpretive answer (vss. 25–27). Vss. 21b–24 are a link to vss. 1–12; "some" in vs. 24 does not really agree with vs. 12. Outwardly, the story follows the schema of a miracle story: the place and characters are introduced (vss. 13–14), the savior appears (vs. 15), the difficulties are emphasized (vss. 16–24), temporary help (vss. 25–27) leads to the sufferers' plea (vss. 28–29), which is answered (vss. 30–31). Confession, confirmation, and proclamation (vss. 33–35) end the story. But this very structure reveals the story's oddity. The conversation in vss. 16–27 is developed to an unusual degree, and the help that is given is not a response to faith in Jesus but the gift of faith itself. Because this is where the interest of the story lies, the conversation concerning it becomes central, and proclamation of the word and the Lord's Supper (vs. 30) can be sensed behind the story. The whole episode is markedly Lukan in style.

In addition, there is a parallel in Acts 8:26–40. Both stories have a road as their setting, and failure to comprehend the Scriptures is met with an interpretation that focuses on Jesus' suffering; a request to stay precedes or follows. Both accounts end with a sacrament—Lord's Supper or baptism—and the disappearance of the helper.

Un-Lukan elements are the localization in Emmaus rather than Jerusalem and the appearance of Jesus to two who are not Apostles (Acts 1:1–4: 10–41), but vss. 26–27 reflect Luke's central interest. The way in which Jesus appears, unrecognized and without heavenly glory, is unusual in an Easter story; also unique are the recognition of him in the context of the meal and the absence of a missionary commission. In content the episode recalls John 21:1–14. There are similar Hellenistic legends: after his death, Romulus is said to have met a peasant on the road, who reported the meeting in Rome (Dionysius of Halicarnassus *Ant. Rom.* 2. 63. 3–4). Other figures appear and disappear: angels (frequently, e.g., Judg. 13:23, 9, 20; 2 Macc. 3:33–34), a deity (Virgil *Aen.* 9. 656 ff.), Helen (Euripides *Hel.* 605ff.; *Or.* 1496ff.). Philostratus (*Apoll.* 8. 11–12) tells a story that involves a journey, the appearance of someone who was thought to be dead but in fact was not, and physical contact, but this story may show Lukan influence.

The following elements are undoubtedly pre-Lukan: Emmaus, the two disciples and the name Cleopas, the meal (roughly vss. 13, 15*b*, 16, 28–31, including the double statement of the time of day in vs. 29, which Luke otherwise omits from his Markan material). It is possible that Luke is working from oral tradition. But the mostly clearly non-Lukan expressions appear precisely in vss. (18), 19, 23–25, where one would most expect Lukan redaction, apart from the statements in vss. 26 and 34, which were already fixed. In addition, "two of them" at the beginning can be correct only if it follows vs. 9 directly, where the Eleven and "all the rest" are mentioned. According to vss. 10–11, presumably added by Luke, the persons involved would have to be "Apostles." If Luke composed the story freely, without following a prototype, would he have been able to speak of the disciples' disbelief in vs. 41 after vss. 34–35, where both groups are convinced of Jesus' resurrection? And it is inconceivable that the scene described in vss. 36–53 took place on the same evening. It is clear that two different traditions have been combined here. Even if it was Luke himself who added the formula in vs. 34 to maintain Jesus' initial appearance to Simon, there is still so much disparity that a written source must be postulated for the two accounts, even though it has been substantially revised and therefore cannot be identified precisely.

[13] The story begins with the "journeying" motif (see the discussion of 9:51). The Sunday after Passover is the day when people return to their homes. There seem to be two sites called Emmaus, one about twenty miles from Jerusalem, the other about four (176 and 35 stadia). Since the disciples return on the same evening (vs. 33), only the latter is possible. Or an earlier text may be right in reading "160 stadia," from which "100" was dropped on account of vs. 33.

[14–15] A journey provides time to think over what has happened. Jesus joins them as they travel. Where he comes from is no clearer than where he vanishes to. As in John 21:4, the reader is told at once who the unknown traveler is and asks only how the two disciples come to meet him. [16] Disbelief has them in its power (see the discussion of 18:34). [17] But it is essential that they express their doubts. [18] Is Cleopas the same as Clopas? According to Eusebius (*Hist. Eccl.* 3. 11), the latter was the brother of Joseph and the father of Simeon, who succeeded James in the leadership of the Jerusalem community. Does this explain why he alone is named? But this is uncertain, and it is even less certain that the second disciple was Jesus' brother James (1 Cor. 15:7). The word translated "visitor" indicates temporary residence; is this because a permanent resident would know, or because Luke conceives Jesus as having no fixed abode?

[19] Acts 2:22 also refers to "Jesus the Nazarene" (as always in Luke except here and 4:34 = Mark 1:24), "a man attested by God with mighty works and wonders and signs"; Luke 4:24; 13:33 (see the conclusion in 3:15–20) refer to him as a "prophet." What is new is the juxtaposition of deeds and words (cf. Moses in Acts 7:22, where the order is reversed). In Acts 2:22 and 10:38 only Jesus' miracles are mentioned; the summaries in Acts speak only of his teaching (4:18–19, 44; 8:1; 15:1; 19:47; 20:1; 21:37) or healing (4:40–

41; 13:32), except where his teaching is added to the tradition of his healings (6:6, 18; 13:10–11). In the case of the disciples, however, both are combined (9:2; 10:9, possibly through the influence of Q).

[20] Again "all the people" are distinguished from the officials (see the discussion of 19:48), who appear to have carried out the crucifixion (see the discussion of 23:25). Neither the Jewish nor the Roman people are guilty.

[21] The "redemption" of Israel is mentioned in 1:68 (2:38). But it is this fixed religious expectation that prevents the disciples from seeing him who "lives" (cf. 20:38; 24:5; Acts 1:3; 25:19). [22–24] The empty tomb does not engender faith (cf. the discussion of vs. 5). [25] Slowness of heart is unable to open itself to something new and unexpected. [26] The destiny of the Christ is reduced to the briefest terms possible: suffering and entrance into glory, which reigns "in the highest" (19:38; cf. the excursus following 22:30, b.1). All this is according to God's will (see the discussion of 9:22), not in the sense of total historical progress from creation to Christ's return and the final consummation but in the sense that he appears everywhere in the wealth of biblical history and teaching. [27] Therefore no specific biblical passages are mentioned; "all the Scriptures" ( = "Moses and the prophets" and the "writings," i.e., the Psalms, etc.; see vs. 44) point to Christ, so that he alone gives meaning to Israel's history (see the excursus following 4:30, b). Scripture therefore interprets the events connected with Jesus, but Luke does not search the Old Testament for references to individual events, as though this would "prove" that God was at work in them.

[28] Once again we have the motif of Jesus' "journeying," which is met by the request to "stay," probably at the home of the two disciples. [29] Jesus appears unexpectedly in vs. 15, but if he is to stay, the request is necessary. The words fit the situation but also point to a deeper truth, described in Revelation 3:20 as the "coming in" of the exalted Christ to the believer to "eat with" him. [30] Vss. 29–30 repeat "with them" three times for emphasis. The guest becomes the host: "[And they made them] sit down [Greek = "reclined at table"]; but taking [the five loaves of] bread . . . , he said the blessing . . . and broke . . . and gave [them] to the disciples,"

we read in 9:15–16; that meal included fish (cf. vs. 42) but no wine, which was not customary at ordinary meals. Both stories recall the Last Supper, which the two did not share (see the conclusion).

[31] The mystery of the Lord's Supper is suggested by the opening of their eyes (not required for table fellowship with Jesus, but given by it) and Jesus' disappearance. In his authoritative interpretation of Scripture and invitation to table fellowship with him the goal of the story has been reached. Jesus cannot be held onto as one would hold onto a friend to keep him always available. He comes in the word and in the fellowship of his table, but he is never simply at our disposal.

[32] When the heart burns (Ps. 39[38]:4; Test. N. 7:4) so that one can no longer escape from Jesus and asks him to stay, Jesus lives there. The two realize in retrospect that the Scriptures were opened before their eyes were opened. [33] They are not sent forth as missionaries but the encounter leads them at once to an act of witness. Their course away from Jerusalem is interrupted and turned around by the risen Lord. [34] Vs. 34 is probably a fixed formula of the Easter tradition. It is important because it maintains that Jesus first appeared to Simon (cf. the introduction to 5:8; 1 Cor. 15:5) even before the Emmaus disciples. Undoubtedly, as in the Old Testament theophanies, actual vision is intended (literally: "he was seen by Simon"); 1 Corinthians 9:1; John 20:18, 25, 29 and all the Easter narratives take it in this sense. The catchword "breaking of bread" is mentioned explicitly at the conclusion: that is where the exalted Lord appears in the midst of his community.

The story begins with the shattering of a "childish faith." The two disciples have been robbed of their illusions. All they have left is words, which are useless. The triumph of the others is visible: the Jewish officials and the Romans have achieved their purpose. Jesus comes into this very situation with his consolation; he is unrecognized, in the form of another traveler. The futility of their discussion leaves a space of time in which he can begin to speak. The two let themselves be questioned, so that their doubt and sorrow can be articulated. What stands in the way of their faith is their belief in an image of the Christ that does not describe Jesus. He should be on the side of help, not the side of distress. For three days—and that can be a long time—the disciples have seen nothing but catastrophe and disgraceful death. They are secure in their error, while the questions come from Jesus' lips. Of course there are some who had some kind of experience of God at the tomb; there were even angels who proclaimed salvation. The two can repeat the statements and even consider them true but for them it is an empty tradition. The turning point does not come through a miracle but through Scripture. Of course it has to be read not with a slow heart but with a responsive heart. In shatters the security of their disbelief so that they do not simply break off the conversation. Outwardly, too, the approach of evening and their arrival home sets a limit to their travel. And so they become receptive indeed. In table fellowship Jesus gives them the reality of his presence; his word takes the form of a visible gift. Table fellowship with the earthly or exalted Jesus is itself decisive; it is no longer possible to make a sharp distinction between an everyday meal eaten in the fellowship of faith and the Lord's Supper in the larger circle of the community, with its festal wine: Luke 5:27–32; 19:1–10; Acts 2:42–46; 20:7–12; 27:35. He was behind the miracle of the "burning heart" and now is even more behind the miracle of opened eyes.

There is no supernatural splendor, even though this is clearly an act of God, a miracle inexplicable in human terms. Quite remarkably, the only "supernatural" phenomenon seen is Jesus' disappearance. This is an extreme way of saying that when God enters into human life and is recognized as God, the divine is never in a position to be apprehended. Therefore the two can only tell what Jesus did; they have no formula to gain control over the living Lord. They experience strengthening through the experience of the others, learning that faith, although granted to individuals, at once creates community. And so the reader is asked where he or she stands along this road: among the perplexed, with whom Jesus nevertheless journeys; among those who reflect and listen to questions, who have heard what others have to say, who allow their hearts to be moved by Scripture, who cannot escape and refuse simply to put an end to their disquiet; or even among those whose eyes have been opened in table fellowship with the risen Lord, so that they can find the road to others.

## The Road into the Future—Gift of the Risen Lord (24:36–53)

[36]As they were saying this, he himself stood in their midst and says to them, "Peace to you." [37]But they were startled and frightened and supposed that they saw a spirit. [38]And he said to them, "Why are you troubled, and why do questionings arise in your hearts? [39]See my hands and my feet, that it is I myself. Touch me and see, for a spirit does not have flesh and bones, as you see that I have." [40]And when he had said this, he showed them his hands and his feet. [41]But since they still disbelieved for joy, and wondered, he said to them, "Have you anything to eat?" [42]They gave him a piece of broiled fish. [43]And he took it and ate before them.

[44]Then he said to them, "These are my words which I spoke to you, while I was still with you, that everything in the law of Moses and the prophets and the Psalms written about me must be fulfilled." [45]Then he opened their minds to understand the Scriptures. [46]And he said to them, "Thus it is written, that the Christ should suffer and on the third day rise from the dead [47]and that in his name repentance for forgiveness of sins must be preached to all nations, beginning in Jerusalem. [48]You are witnesses of these things. [49]And behold, I send the promise of my Father upon you; but stay in the city until you are clothed with power from on high."

[50]Then he led them out as far as Bethany, and lifting up his hands he blessed them. [51]And it happened, while he blessed them, he parted from them and was taken up into heaven. [52]And having knelt before him in worship, they returned to Jerusalem with great joy [53]and were continually in the temple blessing God.

The episode begins with the appearance of the helper. Distress of a sort does not appear until the reaction (vs. 37, again in vs. 41; cf. the discussion of 5:8). Help comes through a question and visible signs (vss. 38–43) but primarily through instruction (from Scripture, vss. 44–48). It is followed by a call to action that confirms that the hoped-for help has been given; this does not take place until Acts (vs. 49). The departure of the helper marks the conclusion (vss.

50–51). The praise of God in Jerusalem (vss. 52–53) concludes the entire book as it began but also represents the beginning of what was predicted in vs. 49. The sequence of initial meeting (vss. 36–43), instruction from Scripture (vss. 44–46), mission to the Gentiles (vs. 47), and ongoing witness (vss. 48–49) appears also in Acts 28 (vss. 17–22; 23–25a; 25b–28; 30–31). The sequence of appearances to individuals followed by appearances to all the disciples is also found in Matthew 28 (vss. 9–10; 16–20) and John 20 (vss. 11–18; 19–29). As in the preceding section, help is not given in response to faith; it consists in the gift of faith. The linkage (vs. 36a) with vss. 34–35 is similar to 22:47 = Mark 14:43 and 22:60 = L. Stylistically it could be pre-Lukan, while the description of fear and disbelief in vss. 37 and 41 is Lukan. Luke is concerned to represent faith as being entirely the gift of Jesus, "the faith which is [given] through him" (Acts 3:16). The tension between this tradition and vss. 34–35 he probably understands to mean that faith always grows through doubt and relapse, new hearing and new seeing, until it finally achieves fulfillment in witness for Jesus.

The earliest papyrus and most manuscripts include vss. 36b (with its striking present tense; see the introduction to 16:23), 40, 51b, 52a, omitted by the group that omits 22:19b, 20; 23:34a; 24:12 (see section 7.2 of the Introduction to Acts in *NTD*, 5). In both cases, it is probably the omission that is late; Acts 1:2 demonstrates that the ascension in vs. 51b was an original part of the Gospel. The greeting of peace may have been omitted because it arouses fear; vs. 40, because disbelief is made to seem even more impossible; and vs. 51b because of Acts 1:11 (not until forty days later). Luke's style is unmistakable; there are few un-Lukan expressions. Vss. 36b, 39–41 largely agree with John 20:19–20. Perhaps we should think in terms of oral tradition containing only a few fixed statements as a nucleus.

[36] Jesus' mysterious appearance parallels his disappearance in vs. 31. He who is already present in the witness of the disciples emerges from his concealment, much as he does in vss. 25–27 and 30–31. His coming brings them peace. Luke probably imagines the scene as taking place at a meal (vss. 41–43; Acts 1:4; 10:41; cf.

John 21:13). **[37]** The notion of the survival of a "spirit" arouses only fear. Ignatius (*Smyrn.* 3:2) speaks in this context of a "disembodied daemon"; for him, as for Luke, that would be nothing but a ghost (the reading of some manuscripts, as in Mark 6:49). The Greeks, for whom incorporeality is paradisiacal (Lucian *Hist.* 2. 212), used this term for the departed. **[38]** For the Bible, this does not represent faith but a chimera. **[39]** It thinks in such corporeal terms that a mere "spirit" cannot be identified with the "I" of Jesus (emphatic, as in Mark 6:50), even when called an "angel" rather than a "daemon" (cf. Acts 12:15; 23:8–9). Vs. 39 is the only biblical passage that speaks of the "flesh and bones" of the risen Lord. For the Greeks, this would prove that he was still alive in the earthly sense (Philostratus; see the introduction to vss. 13–35). This is, of course, at odds with 1 Corinthians 15:50; the resurrection is conceived of as being bodily, but the new body is so different (1 Cor. 15:35–45) that it cannot be identified with "flesh and bones" (Luke 20:35–36). In fact this is true here, as Jesus' disappearance and appearance show; the Greek notion of a purely spiritual resurrection is simply being rejected in very direct language. Here, too, the "flesh and bones" of Jesus differ totally from those of earthly humanity. But the terminology and the demonstration of Jesus' eating can easily mislead one into picturing the resurrection as mere resuscitation, without taking seriously its humanly inconceivable otherness. This is the source of the phrase "resurrection of the flesh" (or: body) in the creed. It is comprehensible as a defense against reducing the resurrection to the survival of some kind of spirit but is highly misleading today. If Luke assumes that Jesus' hands and feet still bear the prints of the nails (cf. John 20:25 and the discussion of Matt. 27:35), he is maintaining (with Rev. 5:6) that the resurrection does not simply cancel out the crucifixion; it is now especially important that Jesus traveled *this* way.

**[40]** Vs. 40 shows that more is involved than touching parts of the body. This touching and the fish that is eaten are related to John 20:27 and 21:10, as is the joy of the disciples (John 20:20). This joy, like the sadness in 22:25, shows that their disbelief is not fundamental but is due to the enormity of what has taken place, which can scarcely be comprehended in human terms (cf. the conclusion to Matt. 28:16–20; similarly Acts 12:14; Livy 39. 49. 5).

[42] Fish were available even in Jerusalem (Neh. 13:16). Some witnesses add honey, possibly because it was associated later with baptism and the Lord's Supper (and the fish became a symbol of Christ). [43] The divine figures in Genesis 18:8 also eat (in contrast to Judg. 13:16; Tob. 12:19).

[44] Only here in the New Testament, following an introduction that resembles Deuteronomy 1:1, are the Psalms (or "writings," i.e., all the remaining books) mentioned alongside the law and prophets (see the discussion of vs. 27). The previous story moved from interpretation of Scripture to personal encounter; here the movement is in the opposite direction. As in 24:6, Jesus' teaching is appealed to, which is authoritative for the interpretation of Scripture. The knowledge brought by Easter is therefore not something absolutely new, even though he who "was among them" in his earthly body (which he no longer is!) can be understood by the disciples only on the basis of the resurrection. This agrees entirely with what John says about the "Paraclete" in John 14:26. In Acts 20:35, Paul also refers to Jesus' teaching, albeit in a different context. [45] What is new is that Jesus now gives the disciples the ability to understand Scripture (see the discussion of vs. 27). Only those who understand him understand Scripture, but this is itself a gift of the risen Lord and cannot simply be demonstrated.

[46] The suffering of the Christ is also spoken of in 24:26; Acts 3:18; 17:3; suffering and rising or (usually) being raised (on the third day: 9:22; 24:7; cf. Acts 10:40) are linked in 9:22 and Acts 17:3. [47] The name of Jesus, (repentance and) the forgiveness of sins, and the witness of the Apostles ( = the Twelve, although in the context of a larger group: 9:33; cf. 6:13; Acts 1:21) also appear together in Acts 2:32–33, 38; 3:15–16, 19; 5:28–32; 10:39, 43. "For forgiveness of sins" is also found in Qumran documents (11QtgJob 38:2–3). It is typical of Luke and shows that he expects forgiveness to come through repentance, not just at the last judgment. Such a view is already attacked by the perfect tense in 7:47–48, not only in the original meaning of the parable, according to which gratitude fol-

lows the granting of forgiveness, but also in Luke's interpretation. And 18:14 says that the tax collector *was* justified. Gentiles (Acts 17:30) and the Jews in Judea are called to "repentance" (see the discussion of 5:32) but not diaspora Jews or Gentiles who have become God-fearers (10:2, 43; 13:16, 38; but cf. 11:18). The important point is that the saving events (Jesus' death and resurrection) include proclamation (also in Acts 17:3; 26:23; 3:15; 5:30–32; 10:41; 13:30–31); vs. 47 is still dependent on "it is written" (cf. *"his* name"; also Acts 10:43; 13:47). In his "name" Jesus himself is present (see the discussion of 10:17). Thus the Christ event therefore includes proclamation in word and deed because the Christ proclaims himself through his messengers. When Jews and God-fearers are addressed, Scripture is cited (Acts 10:43; 13:29); when Greeks are addressed, Greek poets are appealed to in support of God's nearness (Acts 17:28).

[49] The Gentile mission is mentioned for the first time (vs. 49; cf. Mark 13:10 [not in Luke]; Matt. 28:19–20), typically together with the term "witnesses" or "martyrs," those who are prepared to die for it (Acts 1:8; 22:20). Justin (*Dial.* 109; possibly also *Dial.* 17. 1, countering missions of the Jews) finds scriptural support in Micah 4:1–7. The Spirit is sent by Jesus (as in Acts 2:33; John 15:26; 16:7; cf. 20:21–23; by God: Acts 5:32; John 14:16, 26). The Spirit is "power," inexplicable in human terms. The image of "being clothed" or "putting on" is common in the Old Testament ("power": Ps. 93[92]:1, and many other passages) and Paul. The Spirit is also said to "put on" or "take possession of" certain individuals (Judg. 6:34; 1 Chron. 12:19; 2 Chron. 24:20). Just as Scripture is referred to at the beginning (vs. 44), so is Jerusalem at the end; it represents continuity with the previous history of God. Therefore also the first step beyond Israel must be confirmed at Jerusalem (Acts 8:14–17; cf. Rom. 15:19–20) although this does not imply any kind of ecclesiastical authority. The collection taken up by the Gentile Christians for Jerusalem, which was also an act recognizing its position (Gal. 2:10), was replaced by Luke (although he knew of it; Acts 27:17) with a purely charitable contribution, initiated by charismatic prophets (Acts 11:27–30).

[50] The book ends with Jesus' doing what the priest could not do in 1:22: he blesses. His blessing will enable his disciples to serve.

The lifting up of his hands (cf. the high priest in Ecclus. 50:20–21) gives the blessing visible, corporeal form. As before Easter, Jesus leads the way (cf. John 21:19–20), this time to Bethany (19:29). **[51]** As in vs. 31, Jesus vanishes, but now his disappearance is described as an ascension. Strictly speaking, it must still be Easter Sunday, but compare the discussion of 3:20. Is the ascension final, or does Luke think in terms of the risen Lord's appearing to his disciples from heaven (for forty or "many" days; Acts 1:3; 13:31)? According to vs. 26, he has already entered into "glory." In the church, the celebration of the ascension was shifted a century later to the fortieth day; earlier it was celebrated on another day, often together with Easter.

**[52–53]** Only now, not in face-to-face encounter during his earthly ministry, is Jesus worshiped as God would be. Luke speaks elsewhere (5:12; 8:28, 41; 17:16) of people falling at Jesus' feet but not in worship as in Mark 5:6 (Matt. 8:2; 9:18; 14:33; 15:25; 20:20). Perhaps he uses the other Greek word here because in Hellenistic stories ascension leads to recognition of divinity (Sophocles *Oed. Col.* 1654; Plutarch *Rom.* 27. 8–9; Lucian *Pereg.* 39; cf. Judg. 13:20; Ecclus. 50:20–22). In it God has "made Jesus Lord" (Acts 2:36); acknowledging this, the disciples worship Jesus and praise God. Just as Acts 1:3–8 mentions the appearances of the risen Lord, so Luke 24 mentions the ascension. Thus the two books are linked together.

As in the other Gospels, Jesus' resurrection is not a fulfillment of human yearning; not a word is said about the resurrection of the disciples. *He* is risen; *he* is the Lord before whom the disciples fall in worship. If anything, the resurrection is a call to service (cf. Gal. 1:16; 1 Cor. 9:1) although for Luke this takes the form of the promise of the Spirit (vs. 49; cf. John 20:22) rather than a direct command. Although Luke avoids the error only narrowly, for him, too, faith is not engendered by experience of a miracle. Even Jesus' showing of his hands and feet does not overcome disbelief (vs. 41; cf. vss. 23–24) but only Jesus' word that opens the Scriptures for the disciples, where Jesus' way through suffering to resurrection is described as God's way. The earthly Jesus had already talked of this. As the risen Lord, therefore, he also gives faith (vss. 44–48; Acts

3:16; 16:14), while to those who already believe, who are already obedient (Acts 2:38; 5:32), the Spirit is given as the power to live in faith, above all in proclaiming Jesus in word and deed. When Luke speaks of flesh and bones, we can no longer picture what he means: Jesus lives in an entirely different dimension, he comes and vanishes, he can simultaneously appear to Peter and journey to Emmaus. What matters is that he shows himself to be alive. It is not just his cause that survives; he lives and can be worshiped. Even with terms like "he himself" or "his person" we can only approximate the reality, without ever being able to describe it entirely. The fact that Acts 1:11 understands his coming at the end of the world as being analogous to his departure underlines this. This, too, cannot be pictured in human terms, but the image of human encounter is obviously best. His disciples will encounter him in person when all of history reaches its consummation. Therefore the Gospel closes with the "great joy" proclaimed by the angels in 2:10: it is now reality, and will be reality wherever we, through faith, encounter the living Lord.

# RETROSPECT

## 1

Luke does not provide a clear Christology. Jesus is a "prophet" (13:13; cf. 7:16; 24:19) or "*the* prophet (like Moses)" (Acts 3:22–23; 7:37), "savior" or "leader" (Luke 2:11; Acts 3:15; 5:31; 13:23). Whether "servant of God" refers to the suffering servant (Acts 3:13, 26) or the king (like David, Acts 4:25–30; Luke 1:69) remains unclear. In contrast to Mark and Q, the earthly Jesus is already called "Lord" (see section 2.c of the Introduction), but Acts 2:36 states that God made him Lord in the resurrection. According to Luke 1:35, he is "son of God" by virtue of his miraculous birth, according to 3:23–38, by virtue of his descent from Adam, and according to Acts 13:33–34, by virtue of his resurrection (see the excursus following Mark 15:39). He is a "man" attested by God (Acts 2:22; 17:31), and as such he is "Christ," "Son of Man," and "son of God," all of which appear to be equivalent in Luke 22:67–70. In any case the situation is not very clear.

Equally unclear is the grounding of salvation (see the discussion of 7:19) in Jesus' death, a concept that appears explicitly only in two mechanically borrowed formulas that are not even adapted to the context (see the excursus following 22:30, a). Nonetheless Luke puts far more emphasis on Jesus' path of suffering than do the other Gospels (see the discussion of 9:31). One might ask whether people like Elizabeth, Simeon, and Anna in Luke 1—2 or Cornelius in Acts 10 are not righteous, lacking nothing but a knowledge of Jesus as the Messiah. But Luke 3:7 makes John's call to repentance apply to everyone; 15:1–2 shows redactionally that the ninety-nine who do not need to repent do not exist, and Acts 11:18; 13:38; 15:9, 11, 19 are aware that even God-fearing Gentiles need repentance and grace. Luke's special parables such as 7:40–47; 15:25–32; 18:9–14 (cf. the conclusion to 11:37—12:1 and the conclusion to 13:1–9) are specifically spoken against the righteous. Above all, Luke is aware of the danger of self-righteousness and self-assurance, not only among the Pharisees (see the excursus following 21:24, b). This is shown by the import of Lukan statements. If faith involves the totality of a person, not just intellect or emotions, head or heart, then there must be analogies between what takes place in the life, death, and resurrection of Jesus, and what takes place in those who read the Gospel: aftertastes (or in the case of Luke 1—2 foretastes) based on the reality of God as shown in Jesus (see the introduction to 1:5—2:52, the excursus following 2:52, b, c, and the excursus following 22:30, b.2, 3).

## 2

Jesus used parables to speak of God and the kingdom, sin and forgiveness, death and the life to come. He never gave his listeners clear, direct statements that they could simply accept, agree with, and carry home—in other words, "master" (see the excursus following Mark 4:1–9). Neither did he give them a title in which his significance could be finally comprehended and accepted intellectually. "Christ" appears more than five hundred times in the New Testament but in the first three Gospels almost never in the mouth of the earthly Jesus: Mark 9:41 (where Matt. 10:42 preserves the earlier form without the title); 12:35 (where it does not refer unambiguously to Jesus); Matthew 23:10 (where vs. 8 contains the earlier, Palestinian form of the same word); and Mark 13:21 and Luke 24:46, which are spoken after Easter. Others call Jesus "son of God" (Mark 14:61; 15:39; Matt. 16:16; 27:43); he himself at most uses the terms "father" and "son," with emphasis on the subordination of the son, not the son's superiority to all others. "Servant of God" appears only in Acts 3—4 and indirectly in the quotation in Matthew 12:18. Probably Jesus spoke of himself as the "Son of Man," but this was not a recognized title. It pointed rather to the mystery of his person: was he simply "a person" like other human beings, or "*the* person," with a uniqueness given by God (see the excursus following Mark 8:27–33 and the discussion of Mark 8:30; 13:32)?

**3**

Luke understood all this. Therefore he makes no direct statements about who Jesus is and how human salvation comes through him. A reader could take such statements as definitions, providing one with knowledge of the truth. But the parables of Jesus speak only when the reader learns to understand them "from within," i.e., when one is so moved and gripped by them that one in some sense lives in them. Then their truth dawns, and although it is a truth that remains fundamentally the same, it will be different tomorrow from the truth understood today. The same thing happens when Luke does not simply record teachings about Christ and salvation but recounts a wealth of stories. They, too, reveal their truth only to those who begin to live in them, to allow themselves to become involved. Today it may be one story, tomorrow another, in which God speaks. Who Jesus is and what he means for faith—this can be stated only in the full wealth of the tradition. It includes Jesus' power demonstrated in healing and his powerlessness on the cross, his fellowship with tax collectors and prostitutes and his rejection by his fellow citizens, the miracle of his birth and his rejection of every demand for a sign, his judgment discourses with their "Woe!" and his parables of God's searching love.

No other New Testament writer provides such a picture of Jesus and thus of the life of the community: the Christmas story, the twelve-year-old boy with his knowledge of the Father, the preacher in Nazareth. He calls Peter through a miracle, raises a widow's only son from death, opens himself to a prostitute and a crucified criminal, struggles in agony in Gethsemane, prays for those who torture him, journeys to Emmaus with his disciples, tells the parables of the good Samaritan, the prodigal son, the Pharisee and the tax collector—all this, a message that has put its stamp on faith through the centuries, we owe to Luke. This concentration on Jesus and the salvation that comes through him sets Luke-Acts apart from the formally similar lives of the philosophers by Diogenes Laertius (third century C.E.!), which record the life of the master, the lives of his pupils, and a summary of his teaching.

**4**

The strengths and weaknesses of the presentation are especially clear in Luke. It is not easy to define the relationship of the cross to the resurrection, of the enormous importance of Jesus' sufferings in the Gospel and of the suffering of the community in Acts to the miracles experienced, or of the gift of faith to the strong emphasis on repentance and conversion (see the introduction to 4:31–44; and the discussion of 9:31; 22:32; Acts 5:32). Undoubtedly Paul dealt more clearly with these and other questions. He gives more help in times of conflict with false doctrine. But how Paul has been misused, for example in the Gnostic movement or in certain branches of modern existential philosphy, which have adopted something like his doctrine of justification but have no need for Jesus of Nazareth! Neither does Luke provide a clear, continuous line of salvation history from the Old Testament to Jesus and from him to the end of all ages. Matthew 1:1–17 and even Paul are clearer on this point (see the excursus following 4:14–30, a). But how this salvation history has been misused by those who found there the justification for the most horrible persecutions of the Jews! In comparison, the misuse of Luke to defend a church attested by miracles and guaranteed to enjoy God's guidance is almost innocuous.

Nevertheless, when what is needed is the clearest possible delineation of the significance of Jesus against misunderstandings, Paul and the writers of the other epistles, as well as the other Gospels, are on the whole more helpful. But when what is needed is a means to genuine faith, involving the whole person, the Lukan concentration on a wealth of stories about what Jesus did and taught, eschewing Christological titles and doctrines that aim to comprehend this vital fullness, is closer to the parables of Jesus and his complex symbolic acts than any other document. Luke learned from Jesus that ultimately the only correct way to speak of God is in the form of a narrative which points constantly to what God did in the midst of our history. In Luke, the Word truly became flesh, God truly became human (cf. John 1:14). However uncertain the historical details may be, this account differs totally from all the myths that merely embody eternal timeless truth in narrative form; for Luke always points clearly to Jesus of Nazareth, who lived, died, and rose again at a particular time in a particular place. This is also why the uniqueness of God is so important to Luke, as even the statistics illustrate: the word "God" is used 48 times in Mark, 51 times in Matthew, 122 times in Luke, and 166 times in Acts. Only God is surrounded by angels (see the discussion of 21:38), not Christ. But this God is found nowhere unambiguously except in Jesus of Nazareth. God is revealed in what happens to those God touches, both in the time of Jesus' earthly ministry and in the community of the risen Lord.

It is a direct consequence of this understanding that Luke wrote not only a Gospel but the book of Acts. Nowhere in the New Testament is the resurrection of Jesus itself described, what God does with Jesus in isolation. What *is* described is what God does with Jesus for the sake of his disciples, and in and through them. In this sense, Mark 16:1–8; Matthew 28; John 20—21; and 1 Corinthians 15:5–11 are every bit as much "Acts of the Apostles" as Luke's second book. But this shows once more that Luke understood very well that the miracle God performed with Jesus, dead and buried, can be told only in the wealth of stories that reflect this act of God.

# INDEX OF NAMES AND SUBJECTS

Acts of the Apostles, 11
Adam, 80
Afterlife. *See* Life after death
Almsgiving, 210
Angels, 21, 23, 27, 50–51, 157, 321, 343, 376
Annas, 69
Antisemitism. *See* Jews
Apostles, 11–12, 87, 115, 304, 336, 367. *See also* Disciples
Augustus, 59, 69
Ascension. *See* Jesus—Ascension
Atonement, 66, 359–360

Baptism, 285
—Synonymous with death, 215
Belief. *See* Faith
Bultmann, Rudolf, 92

Caiaphas, 69
Call (narrative), 20, 101–103, 105
Catchwords, 204, 212
Chiasmus, 40
Children of light. *See* Light, Children of
Choice (Divine). *See* Election
Christ. *See* Jesus—Christ
Christmas, 27, 46–47, 59
Commandments. *See* Law
Completion, 223
Confession, 291
Conversion. *See* Repentance
Covenant, 223, 336–37
Creation, 180–81, 327–28
Crucifixion. *See* Jesus—Crucifixion

David. *See* Jesus—Son of David
Death and baptism. *See* Baptism—Synonymous with death
Death of Jesus. *See* Jesus—Death
Deliverer, 50
Demons, 178, 194–95
Devil. *See* Satan

Disciples, 119, 145, 164, 174, 210, 213, 241–42, 286, 288, 345. *See also* Apostles

Discipleship, 84, 101–104, 106, 117, 157–58, 164, 171–72, 241–42, 286–87, 291–92, 357, 364

Divine Sonship. *See* Jesus—Son of God

Easter, 103, 133, 372

Election, 29, 51–52, 57, 161, 178, 277

Elijah, 16, 22, 43, 76, 132–33, 153, 160, 171, 360

Elishah, 42, 170

Eschatology, 59, 65, 87, 89, 119–210, 135, 161, 178, 215, 231, 263, 276, 311, 314, 317, 322, 324–25, 335. *See also* Jesus—Coming; Judgment

Ethics, 75–76, 117, 258

Eucharist. *See* Lord's Supper

Exaltation. *See* Jesus—Ascension

Experience, 94, 106, 181, 183, 340, 382

Eyewitness. *See* Witness

Faith, 30–31, 34, 39, 47, 51–53, 65, 91, 94, 106, 110, 131, 141, 146, 149, 150, 263–65, 268, 292, 319, 327, 340–41, 344, 360, 363, 368, 372, 375, 379, 384
—Lack of, 24, 162

Farewell discourses, 336–37, 339

Fear of God, 35, 50

Force, 341, 345

Forgiveness of sins, 45, 72, 88–89, 105, 107, 137–38, 140, 249, 264, 359–360, 377

Freedom, 248, 354

Fulfillment, 38, 42, 56, 87, 135, 317, 327

Galileans, 219, 351, 366

Gentiles, 56, 58, 60–61, 86, 91, 116, 149, 174, 176, 185, 203, 238–39, 317–19, 324, 359, 378
—Mission to, 58, 104, 131, 238, 378

Gnosticism, 7, 92, 327, 384

God
—Fear. *See* Fear of God
—Grace, 57, 60, 66, 72, 90–91, 291
—Greatness, 195
—Incarnation. *See* Incarnation
—Independence, 92–93, 220, 251, 283, 373
—Judgment. *See* Judgment

—Justice, 219, 262
—Kingdom. *See* Kingdom of God
—Love. *See* Love of God
—Name, 35, 179–180
—People. *See* People—Of God
—Praise. *See* Praise of God
—Son of. *See* Jesus—Son of God
—Sovereignty. *See* Kingdom of God
—Uniqueness, 385
Good news. *See* Gospel
Gospel, 22–24, 59, 76, 92, 99, 318
Gospel of John. *See* John (Gospel)
Grace. *See* God—Grace
Greeks. *See* Hellenism

Healing, 268
*Heilsgeschichte. See* History—Sacred
Hellenism, 59, 133–34, 145, 318, 379
Herod, 75, 153, 229, 313, 351–53
History, 12–14, 48, 50, 317
—of Israel. *See* Israel
—Sacred, 12, 24, 66–67, 92–96, 326–27, 384–85
Holy Spirit. *See* Spirit

Incarnation, 17
Infancy narratives. *See* Jesus—Infancy narratives
Inner light. *See* Light, Inner
Interim, 293–94, 296, 326–27, 361
Israel, 36, 50, 56–57, 58–60, 66, 72–73, 90–91, 95–96, 202–203, 209,
    223, 230–31, 238, 241–42, 318–320

Jerusalem, 2, 110, 160, 165, 168, 215, 219–20, 224, 230–32, 267, 294,
    296, 299–300, 302, 312, 314, 316–17, 318, 323–24, 357, 378
Jesus
—Ascension, 160, 169, 301, 379
—Christ, 88–89, 156, 158, 360, 382
—Coming, 212, 214, 271, 273–76, 294–95, 321–22, 323–29
—Crucifixion, 338–340, 353, 357, 362–63
—Death, 215, 338–340
—Disciples. *See* Disciples
—Exaltation. *See* Jesus—Ascension
—Farewell discourses. *See* Farewell discourses
—Infancy narratives, 4, 15–17, 65–67

—**Journeying,** 165, 168, 170, 172, 213, 215, 224, 230, 298, 306, 370, 371
—**Lord** (*Kyrios*), 50, 104, 189, 315–16
—**Messiah.** *See* Messiah
—**Name,** 93, 179, 377
—**Parables.** *See* Parables
—**Passion,** 160, 288, 338–340
—**Presentation,** 55
—**Resurrection,** 261, 376, 379–380
—**Savior,** 50, 58–59
—**Second coming.** *See* Jesus—Coming
—**Son of David,** 26, 28, 42, 44, 48, 289
—**Son of God,** 26, 28–29, 31, 52, 62, 64, 79–80, 161, 183, 304, 348, 382
—**Son of Man,** 157, 205, 273–75, 291, 321, 348, 382
—**Teaching,** 180, 302, 323, 371, 377, 383
—**Virgin birth,** 16, 27–30, 31, 46, 49, 51
**Jews,** 185, 202–203, 220, 239, 281, 318–320, 322, 353, 378, 384
**John (Gospel),** 3, 328, 355, 365
**John the Baptist,** 22–23, 56, 65–66, 70, 72, 76, 135, 153, 191, 258
—**Followers,** 15, 65
**Journeying.** *See* Jesus—Journeying
**Joy,** 22, 24, 50, 245, 249–251, 300, 380
**Judgment,** 57, 60, 72, 75, 87, 146, 205, 216, 255, 275, 282, 296, 324–25
**Justice of God.** *See* God—Justice
**Justification,** 35, 236, 250–52, 281–82, 319–320

**Kingdom of God,** 77, 99, 120, 152, 158, 176, 179, 181, 237, 250, 258, 271–72, 276–77, 280, 293–94, 296, 321, 325–26, 335, 337, 361
*Kyrios.* *See* Jesus—Lord

**L (Source),** 2–4, 263, 354–56
**Last judgment.** *See* Judgment
**Last Supper.** *See* Lord's Supper
**Law,** 20, 24, 55, 60, 92, 109, 113, 186, 200, 258, 286, 319, 341
**Law of love.** *See* Love, Law of
**Legal maxims,** 204
**Life after death,** 205, 261, 308, 361–62, 376
**Light, Children of,** 255
**Light, Inner,** 196–97
**Lord.** *See* Jesus—Lord
**Lord's Supper,** 233, 236–37, 332–38, 372–73

**Love, Law of,** 123, 140, 185–88, 264
**Love as a gift,** 216
**Love of God,** 242, 250–51
**Luke**
—**Identity,** 6–7
—**Sources,** 1–6. *See also* L. (Source
—**Style,** 1–4, 10, 46, 109, 138–39, 159, 204, 243–44, 354–56, 375

**Macarism,** 212
**Marcion,** 7, 98, 182, 200, 258
**Mary,** 16–17, 25–27, 29–30, 46–47, 49, 52, 57, 63–64, 65–67, 195–96
**Mary of Magdala,** 142
**Mercy.** *See* God—Grace
**Messiah,** 42–43, 49–50, 76, 81–82, 88–89, 156, 296
**Miracles,** 19, 98, 101–102, 133–34, 135, 137–38, 163, 170, 179–180, 182, 221, 234, 360, 368–69, 370–71
**Mission,** 146, 177, 324, 341
—**to the Gentiles.** *See* Gentiles—Mission to
**Mountain,** 114, 159

**Name**
—**of God.** *See* God—Name
—**of Jesus.** *See* Jesus—Name
**Naming,** 20, 28, 38
**Narrative,** 15, 46, 93, 384
**Nations.** *See* Gentiles
**Nazareth,** 86, 91
**Nazirites,** 22

**Old Testament,** 14, 40, 59, 96, 98, 165–66, 178–79, 259. *See also* Law

**Parables,** 213, 243, 252, 383
**Parousia.** *See* Jesus—Coming
**Passover,** 62–63, 330, 332–33, 335–36
**Peace,** 44, 51, 56, 60, 175, 216, 299
**People,** 119, 136, 145, 351, 371
—**of God,** 56, 58–60, 302–303, 360. *See also* Israel
**Persecution,** 315–16
**Peter,** 101–102, 114–15, 150, 157, 161, 286, 334, 340, 347, 366–67
**Pharisees,** 199, 229, 231, 245, 281–83, 318
**Politics and religion,** 305–306
**Poor,** 119–120, 259–262
**Possessions,** 207, 242, 254–56, 287
**Praise of God,** 34, 38, 42, 52, 268
**Prayer,** 111, 156, 174, 190, 279–281, 342–43

**Preaching,** 177, 181
**Presentation.** *See* Jesus—Presentation
**Priests,** 21
**Profession,** 290
**Promise,** 213
**Prophets,** 22–23, 43, 55–56, 65, 76, 133, 139, 153, 157, 178–79, 202–203, 228, 230–32, 305, 358

**Q (Source),** 1–6, 76, 105
**Qumran,** 29, 44, 59, 81, 244

**Rahner, Karl,** 92
**Reconciliation,** 282, 292
**Repentance,** 22, 72–73, 75, 111, 202–203, 243–44, 289–291, 341, 377
**Resurrection,** 153, 235, 261, 307–308, 324–25, 376. *See also* Jesus—Resurrection
**Rich,** 259–62; 286–87
**Righteous(ness),** 244–45, 358, 362, 364, 381
**Righteousness of God.** *See* God—Justice

**Sabbath,** 88, 112–13, 221–23
**Sacred history.** *See* History—Sacred
**Salvation,** 141, 268, 381
**Samaritans,** 169–70
**Satan,** 2, 82–84, 145, 178–180, 330
**Savior.** *See* Jesus—Savior
**Scribes,** 245
**Scripture**
    **—Authority,** 200, 202–203
    **—Interpretation,** 316–17, 371–73, 377
**Second coming.** *See* Jesus—Coming
**Signs of the times,** 276–77, 320
**Simon.** *See* Peter
**Sin,** 105–107, 139–141. *See also* Forgiveness of sins
**Sinners,** 245–46
**Social conditions,** 35–36, 44–45, 73–76, 119–120, 142–143, 276–77
**Son of David.** *See* Jesus—Son of David
**Son of God.** *See* Jesus—Son of God
**Son of Man.** *See* Jesus—Son of Man
**Sonship (Divine).** *See* Jesus—Son of God
**Soul,** 151, 205, 307
**Sources.** *See* Luke—Sources
**Spirit.** *See* Life after death

**Spirit (Holy),** 22, 26, 34, 41, 44, 56, 60, 74, 79, 82, 157, 192, 205–206, 315–16, 214, 378, 380
**Spirits,** 178, 376. *See also* Demons
**Story.** *See* Narrative
**Style.** *See* Luke—Style
**Suffering,** 121. *See also* Jesus—Passion

**Tax collectors,** 73–76, 136, 245, 259–260, 282–84, 290–92
**Teaching of Jesus.** *See* Jesus—Teaching
**Teilhard de Chardin, Pierre,** 92
**Temple,** 20–21, 24, 55–56, 60, 63, 83, 88, 93, 299, 301–302, 313–14
**Temptation,** 82, 84
**Time,** 217
**Tradition,** 11–12, 14, 372–73
**Trinity,** 31
**Truth,** 383–85
**Twelve, The.** *See* Apostles

**Violence.** *See* Force
**Virgin birth.** *See* Jesus—Virgin birth
**Visitation of God,** 42, 44, 133, 300

**Wealth.** *See* Possessions
**Wisdom,** 62, 76–77, 136, 228, 241
**Witness,** 11, 52–53, 115, 378
**Women,** 25, 34, 36, 57, 141–42, 189, 221–22, 241, 357, 362, 366
**Word**
   **—of God,** 12, 30–31, 42–43, 51–52, 70, 88–89, 98–99, 104, 177, 261
   **—of Jesus,** 189, 372–73
**Worship,** 88, 93